A History of British Railways' North Eastern Region

Comprising Papers by John F Addyman, David Bradwell, Reg Davies, Bill Fawcett,
Illtyd Lloyd Gray-Jones, John P McCrickard, James Rogers,
John G Teasdale and Chris J Woolstenholmes.

Edited by John G Teasdale.

NORTH EASTERN RAILWAY ASSOCIATION

© John F Addyman, David Bradwell, Reg Davies, Bill Fawcett, Illtyd Lloyd Gray-Jones,
John P McCrickard, James Rogers, John G Teasdale and Chris J Woolstenholmes.

All rights reserved. No part of this publication may be reproduced, stored in a retrieval system or transmitted, in any form or by any means, electronic, mechanical, photocopying, recording or otherwise without prior written permission of the publisher.

Published by John G Teasdale, 2009.

ISBN 978-0-9561867-0-6

Printed in Great Britain by The Amadeus Press, Ezra House, West 26 Business Park, Cleckheaton, BD19 4TQ.

The North Eastern Railway Association

Formed in 1961, the North Eastern Railway Association caters for all those interested in the railways of north-east England, in particular the North Eastern Railway and the Hull & Barnsley Railway, from their early history down to the present day. This also extends to the many industrial and smaller railways that operated alongside them. Interests range over all aspects of development, operation and infrastructure of the railways, including such diverse subjects as locomotives, rolling stock, train services, architecture, signalling, shipping, road vehicles and staff matters – both for the general enthusiast and the model maker.

With in excess of 700 members, regular meetings are held in York, Darlington, Hull and London. A programme of outdoor tours and walks is also arranged.

Members receive a quarterly illustrated journal, the *North Eastern Express*, and a newsletter covering membership topics, forthcoming meetings and events in the region together with book reviews and a bibliography of recent articles of interest. Over 190 issues of the *Express* have been published to date.

The Association owns an extensive library of books, documents, photographs and drawings; these are available for study both by members and non-members alike. The Association also markets an extensive range of facsimiles of railway company documents, including diagram books, timetables and other booklets, while at the same time it is developing an expanding range of original publications, available to members at discounted prices.

For a membership prospectus, please contact:

T Morrell, Esq, 8 Prunus Avenue, Kingston Road, Willerby, Hull, HU10 6PH.

A list of NERA publications is available from the Sales Officer. Please send SAE to:

T Mumford, Barbeck Farmhouse, 1 St. Giles Close, Thirsk, YO7 3BU.

NERA Website : www.ner.org.uk

Front cover photograph: A significant achievement pertaining to the modernisation of working practices in the North Eastern Region was the improvements made to the conveyance of iron ore from Tyne Dock to Consett. Seen here is the Iron Ore Handling Facility at Tyne Dock. Hidden in the shadows is a rake of modern iron ore hopper wagons; two Type 2 diesel-electric locomotives are coupled at their head. See the Case Study by David Bradwell beginning on page 64. (MC Crawley)

Rear cover photograph, upper: Class A3 No 60086 'Gainsborough' departs Sunderland station with a Bank Holiday extra to Manchester in June 1963. The view looks northwards towards the south entrance to the station as re-built in 1953. This entrance would be demolished in 1964 when work began to re-build the station once again. The splendid clock tower, part of the North Eastern Railway's 1879 entrance to the station, would also be demolished, to be replaced by a department store. (GW Sharpe Collection / Colour Rail, per CE Williamson)

Rear cover photograph, lower: A Trans-Pennine diesel multiple-unit at Leeds City station in July 1963; note the roof boards carried by the nearest two cars. On every side, work proceeds on the re-building of the station. (AG Forsyth / Colour Rail, per CE Williamson)

*This book is
dedicated to the hard-working
railwaymen and women of the
North Eastern Region*

Contents

Introduction	4
The North Eastern Region in Context :	
An Overview of the History of British Railways, 1948 – 1967. John G Teasdale	5
The Organisation of the North Eastern Region. Reg Davies	26
Evolution and Diminution : The Changing Nature of the	
Freight Traffic Conveyed by the Trains of the North Eastern Region. John G Teasdale	35
Freight Traffic in the North Eastern Region. A Case Study : Tyne Dock to Consett Iron Ore. David Bradwell	64
Passenger Traffic in the North Eastern Region. John P McCrickard.	
From Austerity to Modernisation	71
From Sentinels to Derby Lightweights : the Diesel Multiple-Unit Revolution	75
The East Coast Main Line	87
Cross-Country	94
Trans-Pennine	97
Sleeper Services, including Car-Sleepers and Car-Carriers	101
Holidays, Excursions, Events and Special Traffics	103
Early Line Closures and Economies	107
The End of the 'Tyneside Electrics'	113
Fares, Marketing and Tickets	115
Conclusions	116
The North Eastern Region's Locomotives and their Maintenance. James Rogers.	
Locomotives of the North Eastern Region	122
Motive Power Depots	132
Workshops	141
Civil Engineering. John F Addyman	145
Notes on North Eastern Region Architecture. Bill Fawcett	160
At the Leading Edge of the New Technologies :	
Signal and Telecommunications Engineering in the North Eastern Region. Chris J Woolstenholmes	164
Ships, Shipping, and the North Eastern Region. John G Teasdale, with contributions by John Edgington	182
The North Eastern Region : A Personal View. Illtyd Lloyd Gray-Jones	184
A Brief Postscript	189
Bibliography	190
Index	191

Acknowledgements

This History is a the result of extensive collaboration. John Richardson, a Vice-President of the North Eastern Railway Association, made a significant contribution at the beginning of the project, helping to co-ordinate the work of editor and co-authors. The co-authors went on to help each other, proffering information and advice during the preparation of the diverse Papers.

    Editor and co-authors also received most welcome advice, assistance, information, photographs and artwork from other people, both members and non-members of the Association. We would like to thank in particular: Stephen Askew; Roger Bastin; Steve Batty; Richard Casserley; Pete Coombs; Malcolm Crawley; Andrew Dow; John Edgington; Ron Goult; Andrew Grantham (*Railway Gazette International Limited*); William Heszelgrave; Tom Kirtley; John Midcalf; Charlie Oxley; Alan Smith; Alan Thompson (JW Armstrong Trust); Dick Warwick; Les West; Mike Wild; Duncan Wilcock; David and Claire Williamson; Alan Young. We also received assistance from staff at diverse institutions: the Ken Hoole Study Centre (Julie Biddlecombe, Lorraine Cornwell and Madi Grout in particular); the Leeds Library; the National Archives; the National Railway Museum.

    Last but not least, the North Eastern Railway Association's Publications Officer, David Williamson, provided financial information pertaining to publication, and other useful advice. Many thanks to you all – the book would have been much less than it is without your most valuable contributions.

John G Teasdale, February 2009.

Introduction

When Britain's railways were nationalised, on 1 January 1948, railways as a business enterprise in their own right (as opposed to an adjunct to such as a mining enterprise) were still relatively young; in the north-east of England public railways dated from 1825 and the opening of the Stockton & Darlington Railway. In 1948 then, the history of the public railways was relatively short, but it was one of extraordinary activity.

What would become the major trunk lines were, for the most part, constructed in the early years of that history. These were followed by the construction of a dense web of branch lines. Many of these branches (and, indeed, some of the main lines) duplicated others already in existence; many were constructed for social reasons or to foil the schemes of rival railway companies rather than for sound commercial reasons. In the north-east of England, this was less of a problem for the newly nationalised railways as since 1854 the area had been largely under the monopolistic sway of the North Eastern Railway Company and its successor, the London & North Eastern Railway Company. Even here, however, potential problems loomed for the railwaymen running the newly-created North Eastern Region of British Railways. In the far north, for example, the Alnwick & Cornhill Branch had made little commercial sense even when it was opened for traffic in 1887; the LNER had already ceased to run passenger trains over the branch. In the south, the main line of the former Hull & Barnsley Railway Company had duplicated (more or less) existing routes between south Yorkshire and Hull; the LNER had ceased to run passenger trains over much of this line too, and its profitability was dependent both upon the vigour of the mining industry in south Yorkshire and a continuing demand for shipment coal. Profitability was, of course, as pertinent to British Railways as it had been to its privately-owned predecessors; by the Act of Parliament that created it, BR was required to be profitable.

In their 120 or so years' history, railways had made extraordinary progress in the way of locomotives and rolling stock. The early steam locomotive engines, slow, hungry for fuel and requiring much maintenance, had been improved almost beyond recognition. However, there were problems. The steam locomotive was inherently inefficient in itself, and required a large labour force to keep it in traffic day to day – disadvantages admittedly compensated for by its being cheap to build. Experience with both diesel and electric locomotives had demonstrated that they were cheaper to operate than steam locomotives, but the North Eastern Region had inherited next to no locomotives of either type.

The goods wagons and passenger carriages were similarly improved over those used by the railway pioneers, capable of carrying much greater loads at much higher speeds. However, there were problems here too, particularly with the wagons. The way that railways had developed in Britain meant that most wagons were very small compared with the wagons used for the same task in Europe and America; this meant that they were more expensive to operate than they could have been. It also meant that the small consignments that they customarily conveyed could just as easily be conveyed in a road-going motor lorry.

The problems associated with such as duplicated main lines, unprofitable branch lines, inefficient steam locomotives, diminutive goods wagons, competition from road-going lorries, *etc.*, applied across British Railways in its entirety. These problems were compounded by the fact that what were now the newly-nationalised railways had in turn suffered the ravages of the First World War, the Depression of the 1930s and the ravages of the Second World War; the newly-nationalised railways were to a great extent obsolescent and anyway worn out. How the railwaymen and women of the North Eastern Region coped with these problems forms the subject of this book.

Abbreviations used in the text:

ASLEF – Associated Society of Locomotive Engineers and Firemen
ATC – Automatic Train Control
AWS – Automatic Warning System
BR – British Railways
BRB – British Railways Board
BRS – British Road Services
BTC – British Transport Commission
CEGB – Central Electricity Generating Board
cps – cycles per second
CTC – Centralised Traffic Control
DMU – diesel multiple-unit
EE – English Electric
GCR – Great Central Railway Company
GNR – Great Northern Railway Company
GWR – Great Western Railway Company
H&BR – Hull & Barnsley Railway Company
ICI – Imperial Chemical Industries Limited
ISO – International Standards Organisation
kV – kilovolt

LMR – London Midland Region
LMSR – London, Midland & Scottish Railway Company
LNER – London & North Eastern Railway Company
MGR – Merry-Go-Round (coal train)
MoT – Ministry of Transport
MoT&CA – Ministry of Transport & Civil Aviation
NCB – National Coal Board
NER – North Eastern Railway Company
NUR – National Union of Railwaymen
PP – Parliamentary Papers
PR&PO – Public Relations & Publicity Officer
RE – Railway Executive
S&T – Signal & Telecommunications
ScR – Scottish Region
SI – Statutory Instrument
SR – Southern Railway Company
SR & O – Statutory Rules & Orders
TOPS – Total Operations Processing System
TPO – Travelling Post Office

The North Eastern Region in Context
An Overview of the History of British Railways, 1948 - 1967
John G Teasdale

Within Great Britain, the acquisition of a privately-owned railway by the State – a process hereinafter described as nationalisation – was first enabled by statute in 1844. On 9 August of that year, Royal Assent was granted to what became known as 'Gladstone's Act' after its promoter, William Ewart Gladstone, President of the Board of Trade.(1) Among other things, the Act sanctioned purchase by the Treasury of any railway constructed after the passing of the Act. Purchase could take place at any time after a period of twenty-one years had elapsed since the passing of the Act that had authorised that railway's construction. However, no such purchase ever took place.

One reason for the lack of any nationalisation during the Nineteenth Century was the belief by successive Governments that competition between private companies produced the best balance between the interests of those running the railways on the one hand, and the interests of industrialists, traders and passengers on the other. (The Governments that Gladstone himself subsequently led as Prime Minister had, overall, the same belief.) In contrast, those who lived with the consequences of competition every day of their working lives – the railway companies' employees – believed otherwise. They were, for the most part, very much in favour of nationalisation. On 3 October 1894, the delegates attending the annual conference of the Amalgamated Society of Railway Servants carried a resolution demanding that every effort be made to have the railways nationalised. On 21 January 1908, the Society's delegate to the Labour Party conference proposed a similar resolution; it was carried. A month later, on 26 February, a small group of back-bench Members of Parliament formed the 'Railway Nationalization Society', which subsequently promoted a series of Bills calling for the nationalisation of Britain's railways, none of which got a second reading in the House of Commons. Nationalisation was seriously considered in 1919 by the coalition Government that struggled to cope with the aftermath of the First World War, but was rejected in favour of grouping the multiplicity of small private railway companies into four large ones. The Grouping was put into effect on 1 January 1923, creating the so-called Big Four railway companies: London, Midland and Scottish (LMSR); London and North Eastern (LNER); Great Western (GWR); Southern (SR).

Prior to the 1920s, the concept of nationalisation had been associated with railway companies only. However, conditions were very different in the post-war world from those pertaining during the Nineteenth Century. Perhaps the most significant difference as far as the railway companies were concerned was that competition from road transport was now very much a factor to be reckoned with. Whereas horse-drawn carts had in most situations been suitable only as feeders to the nearest railway station, in the 1920s motor lorries were more and more frequently by-passing the railways by delivering goods directly from producers to consumers. Motor buses and electric tramways were abstracting local passenger traffic that had hitherto been conveyed on the railways. The idea therefore arose that nationalisation should apply to all modes of inland transport, so that transport tasks could be allocated rationally between the various modes. This idea was to come to fruition in the aftermath of the Second World War.

Plate 1.1. 11 October 1947, and No 5812 rolls through Newcastle with a short freight. It had been built in 1908; it worked as well as when it was new, but was by no means as economical to operate as a modern locomotive. The Rectank wagon, unbraked but for a handbrake, had been built for military use during the First World War. The LNER's modernisation is represented by the brake van, built with a long wheelbase to make it suitable for fast-running freight trains. (HC Casserley, courtesy RM Casserley)

In the general election of 26 July 1945, the Labour Party was elected with a large majority. As promised in Labour's election manifesto, Minister of Transport Alfred Barnes and his advisers then set about the preparation of a Bill for the nationalisation of inland transport. The undertakings to be nationalised included the Big Four railway companies, the inland waterways, omnibus companies, road haulage companies whose business was predominantly for hire and reward over long distances. This latter qualification was important – even after the proposed Act took effect traders would be permitted, under the provisions of the Ministry of Transport's 'C' licence, to carry their own goods in their own lorries over any distance.

5

A prime provision of the Bill placed overall control of the nationalised transport industries in the hands of a British Transport Commission (BTC). In order to manage effectively the vast extent of its undertaking, the BTC would have to be subdivided into manageable units. How that subdivision should be effected was of great concern to the politicians and civil servants drawing up the Bill. The worry was that the railways would comprise such a large a part of the undertaking that their management would take up so much time and energy that other modes of transport would be neglected. For this reason, it was decided that the Bill would stipulate that the BTC be divided not by function, but by transport mode. Thus there was provision for the following: a Railway Executive; a Road Transport Executive; a London Transport Executive; a Docks and Inland Waterways Executive.(2) In addition, there was to be a Hotels Executive, to manage the railway-owned hotels. This scheme of division inevitably meant that the officers of the Railway Executive would be likely to concern themselves mostly with railway problems; officers of the Road Transport Executive would be likely to be similarly self-absorbed. A principle aim of the nationalisation of all inland transport – that transport tasks should be allocated rationally between modes – was therefore not likely to be fulfilled, unless the Chairman of the BTC made sure that this aim was firmly adhered to by the Chairmen of the diverse Executives. The Bill was enacted by the granting of Royal Assent on 6 August 1947.(3)

On 8 August, Barnes appointed Sir Cyril Hurcomb as Chairman of the BTC. Hurcomb was a civil servant, and as Director-General of the Ministry of Transport had played a large part in the drafting of the Nationalisation Bill. Barnes and Hurcomb then had to decide upon the remaining appointments to the BTC, and all the appointments to the Executives. Concerning the Railway Executive, most of the appointments were made from the ranks of the Big Four, but selection was complicated by the fact that some men refused to serve a nationalised undertaking. Sir James Milne, Chairman of the GWR, was offered the post of Chairman of the Railway Executive, but refused it. Appointment to the post was subsequently accepted by Sir Eustace Missenden, Chairman of the SR. The remaining appointments were made so as to provide an approximate balance between the Big Four. The appointees – known as Members – were each charged with a functional task such as operating, mechanical engineering, civil engineering, and so on.

Having formed a Railway Executive, the Members of that body and of the BTC had to decide how the railways were going to subdivided into manageable units. The decision-making was complicated by the fact that Hurcomb believed the BTC should closely supervise the Railway Executive, but Missenden believed the Executive should be left to get on with the job without that close supervision. Despite these conflicting views, both the BTC and the Railway Executive quickly reached agreement that the railways should be subdivided geographically into Regions based upon the territories of the Big Four. There was disagreement though as to how many Regions there should be, and how much power should be devolved down to them. The Railway Executive's view was that each of the Regions should be headed by an officer with the powers of a General Manager. The BTC's view was that the Executive's Members would act as General Managers in their respective fields, and that the Regions would therefore be headed by an officer with the role of co-ordinator rather than manager. The BTC, which held ultimate authority, prevailed in the matter of devolution of power down to the Regions – initially at least, it would not happen. Each Region's Chief Regional Officer would co-ordinate the activities of his departmental officers, and ensure that they implemented the policies as handed down by the Executive. Concerning the number of Regions, a compromise was reached. Instead of the eight as suggested by the BTC, there would be six as the Railway Executive refused to countenance any more subdivision of the LMSR than was necessitated by the creation of a Scottish Region. (This latter would be formed by merging the Scottish lines of the LMSR and the LNER.) The six Regions would comprise: Eastern; London Midland; North Eastern; Scottish; Southern; Western.(4) One further decision to make was by what name Britain's

Plate 1.2. A signalman, sadly unidentified, on duty in Crimple box. (JW Armstrong / JW Armstrong Trust, per AR Thompson)

nationalised railways would be known. The title 'Railway Executive' was thought to be inappropriate for use in dealing with the public, and 'British Railways' was therefore adopted as a trading title.

North Eastern Region

The provisions of the Transport Act, 1947 took effect on 1 January 1948. On that day, therefore, British Railways (BR) and its Regions officially came into being. The North Eastern Region was originally based on the LNER's North Eastern Area, and encompassed Northumberland, Durham, the North and East Ridings of Yorkshire, and all but the southernmost part of the West Riding. Subsequent boundary changes (in 1950 and 1956) brought former LMSR and LNER Southern Area lines into the Region. (See the map on page 20 for a view of the Region in 1955.) Even before these boundary changes however, by no means was the Region the North Eastern Area under another name. The LNER's hotel and dock assets were stripped from it and allocated to the appropriate Executive.(5) Nor did the Region have jurisdiction over all the railways in the north-east of England. Colliery railways had been nationalised with effect from 1 January 1947 and allocated to the National Coal Board; industrial railways, and private railway companies which had remained outside Government control during the last war, remained privately owned.(6)

The North Eastern Region's headquarters were established at York – a city that had been a home to railway company headquarters since the incorporation of the York & North Midland Railway Company on 21 June 1836. Appointed Chief Regional Officer was Charles P Hopkins, one of those young men who had been groomed by the LNER for high office, and whose previous post had been that company's Assistant General Manager (Traffic and Statistics). The Region for which Hopkins was responsible was the smallest of the six. It comprised only 9% of BR's track miles, ran only 8% of train miles per annum, and employed only 9% of the total number of staff.(7) The Region was by no means insignificant though; the north-east of England was heavily industrialised, and generated a very heavy traffic in raw materials, finished goods, and passengers.

The range of problems facing Hopkins when he took up his new appointment were daunting. During its brief existence, the LNER had not been a profitable undertaking. Investment therefore, in new methods of working, in new locomotives and rolling stock, had been relatively modest. During the arduous years of the Second World War, there had been next to no investment, and precious little maintenance. Thus the railway assets that the North Eastern Region inherited were old, under-maintained, or just plain worn out. Another problem was that the Region's railway assets, like those of BR as a whole, were too extensive. Throughout Great Britain, railways had not been constructed in accordance with well-considered plans drawn up by central Government, but had been constructed by private enterprise to very little plan at all. In the north-east of England, the North Eastern Railway Company (NER) had held a virtual monopoly from its incorporation on 31 July 1854 until the Grouping of 1923. Thus the railways here were constructed more rationally than elsewhere. But even here, a competing, entirely unnecessary, main line had been constructed by the Hull & Barnsley Railway Company. In the West Riding south of Leeds there was a crazy tangle of lines constructed by diverse companies all engaged in ruthless, and often self-defeating, competition. In contrast to this tangle in the West Riding, the NER's branch lines had been constructed more rationally. However, they had been constructed when the alternative mode of transport was the horse-drawn cart. Thus, on average, railway stations were located only two to three miles apart. By 1948, motor lorries were capable of making much longer journeys than their horse-drawn predecessors, rendering many stations and even branch lines redundant.

Plate 1.3. A wheeltapper stands clear of A1 No 60158 'Aberdonian' as it rolls into York with an Up express on 23 April 1952. (RG Warwick)

Unhappily for Hopkins, his authority to authorise investment or closure of redundant facilities was severely circumscribed. In the instructions he received from the Railway Executive on 1 January, he was given permission to spend up to £2000 on works and equipment, to make appointments up to a salary of £1000, and to accept tenders and approve contracts up to the sum of £5000.(8) He also had to accept the fact that Members of the Executive could – and usually did – arrange matters with his departmental officers directly without any reference to him. The same restrictions and working arrangements applied to all the Chief Regional Officers, and were much resented by them. Several of the Officers had held positions of higher status in the Big Four than had Executive Members who were now conspicuously failing to consult them in dealings with departmental officers. The Chief Regional Officers did not keep their unhappiness to themselves, and articles critical of the way BR was organised at regional level were published in the press.(9) These articles had an effect, and from 29 July 1948 the Chief Regional Officers were invited to attend meetings of the Railway Executive every fortnight. (Previously, the CROs had been invited to meetings of the Executive only once a month.) Unfortunately, Members of the Executive still tended to deal directly with departmental officers, and the Chief Regional Officers remained unhappy with their lot.

A field in which close working relations were maintained between a Member of the Railway Executive and the officers in the Regions was mechanical and electrical engineering; this continuing closeness was inevitable given that mechanical and electrical engineering had been strongly centralised within the hierarchies of the Big Four and its predecessors. The responsible Member was Robert A Riddles, and it was for him to decide upon BR's future traction policy. In order to guide him, a Locomotive Standards Committee was established on 8 January 1948. Riddles selected the Chairman of the committee; the Chief Mechanical and Electrical Engineers (CMEEs) in the Regions selected the remaining committee members. (The North Eastern Region's CMEE was Arthur H Peppercorn, who was based in Doncaster. This location was due to the fact that Peppercorn served also as CMEE of the Eastern Region.) The Locomotive Standards Committee quickly came to the conclusion that existing designs of steam locomotive should be built until new standard designs could be drawn up. Existing designs would indeed built by BR, but Riddles decided that standard designs would be drawn up sooner rather than later. By mid-1948, a range of standard steam locomotives had been sketched out. The BTC was deeply concerned at what it regarded as a premature decision. Hurcomb in particular thought that there should be an investigation into the merits of diesel and electric traction. Hurcomb's concern led to the appointment of another committee – a committee that worked in such a dilatory fashion that it would not report until 1951. By this time, the building of standard steam locomotives was well under way. In deciding that steam locomotion should prevail upon BR, Riddles was profoundly influenced by his previous experience; he was emotionally

Plate 1.4. On a bleak day in February 1954, an unidentified railwayman waits in the bitter cold while a freight train by-passes Newcastle Central station. (IL Gray-Jones)

attached to steam. He was also influenced by diverse Government policies, one of which was that imports should be restricted (which limited the potential for oil imports), and another which was that jobs should be preserved in the coal industry. Riddles did not anyway favour main line dieselisation, believing that such would delay electrification, which latter he regarded as a superior form of traction.

Following the retirement of the London Midland Region's Chief Regional Officer, effective from 1 January 1950 the Railway Executive instituted a management re-shuffle. As it affected the North Eastern Region, the consequence was that Hopkins became Chief Regional Officer of the Southern Region; he was replaced by Herbert A Short, an ex-SR officer, previously the Executive's Acting Chief Officer (Docks). The switching between Regions was an important part of the Executive's policy in trying to prevent the insular mentality that had characterised each of the private railway companies from being perpetuated in BR's Regions. The policy could only be regarded as a palliative, however, as insularity of thought was practically guaranteed by the subdivision of the railways geographically into Regions, rather than by, say, business sectors. Insularity of thought was also reinforced by the Executive's own policy of giving Regions their own distinct identities in the form of regional colour schemes. The colour chosen for the North Eastern Region was Deep Orange.(10)

A month later, Missenden retired as Chairman of the Railway Executive. The appointment of a new chairman did not lead to much of an improvement in relations between the Executive and the BTC. In view of the obvious difficulties that also continued to exist in the relations between the Railway Executive and the Chief Regional Officers, the BTC asked the former to review regional organisation. An ad hoc committee was therefore formed to study the possible benefits of merging the Eastern and the North Eastern Regions; this committee found in favour of leaving things just as they were.(11) A separate study proposed that the Chief Regional Officer be the Executive's principal officer in a Region, and that he be re-designated Regional Manager in order to signify his increased status.(12) This re-designation did not take place, but during 1951 more authority was delegated to the Chief Regional Officers, who were permitted to more closely supervise regional budgets, and to recommend redundant stations and branch lines for closure. Some modest progress in

Plate 1.5. Selby New Yard, circa 1962. Inspector GS West and Shunter G Walker stand clear of Class B16 No 61463 as it departs with an express non-fitted freight. (LM West Collection)

this latter regard had begun already. From 25 September 1950, for example, passenger services between Knaresborough and Pilmoor had been withdrawn, and the intermediate stations closed to passengers. The tinkerings, both proposed and actual, with details of organisation were, however, dwarfed in importance by the Conservative Party's victory in the general election of 25 October 1951. The Conservatives did not approve of Nationalisation, and were determined to reverse it wherever possible. In the case of the railways that was not likely to be possible at all – given their poor condition and marginal profitability, it was unlikely that anybody would want to buy them. In May 1952, the Conservatives published a White Paper entitled *Transport Policy* stating the Government's intentions: nationalised road haulage companies would be sold to entrepreneurs; the railways would be re-organised into 'an appropriate number of regional railway systems, each with its own pride of identity'. The White Paper led in turn to a transport Bill, which was enacted on 6 May 1953.(13)

The new Act had two main aims. The first was to terminate Labour's policy of integration between modes of transport, and to institute instead a policy promoting competition between them. The second was to decentralise the management of the railways, and to abolish the Railway Executive. Concerning the second, the BTC was required within twelve months to submit to the Ministry of Transport a re-organisation scheme. Given that the present organisation was not working, re-organisation was no doubt a good thing. What was unequivocally a good thing for the railways was that the tight control exercised by legislation over railway charges was relaxed somewhat.

The Transport Act, 1947, that had established the BTC had also stipulated that the BTC as a whole should make a profit. As the railways were such a large part of the undertaking, there was no question of the railways making a loss, and of their being cross-subsidised by other modes of transport sufficient to produce a profit for the BTC as a whole. In effect, the railways were ordered by Act of Parliament to make a profit. But Parliament made it very difficult for the railways to do so – the railways' ability to charge for the conveyance of passengers and freight was severely circumscribed by legislation. At the time of Nationalisation, the LNER's charges were based on an Order made 6 July 1927.(14) The provisions of this Order had not been generous in 1927, and an increase in charges had been permitted by Government in 1937. From 1 October 1947 another increase in charges, of 55%, had been sanctioned. Inflation though had increased costs by at least 80%. The Labour Government however, like Governments before it, was reluctant to court public displeasure by sanctioning the increases in railway charges that would give the railways adequate remuneration. The Transport Act, 1953, began to tackle the problem. From henceforth, the various undertakings of the BTC would be required to publish only their maximum charges for the conveyance of freight; this measure would prevent privately-owned road haulage companies, for example, from simply undercutting BR's published rate by a few shillings and thereby winning traffic. Also, the BTC was henceforth to be permitted to set charges for the conveyance of passengers and freight at its own discretion (though, in practice, it still remained subject to the strictures of the Transport Tribunal) and was permitted to give preference to particular traffics in the way of charges – a measure that had not been permitted before, when legislation specifically forbade railway and canal companies from the giving of 'undue preference'.(15) The railways' common carriers obligations, however, still applied.

On 15 September 1953, General Sir Brian Robertson took over as Chairman of the BTC. A few weeks later, on 1 October, the British Transport Commission (Executives) Order took effect; this Ministerial Order abolished all the BTC's Executives apart from that running London Transport. In effect, the BTC absorbed the Railway Executive. As a new organisational scheme had not yet been agreed upon and instituted, the BTC now established an interim organisation, and dealt directly with the Regions. Within each Region, the power of the Chief Regional Officer was strengthened by giving him authority over his departmental officers, and by the BTC agreeing that all dealings with those officers would be done through him. In order to reflect that strengthened authority, the Chief Regional Officer was re-designated the Chief Regional Manager.

This interim organisation was in effect for just over a year. On 25 November 1954 the British Transport Commission (Organisation) Scheme Order was made, and implemented with effect from 1 January 1955.(16) A significant part of the scheme involved the establishment of an Area Board for each Region. Each Board was intended: to manage the railways in its Region; to promote initiatives that would improve services and reduce costs; to maintain commercial contacts with users of the railways so that their interests could be met to the fullest extent consistent with the duty imposed by statute on the BTC; to ensure the safety of employees. Day-to-day management of the railways in each Region would be in the hands of the General Manager (as the Chief Regional Manager was re-designated from 1 January) and his departmental officers. Appointments to a Board were to be made by the BTC, to which the appointees were ultimately responsible. The man appointed Chairman was to be a

Plate 1.6. Perhaps the best of the diesel shunters bought by BR were the 400 hp 0-6-0 diesel-electrics of the type seen here at Alexandra Dock in 1953. However, even these paragons was not immune to faulty track; Fitter's Assistant F Jackson (left), Fitter J Porter and colleagues set about the task of re-railing. (CW Oxley)

Plate 1.7. Alexandra Dock shed tool van crew, circa 1953. Standing, from left: Labourer A Heckingbottom; Fitter J Porter; C&W; Charlie Oxley; C&W; Fitter's Assistant Fred Jackson. (CW Oxley Collection)

BTC Member; other appointees were to be drawn from the ranks of the great and good in local trade and industry, as had been the case with directors of such as the NER and LNER. Appointed Chairman of the North Eastern Area Board was a steel magnate, Thomas H Summerson.(17) Another appointee was Sir Mark Hodgson, formerly President of the Confederation of Engineering and Shipbuilding Unions – a man who would, perhaps, not have been elected a director of either the NER or the LNER. A total of six men were appointed to the Board, which first met at York on 7 February 1955. These men did not have an entirely free hand in managing the railways in the Region; the BTC reserved to itself the right to determine BR's policy on charges, wages and salaries, building of new locomotives and rolling stock, and so on.

Investment and the Modernisation Plan

When the railways were nationalised, they desperately required substantial investment to replace worn out track and rolling stock, and to install the facilities required to expedite modern methods of working. By and large, they did not get it. The Labour Government in office from 1945 to 1951 gave priority instead to the National Health Service, and to such as the electricity and coal industries. The BTC had difficulty in challenging those priorities because the Railway Executive, determined to be as independent as possible, failed for the most part to supply it with the facts and figures that would have supported the case for investing in the railways. Some money was spent on the railways however. In the North Eastern Region, limited track renewal programmes were agreed, railway workshops were given orders for new rolling stock, and there was investment in new freight facilities for Imperial Chemical Industries Limited (ICI) and for Dorman Long and Company Limited on Teesside. Completion of these various works were hindered to a greater or lesser degree by a post-war shortage of steel.(18) The recommendation by the United Nations Security Council on 27 June 1950 that the free world intervene in the fighting in Korea made matters worse still; in Britain, re-armament absorbed money and steel that might otherwise have been invested in and used on the railways. Fortunately, the Korean War was all but over by the end of June 1951. Modest investment funds and allocations of steel eventually became available once again.

Meanwhile, neither the Labour nor the Conservative post-war Governments had adequately tackled the problems of railway charges for the conveyance of freight and passengers. Between 1948 and 1952, four Statutory Instruments had been made increasing by various percentages BR's freight charges.(19) Similarly, passenger fares had been intermittently increased. None of these increases had been sufficient to provide adequate remuneration for the railways. Thus, BR's overall financial performance steadily deteriorated into deficit. (The North Eastern Region's financial performance remained respectable, partly because, in order to minimise BR's overall accountancy costs, each Region was allocated all the revenue for its originating freight traffic, even when that traffic terminated in another Region. As the North Eastern Region was a net exporter of freight traffic, its figures were much better than, say, the Western Region's, which was a net importer.)

There were several ways in which BR's accumulating deficit could be dealt with – and dealt with it had to be, as the undertaking was effectively bound by statute not to run at a loss. A relatively easy way to reduce losses was not to run loss-making passenger and freight services, and to close redundant stations and branch lines. Concerning passenger services, a census taken during the week ending 11 October 1952 produced, on the North Eastern Region, the following statistics:

Fast passenger trains margin : £22,690
(Operating ratio : 28)
Semi-fast passenger trains margin : £10,967
(Operating ratio : 73)
Stopping passenger trains margin : minus £30,417
(Operating ratio : 231)
Total passenger-miles as a percentage
of seat-miles provided : 29%(20)

The statistics for freight traffic were similarly depressing. General merchandise traffic in particular failed to cover its indirect costs. (As early as 1948, the BTC had concluded that there was excess capacity in inland transport for the conveyance of general merchandise, largely due to the ever increasing numbers of 'C' licence lorries.)(21) However, the ethos inherited by the men running the nationalised railways predisposed them towards public service, not rationalisation of facilities. Trains were removed from the timetable, and stations and branch lines closed, but progress made was not great.

Another way of reducing the deficit was to increase receipts. The difficulties experienced in this regard by the BTC have already been mentioned. Yet another way was to increase the investment in facilities that would expedite modern methods of working. On the North Eastern Region, a massive step forward in this regard was the ordering of diesel multiple-units which would, it was calculated, reduce significantly the cost of operating passenger trains. That such units be ordered and introduced was not the initiative of RA Riddles, but of BTC Member Frank A Pope. The first of the new units were scheduled to enter service in the West Riding during mid-1954. Sir Brian Robertson, Chairman of the BTC, came to the conclusion that the only hope of returning BR to profit lay in more investment such as this. On 14 April 1954 the BTC set up a Planning Committee, charged with the task of drawing up a plan for modernising the railways. The committee comprised officers from both the BTC and from the Regions, who all liaised closely with the Chief Regional Managers. The committee did not have to start quite from scratch; the Railway Executive had undertaken a similar exercise early in 1953. However, because of the poor relationships that had existed from the very beginning of BR between the BTC and the Railway Executive, and between the Executive and the Chief Regional Officers, no strategic planning for the railways had ever been undertaken. Nor had the consequences for the railways of the Conservative's policy of competition between modes of transport been thoroughly considered. In the absence of any strategic planning, and of any deep consideration as to how increasing competition from road transport would effect the railways, any plan produced by the committee was likely to be flawed.

That committee's Modernisation Plan was submitted to the Minister of Transport and Civil Aviation on 21 December 1954.(22) The Plan was published on 25 January 1955 as a booklet entitled *Modernisation and Re-Equipment of British Railways*. Broadly, over a fifteen-year period, the Plan prescribed:

* Investment in modern track and signalling, Centralised Traffic Control where suitable, and modern telecommunication services. Estimated cost: £210 million.
* The rapid replacement of steam locomotion with diesel or electric. Estimated cost: £345 million.
* The replacement of most of the locomotive-hauled carriages with diesel or electric multiple-units, and modernisation of the remainder. The modernisation of the main passenger stations and parcels depots. Estimated cost: £285 million.

Plate 1.8. Jervaulx station on the Hawes Branch, September 1953. The two passenger trains, hauled by Class G5 No 67312 and Class D20 No 62388, are passing at the station on the single-track branch. The crews take the opportunity to chat. (JW Armstrong / JW Armstrong Trust, per AR Thompson)

Plate 1.9. Starbeck shed staff and enginemen gather around No 62727 'The Quorn' to have their photograph taken on 3 March 1951. (HC Whitby / ST Askew Collection)

* The drastic re-modelling of freight services, involving: the fitting of continuous brakes to all wagons; the introduction of wagons with larger carrying capacities; the modernisation of freight handling facilities; the closure of small freight yards, and the re-siting and modernisation of marshalling yards. Estimated cost: £365 million.
* Miscellaneous measures, including improvements in office equipment, staff facilities, and research and development. Estimated cost: £35 million.

Specifically as regard to the North Eastern Region, the Plan envisaged:

* More orders for diesel multiple-units, in addition to those already in service in the West Riding.
* The withdrawal of passenger services which would not be profitable even if operated by diesel multiple-units.
* The replacement of steam locomotion by diesel on the passenger trains serving the route Liverpool Exchange - Bradford Exchange - Leeds - Hull.
* Provision was to be made for the accommodation of diesel locomotives at the new Thornaby motive power depot, currently being built. Major changes were going to be required at the Region's existing depots in order to accommodate diesel locomotives, though no date was set for a change over from steam locomotion to diesel on the main lines. For shunting, steam was definitely to be replaced by diesel at an increased rate.
* The Newcastle area was to be re-signalled on modern principles, following the success of a similar scheme at York. The work of re-signalling the East Coast Main Line was to be completed. Other signalling projects were to be undertaken, involving the installation of modern equipment and the concentration of signalling in large power signal boxes.
* As part of the BR's overall scheme to modernise the working of freight trains, hump marshalling yards were to be built at Newport (Teesside), and facilities were to be rationalised at Hull and in the West Riding.
* As part of the same scheme, general merchandise traffic was to be concentrated at large modern depots, each fully provided with mechanical handling equipment.
* The coal staiths at Blyth and Dunston were to be strengthened in order to accommodate $24^{1}/_{2}$ ton capacity wagons.
* Track on the East Coast Main Line subject to severe speed restrictions, such as at Selby, Durham and Morpeth, was to be re-aligned to permit increased speed. Also on the Main Line, a fourth track was to be constructed between Pilmoor and Alne to complete the quadrupling there, and running loops were to be constructed at Balne. Running loops were to be constructed also between Northallerton and Eaglescliffe.
* Passenger stations were to be improved, as was already in hand at Middlesbrough and Bradford Forster Square.
* A modern telecommunications network was to be installed.

In connection with the Plan, a scheme prepared jointly with the Eastern Region for electrification of the East Coast Main Line between King's Cross and Newcastle, and of the route Doncaster - Leeds, was accepted by the BTC. However, the Ministry of Transport and Civil Aviation did not accept the scheme, which was eventually abandoned in favour of dieselisation.

The Modernisation Plan was initially welcomed by Government and press alike. This welcome did not last long. Potentially the most influential of the critics was Hugh P Barker, a part-time Member of the BTC. Barker was not a railwayman, but a distinguished gas and electrical engineer. In a memorandum of November 1954, he criticised railwaymen's obsession with equipment rather than operation, and pointed out that many passenger and freight services would always loose money no matter how much was invested in them. Barker was particularly critical of railwaymen's belief that the provision of modern marshalling yards would make profitable general merchandise traffic.(23) Unfortunately, Barker was not listened to at the time. The Ministry approved the Plan, though without having scrutinised it to any great extent.

When fully implemented, the Modernisation Plan was intended to return BR to profitability – the additional net revenue that was predicted to be earned as a result of the Plan was at least £85 million per annum. Work done on the North Eastern Region made its contribution towards the attainment of this additional revenue. In particular, the extensive introduction of diesel multiple-units dramatically improved receipts and passenger numbers. Progress was made also in cutting down the Region's approximate annual total of 2¼ million unprofitable train miles by the withdrawal of services – progress which was, admittedly, inhibited by the need to seek approval from Transport Users' Consultative Committees, and by railwaymen's inherited mindset that the railways were there to provide a service to all sections of the public, not just those who happened to live on profitable routes.

Plate 1.10. An intended consequence of the mechanisation of work on the Permanent Way: where once many men would have been at work, a mere handful dig out the trackbed at an unidentified station. (BR (NER), per A Dow)

An important component of the Modernisation Plan was the replacement of steam locomotion by diesel or electric. BR had acquired five main line Co-Co diesel-electric locomotives from orders placed just prior to Nationalisation by the LMSR and the SR. As this handful of locomotives had not been added to by Riddles, it had proved impossible for train operators to dieselise an entire train service. Instead, the diesel locomotives had formed only part of a pool formed largely by steam locomotives. In such a circumstance, the diesel locomotives had been a nuisance, not an asset. Little effort had been made by engineers or operators to find out what diesel locomotives could or could not do when rostered and worked intensively. Thus, when the Ministry accepted the Modernisation Plan, and when significant investment was at last in prospect, BR's knowledge of diesel locomotion was less than complete. This was despite the fact that experience in the United States and in continental Europe had convincingly demonstrated how much more economical diesel traction was than steam. Riddles by now having retired, his successor, Roland C Bond, therefore approved a programme for the building of 174 diverse diesel locomotives. These would be tested over three years, and the best then selected as standard designs. This prudent programme had come far too late though. BR's trading account for the year 1954, after the inclusion of central charges, showed a deficit of £21.6 million.(24) The deficit for the year 1955 was even worse: £38.2 million.(25) The increasing deficits triggered something akin to panic within Government and the BTC, and led in 1956 to the BTC's decision to abandon the three-year testing period. Henceforth, dieselisation would proceed as fast as possible in order to reduce the costs of train operation, and, therefore, BR's deficit. This imprudent policy would saddle BR with many expensive, non-standard diesel locomotives that were next to useless. The North Eastern Region would get its share of these.

Concerning the funding for the Modernisation Plan, the initial intention was that the BTC would fund one third of it, the remaining two thirds would come from the Government. Early in 1956 however, it became apparent that BR's financial position was worsening, and that the BTC would not be able to fund the Plan to the expected extent. The Ministry therefore asked the BTC to re-examine the Plan. The result was the White Paper *Proposals for the Railways*, published in October 1956.(26) The drafting of the Plan had been done hurriedly, over a period of about six months. As a result, no detailed costings of the various schemes had been done for it. In the preparation of the White Paper, the costings were done, and presented to the Ministry as a sound commercial proposition. The expectation now was that BR's revenue account would achieve a balance by 1961 or 1962. Reassured, the Ministry gave its approval. The Government as a whole played its part also by introducing a new system of financing, whereby it undertook to advance money to meet deficits incurred during current operations as well as to defray expenditure.(27) Such confidence as the Government had in the planning skills of the BTC and its railwaymen took a knock when, late in 1957, the BTC informed the Minister of Transport and Civil Aviation that the total cost of implementing the Plan had risen from £1240 to £1500 million. Part of the rise was accounted for by inflation, but some was due to more precise costings of the Plan's diverse schemes. In addition, the conclusion had been reached that the best results would be obtained by additional expenditure on continuous brakes on freight wagons, and on expanded provision at maintenance depots for the new types of locomotive and rolling now being introduced. The proposed additional expenditure totalled about £160 million.

Plate 1.11. A steam breakdown crane re-rails an unidentified member of Class Q6. (JW Armstrong / JW Armstrong Trust, per AR Thompson)

Implementation of the Plan did not, unfortunately, manifest itself in a rapid reduction in BR's deficit, Indeed, it got worse. The trading account for the year 1957, after the inclusion of central charges, showed a deficit of £68.1 million.(28) By December 1958, it was already apparent that the deficit for the year was going to be even worse. In the House of Commons on 11 December, the Minister of Transport and Civil Aviation announced that the BTC was therefore undertaking a 'full, detailed and urgent review of the whole Modernisation Plan'. The result was the White Paper *Re-appraisal of the Plan for the Modernisation and Re-equipment of British Railways*, presented to Parliament in July 1959.(29) This included details of the progress made so for with the implementation of the Plan. Concerning the North Eastern Region, progress included the following:

* Track had been laid with continuously-welded rail, and concrete sleepers installed. Track maintenance had been mechanised to a significant extent by the introduction of machines to tamp ballast, to clean ballast, and to relay track.
* Colour-light signals had been installed at Newcastle, and the Automatic Warning Control system installed on the fast lines on the East Coast Main Line between King's Cross and York.
* By the end of 1958, the Region was operating two thirds of its local passenger train mileage using diesel multiple-units. On the route Bradford - Leeds - Harrogate, such units were bringing in receipts five times greater than had been obtained when steam locomotion was used.
* There had been an increase in the proportion of freight train mileage run by expresses.
* The replacement of low capacity wagons by modern steel high capacity wagons was proceeding apace, permitting a reduction in the size of the wagon fleet.
* The container fleet had been increased, and high capacity fork-lift trucks and mobile cranes had been put into service to handle them.
* York freight depot had been modernised.

Over the next five years, the Plan would be implemented in the Region in the following ways:
* There would be further rationalisation of facilities, including the closure of Leeds Central station and of much of the former Hull & Barnsley Railway. Centralised Traffic Control would be installed over the route York - Hull via Market Weighton, and the line singled in order reduce operating costs to the extent that passenger services would be profitable. Over the Region as a whole, the route mileage open to passengers would be reduced from about 1750 in 1950 to about 1100 in 1963. Over the period 1958 to 1963, the number of passenger stations would be reduced from 520 to about 400. Railway workshops would also be closed.
* More continuously-welded rail would be laid and more concrete sleepers installed.
* By 1963, most of the East Coast Main Line between Doncaster and Berwick would be equipped with a modern signalling system. Most level crossings would be protected by lifting half-barriers, operated automatically by approaching trains. The East Coast Main Line between King's Cross and York, and the route Doncaster - Leeds would be electrified some time after 1964.
* Passenger stations, including those at Leeds, Sunderland and Wakefield, would be improved. Parcels traffic would be segregated from passengers at stations; new parcels concentration depots would be provided at Leeds and York.
* Dieselisation would increase, permitting an increase in the speed of freight trains. By 1960, nearly all merchandise wagons would be vacuum-braked. The Region's ninety sundries depots would be reduced to sixty in accordance with the policy of concentrating general merchandise traffic; the depots at Bradford, Hull, Leeds, Newcastle, Stockton and Sunderland would be reconstructed and mechanised. The cartage fleet, which at present largely comprised three-wheeled tractors, would in the future be equipped with a larger proportion of four-wheeled tractors better suited to longer distance runs. The number of specialised door-to-door containers would be increased, and 'Freight Liner' trains introduced. The number of goods yards would be reduced. Yards that remained open would be modernised; new hump marshalling yards would be built at Healey Mills, Lamesley, Newport and Stourton.

Plate 1.12. The crew of Class G5 No 67278 replenish its water tanks at Garsdale (London Midland Region) on 20 March 1954. They have just worked the 9.50 am train from Northallerton via the North Eastern Region's Hawes Branch, and are preparing to work back. (TJ Edgington)

On 8 October 1959 there was a general election, as a result of which the Conservatives were re-elected. The formation of the new Government was accompanied by the appointment of a new Minister of Transport.(30) The new appointee was Ernest Marples, one of a growing number of politicians and civil servants who believed that roads were superseding railways in exactly the same way that railways had superseded canals. Indeed, the contracting company of which he was a director, Marples, Ridgeway, and Partners, was now well-known as a constructor of new trunk roads. (Marples temporarily relinquished this directorship while he was a Minister in order to avoid an overt conflict of interests.) When the White Paper was studied by the new Minister and his civil servants, it became apparent to them that the profits that were predicted to accrue from implementation of the Plan were dubious. Marples therefore asked that detailed costings of all schemes amounting to £250,000 or more be submitted to him. When these were submitted, they came as a shock. By the Ministry's own calculations, the expected return on the schemes was nothing like that predicted by the BTC. There seemed no prospect of the schemes implemented in accordance with the Plan generating sufficient revenue to service the new expenditure, never mind pay off the old capital.

The BTC was not the only nationalised undertaking that was in financial difficulties. On 30 November 1959 the House of Commons appointed a Select Committee to investigate on its behalf how the undertakings were faring, and to make comment as appropriate. The Committee's report on BR was published in July 1960.(31) A pertinent point made in the report was that, as the Plan was not fully implemented, final conclusions upon its success or otherwise could not yet be made. It was, though, already very apparent that schemes such as the North Eastern Region's replacing steam locomotion by diesel multiple-units were proving very successful in increasing receipts and passenger numbers. However, the Committee wanted to know if the increased receipts were commensurate with the capital cost of such schemes. Unfortunately, it did not seem as though they were. In the words of the report: 'large expenditures have been undertaken on modernising parts of the undertaking without any precise calculation of what the profitability of those parts will be on completion'. The Committee also observed that there was 'a confusion in judging what is economically right and what is socially desirable'. According to the Transport Act, 1947, BR was, of course, effectively bound by statute to be profitable. Given that there was now so much competition from road transport for all types of traffic, no one part of the railway was so profitable that it could cross-subsidise another. Therefore, railwaymen were effectively bound by statue to run the trains that were profitable, and to stop running those that were not. In practice, BR for the most part was running the trains that its predecessors had run, whether they were now profitable or not, in order to provide what railwaymen saw as a service to the nation as a whole. In their report, the members of the Select Committee made the point that the running by BR of some loss-making passenger and freight services might well be in the national interest, but that decisions on these were for Parliament to make. The decisions were not those that either the BTC or BR should have made on their own.

Plate 1.13. Driver J Hill oils his locomotive, a member of Class B1, at Scarborough shed. (Ken Hoole Study Centre Collection)

Doctor Richard Beeching

Even before the Select Committee published its report, Marples set up in March 1960 a Special Advisory Group to assist him in an examination of the structure, finances and workings of the BTC. One of the men he appointed to the Group was Doctor Richard Beeching, ICI's Technical Director. Beeching was a physicist with no experience in the transport industry, but a proven record in business management. The specific trigger causing Marples to set up the Group was the publication on 2 March of the Guillebaud Report, which recommended increases in the wages of BR's employees of between 8 and 18%. However, a factor by no means insignificant was BR's worsening deficit. The trading account for the year 1959, after the inclusion of central charges, showed a deficit of £84 million. Admittedly, this was better than for the year 1958, which had shown a deficit of £90.1 million, but by now the railways should have been approaching a break-even position, not continuing to make an enormous loss.(32)

While the Group undertook its study, the Modernisation Plan was put on hold. By July 1960, the Group had learned enough to recommend to Marples that those modernisation schemes which were well-advanced, were self-evidently justified, or involved replacement of assets that were worn out, should be completed; schemes only just started should be stopped. The BTC responded by preparing a modernisation plan to be implemented over the period 1961 to 1964. The Ministry was still mulling over this plan when it was overtaken by events.

In their consideration of the structure of the BTC, the Group's members had differing views. All members were though in broad agreement that the BTC and the Area Boards should be abolished. The failings of the former were, given the size of BR's deficit, all too apparent. The failings of the latter were more modest. The Boards had performed well enough, but as their members served part-time, they had not been able to devote as much effort to their appointed tasks as was warranted by the situation in which the railways found themselves. The Groups' recommendations as to future organisation were published in December 1960 in the White Paper *Reorganisation of the Nationalised Transport Undertakings*.(33) Within, it was observed that BR was such a large undertaking that its affairs had tended to dominate those of the BTC (which was, of course, still responsible for those nationalised road transport undertakings that had not been sold back to private industry, as well as for docks, inland waterways, transport hotels, and London Transport).

Plate 1.14. Mickleton on a damp and gloomy 25 October 1952. The weather might be miserable, but the station is neatly tended, and the railwayman on duty is smartly dressed. (JW Armstrong / JW Armstrong Trust, per AR Thompson)

Concerning the railways, the Group's recommendations were that a British Railways Board be established to perform those functions best managed centrally. All other functions would be delegated to Regional Railway Boards, which would replace the existing Area Boards; some of the appointees to the new Boards would serve full-time.

These recommendations were very much influenced by Beeching's views. The White Paper also recommended that the nationalised undertakings be given the maximum practicable freedom of operation in conducting their affairs. Although the Transport Act, 1953, had in theory given the BTC the freedom to charge for the conveyance of passengers and freight at rates it thought appropriate, in practice procrastination by the Transport Tribunal had not permitted the implementation of the BTC's new Railway Merchandise Charges Scheme until 1 July 1957. Further liberalisation in the way of charging would be welcomed as a way of reducing BR's deficit.

Marples was very impressed by Beeching and the part he had played in the preparation of the White Paper, and offered him the Chairmanship of the proposed British Railways Board (BRB). To tempt Beeching, he was offered a salary matching that paid to him by ICI – £24,000. Marples' own salary as a Government Minister was only £5000; the present Chairman of the BTC, Sir Brian Robertson, was paid £10,000. The huge salary offered to Beeching was in line with the huge impact he was expected to make on BR. Such an impact was deemed necessary given the enormous deficits being incurred annually in the operation of the railways. Despite the scale of the task of turning these deficits into profits, Beeching accepted the challenge, and the appointment to the proposed BRB. On 15 March 1961 it was announced that he was to be appointed a part-time Member of the BTC, and that he was to take over as Chairman on 1 June when Robertson retired. In due course, Beeching would be appointed Chairman of the BRB.

In April 1962, while the Bill that would abolish the BTC and sanction the formation of the BRB was in preparation, Beeching established the British Railways Committee; this would function as a precursor to the BRB. Beeching recommended to Marples that some at least of the members of this Committee be drawn from outside the railway industry. As railwaymen had made such a hash of the planning of the Modernisation Plan, this was a recommendation that Marples was happy to accept. One of the appointees from outside was Sir Steuart Mitchell, trained in naval engineering and, latterly, serving as the Ministry of Aviation's Controller of Guided Weapons and Electronics. Mitchell was appointed to the Committee as Beeching's Vice-Chairman, and with the specific intention that he take over from the Area Boards responsibility for BR's main workshops. Other functions, such as purchasing, were also to be withdrawn from the Area Boards and placed in the hands of members of the Committee; this was in accordance with Beeching's view that there should be strong central control of BR. In order to involve the existing regional management in the proposed BRB, the six Chairmen of the Area Boards were also appointed to the Committee. From the North Eastern Area Board, the appointee was TH Summerson. Last, but not necessarily least, space was found on the Committee for three railwaymen. One of those was Frederick C Margetts, who since 1 September 1961 had been the North Eastern Region's General Manager.

Colour Plate 1.
The regional colour chosen for the North Eastern Region was variously described as Deep Orange or Tangerine. It was seen predominantly on station signs, as seen here at Stockton on 3 August 1964. (JM Boyes / JW Armstrong Trust, per JR Midcalf)

Colour Plate 2.
The colour was widely applied, and in some cases lasted a very long time; it is seen here on 10 March 1995 on a North Eastern Railway 'Public Warning' sign. The sign was placed next to an unmanned level crossing giving access to Norden Barn farm east of South Milford; it remained in place until removed by persons unknown in the late 1990s. (JG Teasdale)

Colour Plate 3.
The regional colour was used on stationery too. (Reproduced at 80% of original size.) (NERA Collection)

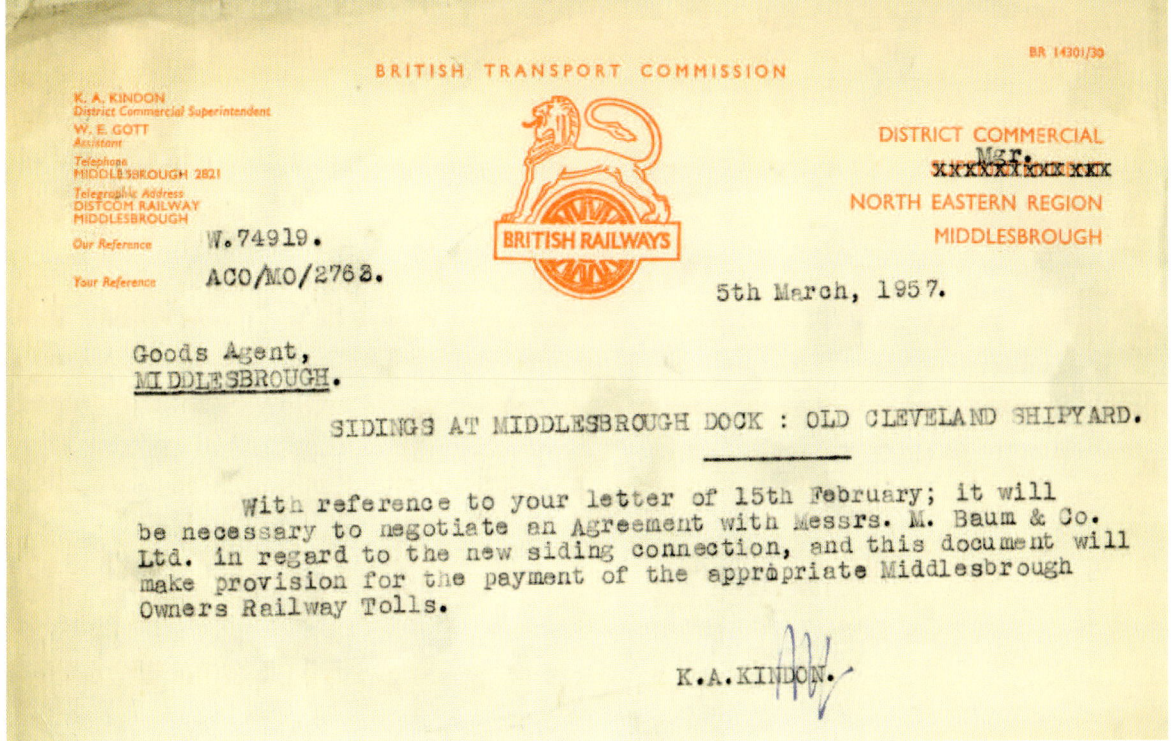

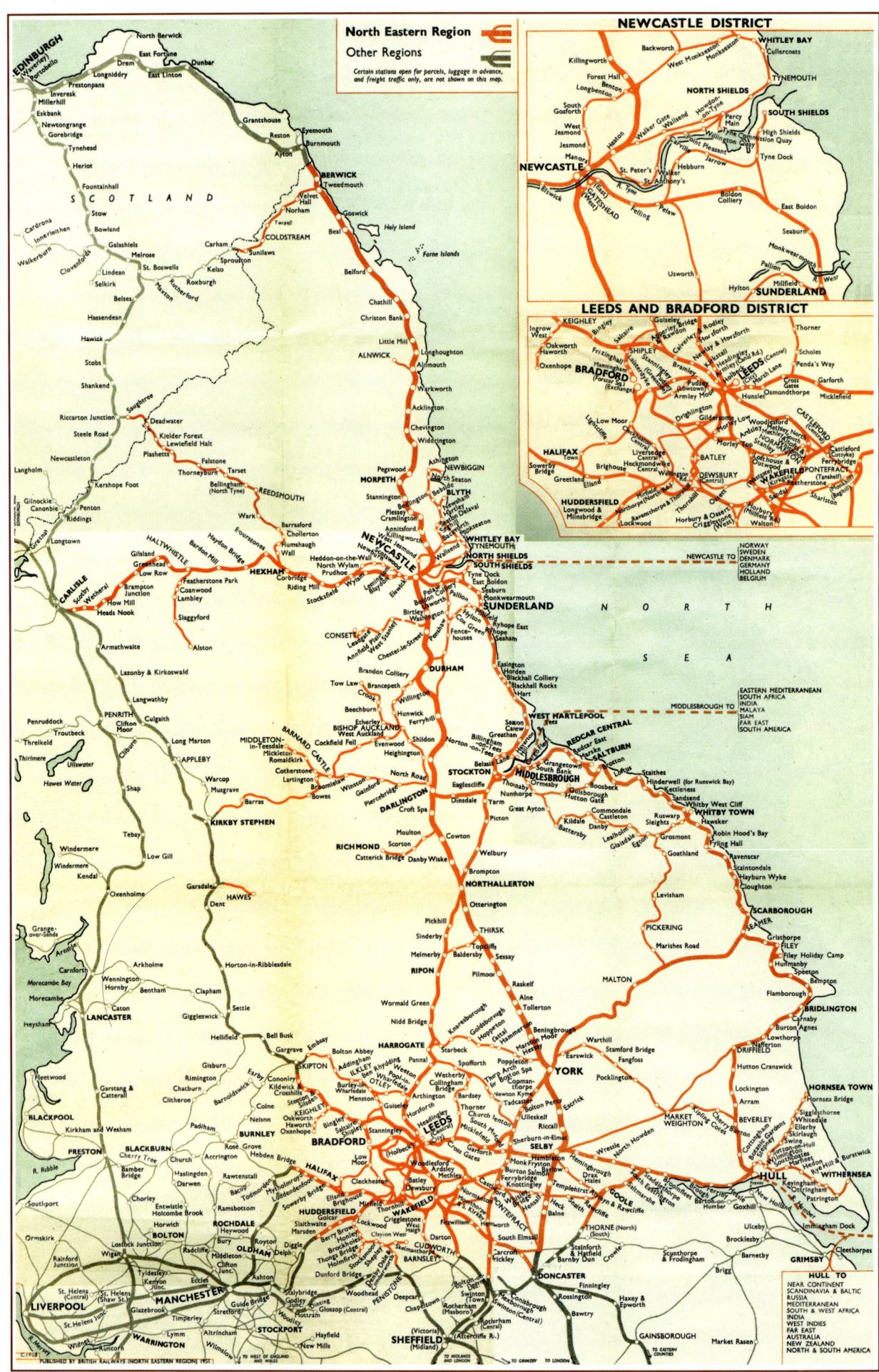

Colour Plate 4. This timetable map, issued to the public in June 1955, shows the North Eastern Region's passenger lines. (For clarity, the freight only lines are omitted; reproduced at 50% of original size.) (BR (NER), per AE Young)

Margetts, who had begun his railway career with the LNER, had been promoted to the general managership from the post of the North Eastern Region's Assistant General Manager (Traffic). Following Margetts' appointment to the Committee, with effect from 30 April 1962 he was replaced as General Manager by Arthur Dean, a civil engineer who had started his railway career with the SR. Like Margetts, Dean was promoted to the general managership from within the Region. In 1951 he had been appointed the Region's Chief Civil Engineer; in 1960 he had been appointed Assistant General Manager (Modernisation). These promotions of Margetts and Dean were in contrast to the earlier policy of promoting to high office from outside a Region.

The establishment of the BRB was authorised by the Transport Act, 1962; it assumed its responsibilities on 1 January 1963 with Beeching as its Chairman.(34) One of the clauses in the Transport Act stipulated that the newly-inaugurated BRB should make a profit – a stipulation inherited from the BTC and the Transport Act, 1947. Another clause stipulated that six Regional Railway Boards be established to manage the railways in the six Regions; TH Summerson was appointed Chairman of the North Eastern Regional Railway Board. Unlike the situation that had pertained with the Area Boards, appointees to the Regional Railway Boards would include railwaymen. Indeed, Arthur Dean was appointed Chairman of the North Eastern Regional Railway Board effective from 1 October 1963, following Summerson's resignation from the post. This increase in status for the railwaymen at regional level was very welcome, but the BRB reserved to itself many important functions. These latter included: negotiations with staff on pay and conditions; appointments of senior officers; determination of the size of the railway system; overall commercial policy; design and procurement of locomotives and rolling stock; management of main workshops; research and development. Concerning BR's charges for the conveyance of passengers and freight, the Act abolished all charges schemes, thus allowing the BRB to set charges at levels it thought appropriate. The Act also abolished the railways' obligations as common carriers. This last was a very useful liberalisation – no longer would BR be compelled to accept traffic that was regarded as uneconomic by such as road haulage companies.

By freeing the BRB to set charges, and by abolishing the common carrier obligation, the Government played its part in allowing BR to become profitable once again. In March 1963, the BRB made known its contribution by publishing *The Reshaping of British Railways* (subsequently known as the Beeching Report). This was based on thoroughgoing investigations made first by the British Railways Committee and then by the BRB into such as: the closure of redundant stations and lines; the single-manning of diesel and electric locomotives; the poor reliability and utilisation of diesel locomotives; the excessive size of the passenger carriage and the freight wagon fleets; the operation of passenger and freight traffic. The basic message of the report was that the route to profitability lay in rationalisation of redundant stations, depots, yards and lines, coupled with a concentration on profitable traffics. Concerning rationalisation, the report made public some extraordinary statistics: the sum of the passenger receipts from 1762 stations (the least busy, and 41% of the total number) contributed only 1% of British Railway's total passenger receipts; the sum of the tonnage of merchandise and minerals forwarded from 2906 stations (58% of the total number) contributed only 1% of British Railway's total such tonnage. From these statistics, it was obvious that the Area Boards and the General Managers between them had signally failed to recommend to the BTC the closure of redundant facilities in their Regions. Unfortunately, since the opportunity to close such facilities on a carefully considered basis had been squandered, the likelihood was that facilities that perhaps ought to remain open would be closed in a desperate attempt to return BR to profit. So it proved; the Beeching Report included a list of 266 routes from which passenger services would be withdrawn, a list of 71 routes over which passenger services would be modified, and a list of 1924 stations which would be closed.

Plate 1.15. A job lacking appeal in post-war Britain: cleaning the char out of a steam locomotive's smokebox, 1963. (RG Warwick)

In the North Eastern Region, a route listed for closure was York - Hull via Market Weighton. The report described current passenger train operations over that route in detail. There were nine trains each way each weekday, mostly worked by diesel multiple-units. On average, there were 57 passengers per train. Total receipts per annum were £90,400. Total movement costs were less than this at £84,400. However, terminal expenses at York and Hull totalled £23,100, track and signalling costs along the route totalled £43,300. The inclusion of these latter sums put the service into deficit. Closure of the route would lead to loss of all receipts from the intermediate stations, but passengers travelling between York and Hull would be able to use an alternative railway route, so retaining some at least of these receipts for BR. As it happened, the North Eastern Region did have plans to make the route more economical to operate. These included the singling of the track, the installation of automatically-operated level crossings, and Centralised Traffic Control. Unfortunately, the preparation of these plans had proceeded at such a slow pace that they had not been fully implemented when the report was published; the route would be closed between York and Beverley on 29 November 1965.

The report was not, however, solely concerned with ruthless rationalisation. As well as ridding itself of unprofitable traffic, BR would actively develop profitable traffic. Such traffic tended to be that which was worked in trainloads rather than wagonloads. In order to increase trainload traffic, there would be investment in new facilities such as new types of freight wagon specifically matched to customers' requirements. For example, the BRB's High Capacity Wagon Design Committee was working with the National Coal Board and the Central Electricity Generating Board on a design for an automatic-discharge coal hopper wagon. Trains of such wagons would work continuously between collieries and power stations. The operation of domestic coal traffic would also be converted to trainload operation by the establishment of coal concentration depots, all provided with modern mechanical coal-handling equipment. (This idea was perhaps less relevant to the North Eastern Region, which had inherited a system in which most stations were equipped with coal cells. These cells were served by bottom-discharge hopper wagons, and allowed much better wagon utilisation than the system applying in much of the rest of the country, in which wagons were unloaded over a period of days or even weeks by a man with a shovel.) BR itself would operate much of its general merchandise traffic in trainloads by the inauguration of a network of Liner Trains. Such trains would convey containerised merchandise to and from newly-built depots, all provided with cranes to transfer containers between railway wagons and the motor lorries that would effect local collection and delivery. In order to haul all trains more economically and at faster speeds, the process of dieselisation would continue. This investment in new methods of working, new equipment and depots, when combined with the rationalisation of redundant facilities, was predicted to eliminate BR's deficit – or at least the greater part of it – by 1970. There was a long way to go; BR's trading account for the year 1962, after the inclusion of central charges, showed a deficit of £159 million.(35)

A New Government

Although Beeching was confident that BR could, eventually, achieve profitability, others were not convinced. On 30 September 1963, TH Summerson resigned his membership of the BRB and his chairmanship of the North Eastern Regional Railway Board, disappointed that Beeching had not accepted his suggestion that the Government subsidise the running of socially-necessary railway passenger services. Not that the Conservative Government was necessarily any more keen than Beeching on the idea. However, at the general election of 15 October 1964, the Labour Party achieved office once again. The concept of such subsidisation was more likely to find favour with the new Government, though for the moment the major closure programme initiated in the wake of the publication of the Beeching Report continued (though at a slower rate, and with increasing ministerial reluctance). In February 1965 the second part of that report was published: *The Development of Major Trunk Routes*. Broadly, this second part recommended that BR concentrate on the development of a core network comprising only 3000 miles out of a total of 7500 miles of presently-operated through routes. Publication of this second report did not result in a particularly forceful response from the Government – a Government that in its election manifesto had promised to halt major railway closures. Nevertheless, Beeching

Plate 1.16. Class G5 No 67315 at Alston on 12 April 1952. Note the former North Eastern Railway snowplough waiting for the next spell of wild winter weather. (JW Armstrong / JW Armstrong Trust, per AR Thompson)

resigned from the BRB with effect from 31 May 1965 and returned to ICI. For a replacement, the Government did not look outside the railway industry as the Conservatives had done; the new appointee as the Chairman of the BRB was Stanley E Raymond, who had at one time been General Manager of the Western Region, and who had sat on the BRB since 1 October 1963. (Incidentally, as Chairman of the BRB, he was paid much less than Beeching had been – £12,500, the same sum as was paid to the Chairman of the National Coal Board.)

Another new appointment concerned the Ministry of Transport. The current Minister, having failed to produce the plan to integrate inland transport that was required of him, was asked to resign. The post was offered to Barbara Castle on 22 December 1965; she accepted it the following day. Castle was no more experienced in transport matters than her predecessor had been, but she was a lot more forceful. She was also a keen advocate of the railways – an advocacy by no means shared by all her ministerial colleagues.(36) Within six months of her appointment, in July 1966, her Ministry published the White Paper *Transport Policy*.(37) This described how the Labour Government proposed to modernise the railways, how it would subsidise socially-necessary passenger services, and how it would integrate publicly-owned road and rail services. During November and December 1967, three more railway-related White Papers were published.(38) All this activity culminated in the Transport Act 1968.(39) The implications of this Act were to have a profound effect upon BR's financial performance; from henceforth, a Minister of Transport was permitted to subsidise loss-making rail passenger services if it was thought necessary to do so for social or economic reasons. By this time the Act had no relevance at all to the North Eastern Region.

Merger

A merger between the North Eastern and the Eastern Regions was first considered in a report by the Railway Executive dated 30 April 1951.(40) This report came down in favour of the status quo. Thereafter the North Eastern Region was well regarded by the BTC – it was compact, profitable, and had its headquarters at York, close to its customers. (All other Regions bar the Scottish had headquarters in London.) However, by 1964 the Region's deficit was on a par with BR's as a whole. The idea of merging the two Regions was, therefore, reconsidered. There were many advantages in such a merger. At present, the management of the East Coast Main Line was divided between three Regions: Eastern, North Eastern, and Scottish. A merger would reduce the number to two, unifying management to a significant extent. The merger would also unify management of the route King's Cross - Leeds, which since 11 June 1956 had been divided between the two English Regions, and of the routes between the south Yorkshire coalfields and the new baseload power stations being built in the lower reaches of the Aire Valley. Headquarters of the merged Region would be in York, close to the heavy industry that still provided large tonnages of freight traffic. Having only one headquarters, instead of the two currently serving the existing Regions, would allow approximately 1500 office and managerial posts to be abolished, and result in the saving of some £1½ million per annum in wages and salaries. The disadvantages were that the re-organisation of two Regions into one was bound to disrupt the day-to-day operation of the railways, and was bound to upset the staff who would lose their jobs. When the BRB considered the merger, these disadvantages were deemed to be outweighed by the advantages. Therefore, Gerard F Fiennes was appointed General Manager of the Eastern Region with effect from 1 January 1966. Part of his brief was to plan with Arthur Dean the merger of the two Regions into one large Eastern Region, and to assume the general managership of it in due course.

The BRB was not free to authorise that merger on its own initiative. The number of Regional Railway Boards, and by implication the number of Regions, had been set at six by Section 2 of the Transport Act, 1962. That same Section though permitted the Minister of Transport to alter the number of Regional Railway Boards. The BRB therefore put the case for the merger to Barbara Castle. The unions, whose members were already losing jobs as stations and lines closed, put the case against. Castle was moved by the unions' arguments, but not, ultimately, swayed by them. She signed on 30 November 1966 a Statutory Instrument abolishing the North Eastern Regional Railway Board.(41) This order came into operation on 1 January 1967. On that day, therefore, the North Eastern Region was abolished also. As an organisational entity, it had lasted six years less than the LNER's North Eastern Area that had preceded it.

Conclusion

The history of BR over the period 1948 to 1967 is, unfortunately, characterised by failure. Perhaps the greatest failure was by the Labour Government which nationalised the railways, and then failed to invest in them. It was also a failure of successive Governments that the British Transport Commission was never given full discretion over how much it charged for the conveyance of passengers and freight. That discretion, and the abolition of the railways' common carrier status, did not come until the passing of the Transport Act, 1962. The British Railways Board benefited from the passing of that Act, but by then BR had been financially ruined by years of being unable to charge economic rates for its passenger and freight services. The Transport Act, 1947 in effect obliged BR to be profitable, but successive Governments' procrastination in liberalising the charging regime made that all but impossible to achieve.

Labour's policy of integrating inland transport also failed. The policy was anyway hardly likely to be fully implemented once the decision was made to subdivide the BTC by transport mode rather than by, say, functions such as passenger transport provision, freight service provision, engineering, *etc*. The Conservative Government of 1951 adopted a policy the antithesis of Labour's, strongly encouraging competition between modes of transport. Significant integration would not be achieved until the passing of the Transport Act 1968. This Act established a National Freight Corporation, which was specifically intended to work in conjunction with the BRB in the task of integrating the conveyance of freight by road and railway. The Act also authorised the establishment of Passenger Transport Authorities, which would work with the BRB to integrate local road and railway passenger services. However, these developments came too late to influence the history of the North Eastern Region.

Railwaymen too contributed their share of failure, particularly in the way dieselisation was handled. The ill-judged dieselisation policy contributed to the failure of the Modernisation Plan to do what it was planned to do – return BR to profitability. This failure had major political ramifications; profitability was important. Although investment in Britain's roads was not expected to turn a profit, investment in the railways was – BR was a transportation business, and was expected to make a profit just like any other business. When profitability was not achieved, politicians and civil servants, many of whom were coming to believe that railways had been superseded by roads, had their beliefs confirmed. This led to the appointment of Doctor Beeching to the BRB, and to the drastic rationalisation of facilities that ensued after the publication of *The Reshaping of British Railways*. That drastic rationalisation too was a result of failures by railwaymen to cope adequately with the problem of redundant stations and lines. Had railwaymen dealt earlier with the problem, some lines which were closed following the publication of the Beeching Report might still be open today.

However, the history of the North Eastern Region is not one of unrelenting failure. The railwaymen and women working in the Region had much to be proud about: they were pioneers in the introduction of diesel multiple-units and in the application of the new technologies to signalling and telecommunications; they were well to the fore in the mechanisation of track maintenance. Such as these are described in the Papers that follow.

Endnotes:

(1) Act of Parliament 7 & 8 Victoriæ, cap. LXXXV. 'An Act to attach certain conditions to the Construction of future Railways authorized or to be authorized by any Act of the present or succeeding Sessions of Parliament; and for other Purposes in relation to Railways.' The Act is better known today for its provision of what came to be known as Parliamentary Trains, for which the adult fare was to be no more than 1d per mile.

(2) In June 1949, the Road Transport Executive was divided to form the Road Haulage and the Road Passenger Executives.

(3) Act of Parliament 10 and 11 Geo. 6. c. 49. 'An Act to provide for the establishment of a British Transport Commission concerned with transport and certain other related matters, to specify their powers and duties, to provide for the transfer to them of undertakings, parts of undertakings, property, rights, obligations and liabilities, to amend the law relating to transport, inland waterways, harbours and port facilities, to make certain consequential provision as to income tax, to make provision as to pensions and gratuities in the case of certain persons who became officers of the Minister of Transport, and for purposes connected with the matters aforesaid.' Short title: 'Transport Act, 1947'.

(4) See memorandum *Inception of the Regions* of February 1951 [National Archives file AN6/58]. Incidentally, the Regions were always listed in alphabetical order in order to avoid arguments over precedence.

(5) The Hotel Executive assumed its responsibilities for all railway-owned hotels, and for the employment of hotel, refreshment room and restaurant car staff, on 1 July 1948. The Docks and Inland Waterways Executive took control of the LNER's docks at Hull on 1 January 1949, and of that company's docks at Hartlepool and Middlesbrough on 1 March 1949.

(6) The private railway companies in the north-east of England that were not nationalised were: the Derwent Valley Light Railway Company; the Easingwold Railway Company; the North Sunderland Railway Company.

(7) The statistics come from a Paper submitted by the Railway Executive to the BTC in June 1948, quoted by MR Bonavia in *The Organisation of British Railways*. The actual figures were: route miles 1823; train miles per annum

Plate 1.17.
The LNER adopted the Scammell Mechanical Horse in the 1930s as part of its plans to mechanise local delivery services. This three-wheeled vehicle was highly manoeuverable, cheap to run, and with its automatic coupling could quickly couple to a variety of trailers. The Mechanical Horse was replaced by the improved Scarab in 1948, and BR bought large numbers of them. There was no regional difference in livery, all being painted maroon and cream. An example is seen here at Durham Gilesgate on 13 October 1962. (Ken Hoole Study Centre Collection)

29,000,000 (both statistics from 1946); number of staff 62,582 (statistic from 1948). The London Midland Region was the largest, having 26% of route miles, running 29% of train miles, and employing 33% of staff.

(8) The figures are as quoted by TR Gourvish in *British Railways 1948 – 73 : A Business History*.

(9) See in particular *The Sunday Express*, 23 May 1948.

(10) Deep Orange was British Standard Colour Number 591. The colour was also described in official documents as Tangerine.

(11) See *Eastern and North Eastern Regions*, 30 April 1951 [National Archives file AN4/8].

(12) See *Review of Present Organisation*, 8 October 1951 [National Archives file AN6/6].

(13) Act of Parliament 1 and 2 Eliz. 2. c.13. 'An Act to require the British Transport Commission to dispose of the property held by them for the purposes of the part of their undertaking which is carried on through the Road Haulage Executive; to amend the law relating to the carriage of goods by road and to provide for a levy, for the benefit of the said Commission and for other purposes, on motor vehicles used on roads; to provide for the re-organisation of the railways operated by the said Commission; to repeal certain provisions of the Transport Act, 1947, and to amend other provisions thereof; to amend section six of the Cheap Trains Act, 1883; and for purposes connected with the matters aforesaid.' Short title: 'Transport Act, 1953.'

(14) See SR & O 1927 N° 850. 'Schedule of Standard Charges.' This applied to the LNER only – other Statutory Rules and Orders applied to the other three companies.

(15) See the Railway and Canal Traffic Act, 1854.

(16) SI 1954 N° 1579.

(17) According to the *List of Members of Public Bodies . . .*, Summerson was appointed to the BTC – in a part-time capacity – on 1 May 1955. [See, for example, PP 1962 – 63 (Cmnd. 1903) volume xxxi, page 771.]

(18) Steel rationing (apart from that of tinplate) ended on 6 May 1953.

(19) See: SI 1950 N° 701; SI 1951 N° 601; SI 1951 N° 2194; SI 1952 N° 2013.

(20) The operating ratio is obtained by expressing the direct costs of providing a particular service as a percentage of receipts obtained from that service. An operating ration approaching 100 indicates that a service is going to be loss-making, once indirect costs have been added; an operating ratio above 100 is loss-making even before indirect costs have been added. For the source of the statistics, see BTC train censuses [National Archives file AN82/81].

(21) See the BTC's *First Annual Report* . . . [PP 1948 – 49 (235) volume xii, page 1].

(22) The Ministry of Transport and the Ministry of Civil Aviation were amalgamated with effect from 1 October 1953. See SI 1953 N° 1204.

(23) See HP Barker, *Re-equipment of British Railways*, 16 November 1954.

(24) See the BTC's *Seventh Annual Report* . . . [PP 1955 – 56 (20) volume xxviii, page 1].

(25) See the BTC's *Eighth Annual Report* . . . [PP 1956 – 57 (290) volume xxviii, page 325].

(26) [PP 1955 – 56 (Cmnd. 9880) volume xxxvi, page 419.]

(27) Act of Parliament 5 and 6 Eliz. 2. c. 9. Royal Assent 26 February 1957. 'An Act to make temporary provision authorising the British Transport Commission to meet interest and other revenue charges by borrowing, and modifying the requirements of the Transport Act, 1947, as to the sufficiency of the Commission's revenue to meet revenue charges, to authorise advances out of the Consolidated Fund of sums so borrowed, and for purposes connected therewith.' Short title: 'Transport (Railway Finances) Act, 1957'.

(28) See the BTC's *Annual Report . . .* [PP 1957 – 58 (215) volume xviii, page 17].

(29) [PP 1958 – 59 (Cmnd. 813) volume xix, page 777.]

(30) Effective from 21 October 1959, the Ministry of Transport and Civil Aviation was split into separate Ministries dealing with transport and with civil aviation. See SI 1959 N° 1768.

(31) [PP 1959 – 60 (254-1) volume vii, page 233.]

(32) For the source of the statistics, see BTC *Annual Report . . . year ended 31st December 1958* [PP 1958 – 59 (216) volume xix, page 397] and BTC *Annual Report . . . year ended 31st December 1959* [PP 1959 – 60 (226) volume xxi, page 43].

(33) [PP 1960 – 61 (Cmnd. 1248) volume xxvii, page 991.]

(34) Act of Parliament 10 and 11 Eliz. 2. c. 46. Royal Assent 1 August 1962. 'An Act to provide for the re-organisation of the nationalised transport undertakings now carried on under the Transport Act, 1947, and for that purpose to provide for the establishment of public authorities as successors to the British Transport Commission, and for the transfer to them of undertakings, parts of undertakings, property, rights, obligations and liabilities; to repeal certain enactments relating to transport, inland waterways, harbours and port facilities, and for purposes connected with the matters aforesaid.' Short title: 'Transport Act, 1962'.

(35) See the BTC's *Annual Report . . .* [PP 1962 – 63 (232) volume xxv, page 1].

(36) The Minister of Technology, for example, who said to Castle: 'If I had my way I'd close the whole lot down and put everything on road'. Quoted in Castle's autobiography *Fighting All the Way*, Macmillan London, 1993.

(37) [PP 1966 – 67 (Cmnd. 3057) volume lix, page 837.]

(38) *The Transport of Freight* [PP 1967 – 68 (Cmnd. 3470) volume xxxix, page 235]; *Public Transport and Traffic* [PP 1967 – 68 (Cmnd. 3481) volume xxxix, page 805]; *Railway Policy* [PP 1967 – 68 (Cmnd. 3439) volume xxxix, page 851].

(39) Act of Parliament 1968 Chapter 73. Royal Assent 12 October 1968. 'An Act to make further provision with respect to transport and related matters.' Short title: 'Transport Act 1968'.

(40) *Eastern and North Eastern Regions* [National Archives file AN4/8].

(41) SI 1966 N° 1508. 'The Regional Railway Boards Order 1966.'

The Organisation of the North Eastern Region
Reg Davies

Introduction

Organisation is not a subject that has the immediate appeal of locomotives, train working or engineering. Yet it often explains why events happened in a particular way and at a particular time. Largely taking place away from public view, policies and decisions as a result are little known or understood.

Whilst the North Eastern Region owed its inception to compromise, its relatively small size, throughout its life, was the ultimate cause of its elimination. In its nineteen years, overall management was successively exercised by four people. Initially the task was to set up a new organisation with minimal disruption to day to day operation. Later, expansion came with the transfer of more lines and the end of shared departments.

The Region's visual identity was one example of where its policy was determined by British Railways headquarters. For the first half of the Region's life, that control was a tight one but it later gained much more autonomy. These themes are developed in this Paper.

Nearly not a Region

As the table below demonstrates, the North Eastern Region was the smallest of the Regions. As such its existence was always questionable. Half-hearted attempts to eliminate it were finally successful in 1967.

The structure of its organisation was one of the first matters the Railway Executive (RE) discussed with the British Transport Commission (BTC). The RE Chairman, Sir Eustace Missenden, proposed on 2 October 1947 that there should be five main areas including a 'North Eastern – corresponding to English portions of L.N.E.R'. Lord Hurcomb, the BTC Chairman, replied 'such a grouping might be advisable…but it would be provisional'. On 27 October a BTC/RE meeting suggested eight Regions including a 'Sub-division existing L.N.E. to be centred, say, on York'. Two days later Missenden wrote to Hurcomb 'it may now be possible for an area to be brought into being as from January 1st next, which…will be named 'North Eastern Railway Area'.' With a ready-made nucleus in the North Eastern Area of the LNER, such an organisation could be set up fairly easily in the two months before Nationalisation became effective.(1)

In June 1948 Missenden wrote again to Hurcomb that 'the time has come to consider afresh the number and boundaries of the railway regions'. Noting that 'on all counts the London Midland Region…is oversize and the North Eastern is too small', he eventually concluded that the organisation should be developed 'by adjustment of the present six regions, without adding to their number'. A sense of uncertainty ran through the document. On one hand the RE 'are in some doubt even now as to the efficacy of the split between the Eastern and North Eastern Regions' but 'The possibility of enlarging the North Eastern Region is also being studied'. Whatever doubts surrounded the process, the outcome was the revision of regional boundaries on 2 April 1950, when the North Eastern Region gained former GC and GN lines from the Eastern Region and LMS lines from the London Midland Region.

But the topic would not go away. In February 1951 the RE, just beginning the new chairmanship of John Elliot, set up a Committee to report on a merger of the Eastern and North Eastern Regions. It was to comprise RE staff, who should consult with the two Chief Regional Officers and who must be able to comment on the report to the RE. If possible, it should be presented in four weeks. In the event the results were not available until June. 'It was decided that no case had been made out for merging the two Regions and no change should be made for the time being'. So a September memorandum to the RE concluded 'The six Regions should continue in their present form, which was only finalised in 1950, and on which agreement was made with the Unions'. It further suggested decentralisation from the RE to the Regions should continue with the re-designation of the Chief Regional Officers to Chief Regional Managers to epitomise the change. From 1955 this process would gather momentum, building up the status of the North Eastern Region. With the exception of a report 'entirely without foundation' in 1962, not until 1966 would the existence of the Region be threatened again.

Region	Staff in 1948 Number	% of Total	Route Miles, 1946 Number	% of Total	Train Miles per Annum, 1946 Millions of Miles	% of Total
Eastern	116,175	17	2,836	15	62	17
London Midland	228,569	33	4,993	26	109	29
North Eastern	62,582	9	1,823	9	29	8
Scottish	79,348	11	3,720	19	46	12
Southern	79,705	12	2,250	12	63	17
Western	123,135	18	3,782	19	62	17
Regional Average	114,919		3,286		62	

Source: *The Railway Regions* [National Archives file AN6/58]

GF Fiennes records that when he was appointed General Manager of the Eastern Region in 1965, the Chairman gave him the remit to merge it with the North Eastern and become General Manager of both.(2) The two Regions had already done a feasibility study; a merger would have many administrative advantages and cost savings of some £1.6m a year. In addition, rationalisation had meant many fewer staff and assets to manage. Fiennes felt the best location for the new Regional headquarters was York, since 80% of the freight business and 70% of the passenger originated within 80 miles of the city. In addition, moving offices out of London was in line with government policy. Since the Transport Act 1962 said there should be six Regional Railway Boards, abolition of the North Eastern required an amendment Order to be made by the Minister of Transport. Although requested in January 1966, it was not made until December. Nominally the new Region began from 1 January 1967 but it was to take a further year before it was fully effective. Of the Assistant General Managers and Chief Officers of the new Region, slightly more came from the Eastern than the North Eastern.

Four General Managers

During the whole of its existence the Region only had four men at its head. From 1 January 1948 the principal post was termed 'Chief Regional Officer' (CRO). Renamed 'Chief Regional Manager' (CRM) from 1 October 1953, it became 'General Manager' (GM) from 1 January 1955. In chronological order the occupants were CP Hopkins, HA Short, FC Margetts and A Dean. Short served the longest at eleven years, Margetts the shortest with one year; Hopkins stayed for two years and Dean for five. Hopkins, Short and Margetts had an operating background, whilst Dean was a civil engineer. Hopkins and Margetts had sprung from the LNER but Short and Dean were Southern Railway men.

Charles Patchett Hopkins was educated at Archbishop Holgate's Grammar School in York and joined the North Eastern Railway in 1916. He became a Traffic Apprentice in 1921 and then served with the newly centralised freight rolling stock organisation of the LNER. In 1932 he began a succession of operating appointments in the Southern Area of the LNER. Transferring to LNER headquarters in 1943, he became Assistant General Manager (Traffic & Statistics) in 1946, from which he was appointed the youngest CRO. His 'personal charm, his capacity for hard work, and his wide knowledge of railway work soon established him as a major figure.(3) However, he moved to the Southern Region from 1 January 1950, as part of a reshuffle of CROs. He stayed in that post until he retired on 1 January 1963. He died on 18 December 1987.

Herbert Arthur (Bill) Short was educated at Bournemouth School and joined the London & South Western Railway in 1913. On the outbreak of war, he served with the Suffolk Regiment until 1919, during which time he won the Military Cross. Rejoining the

Plate 2.1. This June 1951 view from York city walls looks out across what remained of the city's first railway station. Beyond can be seen the North Eastern Railway Company's Headquarters building, now in use for the same purpose by British Railways' North Eastern Region. As had been the case before Nationalisation and even before the Grouping, the former station hotel at the head end of the station was also in use by Headquarters staff. To the left, members of the public attend an exhibition of modern locomotives and rolling stock, put on in connection with the Festival of Britain; BR Standard No 70000 'Britannia' is clearly visible. (RG Warwick)

LSWR, he had experience in the operating and commercial departments of that company and the Southern Railway. Becoming Assistant Docks & Marine Manager in 1936, he was promoted to Docks & Marine Manager in 1941. Perhaps significantly Sir Eustace Missenden, the RE Chairman, had once occupied the latter post. Certainly Short was a great friend of Missenden. Short's last appointment with the Southern Railway was as Deputy Traffic Manager in 1945. On Nationalisation, he became Acting Chief Officer (Docks) from which post he joined the North Eastern Region as part of the reshuffle of CROs. Despite his Southern Railway background he 'once again identified himself closely with the team he was to co-ordinate if not to lead, and after a time people forgot that he had ever been an outsider'.(4) He retired on 31 August 1961 and died on 15 November 1967.

Frederick Chilton (Freddie) Margetts began his railway career with the LNER in Hull in 1923 and became a traffic apprentice in 1927. From 1932 to 1943 he had a succession of posts in the North Eastern Area of the LNER in commercial, operating and motive power departments. He joined the Southern Area in 1943, leaving for Scotland in 1945. His time there, associated particularly with modernisation of marshalling yards, culminated as Chief Operating Superintendent, Scottish Region. Returning to York in 1958 as Chief Traffic Manager, later re-styled Assistant General Manager (Traffic), his considerable impact made him the obvious candidate to succeed Short. Margetts was 'essentially a Traffic Officer who has achieved a deservedly high reputation for his energy and initiative and for his forward thinking on railway affairs'.(5) This reputation meant he was not to stay as General Manager for long. Dr Beeching gave him responsibility for operations as a member of the British Railways Committee in April 1962 and of the Board that succeeded it from 1 January 1963. Margetts retired from the Board on 1 January 1968 and died on 28 March 1989.

Although born in Halifax and studying for an engineering degree there, Arthur Dean subsequently left for post-graduate work at Imperial College, London. He joined the Civil Engineering Department of the Southern Railway in 1924, becoming Divisional Engineer (London East) in 1939. Promoted to Maintenance Engineer in 1942 and Assistant Chief Civil Engineer in 1946, he became Chief Officer Engineering (Works) on Nationalisation. His connection with the North Eastern Region began in 1951, when he became its Chief Civil Engineer. Leaving that field in 1960, he became Assistant General Manager (Modernisation) and, on 30 April 1962, General Manager. He seems to have been a man who inspired very mixed feelings. To one man, Dean and he on occasions were 'in open conflict'(6); to another Dean 'could behave strangely'.(7) After the merger with the Eastern Region, when GF Fiennes became GM of the larger Eastern Region from 1 January 1967, Dean undertook analysis and planning for the freight business at Board headquarters. He retired in June 1967 and died on 14 August 1968.

1948 – The Immediate Task
(Changes to the LNER Structure)

As we have already seen, the North Eastern Region had its nucleus in the North Eastern Area of the LNER. That reflected the Railway Executive's need to ensure an organisation that would keep the railways running. At least as a start, the RE decided not to change the Big Four companies' administration fundamentally. At its inception, the Region showed few changes to the existing LNER structure and covered only former LNER lines. Only as time went on did the organisation change and other lines were added. To consider the first, it is necessary to return to the LNER organisation briefly.

This was a fairly decentralised one. Three Divisional General Managers (DGM), responsible for day to day operation in their Area, and a number of 'all line' Officers, responsible for activities throughout the company, reported to a Chief General Manager (CGM), who set policy under the general direction of the Board of Directors. The North Eastern Area organisation, already fairly self-contained, became the basis of the North Eastern Region. However, a number of changes had to be made.

Personnel (or 'staff') work on the LNER had been included within each Department. The Staff Assistant to the CGM made policy and the Staff Assistant to the DGM controlled the work of each departmental staff section. In the new Region staff work, including welfare and medical services, became on 1 January 1948 a separate department under a Regional Staff Officer. In the LNER Signal & Telecommunications engineering was part of the Civil Engineering department. In the new Region, it became a separate department on 1 January 1948 under a Chief Signal & Telecommunications Engineer.

Plate 2.2. Arthur Dean, the North Eastern Region's last General Manager. (Courtesy Mrs Annette Dean)

Plate 2.3. The North Eastern Region inherited a fine collection of vintage Inspection Saloons for use by senior officers and their staff. This is six-wheeler No DE902178, stabled at Durham on 26 July 1952 in connection with the running of trains to and from the Durham Miners' Gala. The saloon served as required both the operating and engineering departments in the Newcastle and Sunderland Districts. It had been built by the North Eastern Railway in 1894 (possibly incorporating parts recovered from four-wheeled Saloon No 853 of 1874), and would remain in service until circa 1960. (IL Gray-Jones)

Former 'all line' officers presented a different problem. As the LNER Scottish Area had been incorporated into the new Scottish Region and the Southern Area became the basis of the Eastern Region, these officers were made responsible jointly to the CROs of the Eastern and North Regions 'to keep down the initial cost of this conversion'. The departments concerned were Mechanical & Electrical Engineering, Accountancy, Law, Treasury, Press Relations & Advertising; all were based in London but, in the case of the last three, local sub-offices were established in the York headquarters. In addition, the Continental Traffic Manager, Eastern Region acted for the North Eastern Region. Subsequent developments in the joint departments will be noticed later.

A relatively minor change within the Region was the transfer of goods terminal work from the operating to the commercial department for which preparations were made during 1948. BTC policy required transfers to two of its other Executives, which affected the Region. On 1 July 1948 all the hotels, refreshment rooms and restaurant car services were handed to the Hotels Executive. Responsibility for Hull Docks passed to the Docks Executive on 1 January 1949. The Hartlepools and Middlesbrough followed on 1 March 1949.

A further change from 1 November 1948 was the introduction of a Motive Power Officer, a result of the RE's decision to standardise the differing practices of the former companies. On the LNER the Locomotive Running Superintendent (LRS) was a departmental officer but was responsible to the Chief Mechanical Engineer for maintenance of locomotives between shoppings. Additionally in the North Eastern Area the LRS had joint responsibilities with the Operating Superintendent for current operations. The new Regional Motive Power Officer was essentially responsible for the provision of motive power including manning, servicing and maintenance. The Operating Superintendent was responsible for locomotive operation outside shed limits and the Regional Mechanical Engineer for technical standards.

Changes in lines controlled by the North Eastern Region from 1 January 1948 were few. It gained two Joint Railways, the Axholme and the Swinton & Knottingley. It incorporated former LNER Scottish Area lines in England. They were the Silloth Branch, Hexham to Saughtree, Reedsmouth to Morpeth and the Rothbury Branch. In exchange, Sprouston and Carham stations in Scotland were given up. Recognising geographical realities, the Silloth line was further transferred to the London Midland Region on 12 June 1948. Subsequent changes are noticed elsewhere.

Expansion – The Take-over of LMSR Lines

Although the RE had little choice other than to continue with existing organisations, it meant that, although Regions appeared to cover specific areas, in practice two Regions could be operating alongside each other. The changes introduced from 2 April 1950 were intended to make each Region self-contained by transferring lines and stations. The North Eastern Region gained considerably from this process.

The former Great Central and Great Northern lines north of Barnsley, Mexborough and Doncaster were transferred from the Eastern Region. All former LMSR lines north of Penistone, Darfield and Denaby and east of Diggle, Eastwood and Skipton were transferred from the London Midland Region. In addition, the North Eastern Region gained the line from Shaftholme Junction to Knottingley. Its only losses were the lines from Kirby Stephen East to Clifton Moor and to Tebay. However, operation of these lines remained with the Region from which they had been transferred, as 'penetrating lines'. This was a concept intended to avoid disruption, as the operating and motive power officers continued to exercise their existing control. But it introduced complications as the staff on a penetrating line were employed by the Region to which they were transferred but controlled by another. These difficulties meant that in time penetrating lines were eliminated.

In its 1955 Report the British Transport Commission noted it intended 'to terminate arrangements whereby certain lines controlled by one Region penetrate into another Region'.[8] In brief, the choice was to revert to the previous situation or to transfer penetrating lines to the geographical Region. The West Riding was a particular area of contention. The Eastern and London Midland Regions favoured the first option, whilst the North Eastern favoured the second. Tellingly, in the light of previous concerns about the size of the Region, the North Eastern would loose 25% of its staff if the first option were adopted. The Commission finally decided on 24 November 1955 to transfer to the North Eastern Region the penetrating lines in its area for all purposes. Consequently the Eastern Region lines were transferred on 11 June 1956.

The London Midland Region transfer was in two stages. The Carriage & Wagon organisation was first on 17 June 1956 and the operating and motive power followed on 17 September 1956.

Tangerine or Orange?

The British Railways totem, designed by AJ White, Advertising Officer, Railway Executive, was shown at a Press conference held by Sir Eustace Missenden, the RE Chairman in February 1948. The background colour of the totem was intended to vary when used by Regions for public display purposes, such as station name boards. The North Eastern Region was to use 'tangerine'. Confusingly the colour changed name over time. A Railway Executive Minute in 1948 records the distinctive colours for the North Eastern Region as 'Tangerine and Black'.[9] The 1948 BTC Report called it 'Orange' and by 1955 the North Eastern Area Board referred to it as 'Deep Orange'.[10] George Dow, who on Nationalisation briefly became Press Relations Officer for the Eastern and North Eastern Regions, thought it introduced a colour 'highly unsuitable for signs… bilious tangerine'.[11] But whatever the description, why was this colour chosen?

One of those around at the time recorded 'the reason was never explained' and no reason has been found in any of the official papers.[12] Three other regional colours bore some affinity to their past history and the Scottish Region's to the national flag. The two Regions formed from the English portion of the LNER may have taken their colours from the company's timetable covers. From 1 May 1939, a new form of LNER timetable had been introduced based on Bradshaw's Railway Guide. Whilst initially there had been some variety, from the edition commencing on 1 April 1940 white lettering on a dark blue ground was used for the rest of the company's existence. This was virtually identical to the colour adopted by the Eastern Region. Before the major change of 1939, the LNER timetable cover was tangerine, virtually identical to the colour adopted by the North Eastern Region. Of course an alternative, simpler, explanation to this timetable theory is the need for a distinctive colour, which had not already been used.

Plate 2.4. D49/1 No 62702 'Oxfordshire' is seen here with an unidentified Inspection Saloon on Monkton Moor in April 1952. (JW Hague / NERA GM Pierson Collection)

Plate 2.5. D49/1 No 62702 'Oxfordshire' and the Inspection Saloon is seen once again a month later, this time near Melmerby. (JW Hague / NERA GM Pierson Collection)

The Siamese Twins : Eastern and North Eastern

In the immediate changes of 1948, a number of departments were set up to serve both the Eastern and North Eastern Regions. Some were taken over by other organisations, whilst others received an impetus to separate by the increasing devolution of authority by the BTC to Regions after 1955. In time all the dual responsibility ceased and separate departments on each Region had to be merged in 1967.

Taking these in turn, the major department was Mechanical & Electrical Engineering. AH Peppercorn, the last Chief Mechanical Engineer of the LNER, had continued in this role, jointly serving the two Regions. When he retired at the end of 1949, the RE took the opportunity to implement its decision that there should be two posts. JF Harrison, a former LNER man, was appointed Mechanical & Electrical Engineer whilst AE Robson, from the former LMSR, was appointed Carriage & Wagon Engineer. Both continued to serve both Regions. This was the position until around 1959, when KJ Cook who had replaced Harrison in 1951, retired. A fundamental change then took place. The two departments were merged but separate Chief Mechanical & Electrical Engineers were appointed for each Region. MG Burrows was appointed to the North Eastern Region post.

Similarly the Road Motor Engineer, who had served both Regions, was replaced by a separate post for each Region. However, instead of being an independent department, a legacy from LNER days, the two new posts were a part of the Chief Mechanical & Electrical Engineer's organisation.

One of the early decisions of the BTC was to set up a single Legal Service for the whole of their undertaking. Accordingly the joint Legal department passed to the Legal Service from 2 January 1950. Similarly the BTC decided to unify the separate Police forces under a Chief Officer (Police), appointed by the RE in 1949. Although the Northern Area of the British Transport Police had its headquarters in York, its area was not co-terminous with any Region but rather was based on civil police boundaries. Its establishment meant the Chief Regional Officer lost his Chief of Police.

A standard organisation for public relations and publicity was brought into operation on 4 April 1949. Separate Public Relations and Publicity Officers were introduced at RE HQ; the Publicity Officer also took responsibility for commercial advertising under the direction of the BTC's centralised organisation, established on 14 March 1949. However, in each Region the roles were combined. So a Public Relations & Publicity Officer was appointed in York, ending the interim arrangement of Press Relations and Advertising departments, located at Marylebone, serving both Regions.

Further complication was added to Operations on 1 February 1949, when the Chief Officer (Operating) Eastern Group, attached to RE Headquarters, was made Operating Superintendent, Eastern & North Eastern Regions, supervising Divisional Operating Superintendents at Liverpool Street and York. This arrangement lasted until the end of 1954. Since VM Barrington-Ward, the operating member of the RE, was known to have been trying to replace the CROs in his function, it is tempting to see his hand in this arrangement, particularly since he had been Temporary Assistant General Manager (Operating) for the whole LNER system during the Second World War.

The Chief Accountant of the LNER had been based at King's Cross and controlled a number of offices in London, Peterborough, Doncaster and Newcastle. After passing accounting work for ex-LNER lines in Scotland to the Scottish Region, the department served both the Eastern and North Eastern Regions, although the Engineer's Accountants at King's Cross and York, as well as the Works' Accountants at Doncaster, Stratford and Darlington only served their respective Region. Although the BTC approved in principle the introduction of separate organisations by stages in 1957, final completion had to wait until March 1962 when independent organisations were established in London and York.

Changes to the Treasurer's organisation were similar to those affecting the Chief Accountant. Based at Liverpool Street in LNER days, the Treasurer was responsible for all banking matters and ensuring that the company had sufficient funds. As well as the division into two organisations, also finally effected in March 1962, the function lost much of the responsibility for funding work to the British Railways Board's headquarters. Regional work then concentrated on banking arrangements and forecasts of cash requirements.

The Stores Superintendent, responsible for the purchasing and control of all technical and traffic material, was located at King's Cross. In the mid 1950s an Assistant to the Stores Superintendent (North Eastern Region) was appointed, based in York, to provide a better liaison with the Region. That process was developed further by the appointment in June 1959 of separate Supplies and Contracts Managers for each Region; the arrangements became effective on 1 November.

In charge of passenger and freight traffic to and from Europe, the Continental Traffic Manager Eastern & North Eastern Regions was based at Liverpool Street. The duties of the Manager (Shipping Services) of the Eastern Region were added in 1956 and the post then became Continental Traffic and Shipping Manager, Eastern Region. No separate department was ever established for the North Eastern Region, though as recorded in the Paper on ships and shipping, proposals were made for such a department.

Agent of the Railway Executive 1948 - 1954

The Railway Executive established a 'functional' organisation where the chain of command passed from the Chairman, who was responsible for all its work, to a number of Members, who each took responsibility for particular aspects. In turn, the Members directed the appropriate Regional Officers. 'Instructions may be given direct to the regional departmental officers by the member of the Railway Executive concerned, just as reports may be made direct by the regional departmental officers to the appropriate member of the Railway Executive.' With this strong line of command, the role of Chief Regional Officers was unclear. Officially their role was 'the co-ordination of the departments at regional level' and 'to secure that the policies laid down and general instructions issued by the Railway Executive are made effective'.(13)

This meant that the CROs, men who in company days had a considerable degree of independence, were stripped of authority. When the habit of Railway Executive Members of paying little regard to CROs was added, the result was to 'create in their minds a sense of frustration and even cynicism, which could easily permeate material sections of the railway organisation'.(14) Missenden attempted to alleviate this by inviting the CROs to attend the fortnightly meetings of the Executive itself. But he did not end it. To be fair, the Executive had to weld together the practices of the Big Four companies quickly, against opposition from Regions which were loath to abandon traditional practices. A functional organisation was the most effective way of doing this. Nevertheless, it is hard not to see the visit of Missenden to the North Eastern Region in Summer 1948 as a colonial inspection with Hopkins as the District Officer.

Matters improved when John Elliot took over as RE Chairman on 1 February 1951. Since he had been CRO on both the Southern and London Midland Regions, he must have decided to reduce the frustration he himself had experienced. Some of his efforts can be seen in a RE memorandum of September 1951. After noting that 'despite much talk to the contrary [the functional organisation] has not proved to be so difficult a method of organisation to operate as was supposed', it concluded 'Decentralisation from the Executive to the Regions has already gone a long way, despite partisan assertions to the contrary'. Continuance of decentralisation imposed an obligation on the RE to regard the Heads of Regions as the principal officers in charge who must not be by-passed on matters of major importance. Likewise the Heads of Regions must accept, 'as they do', that the top management of the Railways rested with the Executive.(15) Regional authority was to be built up by channelling RE communication through Heads of Regions, re-titling their posts along with certain increases in salary, giving more authority to make appointments and grant pay increases, together with greater responsibility for investment schemes.

However, the election of a Conservative government in October 1951 led to major changes in the organisation established by the Transport Act 1947. Most notably, it abolished the Railway Executive and set up an Interim Organisation for British Railways from 1 October 1953. Chief Regional Officers were renamed Chief Regional Managers and became responsible for the management of all departments in their Regions. They were responsible directly to the British Transport Commission, which exercised general financial and policy control and set technical standards. This looser supervision would be seen more in the final organisation, introduced in 1955.

So for the first seven years of its life, the North Eastern Region was allowed little scope for initiative and the RE fairly closely controlled its activities. That control was at first drawn tight but loosened from around the early fifties. Nevertheless it was always present. In 1953 HA Short suddenly changed his mind and told the RE he wished to withdraw from the experimental introduction of diesel multiple units in the West Riding. Elliot told him in no uncertain terms that it was out of the question.(16)

Independence 1955 - 1967

The new organisation introduced by the British Transport Commission on 1 January 1955 was intended to decentralise the management of British Railways to Area Boards. Only reserved matters, largely standards and policies, were to be retained by a British Railways Division of the Commission. The Area Boards, corresponding to the Regions, were directly responsible to the BTC. None of the Area Board Chairmen were BTC members at the time of their appointment but they subsequently became part-time Commission members; TH Summerson fulfilled this role for the North Eastern Area Board, which met for the first time in York on 7 February 1955.

In addition to Summerson, its members were Dr James W Armit, Sir Mark Hodgson, Sir John

Plate 2.6. An unidentified tank locomotive departs York with Inspection Saloon No E902179E. This saloon started life on the Stockton & Darlington Railway in 1871 as a six-wheeled Third Class Saloon. In 1884 it was converted for use by the Locomotive Superintendent. Subsequent modifications included lengthening to 40' by the addition of a kitchen at one end, replacement of the six wheelsets by a pair of bogies, the replacement of the original windows and the installation of underfloor equipment to allow use as a simple type of dynamometer car. The Saloon would be withdrawn in 1969, and be preserved on the Keighley & Worth Valley Railway. (NERA GM Pierson Collection)

Benstead (who was Deputy Chairman of the BTC), GH Kitson and PD Priestman. At a press conference Summerson explained that the objects of the Board were to bring customers 'right into the railway organisation' and to bring control of the organisation nearer home. The Board hoped to get about the Region as soon and as often as possible to see what was going on and to meet railwaymen of all grades. The first visit was to Hull on 14-15 April. Trading Associations and railway staff were met and inspections made of installations, depots and stations, such as New Inward Yard. Subsequent visits that year were to Newcastle and the North East, Northumberland, Darlington and York. In addition, the BTC met in York for the first time on September 15. After the meeting Sir Brian Robertson, BTC Chairman, accompanied by Summerson and Short, visited the Lord Mayor, a retired railwayman, at the Mansion House.

The BTC gave the Area Boards the task of preparing schemes to devolve general management below regional level. In the North Eastern Region this was done on a geographical basis. As a first step, a Chief Traffic Manager, Frank Grundy, was appointed on 1 April 1957, who controlled Traffic Managers in four areas. The new organisation was claimed to produce quicker decisions for customers, encourage local officers by delegating more authority and give flexibility in working by integrating the Commercial, Operating and Motive Power departments. The four areas were based on Newcastle, Darlington, Leeds and Hull. Ominously 'Full details of the new organisation have not, it seems, been worked out'.(17) In 1958 an Assistant General Manager (Traffic) replaced the Chief Traffic Manager.

By 1960 Summerson was able to announce that in the Region modernisation, short of electrification, was intended to be complete by the end of 1964. The guiding principle was to concentrate on those passenger and freight services, which the railways did best. There were four major tasks. They were to modernise technical equipment, to rationalise the system, to decentralise within the Region; to use road haulage for local collection and delivery. In addition, the Region wanted better public relations, attractive buildings and equipment, clean carriages and better train running information. Short was able to illustrate progress so far in a number of ways. The introduction of diesel locomotives and multiple units, colour-light signalling from Newcastle to Berwick, construction of three new marshalling yards and the combination of the Leeds stations were just four examples.

Better public relations were fostered by a series of public meetings. Frank Hick, then Assistant Operating Officer, records how he discussed the problem with Short and Margetts, the Assistant General Manager (Traffic), in a taxi. They decided to arrange the first of these at Huddersfield, where there was much criticism of local and main line services. Held on 29 February 1960, the format of the two hour meeting mixed talks, a film and a panel discussion, presided over by the Mayor and Mayoress. St Patrick's Parochial Hall was filled to capacity and beyond, whilst 'many questions were brisk and interesting'.(18) Hick gave a talk on the traffic developments on the Region. After the success of this pilot, a series of similar meetings were held the next year in such places as Harrogate, Newcastle, Halifax, Sunderland, Wakefield and Brighouse. Over 1,000 people attended the Newcastle event and 400 in Wakefield despite pouring rain. At Sunderland

Summerson, Short and Kitson from the Area Board attended and were accompanied by the Mayor. These meetings came of age when the twenty-first meeting was held at Harrogate on 25 April 1962, which included the film 'The North Eastern goes forward'. This 20 minute British Transport film was intended for showing to the public, Chambers of Commerce, Trade Organisations and railway staff.

To accommodate the new Traffic Manager for Teesside, Sir Ellis Hunter, Chairman and Managing Director of Dorman Long & Company Limited, the contractor for the structural steel framework, formally opened new offices on 22 July 1960. Zetland House at Middlesbrough was designed by the Architect's Office of the Regional Chief Civil Engineer. Speaking at the opening Summerson referred to the new feeling that there should be greater autonomy given to Regions and decentralisation within them. The new offices were a symbol of the North Eastern Region's acceptance of that principle. KA Kindon, the Traffic Manager, possessed a very high degree of autonomy and authority to quote rates and organise transits. Zetland House was a significant part of modernisation, which would be completed by the new yards at Newport. Already more than half of the Region's freight reached its destination the next day; the target was all of it.

The replacement of the BTC by the British Railways Board had some effect on the Region. At the top a North Eastern Railway Board replaced the Area Board from 1 January 1963. Although Summerson initially remained Chairman, Dean, the General Manager replaced him from 1 October of that year. This was the culmination of a gradual process. Short had never been a member of the Area Board. Margetts became one on 1 January 1962 and, as the next General Manager, Dean followed him on 30 April. Dean was an initial member of the North Eastern Railway Board. His assumption of the Chairmanship replaced an outside industrialist with an internal manager.

As part of a uniform organisation within Regions, four Assistant General Managers were established to supervise respectively Finance, Commercial, Movements (renamed from Operations) and Technical activities. Divisional Managers replaced Traffic Managers, within the Region and were responsible for commercial, movements and maintenance staff within their area. In turn, Station or Area Managers responded to Divisional Managers. However, regional departmental officers controlled all Civil and Signal Engineering. In the North Eastern Region Divisions were originally set up at Newcastle, Middlesbrough, Leeds and Hull. From 5 December 1966, in advance of the merger of the North Eastern and Eastern Regions, the Newcastle and Middlesbrough Divisions were themselves merged.

Envoi

Organisationally the North Eastern Region must be judged a success. Its compact size, based on long established predecessors, made its staff feel part of a cohesive whole. Located at a distance from BR Headquarters, it was thus better able to exercise the independence and enterprise that became its hallmark.

Continuity of management meant consistent policies had time to take effect. The view that 'There was rejoicing in York when "NER" once more became meaningful initials'(19), was borne out by the Area Board in 1962. It minuted that 'whilst there was no strong feeling on the part of members, the title "The North Eastern Railway" was preferred to that of "The North Eastern Region" at least for publicity and public relations purposes'.(20) The builders of the Region's offices must have been proud.

Endnotes:
(1) *Inception of the Regions* [National Archives file AN6/58].
(2) Fiennes, GF. *I tried to run a railway.* Ian Allan, 1973.
(3) Bonavia, MR. *The Birth of British Rail.* George Allen & Unwin, 1979.
(4) *Ibid.*
(5) *The Railway Gazette,* 11 August 1961.
(6) Hick, FL. *That was my Railway.* Silver Link Publishing, 1991.
(7) Letter from IL Gray-Jones of 17 April 2003.
(8) *British Transport Commission Eighth Annual Report and Accounts, 1955. Volume I : Report.*
(9) Railway Executive Minute 202, 2 February 1948 [National Archives file AN 4/1].
(10) *British Transport Commission Report and Accounts for 1948* and *North Eastern Area Board Minutes* [National Archives file AN 117/1].
(11) Dow, G. *Railway Heraldry.* David & Charles, 1973.
(12) Bonavia, MR. *The Birth of British Rail.*
(13) *The Railway Gazette,* 19 March 1948.
(14) *Memorandum from David Blee,* 13 May 1948 [National Archives file AN6/10].
(15) *Review of Present Organisation* [National Archives file AN6/6].
(16) Bonavia, MR. *British Rail, the First 25 Years.* David & Charles, 1981.
(17) *The Railway Gazette,* 24 May 1957.
(18) *The Railway Gazette,* 4 March 1960.
(19) Bonavia, MR. *British Rail, the First 25 Years.*
(20) *North Eastern Board Minutes* [National Archives file AN117/7].

Bibliography : The National Archives
(see also the Bibliography at the end of this book)
A Step Forward – Revision of Regional Boundaries, Railway Executive, 1950 [National Archives file ZLIB15/46/12].
AGMs and Chief Officers – Eastern and North Eastern Regions [National Archives file AN174/861].
British Railways Eastern Region Stores Superintendents Organisation, January 1956 [National Archives file AN24/39].
Inception of the Regions [National Archives file AN6/58].
Informal Meeting of Full-Time Members of R.E. [National Archives file AN4/8].
Memorandum from David Blee, 13 May 1948 [National Archives file AN6/10].
North Eastern Area Board and Railway Board Minutes and General Purposes Committee Minutes [National Archives files AN 117/1 to AN117/11].
North Eastern Region Departmental Officers' Conferences 28 November 1955 [National Archives file AN 105/1].
Railway Executive Minutes of Meetings [National Archives file AN 4/1].
Railway Regions, The [National Archives file AN6/58].
RE Instruction No 3 North Eastern Region [National Archives file AN13/592].
Review of Present Organisation [National Archives file AN6/6].

Evolution and Diminution
The Changing Nature of the Freight Traffic Conveyed by the Trains of the North Eastern Region
John G Teasdale

On the eve of Nationalisation, when railwaymen considered the nature of the freight traffic that would in the future be conveyed by the North Eastern Region's trains, they were aware that much depended upon the nature of the industrial enterprises at work within the Region's territory. Those enterprises were in turn profoundly influenced by the natural resources available to them.

The fuel that lit the fire of industrialisation was coal. Within the territory to be allocated to the Region there were two main coalfields. The Great Northern Coalfield was approximately triangular in shape; its base stretched between Shildon and Hartlepool, and its tip reached northwards to Shilbottle (a short distance south of Alnwick). The coal mined in the northern part of the field was ideal for steam-raising. The various grades of coal mined in and around Tyneside were suitable for domestic and industrial use, and for making coke and coal gas. Coals mined in the southern part of the field, in County Durham, were suitable for steam-raising, domestic and industrial use, and for making coke and coal gas. Coals from all parts of the field were consumed locally; they were also conveyed by sea to markets in the south of England, and, in normal times, to markets overseas. This latter trade, however, had ceased during the Second World War, and on the eve of Nationalisation had barely recommenced. Of the millions of tons of coal produced annually from the Great Northern Coalfield, not all would be available for conveyance by the North Eastern Region's trains. The National Coal Board had its own railway systems, and more than half of the production was conveyed over those systems directly to its own staiths and coal drops for shipping to the south of England or overseas.

The Yorkshire Coalfield was approximately rectangular in shape, and stretched from the area around Leeds southwards to the County boundary, and, indeed, far beyond into Derbyshire and Nottinghamshire. Relatively little of the production of the coalfield would, therefore, be available as originating traffic to the North Eastern Region. However, huge tonnages would be forwarded from the southern part of the West Riding for conveyance to Hull via the former Hull & Barnsley Railway, to Lancashire via the Calder Valley Line, and, to a much lesser extent, to the rest of the Yorkshire and the north-east of England. The various grades coal mined in and around Leeds were suitable for domestic and industrial use, and for making coke and coal gas; much of these coals were consumed locally. The coals mined in south Yorkshire were mostly ideal for steam-raising, though some were more suited to domestic and industrial use; both grades of coal were consumed locally, and the steam-coal in particular was also in demand in the south of England and overseas.

The principal local industry fuelled by the North of England's coal was the making of iron and steel. This industry was primarily located on Teesside, though there was also large-scale production at Consett. A declining proportion of the industry's basic raw material, iron ore, was extracted from the Cleveland Hills; much more significant supplies were obtained from Northamptonshire. Home-produced ore was relatively impure however, and increasing quantities of purer ore were being imported from overseas; this imported ore was handled at facilities on the Rivers Tyne and Tees. The limestone required as a flux in the blast furnaces was obtained from quarries in the Cleveland Hills and in the Yorkshire Dales. The blast furnaces were fuelled by coke. The iron and steel-making companies had their own coke ovens, and the coal required for processing in these ovens was

Plate 3.1. The North Eastern Region would inherit a system whereby consignments large and small could be conveyed by rail to a railway-owned goods shed located in most cities and towns (and in many villages too). From the goods shed, road transport would be used for the final delivery to the recipient. The system worked well, but compared with direct conveyance door to door by a road-going vehicle, it was slow and goods were more susceptible to damage. If the system was to survive, the nationalised British Railways and British Road Services would have to co-operate, not compete. The goods shed here is at Brampton Junction, photographed in March 1956. (IL Gray-Jones)

supplied from the coalfields located within the territory served by the North Eastern Region; some coke was also bought ready-made from the National Coal Board. A large proportion of the iron and steel produced was consumed by the shipbuilding industry, an industry largely concentrated on the Rivers Tyne, Wear, and Tees, but also at Blyth, the Hartlepools, Hull, and Selby. Heavy engineering industries, principally located on Tyneside, Wearside, Teesside, and in the West Riding in and around Leeds, consumed significant amounts of iron and steel too. Other industries included the manufacture of diverse chemicals, an industry concentrated in the hands of Imperial Chemical Industries Limited (ICI) at Haverton Hill and at Wilton on Teesside, and the manufacture of clothing and other textile products in the West Riding.

Although parts of the North-East of England were heavily industrialised, much of the countryside in between was still given over to agriculture. Wheat, barley, oats, hay, root crops such as potatoes and turnips were all grown, and cattle, sheep, pigs, and poultry reared. Timber production was not an important industry locally, much of the usable forest having been cleared during the Second World War. Timber was, however, imported into the east coast ports in large quantities. The fishing industry was very important in all the ports down the east coast, especially at Berwick, Blyth, North Shields, Hartlepool, Scarborough, and Hull. (The tonnages handled at North Shields and Hull dwarfed those handled at the other places.)

Another source of freight traffic within the north-east of England was the everyday requirements of the people who dwelt there. This general merchandise traffic comprised such as apples and adhesives, biscuits and buttons, cups and coats – the list was nigh on endless.

Nationalisation

When the North Eastern Region formally came into being, on 1 January 1948, much of the freight that could be conveyed by rail was so conveyed. Competition from road hauliers had gradually intensified during the 1920s and 30s, but had been eliminated during the war by the restrictions placed on the supply of petrol and diesel. That competition would re-emerge in the post-war period, though following the nationalisation of the long-distance road haulage companies, such competition could be expected by railwaymen to be carefully moderated. A recent Government initiative had though resulted in the diversion of traffic away from the railways and on to the roads. During the severe winter of 1946 - 47, the war-worn railways had experienced great difficulties in maintaining supplies of coal to domestic and industrial users. In the autumn of 1947 therefore, the Government had established a Winter Transport Emergency Committee. The Committee diverted some 10,000 tons of coal traffic per week away from the railways and on to the roads. Railwaymen had also been instructed to give priority to the movement of the tens of thousands of tons of coal traffic for which they remained responsible. By these means, the Government hoped that supplies could be maintained during another severe winter. As matters transpired however, the winter of 1947 - 1948 proved to be mild. In consequence, the Committee was disbanded even before the winter was fully over, and the absolute priority to be given to coal traffic on the railways ended on 1 March 1948. From that date, therefore, the Railway and the Road Transport Executives gained full control over their commercial activities. Naturally, the Railway Executive, and the railwaymen of the North Eastern Region, then sought to win back to the railways the diverted traffic.

Plate 3.2. Goods conveyed by rail were liable to damage each time they were handled, but more so if they were loaded badly in a wagon. In order to remind staff how goods should be loaded, in 1956 two 12 ton vans were fitted at Faverdale wagon works with transparent sides so that what happened within could be observed. One van was correctly loaded with representative packages, the other incorrectly. The two vans were sent on a tour of all Regions, spending about two months in each. The scene here is New Bridge Street in September 1956. The so-called 'Fishbowl' vans are being rough shunted so that the effect upon the goods inside may be observed. (IL Gray-Jones)

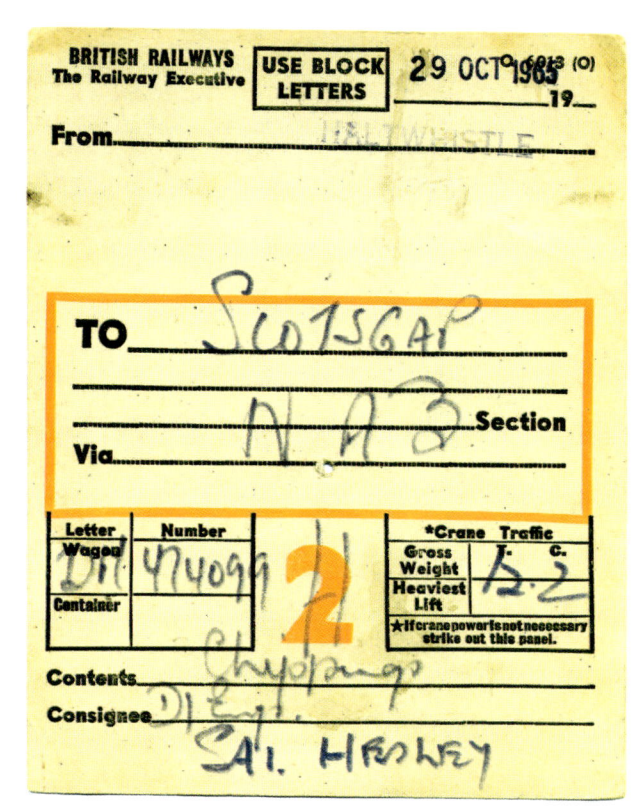

*Colour Plates 5 and 6. British Railways inherited a system whereby a wagon in traffic had clipped to it a wagon label giving details of load, route, etc. Labels were printed bearing the numbers **1** (for loads comprising coal, coke and patent fuel), **2** (for other minerals) and **3** (other commodities). Colour coding within these categories was used to give an indication of weight: orange = heavy; green = medium; black = ordinary. A huge variety of labels was pre-printed, leaving just the details to be added in thick black pencil by the railwayman loading the wagon.*

The label above left, used on a wagon conveying chippings for the District Engineer, is an early example; note that it still has the LNER stationery re-order number O.6013 (O).

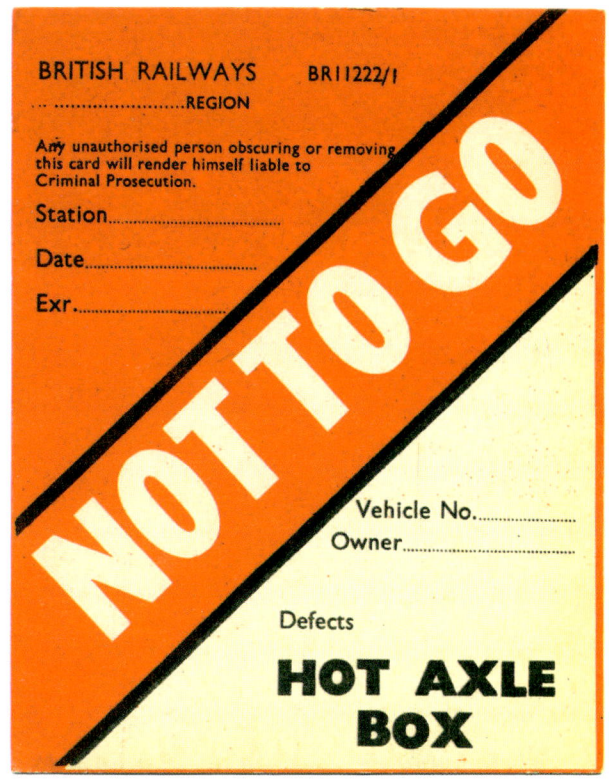

*The system of load categories and colour-coding used to indicate weight was subsequently replaced by one indicating weight alone; from 6 April 1964, labels bore the letters **H**, **M**, **L** or **E**.*

Unfortunately, such were the uncertainties of lubrication for the plain bearings of most wagons, hot boxes were sufficiently common as to warrant the printing of the label above right. (Labels reproduced at 80% of original size.) (JG Teasdale Collection)

Colour Plate 7. Class J72 No 68723 shunts at Newcastle Central in July 1961. Note the special livery, adopted in May 1960 as the locomotive was very much on public view during its regular duty as station pilot. No 68736, stationed at York, was given the same livery. (RG Warwick)

37

Colour Plate 8.
This coal staith at West Hartlepool, photographed on 31 December 1966, is typical of those bequeathed by the North Eastern Railway. Note the 21 ton wagons; the staiths in the north-east of England were readily adaptable for use by high-capacity wagons, unlike most of the end-door discharge facilities elsewhere. (JM Boyes / JW Armstrong Trust, per JR Midcalf)

Colour Plate 9.
On a damp and gloomy 13 November 1964, 4MT Ivatt 1947 Class Mogul No 43036 passes through Piercebridge with the Forcett Branch pick-up. The train is returning to Darlington with a depressingly short train. The situation is even worse than it looks; only the van is revenue-earning, as the three wagons heavily loaded with ballast from Forcett Quarry are for BR's own Civil Engineer. (JM Boyes / JW Armstrong Trust, per JR Midcalf)

Colour Plate 10. WD Class No 90135 runs past Newburn signal box, West Hartlepool, on 14 June 1967 with a Hawthorn Colliery - Tees Yard mineral train. (JM Boyes / JW Armstrong Trust, per JR Midcalf)

In the Region, as elsewhere on British Railways (BR), the ability of railwaymen to win back that traffic was hampered by adverse circumstances. Men, women, and machinery were worn out, and the railways' ability to charge economic rates for the conveyance of traffic was severely restricted by legislation. The cure for the latter ailment would come in stages, culminating in the passing of the Transport Act, 1962. The cure for the worn out machinery was a revitalised maintenance programme, and the building of new wagons. The cure for the railwaymen and women was less specific, but, for the most part, the nationalisation of the railways was in itself a highly-charged tonic. Its effect, however, did not last all that long. On successive Sundays from 15 May until 12 June 1949, footplate staff based at Gateshead, Heaton, York and Grantham (in the Eastern Region) refused to work in a protest over lodging turns. Much more damaging to the railways was a dispute concerning wage differentials that led to railwaymen striking from midnight on 28 May 1955. By the time the dispute was settled on 14 June a significant volume of traffic had been lost to road-based competitors, guaranteeing that fewer railwaymen would be drawing wages from BR in the future.

By the end of May 1948, the coal traffic diverted on to the roads had been won back on to the Region's rails. Exports of coal to Europe and to overseas bunkering ports had been resumed the previous December, and gradually the staiths began to handle more and more of this traffic. Over the whole of 1948, the Region's trains conveyed 30,429,000 tons of originating coal and coke – an increase of 11.74% over the previous year. As demand for iron and steel rose during 1948, so too did the tonnages of iron ore, scrap metal and limestone conveyed by the railways; over the year as a whole, the Region's trains conveyed 10,724,000 tons of originating mineral traffic – an increase of 20.19% over the previous year. The Region's originating general merchandise traffic, which included the semi-finished products of the iron and steel industry, amounted to 7,481,000 tons over the year – a mere 4.18% greater than the tonnage conveyed in 1947. This relatively poor showing was deemed by the British Transport Commission (BTC) to be an indication that there was in Britain excess capacity for the conveyance of general merchandise, an excess capacity brought about by the progressive growth in the number of 'C' licence motor lorries.(1) As part of the railways' effort to compete against those lorries and the State-owned lorries belonging to British Road Services, it was determined that a high quality of service should be offered. To that end, new freight train services were instituted, and some of the existing trains accelerated. Progress in this latter regard was, however, largely dependent upon the restoration of the track to its pre-war standard of maintenance.

Track renewals were dependent upon allocations of steel by the Government. Allocations to the railways of steel for all purposes were restricted; steel was in great demand for such purposes as rebuilding the nation's merchant shipping fleet and the building of cars for export. Steel supplied for such purposes provided freight traffic for the railways, but did nothing to help shift that traffic. However, the Government gradually relaxed its war-time restrictions on the supply and use of all manner of commodities. This led to a gradual increase in the railways' carryings of such as building materials, consumer goods, and imported fruit.

Plate 3.3. Class B16/1 No 61473 with a Class D express freight at Croft Spa in July 1955. Note the cattle van marshalled at the front of the train. (R Goult)

There was, in these early days of the nationalised railways, no large-scale investment in modern facilities that would expedite the conveyance of such freight. However, there was modest investment in new facilities for specific customers, such as on Teesside for ICI and for the steel manufacturing firm Dorman Long & Company Limited, and at Hull Saltend for the Petroleum Board. BR also conducted experiments during 1950 and 1951 to see if the handling of general merchandise traffic could be usefully expedited by the use of timber pallets. Merchandise was loaded on to such pallets by hand, but thereafter pallets were handled mechanically using a fork-lift truck. The experiments were deemed successful, and during 1952 traffic was palletised at major depots and warehouses in all of BR's Regions. From the beginning of 1954, the weight of a customer's pallets was excluded from the chargeable weight of a palletised consignment, and empty pallets being returned to a customer were conveyed free of charge.

Marshalling Yards

The publication of the Modernisation Plan in January 1955 at last offered the prospect of significant investment. This was not before time. BR was steadily losing traffic to road-based competitors. Some of this loss was due to a shortage of all types of wagons – a shortage in part due to antiquated working practices that resulted in very poor utilisation of wagons. Many of the proposed investment schemes would be of indirect benefit to the operation of freight trains – the installation of colour-light signals, and dieselisation, for example – but there were schemes specific to the operation of freight trains: the introduction of wagons with greater carrying capacities; the fitting of automatic brakes to all wagons; the modernisation of handling facilities; the replacement of the present multitude of small goods yards by a limited number of either modernised yards or newly-built hump marshalling yards. Modernised marshalling yards were indeed desperately needed. At the time that the Plan was published, there were seventy-five yards in the North Eastern Region. The working of freight trains between these yards was both expensive and slow. Given the vigour of the railways' road-based competitors, given free rein by the current Conservative Government, neither expense nor slowness could be tolerated.

The building of new hump marshalling yards would be hugely expensive. For that expense, the Region intended to benefit in four main ways:

* Transit times for individual wagons would be significantly shortened, as freight trains would work between a limited number of brand new or modernised yards rather than a large number of small antiquated yards. The shortened journey times would allow the railways to compete against the inherent rapidity of road transport, and would allow increased wagon utilisation.
* The incorporation of Up and Down staging sidings on the perimeters of the new marshalling yards would allow efficient crew and locomotive changes for through freight trains.
* Urgent or perishable traffic could be attached easily to express through freight trains temporarily halted in the staging sidings, again allowing the railways to compete against road transport.
* The making-up of trains in large modern yards would facilitate the grouping into sections of those wagons bound for the same destination area. If a change of train was required en route (because the destination area was not served directly by the originating yard), the grouping of wagons in sections would ease the change of trains at the appropriate intermediate yard.

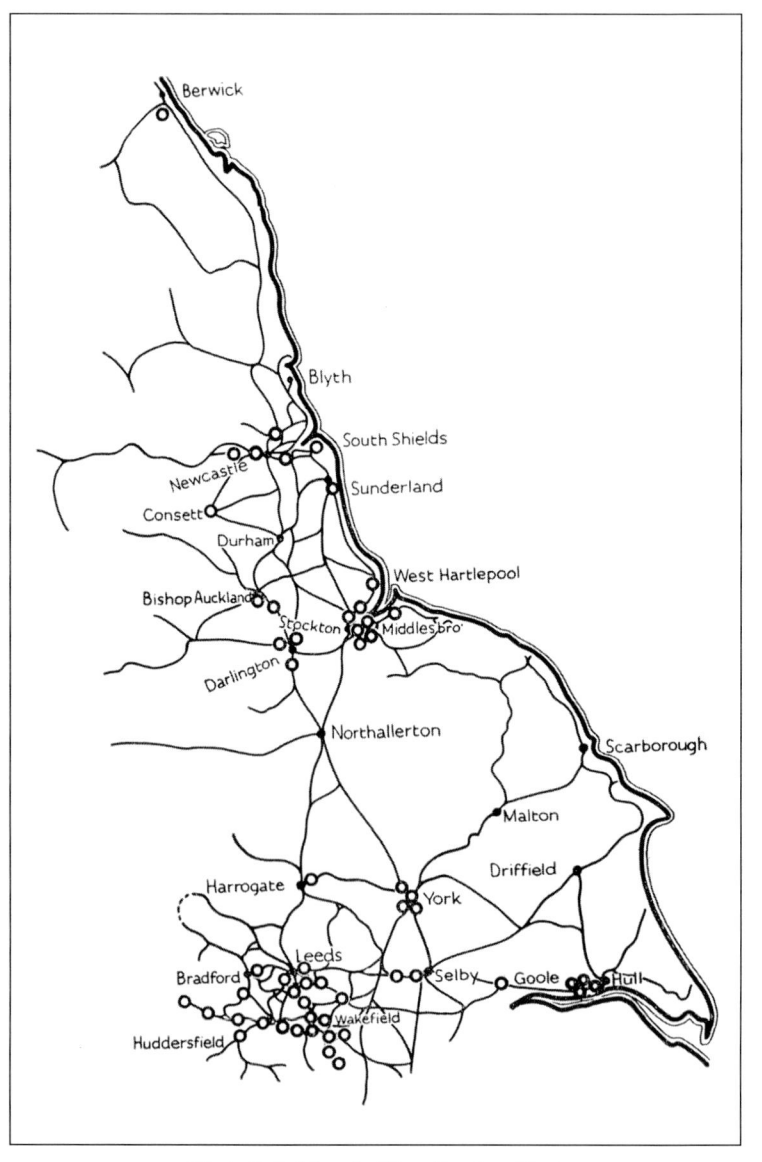

Plate 3.4. Marshalling Yards – Past
◯ : *Main marshalling yards*
Source: 'Healey Mills Marshalling Yard', published by BR (NER) July1963. (R Davies Collection).

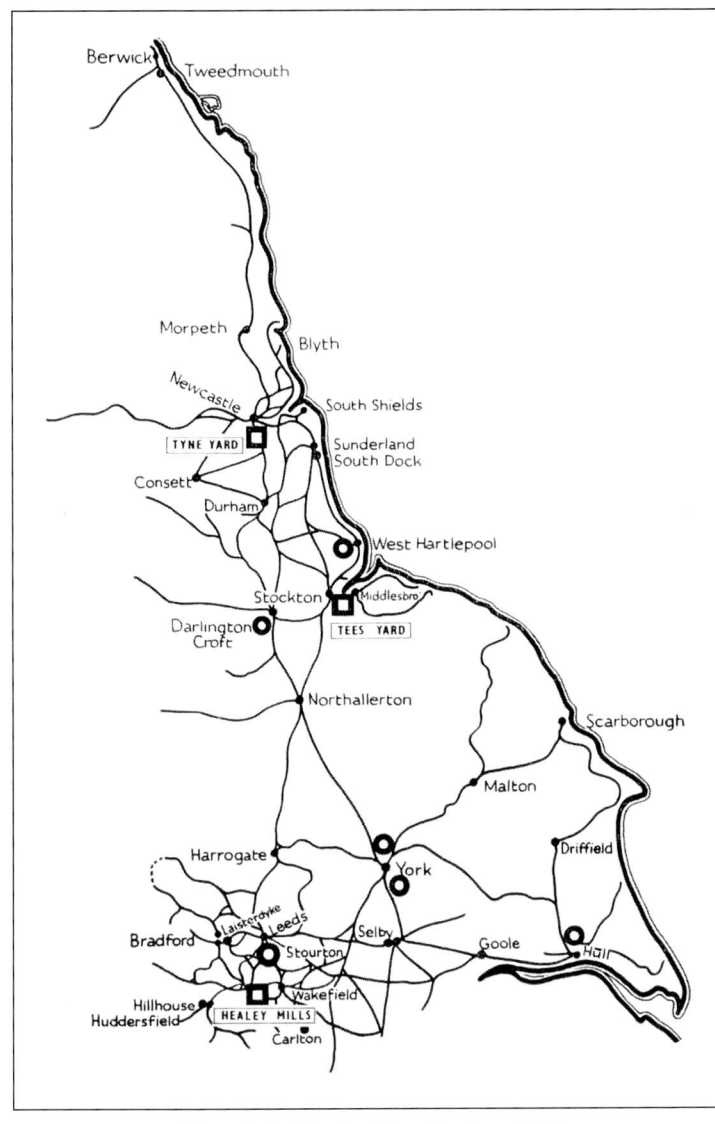

Plate 3.5. Marshalling Yards – 1965
☐ : New yards
○ : Existing yards modified or to be modified
• : Existing yards to continue
Source: 'Healey Mills Marshalling Yard'. (R Davies Collection)

As the Modernisation Plan was developed, the Region ultimately planned to build new hump marshalling yards at Lamesley, Newport, Healey Mills, and Stourton. The planning was greatly assisted by the fact that the Region already had practical experience of operating such a yard: Hull Inward Yard at Hessle had been modernised by the LNER and had opened for traffic on 9 December 1935.

Tyne Yard would be built at Lamesley, in the Team Valley south of Gateshead, and would serve the industrial areas of Tyneside and Wearside. Tees Yard, comprising separate Up and Down Yards, would be built at Newport, on the right bank of the River Tees near Middlesbrough, and would serve Teesside's extensive steel and petrochemical industries. Healey Mills Yard would be located to the west of Wakefield, and would be a natural focus for Trans-Pennine freight services connecting the east coast ports of Hull and Goole both with the west coast ports on Merseyside and with the industrial areas of Lancashire. In the latter regard, coal traffic from Yorkshire collieries would be a staple traffic. Stourton Yard would be built on the south-eastern periphery of Leeds, and would serve the industrial West Riding of Yorkshire.

In addition to these four marshalling yards, yards at Darlington, Hull, West Hartlepool, and York would be modernised. The new and the modernised yards would allow up to sixty-five smaller yards to be closed.

Traffic dealt with at present in the Region's diverse yards originated from collieries, private sidings, and the Region's own depots. As with the Region's yards, so too did the Modernisation Plan provide for the building of new large-scale depots, and the closure of a multitude of smaller ones. As the Plan was developed, the Region ultimately planned to build large new concentration depots for general merchandise and wagonload traffic at Newcastle, Sunderland, Stockton, York, Bradford, Leeds, and Hull. The new depots would be fully mechanised, and would be served by the Region's own cartage fleet ranging over a wide area of the surrounding countryside.

Tees Yard

After the Second World War, the already extensive steel and petrochemical industries on Teesside expanded further. Freight traffic both inward and outward was already very heavy, and the expectation of the Region's traffic officers was that it would become heavier still. Inward traffic included coal from Northumberland and Durham, iron ore from Cleveland, limestone from Wensleydale. Outward traffic included semi-finished steel products and petrochemicals. In order to cope with this traffic, the traffic officers proposed the building of two new hump marshalling yards – collectively, Tees Yard – and a greater effort to work block trains. These latter comprised a whole train of one commodity bound for one destination, and did not need to work through marshalling yards. Already, the large-scale nature of the steel and petrochemical industries on Teesside meant that more block trains were despatched by the North Eastern Region's Middlesbrough Division than by any other on BR.(2)

The North Eastern Region's Area Board did not have the authority to sanction expenditure on the scale required for a new mechanised marshalling yard – approval had to be sought from the BTC. Approval to spend £3,735,634 on the new Tees Yard was obtained on 18 September 1958, along with the stipulation that not all of the intended sidings would be actually laid if traffic did not increase in line with expectations.(3) The only practicable site for Tees Yard was Newport, where there were already four small yards and a motive power depot. The design and construction of the new 200 acre yard therefore had to take into account the need not to upset the existing means of handling the traffic more than was absolutely necessary.

Plate 3.6.
The LNER's Shildon Works began to build 'all steel' 13 ton open wagons in May 1945. (They had a wooden floor, and early ones had wooden doors.) The design was perpetuated by BR, with the addition of this shock-absorbing variant. It was intended for use in conveying fragile commodities. Wagon B720000 was built early in 1948; note that this non-common user wagon is branded 'Eastern Group', i.e. the Eastern and North Eastern Regions. (BR (NER), per CE Williamson)

Plate 3.7.
Loading individual items into such as the open wagon seen above was the traditional way of doing things. In order to avoid the effort and expense of loading individual bags of cement into a wagon, BR developed the bulk cement 'Presflo' wagon; this particular wagon, B888000, is the prototype, built in 1953 at Shildon Works. The load was discharged either directly into a road-going lorry or storage tank by an external source of compressed air. The same design of wagon was later adapted to convey salt. (BR (WR), per CE Williamson)

Plate 3.8.
BR adopted the LNER's 20 ton brake van as standard. This van featured a long wheelbase to give the guard a good ride. As there was only one guard to accommodate, the body of the van was much shorter than the wheelbase in order that it be easy to heat (and be as cheap as possible to build). This particular van was built at Darlington in November 1954; note the non-standard 'London Midland' branding, possibly associated with the branding 'Return to Earlestown for Inspection. Nov, 1955.' (BR (NER), per CE Williamson)

Construction took place in stages during 1958 and 1959. When the tracks were laid, they were so spaced as to allow the installation of masts should the lines serving the yard be electrified at a later date; bridges spanning tracks within the yard were also built with sufficient clearance for the subsequent installation of overhead live wires.

In the Up Yard twelve reception sidings gave access to the hump, from which radiated forty sorting sidings. Wagons rolling over the hump and into the sorting sidings were controlled by a system of primary and secondary hydraulic retarders. Twelve departure sidings could also be used as staging sidings for block trains requiring new crews or locomotives. The Down Yard also had twelve reception sidings, but in this case there were two humps in order to allow two trains to be dealt with at once. Wagons rolling over the main hump and into the forty sorting sidings were controlled by a system of primary and secondary hydraulic retarders. The smaller of the two humps was intended for the sorting of empty wagons being returned to Teesside for re-loading. Access to this hump was from any of the three northernmost reception sidings. Wagons rolling over the hump were controlled by one of the main hump's secondary retarders, and ran into either of the two northernmost sorting sidings. The Down Yard was also provided with eight departure and six staging sidings. Of the track used in the yard, some 75% had been recovered from closed railway lines. The yard was formally opened for traffic on 21 May 1963 by Edward T Judge, Chairman and Managing Director of Dorman Long & Company Limited. Planned capacity of the yard was 7500 wagons per day, making it the largest marshalling yard in Europe at the time it was opened. At the south-west corner of the yard was Thornaby motive power depot, a modern replacement for an old engine shed demolished to make room for Tees Yard.

Tyne Yard

Approval to spend £2,975,900 on the future Tyne Yard was obtained from the BTC on 23 July 1959, along with the stipulation that money be saved by using second-hand rails in sidings wherever possible.(4) Design of the new yard took into account the fact that the greatest volume of freight traffic destined to flow into it would comprise raw materials despatched from sources south of the Tyneside and Wearside areas. For example, millions of tons of steel were conveyed northwards from the steelworks on Teesside to the shipyards on the Rivers Tyne and Wear; the finished products were not despatched by rail, of course, but steamed away downstream under their own power. Many other types of finished product built on a smaller scale, such as the Centurion tanks built by Vickers-Armstrong Limited at Elswick, were manufactured from raw materials brought in by rail, but were delivered by road. For operational convenience therefore, the design of the new 135 acre yard located the reception sidings for traffic arriving both from the south and the north at the south end of the yard. Actual building work on the yard began in December 1959. Two humps for shunting wagons were provided. The main hump at the south end of the yard was served by fourteen reception sidings; beyond the hump radiated forty-eight sorting sidings, grouped into eight fans. Wagons rolling over the hump and into the sorting sidings were controlled by a system of primary and secondary hydraulic retarders. Trains assembled in these sorting sidings would subsequently be shunted into twelve departure sidings. A smaller secondary hump was built at the north end of the yard to deal with local traffic; wagons rolling over this hump were controlled by primary retarders only. In addition, staging sidings were provided. Planned capacity of the yard was from between 3000 and 4000 wagons per day.

Plate 3.9. Tyne Yard, not too far off completion; the view is looking northwards. The East Coast Main Line, which had to be diverted round the site of the new yard, is on the right. (IH Hodgson / JW Armstrong Trust, per AR Thompson)

Tyne Yard was formally opened for traffic on 28 June 1963 by Viscount Hailsham, the Minister for Science and Technology. Upon the yard's opening, it took over the freight traffic formerly worked out of the small Addison, Blaydon, Heaton, Low Fell, Park Lane, Tyne Dock, and West Dunston Yards. At the new yard, trunk freight trains were assembled, bound for the Carlisle, Darlington, Doncaster, Edinburgh, Glasgow, Healey Mills, Hull, King's Cross, Tees, Whitemoor, and York Yards. Other yards were served indirectly by the transfer at intermediate yards of grouped sections of wagons. One of those intermediate yards was the modernised Dringhouses Yard, on the East Coast Main Line south of York. Modernisation of this yard allowed the yards at Shildon and at Croft (near Darlington) to be downgraded; henceforth, these two yards would deal with only local traffic rather than being served by trunk freight trains.

Healey Mills Yard

Approval to spend £3,310,000 on the future Healey Mills Yard was obtained from the BTC on 13 August 1959, along with the proviso that the Region's traffic officers working in the West Riding consult closely with their counterparts in the Eastern and the London Midland Regions.(5) A significant volume of the traffic expected to pass through the new yard would be coal. Coincidentally, the land upon which the yard would be built was underlain by coal-bearing strata. In negotiations with the National Coal Board, it was agreed that extraction of as much of this coal as was economically viable would take place before 1962, after which time the Region's contractors would complete the grading of the 140 acre site of the new yard. In this way, the newly-built yard would not suffer subsidence from continuing coal extraction. Building work began in 1959, commencing with the building of a road bridge over the east end of the site, the diversion of the River Calder, and the relocation of Ossett Sewage Disposal Works. The two existing Down lines past the site of the new yard were shifted a short distance northwards to pass round the northern perimeter; the two Up lines were relocated in order to pass round the southern perimeter.

This work having been completed, approximately 1,048,000 tons of fill were used to level the site, and four separate bridges built to carry the diverse tracks over the Calder. The fill having been compacted, a hump was built on one of the bridges, and the tracks laid. At the west end of the yard, on the river's right bank, fourteen reception sidings gave access to the hump, from which radiated fifty main sorting sidings located on the river's left bank. Wagons rolling over the hump and into the sorting sidings were controlled by a system of primary and secondary hydraulic retarders. Trains assembled in those sidings could subsequently be shunted into thirteen departure sidings. Twenty-five secondary sorting sidings were provided, where wagons fitted with continuous brakes could be assembled at the front of a train (so that at least some of the train could be braked). Fifteen staging sidings were also provided.

To turn the steam locomotives that still provided much of the area's traction, a turntable was installed. There was no provision for a motive power depot, though it was planned that a maintenance depot for diesel locomotives would be built at some time in the not too distant future. Planned capacity of the new yard was 4000 wagons per day; it was formally opened for traffic on 23 July 1963 by Lord Robens, Chairman of the National Coal Board.

Plate 3.10. Tyne Yard on 29 August 1963. To the left is A3 No 60045 'Lemberg' and to the right Type 2 No D5107. The latter propels a Diesel Brake Tender, which will provide additional brake force for the unfitted train. (RG Warwick)

Over half the traffic handled comprised loaded coal wagons and the returning empties. Much of the coal was conveyed over the Pennines into Lancashire, but some was conveyed to industries and power stations in the north-east of England. The new yard also despatched and received trunk freight trains to and from yards in Lancashire, the north-east of England, south Yorkshire, and Goole and Hull. Passing trunk freight trains exchanged grouped sections of wagons. After the yard was opened, some trans-Pennine traffic that had previously been handled at York was henceforth handled at Healey Mills. Nearby yards – Brighouse, Crofton Laden, Horbury Junction Sidings, Low Moor, Mirfield, Mytholmroyd, New Withams, Turners Lane, and Wakefield Exchange – were closed. Three other yards – Copley Hill, Crofton Empty, and Hillhouse – henceforth worked at lower capacity.

Tyneside Central Freight Depot

To complement the Region's new and modernised yards were modernised depots for the handling of general merchandise and wagonload traffic. Ultimately, it was planned that there would be twenty-nine goods depots in the Region, seven of which would be main concentration depots. These would be located at Stockton, York, Bradford, Leeds, Huddersfield, Hull, and, as described here, on Tyneside.

Tyneside Central Freight Depot was initially intended to be established at Newcastle Forth, but detailed costings revealed that adaptation of the existing goods depot at this location would be more expensive than building a new one from scratch. Therefore, Tyneside Central Freight Depot was built in Gateshead upon the site formerly occupied by Park Lane Yard and Borough Gardens motive power depot. The twenty-two acre site had good access for both trains and lorries; it was adjacent to the Sunderland - Newcastle line, and close to the main Sunderland road. Opened officially by Dr Beeching on 15 October 1963, the new depot served an area extending over approximately 700 square miles – this area encompassed the entire Tyneside region. Upon opening, the small depots of Annfield Plain, Birtley, Blaydon, Blyth, Chester-le-Street, Consett, Fencehouses, Gateshead Eldon Street, Newcastle Forth, and South Shields were closed. (Eldon Street depot was used henceforth for warehousing rather than for handling traffic as previously.) At the heart of the depot were large sheds where the merchandise traffic was dealt with. Incoming wagons were spotted by a shunting locomotive on four of the six tracks in front of the freight received shed. (The other two tracks were for the accommodation of empty wagons discharged from the shed after unloading.) The single-storey shed was 818 feet long by 170 feet 6 inches wide. When required, wagons were winched by two tons capacity capstans on to the two wagon-discharge sidings within the shed. Each of these sidings could accommodate fourteen wagons. Once inside the shed, the depot staff unloaded the wagons on to a deck located between the two sidings. This deck was provided with two electrically-operated slat conveyors, each three feet wide and running at a speed of forty feet per minute. One conveyor was for northbound traffic, the other for southbound. Thus preliminary rough sorting of the merchandise took place immediately. As items of merchandise passed along each conveyor, they were marked up for their final destination. The conveyors led to loading bays for the lorries of the Region's cartage fleet, and marked-up merchandise was removed from the conveyors at the appropriate point. One hundred and eight lorries could be accommodated at any one time; each lorry was loaded with merchandise destined for the same area. The shed also encompassed one more siding, long enough to hold eleven wagons, which served a separate fully-enclosed deck. This deck had its own conveyor, and was used for the handling of tobacco, wines and spirits.

A separate freight forwarded shed, also single-storey, was 870 feet long by 96 feet 6 inches wide. This shed encompassed four sidings widely spaced so that wagons could be loaded directly from lorries; a deck was also provided to handle merchandise not suitable for direct loading from lorries. A total of 146 wagons could be accommodated within the shed. In the yard beyond the sheds there were two sidings either side of a concrete pad, to be used for the loading and unloading of wagons by the depot's complement of mobile cranes; items handled in this way included BR's own containers as well as large pieces of machinery and timber. A total of eight wagons could be accommodated in these two sidings. A further five tracks, with road access between, could accommodate ninety-two wagons; these wagons could be loaded and unloaded by hand directly from and to lorries. Diverse reception, holding, and departure sidings completed the depot's railway infrastructure; a garage, a fuel pad, a weigh office and diverse office and accommodation buildings completed the depot's cartage and personnel infrastructure. Daily throughput of the depot was 400 to 500 wagons loaded with general merchandise, plus up to another 200 wagons loaded with a commodity, such as timber or machinery, bound for one individual customer.

Brakes

In order to work a train rapidly between the diverse yards, it was necessary that the wagons making up that train be fitted with brakes under the direct control of the driver. However, the traditional type of wagon was equipped with a handbrake only; a train comprising such wagons could not run rapidly as it could not be stopped within a safe distance (or even at all). The Big Four had made a start in the right direction, fitting an automatic brake to some at least of the wagons used on express freight trains. In normal operation, an automatic brake was under the direct control of the driver; continuity of that control between wagons was effected by means of rubber connecting hoses. If a train parted due to such as a failed coupling, the hoses adjacent to the failed coupling parted also, and all the brakes applied automatically. Ideally, an express freight train would comprise only those wagons fitted with an automatic brake; this type of train was described as fully-fitted. More often than not though, some of the wagons in a train had handbrakes only. In that case, those wagons fitted with an automatic brake were assembled at the front of a train, and formed what was known as a fitted head to a partially-fitted train. The use of a fitted head allowed a train to run faster than one comprising wagons equipped with handbrakes only. (The maximum permissible speed of a partially-fitted train depended upon the size of the fitted head in relation to the size of the train as a whole.) Unfortunately, because the majority of pre-Grouping companies had standardised on the automatic vacuum brake, the Big Four had fitted its wagons likewise, rather than with the more powerful air brake.

From 1950 until the early part of 1952, tests were performed on the London Midland Region at the behest of the Railway Executive to determine whether BR should standardise on the automatic vacuum or air brake. The test trains comprised rakes of 16 tons capacity coal wagons, fitted either with automatic vacuum or air brakes. Although the value of running fully-fitted freight trains was not in doubt, that value was amply confirmed by the tests. On 6 January 1952, for example, an 850 tons vacuum-braked coal train hauled by two Class 5 steam locomotives averaged 38 miles per hour over its journey from Toton to Brent; an unfitted coal train averaged 15 miles per hour over the same journey.(6) The tests also demonstrated that whereas the vacuum brake was at or even beyond the limits of its capabilities with a seventy-wagon train, the air brake could cope not only with such a train, but one heavier and running faster. Given the lack of money for large-scale investment in either system however, no decision was made once the tests were concluded.

The Modernisation Plan stated that all of BR's wagons would be fitted with automatic brakes. A decision in favour of one or other of the two brake systems was now therefore required. Basing its decision largely on the tests done on the London Midland Region, the BTC's Power Brakes Committee unequivocally recommended that BR standardise on the automatic air brake. The committee's recommendation was endorsed by the Technical Development and Research Committee, which urged BR's traffic officers to take the long-term view, and to embrace the system that would be most appropriate for the trains of the future. Unfortunately, the decision by the Big Four to standardise on the vacuum brake meant that by the end of 1955, 181,424 of BR's 1,124,812 wagons were already so fitted.(7) To standardise on the air brake now threatened years of chaos in depots and yards as railwaymen grappled with the problems inherent in forming trains using wagons fitted with vacuum brakes, with air brakes, and with no automatic brakes at all. Eventually of course, those problems would disappear when all wagons were fitted with air brakes. In the meantime though, the problems would be immense. For this reason the Chief Regional Managers (except that of the Southern Region, which ran relatively few freight trains) put pressure on the BTC to retain the vacuum brake. The BTC was influenced by this pressure, and was aware too that to standardise on the air brake would add two years to the conversion period, and would cost an extra £30 million above the sum required to standardise on the vacuum brake.(8) Thus the BTC decided on 16 February 1956 to standardise on the latter. In accordance with the Modernisation Plan, the automatic vacuum brake would therefore be fitted to all of BR's wagons; £75 million was allocated for that purpose.

The decision to fit all wagons with automatic brakes meant that staff on the ground would, in the near future, be faced with the huge task of coupling and uncoupling tens of thousands of hoses as they made up trains in depots and yards. Railwaymen did not take to the prospect with much enthusiasm; non-railwaymen did not take to it at all. Staff of the National Coal Board, for example, normally loaded a coal train in batches of four or five wagons (sidings serving colliery screens not having the capacity to accommodate more than that number). If the train was fully-fitted, with all hoses connected, then uncoupling batches of wagons would take longer and be more arduous than if the train comprised wagons fitted with handbrakes only (as was

Plate 3.11. Class K3 No 61899 with a freight train at Selby, circa 1962. Although the front two wagons of the train are fitted with vacuum brakes, the hoses are not connected; the train is running unfitted. (LM West)

traditional in the coal industry). More work would also be required when the batches of wagons were re-combined to form the fully-loaded train. So the Coal Board's staff refused to do it. Railwaymen working on such as the North Eastern Region's coal staiths on the Rivers Blyth and Tyne, whereon empty wagons were worked individually off the discharge point, also resisted the adoption of automatic brakes on all wagons. The need for brakes on all wagons was also questionable, given the short distance travelled by so many of the Region's coal trains from colliery to staith. (The collieries in the Ashington area, for example, were less than ten miles from the staiths on the River Blyth at Cambois.)

As a consequence of the resistance by staff on the ground, of the huge cost of fitting automatic brakes to BR's vast wagon fleet, and of the wisdom of doing so anyway, the policy of fitting brakes to all wagons was abandoned in May 1960. By the end of 1959, 296,253 of BR's current fleet of 960,353 wagons were fitted with automatic brakes. These wagons were used to increase the number of fitted and partially-fitted express freight trains. The efficiency of the operation of fitted freight trains had been improved from the beginning of 1958 when agreement was reached between the BTC and the railway unions that in certain circumstances diesel and electric locomotives could be single-manned. Concerning freight, the agreement pertained to the non-stop run of a fitted freight train provided that the journey did not exceed 75 miles or two hours; the agreement only applied between 6.00 am and midnight. (A two-man crew was required between midnight and 6.00 am, unless the train started its journey between 5.00 and 6.00 am, or was due to complete it before 1.00 am.) The agreement did not apply to partially-fitted or unfitted freight trains.(9)

Problems of Profitability

Unfortunately, these marshalling yards, concentration depots and brake-fitted wagons – splendid fruits of the Modernisation Plan – did not do what they were supposed to do. They did not make the Region's freight traffic profitable. In particular, they did not make profitable the Region's general merchandise and wagonload traffic.

Prior to the Grouping, the private railway companies had competed with each other largely upon service. Thus a trader despatching his goods over a distance had often been able to choose between rival companies offering fast and frequent freight services. The result of this had been good for manufacturing and retail industries, in that it had not been necessary to maintain large stocks; new stock, either for the manufacturing process or for retail, had been quickly obtainable. The competition on service had proved bad for the railway companies however, as individual consignments despatched had remained relatively small, and the companies had therefore not been able to make much progress in increasing their efficiency by introducing larger-capacity wagons. After the Grouping, the cash-strapped Big Four made little progress in that direction either. When the Big Four were nationalised, the average open or covered railway wagon conveyed a maximum of twelve tons (most ran part-loaded). As part of the Modernisation Plan, BR intended to increase the carrying capacity of its freight wagons. However, progress was slow, partly because the small size of the average consignment was ideally suited to conveyance by motor lorry; there was little incentive for manufacturers and retailers to accept the inconvenience of bulk deliveries in large railway wagons when road hauliers would continue to convey small consignments.

Plate 3.12. The Eastern Region's Class A4 No 60034 'Lord Faringdon' runs into York from the south with a Class C vacuum-fitted express freight in June 1961; at least half of the wagons forming this train have their vacuum hoses connected and have fully functioning automatic brakes. (RG Warwick)

47

The North Eastern Region's new marshalling yards and such as Tyneside Central Freight Depot opened in 1963. During 1962, the Region's trains had conveyed 4,720,000 tons of originating general merchandise compared to 7,481,000 tons during 1948. The reduction in livestock traffic was even more marked. During 1948 livestock weighing in total 92,000 tons were loaded into the Region's trains. By 1962 the tonnage was so low it was not recorded separately in the BTC's annual report.(10) The differences were largely due to competition from lorries. The new marshalling yards and depots, although efficient in themselves, would not allow the Region – nor BR as a whole – to win back much traffic. Indeed, in many cases the opening of the new depots accelerated the shift from rail to road. When the new depots were fully commissioned, many small depots were closed. A trader who had used one of those small, local depots now had his consignment collected by a lorry of the Region's cartage fleet. The lorry often had to travel some distance to the new depot, where the trader's consignment was transhipped into a wagon. At the receiving depot, the consignment was transhipped again into another lorry, and finally conveyed to its destination. The multiple handling did not make for cheap operation for the railways, nor did it provide speedy service for the trader. In many instances the trader decided that it might as well go all the way in one lorry.

Stourton Yard Cancelled

Fortunately for the Region's finances, it had been realised that to spend some £3,976,000 building a large hump marshalling yard at Stourton would be a waste of resources, given the proximity to Healey Mills and the determination to increase the number of block trains. The BTC had approved the building of the new yard on 27 October 1960.(11) Subsequently, the North Eastern Region's Area Board had signed contracts for ground clearance and drainage works, and for hydraulic wagon-retarding equipment. Work commenced on earthmoving and bridge building, but all work was suspended in February 1963, and on 7 September 1965 the Board agreed with a recommendation from the General Manager that the BTC's approval to build the yard be rescinded. The planned establishment of a main concentration depot in Leeds of the same type as that built on Tyneside was also cancelled, the local railwaymen having to make do with modernisation of the existing facilities. In this latter case, the cancellation of the plan was partly because a new method of working the traffic was in the offing.

Containerisation

One of the positive proposals contained within the Beeching Report was that studies should be carried out with regard to the creation of a network of Liner Train services and their associated depots; these studies would be a continuation of those instituted following the publication of the White Paper *Re-appraisal of the Plan for the Modernisation and Re-equipment of British Railways*. The Liner Trains would convey containerised general merchandise between depots specifically adapted for the transhipment of containers between railway wagons and road-going lorries. The basic idea was not new – the concept of loading freight into a container in order to expedite transhipment between modes of transport was old as the idea of railways themselves. However, containerisation was hardly developed until after the Grouping of 1923. In the face of growing competition from road transport, the Big Four railway companies began the process of inducing their customers to load their consignments in containers. The Railway Clearing House approved designs of containers that would be acceptable to each of the Big Four, and those companies built them and the two-axle flat wagons that would convey them. Most of the containers built were boxes, having doors at the ends or the sides or both as appropriate. Some containers, corresponding to the conventional open merchandise wagons, were open. At first, containers were built of wood; from 1929, containers were built of pressed steel. The advantages of building containers from steel were that they were more robust, and that they were lighter than their wooden equivalents. However, even a steel container was rated to carry no more than four tons.

Plate 3.13. An 0-6-0 diesel-mechanical shunter shunts a rake of container-carrying Conflats at Selby Canal circa 1962. (LM West)

Other disadvantages associated with the containers were that they were lifted by means of lugs attached to their upper parts (necessitating a potentially perilous climb up a ladder for the railwaymen charged with the task of attaching the crane hooks), and that they had to be individually chained down on to the wagons or lorries that conveyed them (not a perilous task, but a time-consuming one). Nonetheless, the use of the containers markedly improved the efficiency with which general merchandise was conveyed. After Nationalisation, BR continued to design and build new containers; many of these were built in the North Eastern Region's workshops at Faverdale and Shildon. Some containers were intended for general merchandise, others for specific traffics. In 1949, for example, Shildon Works built tank containers for the conveyance of beer; in 1951, Faverdale Works built insulated containers for the conveyance of frozen meat. Not all of the containers used on BR were built in its workshops however. For example, in 1960 Carmichael and Company Limited built six tank containers for the conveyance of malt liquor from Tyneside to Scotland. There was modest experimentation too. In 1960, the North Eastern Region commissioned the manufacture of two five tons capacity containers built of glass fibre-reinforced plastic; these containers were only half the weight of a wooden four tons capacity container having the same dimensions. The plastic was impregnated with an orange-coloured dye so no painting was required. However, no series production took place.

In order to convey containerised general merchandise traffic rapidly, the programme of accelerating freight trains was continued, and new dedicated services were instituted. The *Export Express* service, introduced on the London Midland Region on 1 July 1956 to expedite the despatch of small consignments to diverse ports, was later reproduced in other Regions. By the end of 1959, the North Eastern Region had its own *Export Express* service, offering guaranteed overnight delivery from its principal freight depots to Hull or to Goole. *The Tees-Tyne Freighter* was inaugurated on 1 July 1960 by the North Eastern and Eastern Regions working in co-operation. The train conveyed containerised or full wagonload traffic from London to Newcastle. It ran every night except Sunday, loaded to a maximum of fifty wagons. The working in the opposite direction was *The King's Cross Freighter*. Another named train, operated in co-operation with the Southern Region, was *The North East Trader*, instituted in November 1964 to convey general merchandise from Brighton, Crawley and Croydon to the north-east of England.(12)

In order to expedite the overall working of containerised merchandise traffic, North Eastern Region traffic officers regularly met their counterparts working for the North Eastern Division of British Road Services (BRS). BRS equipped lorries and trailers at its principal depots to handle railway containers, and actively sought containerised traffic that could be conveyed via such as *The King's Cross Freighter*.

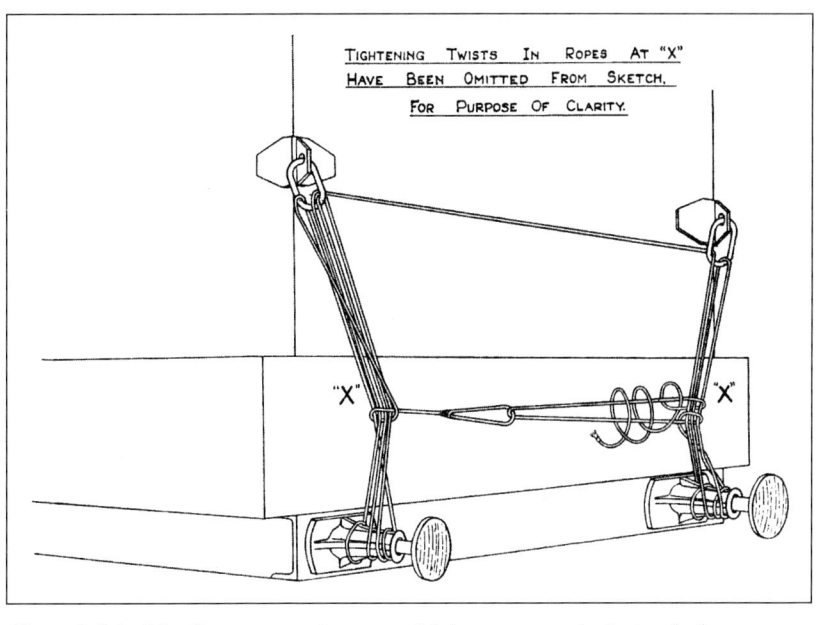

Plate 3.14. Ideally, a container would be conveyed chained down on a purpose-built Conflat wagon. However, if required, a container could be conveyed in an ordinary merchandise wagon. This drawing shows how to rope a container into such a wagon. ('Instructions for the Loading and Securing of Containers in Rail Vehicles', BR20427, February 1961)

Roadrailer

Containerisation of merchandise traffic, and its conveyance by rail, was undeniably an efficient process. However, the cranes required at depots were expensive to buy and maintain. Cranes were no less expensive in the United States, so a road/rail inter-modal system that did not require cranes was developed as an alternative. This system, christened Roadrailer, was adopted and fully developed by the Chesapeake and Ohio Railway Company during the 1950s. It comprised road-going semi-trailer vans, each van fitted with set of rubber-tyred wheels for use on the road, and a set of steel wheels for use on the railway. The sets of wheels were mounted at either end of a rocking beam – when one set of wheels was down and in use, the other set was up and out of the way. The advantage of the system was that no cranes were required, merely a yard with tracks so ballasted or concreted that lorries could drive Roadrailer vans on to and off the railway. Disadvantages were that each van was heavy, being fitted with both rubber tyres and steel wheels, and that no other types of wagon could be coupled behind a Roadrailer train. (A Roadrailer train could be coupled safely to the rear of a conventional freight train.) Nevertheless, when BR traffic officers visited the United States to see the system at work, they were sufficiently impressed as to recommend it be adopted on BR.

Working in co-operation with British Road Services, the Eastern, North Eastern, and Scottish Regions planned a Roadrailer service between King's Cross, Pelaw, and Portobello. A Roadrailer train was built by the Pressed Steel Company Limited, and tested on the Eastern Region. Individual Roadrailer vans were demonstrated to potential customers; in the North Eastern Region, for example, the Roadrailer was demonstrated on 21 October 1961 at the opening ceremony for the modernised Hull Central Goods Depot. Inauguration of the inter-regional Roadrailer service was provisionally scheduled for August 1963. However, although a suitable depot was built at Pelaw, the service was never implemented. The Liner Train, conveying new designs of container, appeared to offer better prospects of success. It was developed instead of the Roadrailer.(13)

Plates 3.15 and 3.16. Roadrailer, in road and rail modes. Note the adaptor wagon between the Roadrailers and the locomotive. (BR, per J Kearney)

Liner Trains

The prototype containers designed for use on the Liner Trains were somewhat different from the traditional types. Two significant differences were the ways whereby an individual container was lifted and then secured upon a railway wagon or road-going lorry. The container was lifted by means of slings hooked into pockets located along its bottom edges, then lowered on to four spigots mounted on the wagon or lorry; once in place, it was clamped. The lifting method allowed the railwayman positioning the slings to remain safely on the ground, and the securing method was much quicker than using chains. Both methods were already tried and tested, having been devised by London Midland Region engineers for that Region's *Speedfreight* containerised freight service which was introduced between London and Manchester on 1 April 1963. During 1964, various prototype box and open containers were fabricated by diverse railway workshops and private manufacturers in ten, twenty, and twenty-seven feet lengths. The tare weight of the containers was kept as low as possible in order to maximise carrying capacity; that capacity ranged from seven and a half tons in a ten foot container to twenty tons in a twenty-seven foot container. A consequence of the low tare weight was that containers were not strong enough to be stacked more than two high, so plenty of space for storage of empty containers would be required at Liner Train depots. Loaded containers could not be stacked at all. To convey the containers by rail, the North Eastern's Shildon Works built four low-height skeletal container-carrying wagons. The reduced height compared with the traditional wagons used to convey containers was necessary as the new box containers were eight feet wide and eight feet tall. Although the new box containers were no taller than the traditional type, the latter had their upper corners rounded in order to pass safely through tunnels. The new containers, being square in cross-section, would foul such as tunnels unless they were carried at a lower height where the loading gauge was wider. The new wagons were permanently coupled by steel bars in a set of four wagons; Liner Trains would be made up of as many sets as the traffic required. The idea behind the bar couplings within the set was that they avoided the slack associated with conventional couplings and hence prevented damage to the merchandise conveyed within the containers. Preventing such damage was very important to BR, as conventional methods of working trains and marshalling wagons (especially using hump shunting) caused a lot of damage. In contrast, merchandise conveyed in rubber-tyred lorries travelling over tarmac roads tended to suffer little or no damage. Each wagon in the set had space for four containers each ten feet long, or a lesser number of longer containers. Concerning the type of brake fitted to the wagons, it was apparent that the automatic vacuum brake was not compatible with the running of heavy and fast Liner Trains. Therefore, in accordance with a decision made by the BRB in 1963 to standardise on the automatic air brake, the wagons were so fitted. This decision was facilitated by the fact that such as the new container-carrying wagons would run in block container trains, and would not be required to couple with other types of wagon. However, the decision to adopt the automatic air brake did mean that the train braking systems of diesel and electric locomotives would have to be modified. (The locomotives were already fitted with air-operated locomotive brakes.)

The prototype wagons and containers demonstrated the practicality of the proposed Liner Trains, and production orders were therefore placed. The production series wagons were not built at Shildon, but at Ashford; the wagons were longer than the prototypes, having a greater carrying capacity and space for more containers. The extra space proved useful in 1966 when a change in the Construction and Use Regulations for road-going lorries permitted the use of thirty-feet long semi-trailers. This in turn allowed the use of thirty-feet long containers, which henceforth were built instead of twenty-seven feet long containers.

At the same time as these railway designs were being developed, the International Standards Organisation (ISO) was developing designs of container for maritime traffic. Such containers would be stacked on top of each other aboard ship, so were designed to be very strong. In consequence, they were also much heavier than the railway designs intended for domestic merchandise traffic. A feature of an ISO-type container was that it had strong castings built in to each corner. Holes in the bottom castings were used to locate the container on spigots on railway wagons or lorries; a simple twistlock rotated the top part of each spigot in order to lock the container in place. The top castings were used to lift the container; a crane-mounted frame had hydraulically-rotatable spigots at its corners, and these were locked into the castings in order to effect the lift. Soon after the first of BR's production wagons were delivered, they were fitted with twistlocks to enable them to carry ISO-type containers. Some of the new production containers built by BR were fitted with ISO-type corner castings as well as lifting pockets. In order to offer a service conveying ISO-type containers to industrial concerns within the North Eastern Region, fifty Lowmac wagons were fitted with twistlocks during the summer of 1966. The modified wagons worked out of Hull in connection with shipping services to and from Scandinavia. Containers were transhipped between railway wagons and road-going lorries at Hull Central Goods Depot; the lorries ferried containers to and from King George Dock.

Progress on the engineering front was good, therefore. Progress with industrial relations was less good. All grades of railwaymen were very anxious at this time as relentless rationalisation was reducing rapidly their numbers. The proposed Liner Trains were objected to by the National Union of Railwaymen as privately-owned road haulage companies would be allowed to work into and out of the proposed new Liner Train depots; this might well lead to redundancies amongst the ranks of the drivers of BR's own cartage fleet. The question of where a Liner Train's guard would travel was also contentious – the BRB wanted guards to travel in the rear cab of the train's diesel or electric locomotive rather than in the traditional brakevan. These problems were eventually resolved however, and on 15 November 1965 the first Liner Trains, operating under the new BR marketing name Freightliner, carried modest commercial loads between London and Glasgow via the West Coast Main Line.

Early development of Freightliner traffic was on the London Midland Region. The first Freightliner depots in the North Eastern Region did not open until 31 July 1967; by this date, of course, the Region had merged with the Eastern Region. One of the depots to open on that date was on Tyneside at Follingsby, located at the northern end of the Leamside Line. Access to the depot by road, would, in the near future, be off a newly-constructed stretch of trunk road connecting to the Tyne Tunnel. Until that was built, access was via local roads. The depot was laid out in a standard design, comprising three parallel terminal sidings flanked on one side by a roadway and container-handling area. Containers were transhipped by means of two overhead gantry cranes,

Plate 3.17. Roadrailer was demonstrated on 21 October 1961 at the opening ceremony for the modernised Hull's English Street Central Goods Depot, as seen here in the left background.(BR (NER), per DR Wilcock)

which straddled both the sidings and the roadway. The cranes were powered by electricity and ran on their own rails. When the depot was laid out, provision was made for future expansion. That expansion would never come however, and the depot would close (along with seven others) on 6 April 1987 as part of a re-organisation of the Freightliner network.

The other depot to open on 31 July was at Stourton, built on the site originally designated for the hump marshalling yard. Unlike Follingsby depot however, Stourton depot remained busy through the 1980s, and remains so today.

On 23 October 1967, a Freightliner depot was opened at Stockton, on Haverton Hill Road. The location was not ideal however, and the depot would close on 27 February 1989. On that same day a new Cleveland Freightliner Terminal would open on land adjacent to ICI Wilton, Freightliner's largest customer on Teesside.

The fourth of the Freightliner depots planned by the former North Eastern Region was opened on 1 January 1968 at Hull, on the site of Priory Yard. The volume of traffic handled by the new depot was initially very encouraging, generated both by the shipping companies using the docks and by BP Chemicals (UK) Limited, which had a plant to the east of Hull at Saltend. However, the Hull dock workers were by no means enamoured with the concept of containerisation, and resisted it. In consequence, maritime traffic would increasingly be handled by Immingham dockers, and traffic levels through the Hull Freightliner depot would diminish accordingly. The depot would close on 6 April 1987.

Coal

Concerning the conveyance of coal, the systems and equipment bequeathed to the North Eastern Region by the North Eastern Railway Company were models of efficiency – at least compared with those pertaining elsewhere on BR. Traditionally, the conveyance of coal in the north-east of England revolved around relatively intense use of bottom-discharge hopper wagons. This tradition had been whole-heartedly adopted by the North Eastern Railway. Across much of the North Eastern Region therefore, hopper wagons were used to discharge coal at riverbank staiths, at industrial sites and power stations, and in coal cells at stations across much of the Region.(14) By and large, only in those parts of the Region where the lines had been constructed by such as the Hull & Barnsley Railway and the Midland Railway Companies, where wagons were either unloaded by hand or by end-tipping, did inefficient methods of working pertain. Fortunately, the tonnage of coal handled in this way within the Region comprised but a small percentage of the whole.

The scope for modernising the way in which coal traffic was handled in the Region seemed, therefore, to be limited. Some modernisation did take place however. The Ideal Stocks Committee, established by the Railway Executive in February 1948 to make recommendations as to the sizes of locomotive, carriage and wagon that would best work diverse traffics, had by the early 1950s come to the conclusion that a wagon of $24^{1}/_{2}$ tons capacity would be the ideal for the conveyance of coal. For a two-axle wagon, this capacity was the largest that could be accommodated within the $17^{1}/_{2}$ tons axle load specified by the Chief

Plate 3.18. J27 No 65862 hauls 21 ton coal hoppers through Backworth on 5 August 1955. Most of the coal mined in the area around Backworth was conveyed to the staiths on the River Tyne. (TJ Edgington)

Civil Engineer. Shildon Works was therefore commissioned to build a prototype 24½ tons capacity hopper wagon; this wagon, based on an LNER design for a 21 tons capacity wagon, was delivered at the end of 1953. The prototype, like the wagons upon which it was based, had two hopper doors. In tests, these were deemed to be insufficient. The design was therefore modified to have four hopper doors. Quantity production of the modified design began at Shildon in 1954.

In pursuit of the Modernisation Plan, the staiths on the River Blyth at Blyth, and on the River Tyne at Dunston, were strengthened in order to take the weight of the new 24½ tons capacity wagons. Millions of tons of coastwise and export coal were discharged annually into colliers at these staiths, and the diverse staiths, drops, and hoists located elsewhere in the Region. The receipts from this traffic were, however, much less than those from coal destined for landsale, so although the increase in efficiency obtained by the larger-capacity wagons was relatively modest, it was very useful in maintaining the profitability of the traffic.(15)

The method of conveying coal for domestic use was also gradually modernised. Stations large and small throughout the North-East of England were provided with a series of coal cells, served by the ubiquitous bottom-discharge hopper wagons. The cells were used by the local coal merchants to store their stock. (Continuing the practice first adopted by the NER, the most prominent of the local coal merchants was often the local station master.) Although the system of coal cells allowed for a quick turn-round of wagons, the annual tonnage handled at country stations was relatively small. Just how small was revealed in the Beeching Report. Across BR as a whole, the 1790 least busy stations handled a maximum of fifty tons of coal traffic per week. The Report therefore advocated the concentration of coal traffic in large mechanised depots. Within the North Eastern Region, the provision of such depots was inhibited by the fact that few users of coal lived or worked much more than fifty miles from the nearest colliery. Therefore, there was limited scope for the building of depots compared with the situation in the south of England, where towns were mostly distant from the coalfields. The building of the depots was also inhibited by other circumstances: railwaymen were loathe to disturb existing traffic patterns in case traffic be lost to road hauliers; the National Coal Board was reluctant to co-operate with the railways by investing its own money in the new depots as the market for domestic coal was perceptibly declining as consumers converted to oil, gas or electricity. Nevertheless, progress was made within the Region on concentrating coal traffic. For example, in co-operation with the local coal merchant Chadwick Hargreaves, in 1962 Scarborough (Belford Road) depot was equipped for the mechanised handling of domestic coal. Four overhead hoppers were built in an arc round a central wagon-discharge point, served by a conveyor belt that could be swung round to serve whichever of the hoppers required replenishment. Lorries working out of the newly-equipped depot served Chadwick's customers in and around Scarborough, Staintondale, Filey, and Bridlington.

The Scarborough scheme was more ambitious than most. When the Beeching Report was published, the Region still had about 640 stations and depots where domestic coal was handled. By the end of 1966, that figure was planned to fall to about 100.(16) However, the only place within the Region where studies by traffic officers showed there to be potential for large mechanised coal concentration depots was Hull. In that city, the Region had inherited sixteen depots where domestic coal was handled. Working with the National

Plate 3.19. Class J39 No 64855 departs Masham for Ripon with the pick-up goods on 2 May 1956. The train comprises two empty coal wagons plus the brake van. (JW Hague / NERA GM Pierson Collection)

Coal Board and local coal merchants, the Region's traffic officers planned to reduce this to two. The first of these, intended to serve consumers living in the western part of Hull, was opened early in 1968 by Stephenson Clarke Limited within the confines of the existing Calvert Lane depot. The new facility was fully mechanised, and equipped to handle 70,000 tons of coal per annum. Coal was delivered in 21 tons capacity hopper wagons, and discharged on to a conveyor feeding a bank of fourteen ten ton capacity bagging hoppers, plus a chute for bulk-loading lorries directly. When the new depot opened, four small ones were closed. However, Calvert Lane depot continued to accommodate the Hull and East Riding Co-operative Society, which received its coal in non-hopper 16 tons capacity wagons; these wagons were unloaded by a crane equipped with a clamshell grab. The second concentration depot, intended to serve consumers living in the eastern part of Hull, was opened the following year in Sculcoates. Opening of the new depot allowed the closure of ten small ones.

The most significant development in the modernisation of the methods of conveying coal was a consequence of a change in the way coal was burned. The traditional design of industrial and power station furnace was designed to burn coal in lumps. If coal in the form of small pieces or dust was shovelled into such a furnace, it either compacted into a mass that would not burn (as combustion air could not pass through it), or it was carried away unburned by the draught and ejected via the chimney. Such coal, known as slack, was therefore largely useless. (Coal in Britain being relatively cheap, it was rarely economically viable to mix the slack with a flammable binding material to make briquettes.) There was every incentive then for coal owners and coal consumers to make sure that lumps of coal were not ground down into slack. The basic precautions taken were to handle coal as gently, and as infrequently, as possible. Thus coal brought to the surface of a colliery was not stockpiled after screening, but was immediately loaded into railway wagons. In this way, multiple-handling of the coal was avoided. If that coal was then immediately sold, the wagons could be despatched to the customer. More often than not though, the wagons stood in a siding for several days before despatch. At the customer's premises, again the coal was not stockpiled, but remained in the wagons until it was actually required in the furnaces. In consequence, even in the north-east of England where hopper wagons could be emptied in a few seconds, wagon utilisation was very poor.

However, in the mid 1920s furnaces were designed specifically to burn coal that had been deliberately pulverised. One advantage of having such a furnace was that it could burn slack; such slack was cheap to buy as it was all but useless otherwise. Another advantage was that coal of low calorific value – also cheap to buy – could be made into a useful fuel by pulverising it and then mixing it with pulverised coal of high calorific value. Dunston Power Station, on the right bank of the River Tyne to the west of Newcastle, was equipped in the early 1930s with such a furnace, and the LNER adapted a fleet of its hopper wagons to serve it. The adaptation comprised the fitting of dust-proof seals to the hopper doors of each wagon, and the fitting of light metal hoops over the top to support a canvas sheet; these adaptations prevented the loss of pulverised coal from the wagon.

In the same way that Britain's railways were nationalised by the post-war Labour Government, so too was the electricity supply industry; the British Electricity Authority assumed its responsibilities on 1 April 1948. The Authority's assets comprised a plethora of small power stations, most towns and cities in the country having at least one such. These power stations, as well as being small, were also for the most part antiquated. The Authority therefore continued with an existing governmental policy of replacing small power stations with large new ones. Within the territory of the North Eastern Region, for example, the Authority built new power stations on Teesside (North Tees C) and Tyneside (Stella A and B). Although the new power stations were to be larger than those they replaced, they were to be supplied with coal in the traditional method. At each power station, this involved fans of sidings all full of wagons waiting for their coal to be discharged directly into the furnaces. The method suited the Authority very well, as it had to generate electricity seven days per week. In contrast, miners hewed coal on only five days per week, and railwaymen conveyed it on only six days per week. To have stocks of coal on hand was essential to the continuous operation of each power station.

Over the years, the nationalised electricity industry gradually evolved. From 1 April 1955, the British Electricity Authority was divided into separate authorities covering Scotland, and England and Wales. The latter entity was named the Central Electricity Authority; from 1 January 1958, it was re-named the Central Electricity Generating Board (CEGB). In the same way that the industry evolved, so too did the policy concerning the building of new power stations. Instead of building large ones, the Board decided to build enormous ones, with a generating capacity of at least 2000 megawatts. These so-called baseload power stations would not necessarily be built close to the towns and cities where electricity was consumed, but close to sources of coal and to rivers (because millions of gallons of water would be needed every day to condense the steam used to drive the power stations' turbines). A high voltage grid of electricity transmission lines would be erected to conduct the electricity to the towns and cities. These baseload power stations would be supplied with coal using the traditional method, though that coal would be pulverised and not in lumps. Given the huge appetite for coal of a baseload power station, the number of wagons required to serve it would also be huge. For example, calculations done by traffic officers in the Scottish Region showed that 550 wagons of $24^1/_2$ tons capacity would be required to service the proposed Cockenzie Power Station. However, traffic officers on the Eastern Region devised a new way of working.

Colour Plate 11. English Electric Type 4 No D283 works a Class C Up express freight through York station on 29 June 1961. The locomotive was almost a year old when the photograph was taken, having been built in July 1960. It was allocated to York MPD. (RG Warwick)

Colour Plate 12. English Electric Type 3 No D6768 is seen here at Wellfield Junction on 14 May 1968 with a Tees Yard - Hawthorn Colliery empties working. Note the use of a brake tender with these unfitted coal wagons. (JM Boyes / JW Armstrong Trust, per JR Midcalf)

Colour Plate 13. As discussed on pages 49 and 50, there were initially high hopes for the Roadrailer. This train is being shunted by a British Road Services Edinburgh District tractor unit on 6 June 1963. Those hopes would not be fulfilled; in due course, the decision would be made that Freightliner containers were more worthy of investment. (JM Boyes / JW Armstrong Trust, per JR Midcalf)

55

Colour Plate 14.
To replace such as jute sacks for the conveyance of powders and granular materials, BR adopted the 'Tote' system of aluminium containers as made by Pressoturn Limited. These containers were robust, and were designed to be lifted by fork lift truck. Various sizes were available, and different types catered for solid and liquid loads. Seen here is the cover of an advertising leaflet extolling the virtues of the system. (Reproduced at 80% of original size.) (JG Teasdale Collection)

Colour Plate 15.
Despite the introduction of such as the Tote system, railwaymen still had to cope with traditional packing materials. This drawing is part of a series showing how to load a wagon with sacks. ('Instructions for Handling and Loading Specified Traffics', May 1957)

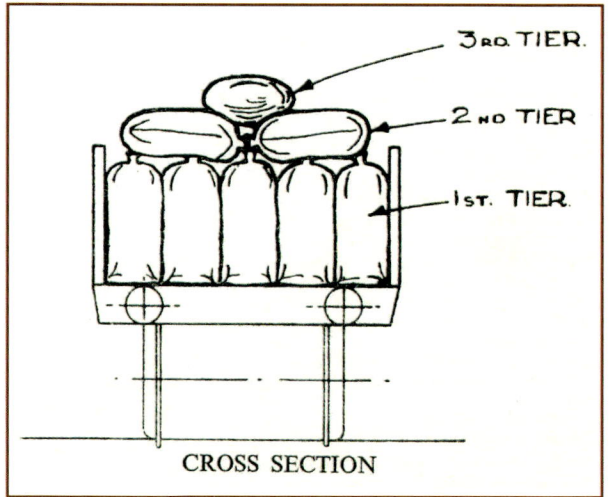

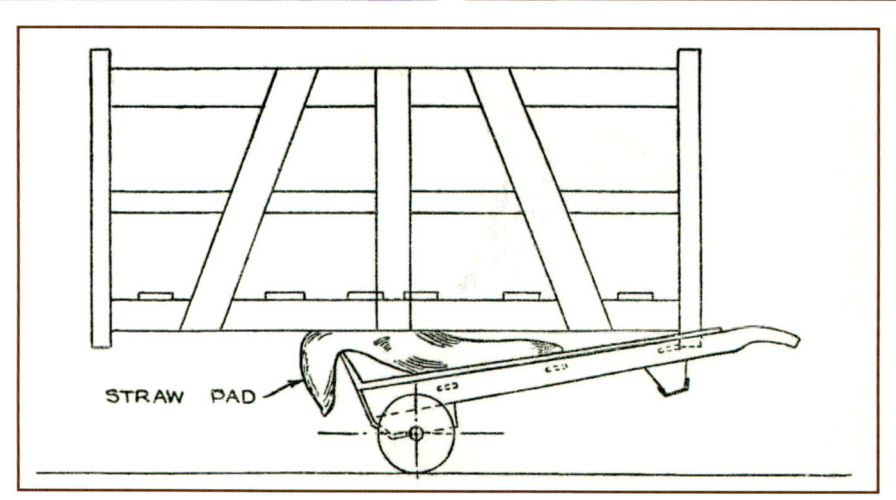

Colour Plate 16.
And despite the introduction of fork lifts and mobile yard cranes, much of the merchandise dealt with by railwaymen still had to be moved by hand. This drawing shows how to barrow a crate of glass plate. ('Instructions for Handling and Loading Specified Traffics', May 1957)

The first of the turbo-generator sets to be installed in the new High Marnham Power Station was commissioned in 1959. The Eastern Region's trains delivered coal to the power station in 24½ tons capacity hopper wagons. These wagons were deposited in the exchange sidings until their loads of coal were required. When that time came, the power station's own locomotive shunted small rafts of wagons through the wagon-discharge shed, within which CEGB staff opened the wagon doors manually. This procedure was inefficient, and decidedly unpleasant for the staff concerned. Traffic officers observing the procedure, and the sidings full of wagons, were not impressed; bringing together several different ideas, they developed the concept of what would be termed Merry-Go-Round (MGR) trains. Such trains made use of the fact that all newly-built power stations would burn pulverised coal, and of the fact that dieselisation of the railways was proceeding apace. The core of the MGR system comprised a limited number of automatic-discharge hopper wagons that were in constant use. At each colliery, coal destined for a power station was stockpiled. Such stockpiling, and the damage to lumps of coal that resulted, was not a problem as the coal was destined to be pulverised anyway. Each stockpile was used to supply a large bunker built above a siding. That siding was in the form of a balloon loop, so that an arriving train could pass under the bunker, be loaded, and then depart without the locomotive having to run round it. Loading took place while the train was moving at a steady half mile per hour – a feat achieved by the Slow Speed Control system installed in the diesel-electric train locomotive constantly compensating for the increasing weight of the train. At the power station the wagons were drawn through a wagon-discharge shed at a constant half mile per hour and unloaded automatically – this latter feat being achieved by means of machines that mechanically operated each wagon's door-opening equipment. The wagon-discharge shed was also built on a balloon loop, again so that an arriving train could arrive and depart without its locomotive having to run round it. Coal discharged from the wagons was either conveyed directly to pulverisation mills and thence to the furnaces, or to a stockpile. Empty wagons were immediately taken back to the colliery for re-loading.

At least, that was what the MGR system was supposed to comprise. The advantage of MGR for the railways was obvious; when the calculations for the wagon requirements of Cockenzie Power Station were re-done, it was found that if advantage was taken of the 22½ tons axle load now pertaining, then only forty-four 32½ tons capacity wagons would be required.(17) MGR would also lead to economies at collieries and power stations in that neither exchange sidings nor shunting locomotives to work them would be required. However, significant investments would be required in automatic-discharge wagons, balloon loops, loading bunkers and wagon-discharge sheds. Concerning the wagons, the investment required would be far less than that required to serve a power station using the traditional method. Because BR would save money if MGR was adopted, it could offer the CEGB favourable rates for the conveyance of coal and still make a profit.

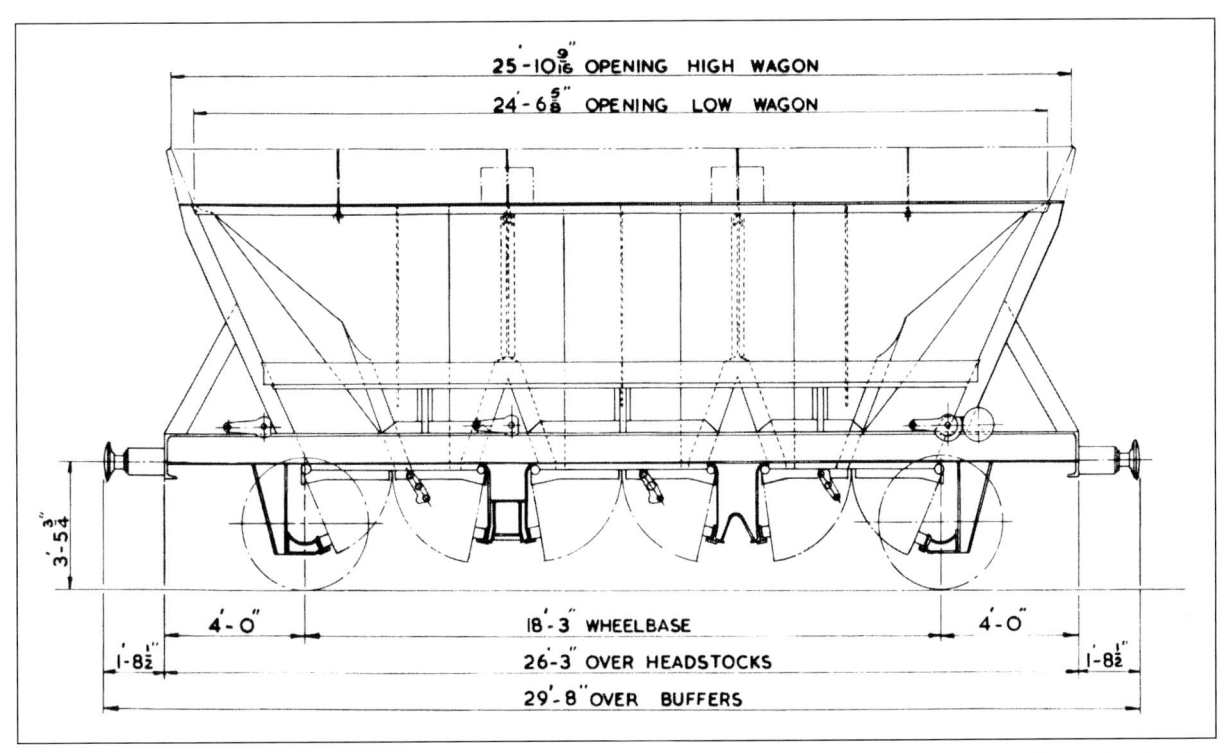

Plate 3.20. This is the wagon designed to work Merry-Go-Round trains. It came in two variants. Those fitted with a canopy had a capacity of 1424 cubic feet and could carry 32 tons of coal; they were designated HOP32 AB. Wagons without the canopy had a capacity of 1156 cubic feet, and could carry between 26 and 32 tons of coal depending upon its density; they were designated HOP AB. The latter variant was always the most numerous as its lower overall height (10' 6" compared with 11' 11½") meant that it would fit under the screens at most collieries. ('High Capacity Coal Wagon Trains, Description & Maintenance', MT/17, February 1969.)

Plate 3.21.
This HOP AB wagon, built at Shildon in 1965, evolved from the traditional type of hopper-bottomed wagon long used to convey coal in the north-east of England. What was new was the fitting of automatic air brakes to a coal wagon and the automatic hopper door opening and closing apparatus. (BR, per CE Williamson)

The CEGB was persuaded of the merits of MGR, and agreed not only to build all new baseload power stations to accommodate the system, but to modify existing power stations where possible. The National Coal Board was not easily persuaded however. Unlike the CEGB, which was building a small number of power stations from scratch, and had a limited number of existing stations to modify, the Coal Board was faced with the prospect of adapting and investing in a large number of existing collieries, few of which were dedicated only to the production of coal for power stations. Such investment would not directly benefit the Coal Board, but BR and the CEGB. Early in 1964 the Coal Board did at last accept MGR, and agreed to build coal loading bunkers at selected collieries. However, agreement was reached only after the BRB agreed to pay a levy on every ton of coal loaded at those bunkers. (In 1966, the levy would be replaced by a joint BRB/NCB investment in such bunkers. The BRB's contribution would be the sum of £3.6 million, to be debited to the accounts of the Eastern, North Eastern, and London Midland Regions.)(18)

To design the automatic-discharge hopper wagons that would be required to make MGR work as intended, the BRB established the High Capacity Wagon Design Committee. Working in collaboration with engineers from both Darlington and Ashford works, the committee produced a wagon that could carry up to 32 tons if fitted with a cowl; this cowl was not fitted as standard, however, as many colliery screens were too low to accommodate a wagon so equipped. Two prototype wagons were built at Darlington early in 1964. Members of the North Eastern Region's Railway Board visited Stooperdale on 2 July to examine them. After various tests, the prototypes were deemed satisfactory, and series production began the following year at Shildon. All the new wagons were fitted with automatic air brakes. To haul them, Brush Type 4 diesel-electric locomotives were equipped by their manufacturer with a Slow Speed Control system.

The traditional methods used to convey industrial and power station coal were costing BR lost business. For example, at the North Eastern Region's Area Board meeting of 17 May 1962, the General Manager reported the loss of 10,000 tons of coal traffic per annum from Ashington Colliery to Jarrow Ironworks. Given the relatively small tonnages and distances involved, the railways were unable to compete with road transport.(19) The development of MGR would allow the railways to regain much lost traffic, and to retain that still existing.

The principal intended role for MGR though was to convey power station coal. In the North-East of England, the CEGB was building a new power station at Blyth, and planned to build baseload stations at Ferrybridge, Eggborough and Drax. Blyth B Power Station was being built on the left bank of the River Blyth adjacent to the existing Blyth A Power Station, and would be rail-connected via the existing spur off the Cambois Branch; the CEGB promised to modify it to accept MGR coal trains. Ferrybridge C and Eggborough Power Stations were to be on the right bank of the River Aire. The former would be rail-connected via the existing spur off the Knottingley - Burton Salmon line; the latter via a newly-constructed spur off the Wakefield - Goole line. Drax Power Station was to be on the right bank of the River Ouse, and rail-connected via a re-instatement of part of the former Hull & Barnsley Railway between Heck (on the Wakefield - Goole line) and Drax. All three baseload power stations would be designed to accept MGR trains from the start. In order to provide traction, wagons and crews for trains to serve the existing power station at Ferrybridge, as well as the new ones planned for there, Eggborough and Drax, the North Eastern Region built a motive power depot and wagon repair workshop at Knottingley. However, apart from the initial commissioning of Blyth B Power Station in December 1962 and of Ferrybridge C in December 1966, none of these projects were completed before the North Eastern Region was absorbed into the Eastern.

Knottingley depot would be commissioned on 6 March 1967 with an allocation of six Brush Type 4 locomotives. That initial allocation would be steadily increased as the new power stations came on line. Eggborough Power Station would first begin to generate electricity in March 1968; Drax A in August 1972. Subsequently, Drax B would be built alongside Drax A. Each power station would, when fully commissioned, typically burn about five million tons of coal per annum. Initially, the coal would come from collieries in south Yorkshire, none of which would be equipped with the balloon loops and overhead bunkers required for full MGR for many years, if ever. From 1983, the power stations would be supplied with coal from the Selby Coalfield via loading bunkers built at Gascoigne Wood. Despite being built specifically to load MGR trains, the new loading facilities would not include a balloon loop – as was the case at so many colliery sites, there would be insufficient space for such a facility.

Oil

The development of MGR ensured that the CEGB would continue to burn coal in the majority of its power stations instead of oil or gas. However, there was no such system that could be devised to keep coal as the preferred fuel for general industrial and domestic use. The quantity of coal consumed in Britain gradually fell as industrial and domestic users converted to oil, gas, and electricity. This conversion occurred at the same time as the heavy industrial base in the north-east of England was declining. The shipbuilding industry began to suffer competition from brand-new yards in Japan, and lost orders as a result. The locomotive-building industry in Leeds declined as the market for steam locomotives both at home and abroad dwindled. The decline of industries such as these led to a reduction in the demand for coal by the steel-making industry. In 1962, the Region's trains conveyed 38,237,000 tons of originating coal and coke compared with 44,949,000 tons in 1950.(20)

As the demand for coal steadily fell therefore, the demand for oil steadily grew. For many years the railways had conveyed oil, and when Dr Beeching took on the chairmanship of the BTC he determined that BR would convey increasing quantities in the future. At this time – mid-1961 – BR moved more than 80% of the oil it conveyed in wagonloads using the oil companies' own tank wagons; most of these wagons were of small capacity and lacked continuous brakes. The method of working, combined with the antiquated nature of the wagons used, meant that the volume of oil being conveyed by BR was not increasing in line with the volume of oil being consumed in the country. BR's competition came from lorries, ships and pipelines. Modern methods that allowed BR to offer an alternative to such competitors were employed in the North Eastern Region, for example, where since 30 August 1960 block oil trains had been worked from the Shell-Mex and BP oil storage depot at Jarrow to Consett Iron Works. (The depot was supplied with oil not by rail, but by sea either from Thameshaven or Grangemouth oil refineries.) Beeching wanted such modern methods of bulk working to be widely adopted by BR, so that an increasing proportion of the oil it moved would be conveyed in block trainloads. To this end Beeching headhunted Terry House – an

Plate 3.22. On 30 August 1960, these Shell-BP 20 ton Class B tank wagons are being filled at Jarrow with heavy fuel oil for delivery to the Consett Iron Company's Hownsgill Plate Mill. This is the first oil train to run to the mill, which is just about to be commissioned. It would appear that the wagons have been painted, or at least thoroughly cleaned, for the event. (BR (NER), per JG Teasdale)

experienced oil man from Shell-Mex and BP Limited – and appointed him to the post of Director of Marketing for Petroleum Products. At the time, this was a controversial appointment. The task of the new appointee was to persuade the oil companies to invest in the new wagons and storage facilities that would make trainload operation possible. During 1963 he succeeded, signing ten or fifteen year contracts with the Petrofina, Gulf, Mobil, Esso, Regent, and Shell Mex-BP oil companies; contracts were eventually signed with all of the major oil companies trading in the British market. By 1963, the maximum permitted axle load had been raised to $22^1/_2$ tons. The new wagons required by the contracts signed that year – all two-axle – were built to take full advantage of this increase. In 1966, the axle load was raised over some routes to 25 tons. This latter led to the introduction of bogie tank wagons. Unfortunately, the BRB's decision to standardise on the automatic air brake was not implemented until 1966, meaning that many recently-built wagons were fitted with the inferior vacuum brake. Despite this, trainload operation of the new wagons permitted BR to win an increasing volume of the available oil traffic. By 1969, more than 80% of the oil moved by BR would be conveyed in trainloads. Not that the traffic turned out to be particularly profitable; much of the money that BR saved by trainload as opposed to wagonload operation had in effect to be handed back to the oil companies in the form of low rates in order to compensate those companies for having to invest in new wagons, storage depots, and the large stocks inherent in accepting bulk deliveries in trainloads. Profitability would, however, improve when the original contracts expired and new ones negotiated.

Within the North Eastern Region, ICI had been making petrol on a relatively small scale since 1935. In the mid-1960s, the company entered into a collaborative agreement with Phillips Petroleum Products Limited to build a new large-scale oil refinery on Seal Sands (at the mouth of the Tees, on the river's left bank). In 1966, BR signed a trainload contract with Phillips-Imperial Petroleum Company Limited. At the new refinery therefore, the two companies built jointly a rail terminal, comprising three 2000 feet long sidings; pipelines and pumps serving this facility could load a train of wagons at a rate of 1200 gallons per minute. The first loaded train, comprising nineteen wagons loaded with 500 tons of gas oil and diesel bound for the Phillips-Imperial storage depot in Birmingham, departed the terminal mid-December 1966.

Two developments came too late to influence the history of the North Eastern Region. Shell Refining Company Limited built a refinery at Teesport; trainload oil traffic would not begin to flow from there to such as the storage depot at Jarrow until 1968. Oil Rail Terminals (Leeds) Limited built a rail-served storage depot at Hunslet, in Leeds, reached by rail via the Hunslet East Branch. A feature of this depot was that its diverse storage tanks were available to rent by different oil companies. In this way, it was hoped that the companies would benefit from the economies of scale inherent in trainload operations and the operation of large storage depots, but would not individually have to bear all the associated costs. The Leeds depot comprised six sidings, sufficient for trains weighing up to 4000 tons gross. On arrival, each wagon of a train would simultaneously be coupled to a tripartite discharge system (for gasolines, for distillates such as kerosene, and for fuel oils) and its contents pumped into the appropriate storage tanks. All trains could be emptied in two hours. The depot would open in 1968, and largely be served by the new Lindsey oil refinery (near Immingham) and the Shell refinery at Stanlow.

Plate 3.23. Clayton Type 1 (later Class 17) No D8594 works a short trip freight (indicated by the 'P' in the headcode) through Wallsend on 29 March 1967. At the front of the train are two Esso Class A 45 ton petroleum tank wagons. (IS Carr / JW Armstrong Trust, per AR Thompson)

Computerisation

One of the significant technological developments of the mid-1950s was the development of computers that were cheap enough, and reliable enough, to be useful business tools. In 1956, BR contracted with Leo Computers Limited to re-calculate the distances between its approximately 7000 stations and depots. The work was required as the distances it had inherited from the Big Four reflected the rivalries between those companies; the distances themselves were required as they provided the foundation for BR's freight charges schemes. When the railways had been nationalised, it had been estimated that at least fifty clerks would take about five years to re-calculate the distances on the basis of the shortest distance between every pairing of station and depot. By 1956 a start had been made; it was anticipated that the Leo computer would complete that task within a year, in time for the inauguration of the new Railway Merchandise Charges Scheme on 1 July 1957. Also in 1956, the North Eastern Area Board obtained the sanction of the BTC to invest in Hollerith punch card equipment in order to mechanise goods and parcels accountancy procedures.

On 15 September 1958, TH Summerson formally inaugurated the use of a computer system in the Chief Accountant's Rolling Stock and Paybills Office at Darlington. Initially, the Hollerith Type 1201 computer was used to calculate the paybills of some 10,000 footplate staff; as the system was developed further, it was used to calculate in addition the paybills of 4000 shed staff. A second computer, a Hollerith 555 plugged-programme computer, was installed to calculate the paybills of some 26,000 commercial and traffic staff. Hollerith 555 computers were installed at York to calculate paybills for such as the Chief Civil Engineer's Department, and in the Revenue Accountant's Office at Newcastle in order to expedite the analysis of coal and passenger traffics.

Taking advantage of the developing computer technology, an IBM 1410 computer was installed at Darlington in 1965. This machine, more powerful than the Hollerith computers, was in use all day, but was free each evening. It occurred to the staff of the Region's Planning (Services) Development Section that the free time could be used to generate freight train timetables, locomotive diagrams and crew rosters. At the time, the work was done manually. In a place like Hull where there was a large volume of traffic, the nature of which varied every day, the work was not done as well as it could have been. This was not the fault of the Hull railwaymen, merely an inevitable result of the number of variables with which they had to grapple. On a typical day in Hull, there were about seventy-five haulage jobs into and out of the multiplicity of docks, railway yards, and private sidings. Some of the jobs remained the same day in and day out; most of them varied to a greater or lesser degree. The current practice was for railway Inspectors to forward each afternoon information concerning the likely traffic to be handled the following day. The information was collated by the Hull Controller and his staff, who then prepared a freight timetable, diagrams and rosters for that following day. Given the volume and the diversity of the traffic, and the number of passenger trains that had to be taken into account (because the line capacity that they absorbed was unavailable to the freight trains), it would normally take about three man-weeks to perfect timetable, diagrams and rosters. Having only an evening in which to do the work – in order to give plenty of notice to motive power depot staff, train

Plate 3.24. English Electric Type 3 (later Class 37) No D6795 is seen here on 29 August 1963 passing Beamish with steel plate hot from the rolling mills at Consett; note the use of a brake tender to give additional braking force to this Class 8 freight train. Train 8K49 is the 11.55 am Consett Low Yard - Low Fell Sidings. (RG Warwick)

crews, shunters, signalmen, *etc.* – it was no surprise that the resulting timetable, diagrams and rosters did not make the most efficient use of the available human and mechanical resources. The Section's staff hoped that what took three man-weeks to do manually could be done in an evening by the IBM computer.

In the summer of 1966, the Section's staff programmed the computer, and established an experimental system for the generation of timetables, diagrams and rosters. At Hull, between 5.00 and 5.30 pm each day the collated information from the Inspectors was transferred on to punched cards. At 5.30, information on the cards was transmitted via an ordinary telephone line to York; from York, the information was re-transmitted to the computer at Darlington via the Region's own newly-installed microwave link. The computer took about an hour and a half to generate the most efficient timetable, diagrams and rosters, then transmitted them to Hull. At Hull, the information was printed off, copied, and distributed to all involved in the next day's workings. Or it would have been, had the experimental system been implemented. It was not, as the Section's staff wished to analyse the results thoroughly before going live.(21)

The experiment was eventually considered to have been successful, but never did go live. This was partly because, using a system bequeathed by the former LNER's North Eastern Area, the imperfections in timetabling freight trains were to some extent overcome by paying bonuses to railwaymen who did more than was expected of them. However, the timetable generated by the computer was, or was supposed to be, that which made the most efficient use of resources. If railwaymen were to try to improve things by, for example, departing earlier from a yard than was timetabled, then potential conflict with such as a passenger train (foreseen by the computer) would make things worse not better. Working to a computer-generated timetable was, therefore, incompatible with the long-standing system of bonus payments. As railwaymen were decidedly hostile to the abolition of bonus payments, computer-generated timetables would have to wait until negotiations concerning a new payment scheme were successfully concluded between the railway unions and the BRB.

The concept of using computers to generate timetables, diagrams and rosters would indeed be applied, but not until after the merger with the Eastern Region. From the beginning of January 1973, an ICL 1904A at Crewe would be used in connection with MGR coal trains running into Drax, Eggborough, and Ferrybridge Power Stations. From 1973, the whole of BR would be computerised, when the Total Operations Processing System came on line.

Conclusion

When the North Eastern Region came into being on 1 January 1948, most of the freight that could be conveyed by railway was so conveyed. However, the competition from motor lorries gradually intensified, and the volume of freight conveyed by the railways steadily diminished. In order to resist that competition, the North Eastern Region modernised the way it dealt with general merchandise and wagonload traffic by building new hump marshalling yards, modernising existing ones, and building such as Tyneside Central Freight Depot. These measures greatly improved the efficiency with which the Region operated its freight trains. It had been the policy of the 1945 Labour Government to allocate tasks rationally between the various modes of inland transport. Had this policy been maintained, then the measures would surely have helped the Region to retain general merchandise and wagonload traffic. But the policy was not maintained – the 1951 Conservative Government substituted a policy

Plate 3.25. In accordance with long-standing agreements, coal trains operated by the National Coal Board also operated over the tracks of the North Eastern Region. This train has come off the Coal Board's Lambton Railway on to the North Eastern Region's Penshaw Branch and is seen here at Cox Green on 27 August 1965 en route to Sunderland. (IS Carr / JW Armstrong Trust, per AR Thompson)

of competition between modes. As a result, the investment in new yards and concentration depots failed to stop the loss of general merchandise and wagonload traffic to the railways' road-based competitors. There was a brief period of optimism late in 1956 when, as a result of the Suez Crisis, supplies of fuel for road-going vehicles were restricted. In consequence, traffic began to return to the railways. The BRB in its *Ninth Annual Report . . .* stated that it detected signs that traders who had increased the size of their 'C' licence lorry fleets were beginning to reconsider their decisions. Unfortunately for railwaymen, such reconsiderations were largely forgotten when supplies of fuel were fully restored. Whereas during 1948 the Region's trains had conveyed 7,481,000 tons of originating general merchandise traffic, during 1962 they conveyed only 4,720,000 tons.(22) BR would finally cease the conveyance of wagonload traffic from 8 July 1991. Although the freight concentration depots would close in consequence, the three marshalling yards at Lamesley, Newport and Healey Mills would remain open (though drastically reduced in size and devoid of their humps).

The tonnage of other traffics conveyed also fell inexorably. Steel traffic dwindled with the decline in the north-east of England's heavy industrial base. Iron ore traffic declined with the contraction of the steel-manufacturing industry, and with the substitution of imported for home-produced ore.(23) Coal traffic declined with the decline in the steel-manufacturing industry, as industrial and domestic consumers switched to electricity, oil and gas, and as coal gas was replaced by natural gas from beneath the North Sea.

However, new traffic was won to the railways, such as in 1965 when the Ford Motor Company Limited established railheads for new cars at Newcastle and Wakefield, and from early in 1966 when cement began to be conveyed from the Associated Portland Cement Company's new works at Eastgate (in Weardale) to depots at Heaton, Leeds, and, occasionally, Northenden in Lancashire. But the volume of traffic won never approached the volume of traffic lost.

The significant developments that would help the railways to maintain their market share of the available freight traffic, or at least, to help them slow the loss of market share, came too late to influence the history of the North Eastern Region. These developments – MGR, Freightliner, computerisation – did influence the history of the railways in the north-east of England. That influence was so powerful that at the dawn of the Twenty-first Century it continued to make relevant the contribution that railways can make to the conveyance of freight in the north-east of England.

Endnotes:
(1) For the quoted statistics and the comment about 'C' licence lorries, see the BTC's *First Annual Report . . . for the year ended 31st December 1948*. [PP 1948 – 49 (235) volume xii, page 1.]
(2) See PF Winding, *Traffic Divisions of British Railways – 7: Middlesbrough* (*Modern Railways*, April and May 1966).

(3) See BTC Board Minute 11/390(b) of 18 September 1958 [National Archives file AN85/12].
(4) See BTC Board Minute 12/294(c) of 23 July 1959 [National Archives file AN85/13].
(5) See BTC Board Minute 12/319(c) of 13 August 1959 [National Archives file AN85/13].
(6) See *The Railway Magazine*, March 1952.
(7) See D Rowland, *British Railways Wagons : the first half million*. The statistics pertain to traffic wagons only, and do not include BR's large fleet of service wagons.
(8) See the BTC's *Ninth Annual Report . . .*, paragraph 113 [PP 1956 – 57 (187) volume xix, page 101].
(9) *The Railway Magazine*, February 1958.
(10) See the BTC's *Annual Report . . . for the year ended 31st December 1962*. [PP 1962 – 63 (232) volume xxv, page 1].
(11) See BTC Board Minute 13/401(b) of 27 October 1960 [National Archives file AN85/15].
(12) *The North East Trader* was introduced by the Commercial Manager of the Southern Region's Central Division, IL Gray-Jones, a railwayman who had begun his career in the North Eastern Region. See the Paper *The North Eastern Region : A Personal View*.
(13) For a recent description of modern Roadrailer services in the United States, see *Trains*, May 2002.
(14) Railway-owned staiths in the North Eastern Region were located: on the River Blyth at Blyth and Cambois; on the River Tyne at Derwenthaugh and Dunston. In addition, the Region's trains conveyed coal to the diverse staiths and coal hoists in Northumberland Dock and Tyne Dock (both on the River Tyne), and those in the docks at Goole, the Hartlepools, Hull, Middlesbrough, and Sunderland. As a consequence of the nationalisation of inland transport, these latter facilities became the property of the Docks and Inland Waterways Executive and its successors.
(15) In 1948, for BR as a whole, the average yield per ton of coal conveyed was 100.5d. In 1949, the originating tonnage of coal increased by 3.8%. This increase was largely due to an increase in the tonnage of export coal conveyed, resulting in the yield per ton of coal conveyed falling to 99.2d. (See the BTC's *Second Annual Report . . .* [PP 1950 (139) volume xiv, page 137].
(16) See interview with Arthur Dean, *Modern Railways* September 1965.
(17) Re Cockenzie Power Station, see GF Fiennes, *I Tried to Run a Railway*.
(18) See BRB Minute 66/94 of 28 April 1966 [National Archives file AN167/3].
(19) See Area Board Minute GPC495 of 17 May 1962 [National Archives file AN117/7].
(20) See the BTC's *Third Annual Report . . .* [PP 1950 51 (21) volume xx, page 361] and *Annual Report . . . year ended 31st December 1962* [PP 1962 – 63 (232) volume xxv, page 1].
(21) See GF Allen, *Hull experiment in local freight train planning by computer* (*Modern Railways*, August 1966).
(22) See the BTC's *Annual Report . . . year ended 31st December 1962* [PP 1962 – 63 (232) volume xxv, page 1].
(23) The last of the ironstone mines in Cleveland, North Skelton Mine, closed on 17 January 1964.

Freight Traffic in the North Eastern Region
A Case Study : Tyne Dock to Consett Iron Ore
David Bradwell

When the iron industry was becoming established in the area now known as Consett, iron ore was available locally. However, by about 1855 increasing amounts of ore were having to be brought from west Cumberland and Cleveland as local supplies ran out; the transport of ore to Consett was to be a major rail traffic for about 125 years. The Cumberland ore was conveyed to Consett via the Newcastle & Carlisle Railway and the Pontop & South Shields Branch (from 1867, via the Consett Branch) but this traffic ended by 1880. The Cleveland ore was conveyed via the Stockton & Darlington line and Crook (from 1862, via Lanchester instead of Crook). This traffic diminished after the 1870s but imported ore from Sunderland substituted.

From 1880, ore for the iron works at Consett began to be imported into Tyne Dock. Concerning the route by which the ore was then conveyed, previous writers on this subject have stated that it was via the Pontop & South Shields Branch. Certainly, when there had been no alternative route, iron ore from Cumberland had been conveyed via this line in the past. However, the line, constructed originally as the Stanhope & Tyne Railway, featured a large number of inclines. These had been a thorough nuisance in working coal traffic down the line to South Shields; they would be an expensive and time-consuming obstacle to overcome in working iron ore up the line to Consett. The more logical route from Tyne Dock was via the Consett Branch, though no evidence either way appears to survive. Iron ore traffic was ultimately conveyed via the Pontop & South Shields Branch, but it seems more than likely that this was after 1893 when the Annfield diversion from South Pelaw Junction through Beamish to Consett was opened (the Birtley, Annfield Plain & Consett Branch).

In 1937, the Tyne Improvement Commission (TIC) acquired Tyne Dock. The TIC invested in two deep water quays, equipping them with 3 and 5 ton cranes. Aided by older quays 400 - 600,000 tons of ore per annum could now be loaded into rail wagons. These wagons were loaded alongside the ship, a slow process requiring manual labour inside the hold and a constant supply of wagons as there was nowhere to store ore at the dock apart from in wagons. Capacity was limited to 1000 tons per shift. Immediately prior to a modernisation of ore handling in 1953, 21 ton wagons were used, latterly 400 Ministry of Transport steel hopper wagons. Trains consisted of 22 loaded wagons and a brake van hauled by a 3-cylinder locomotive of Class Q7, with a similar locomotive as banker from South Pelaw as gradients were as steep as 1 in 35. (Consett is some 880 feet above sea level.) Assistance was also required from Tyne Dock Bottom to Bank Top, usually by a smaller type such as J72 or J21, *etc.*

When the Consett Iron Company opened a third blast furnace, it was realised that a complete overhaul of the facilities at Tyne Dock would be needed to reduce trans-shipment costs and to meet the increased demand for ore of 1,000,000 tons or more per annum. New dock facilities for larger, specialised ships with a faster turnaround would be needed.

As partner in the task of conveying iron ore from dockside to steel works, British Railways was intimately involved in the negotiations between the Consett Iron Company and the Tyne Improvement Commission. The 1953 Transport Act did away with the requirement that railway and canal companies not give undue preference to any company when setting rates. Unfortunately, this came too late for the

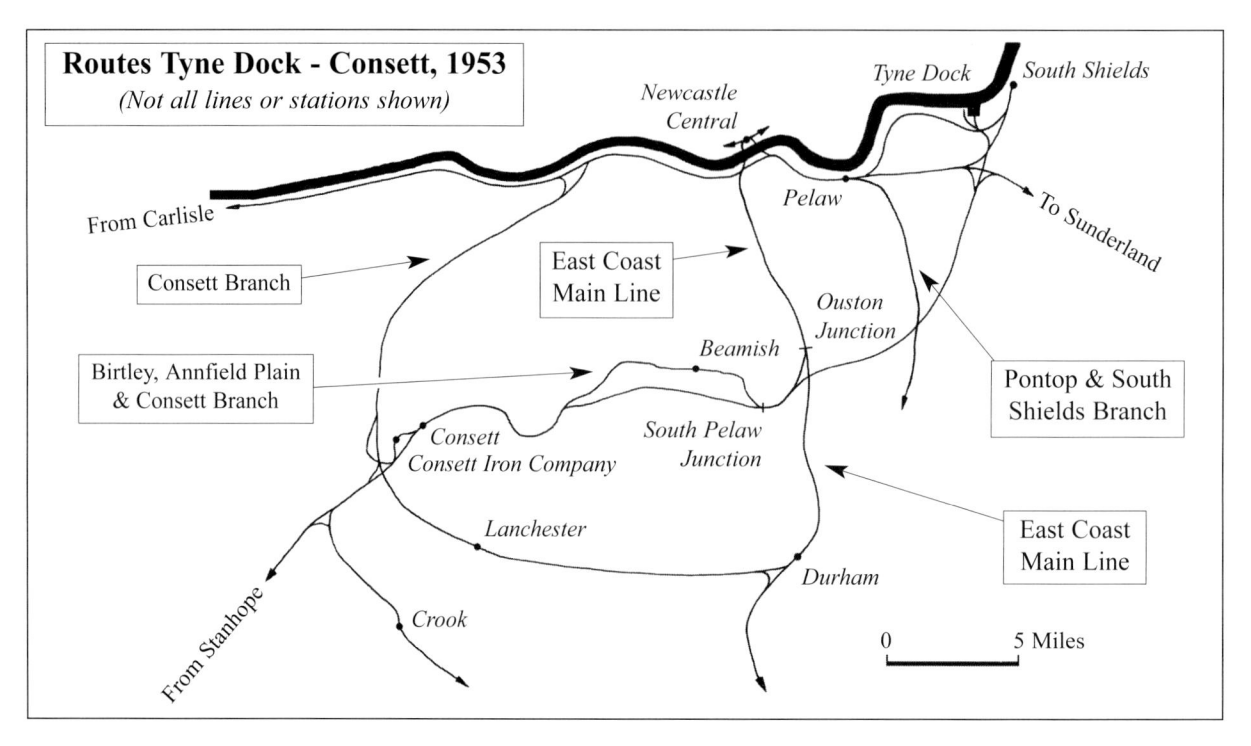

Plate 4.1.
In January 1952, 56 ton iron ore wagon No 446000 was brought specially to Tyne Dock Bottom for inspection by British Railways and Tyne Improvement Commission staff. This is a view of the wagon with its doors open. Before the wagon entered traffic, it and its fellows were fitted with deflector plates below the door openings in order to throw discharged iron ore further away from the wagon. (IL Gray-Jones)

negotiations, which took place when BR was still subject to the old legislation, and it was compelled to inform the Transport Tribunal of the rates it would charge for the conveyance of ore to Consett using the new dock facilities and a new fleet of wagons. These rates were much lower than were charged to other steel companies, reflecting the economies expected following the substantial investment. All those other companies therefore complained bitterly to the Tribunal, complicating BR's negotiations enormously.

Negotiations were successfully concluded, however, and 1953 a new deep water quay and ore handling facility were completed as a joint collaboration between the Consett Iron Company, British Railways and the Tyne Improvement Commission. This new quay allowed ships up to 20,000 (later 30,000) tons to be unloaded by five 10 ton grabbing cranes of the 'kangaroo' type. These discharged the load into an unloading hopper below the jib (like a pouch – hence the name) which passed ore to an integral transfer conveyor and avoided the need to slew the whole crane. Rated capacity of each crane was 300 tons per hour based on a 60-second cycle. Ore was taken by conveyors into ten storage bins which straddled the loading tracks (see drawing on next page). These bins had a total capacity of up to 13,000 tons, depending on ore density. Ore was drawn from the bins into one of two scale cars; these cars were fitted with weighing machines, and were loaded with exactly 28 tons of ore. The scale cars transferred their loads to 36 loading-out hoppers below. When these loading-out hoppers were all charged, the facility was ready for the next train; opening the hopper doors discharged the contents into the wagons below in a few seconds.

The 56 ton bogie wagons were specially designed for the upgraded facility and were arranged for side discharge at Consett using compressed air to operate two doors on each side under the control of the driver – see photograph above. Thirty wagons were built at Shildon to Diagram 1/182 and numbered 446000 - 446029. Continuous vacuum brakes were fitted. The first wagon was inspected by officials of the Railway Executive at Marylebone Goods Yard, London on 10 December 1951. Tare weight was quoted as 28 tons 13 cwt in contemporary press releases; the official diagram records that weight increased to 28 tons 19 cwt as the result of diverse modifications.

The wagons were unusual for this country. Generally, bogie wagons were used for iron ore in Europe and America but here two-axle vehicles were normally employed as home-produced ore was of lower density and there was no advantage in using the bogie type due to the size of body required; the load was limited by the loading gauge rather than by the number of axles. However, with high density imported ore, bogie wagons permitted a greater capacity for a given train length.

Plate 4.2.
Inspections concluded, wagon No 446000 is conveyed back to Shildon. Note the 'British Railways' totem on one of the wagon doors. (IL Gray-Jones)

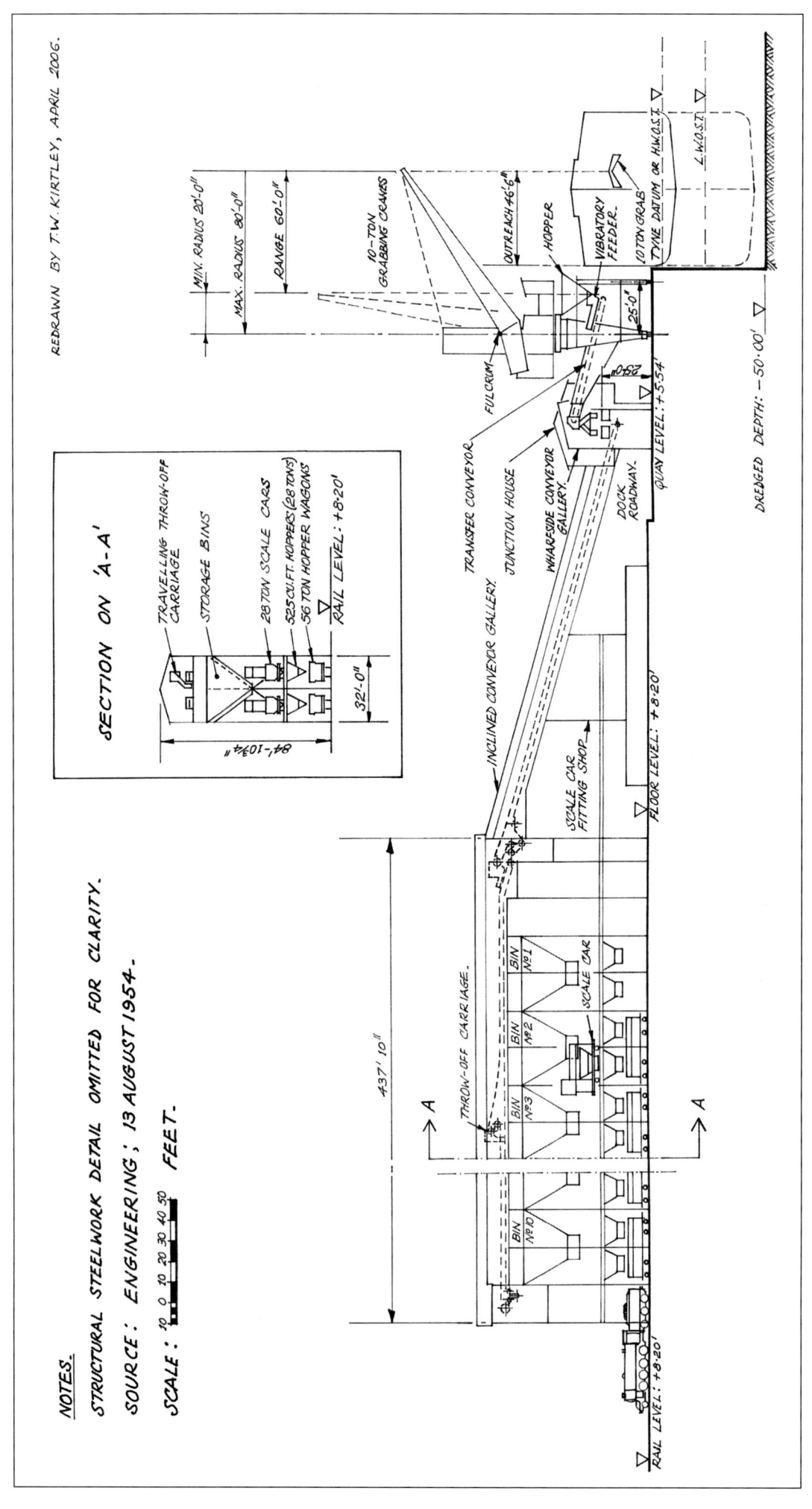

Plate 4.3. Tyne Dock, New Deep Water Quay and Iron Ore Handling Facility, 1953. (TW Kirtley, from a drawing in 'Engineering')

Instructions Relating to the Working of 56-ton Wagons Between Tyne Dock and Consett (1)

Wagon doors are operated by levers attached to compressed air door engines – four per wagon: two at the centre and one at each end. Each engine has separate 16 inch and 14 inch cylinders. To keep the doors **closed**, air is fed through No 1 pipe to the 14 inch cylinders. To **open** the doors, air is fed through No 2 pipe to the 16 inch cylinders. The doors cannot be operated independently. Manually operated safety locking levers are provided at each end and both on the same side of the wagon. These levers must only be raised to the top of their guides prior the opening of the doors. The air pressure is obtained directly from 10 inch air compressors and reservoirs fitted to certain locomotives: O1 class 63712, 63755, 63760, 63856, 63874, and Q7 class 63460, 63463, 63465, 63469, 63473.

The additional cab equipment in the locomotive is painted red. An isolating cock in No 2 pipe prevents the doors being opened accidentally. No 1 pipe appears under the buffer beams – connections and cocks are painted black. No 2 pipe is the swan necked pipe above the buffer beams – fittings are painted yellow. Only one pipe – the vacuum hosepipe, is connected to the brake van.

Empty trains terminate at Tyne Dock Bottom Yard reception lines, the locomotive is released and the guard's van is removed by the pilot and placed on the van kip. Each wagon is examined. The outward train locomotive is attached, pipes coupled and the train is propelled to the bunker line, or placed on the bunker line by a pilot. Both air hose cocks are closed on the last wagon. A marker board is provided to enable the wagons to be positioned correctly. The guard's van must not be attached as vans and engines are not allowed to pass under the bunkers. Air pressure of 86 psi must be created and maintained in No 1 pipe before loading can commence. The guard must ensure safety lock levers are pinned down before loading – and after.

TIC staff operate the ore bunkers and advise the guard when the train is loaded. They will give duplicate copies of the weight slip to the guard. After the loaded train is drawn from the bunker line, the van gravitates from the kip and the vacuum hose connected. The complete train is drawn forward to enable the assisting engine to be placed at the rear. Trains must not exceed eight wagons and van.

If replacement wagons are required, the Yard Inspector must advise the C&W Foreman which side the safety catch handles are required so that all handles on the set are on the same side. Guards are required to insert the individual number of each wagon in the train journal. During the journey to and from Consett the compressors on the locomotive must be in operation to maintain the air pressure of 85 psi to ensure the wagon doors are held closed. [This pressure ambiguity is in the original document.]

The new ore gantry at Consett is approached from Carr House West Box and the new lines between this box and Fell Box (CIC) will be worked under the no block regulations. Fell Box is owned by the CIC but is worked by BR signalmen. After passing this box there are three reception lines. Normally ore trains will arrive on No 1 line (right hand). After the train stops CIC staff raise the safety catch handles to the release position. They advise the guard when this is complete and he signals the driver to draw forward onto the ore gantry. After the Gantry Leading man has given an assurance that the train is in the correct position, the guard instructs the driver to open the doors. The person in charge checks the wagons are empty before the guard instructs the driver to close the doors. The train is then propelled clear of the gantry. When clear of the points, CIC staff return locking levers to the lower position. The train travels around the rest of the triangular track plan, the guard working the ground frames, before departing when authorised by Fell Box.

Wagons are in seven groups of four each – each stencilled with letters A, B, C, D, E, F and S. Two spare wagons are lettered Y and Z and will normally be at Tyne Dock Bottom for use at short notice in the event of wagons having to be taken out of service outside their rostered maintenance period. Each Friday one group of four wagons will be withdrawn for maintenance and replaced by a serviced set. Maintenance is carried out at a special depot provided inside Tyne Dock Motive Power Depot.

Comments on above. There was very little clearance between the bottom of the loading hoppers and the tops of the wagons, presumably in an attempt to control dust. When fine grades of ore were carried, leather covers were fitted over the bogie sides to keep the dust out of moving parts. There were electrical interlocks so that the bottom doors of the loading hoppers could not be opened unless the wagons below were in the correct position.

In practice the banking locomotive usually attached the brake van at Tyne Dock. Initially three brake vans were set aside at Tyne Dock for this service, although there were no special fittings or lettering.(2) Occasionally a second brake van was added when groups of enthusiasts were carried.

Water for the return journey was taken on the second side of the triangle at Consett; a room beneath the water tank provided for the crew's 'physical needs break'. The locomotive was not normally uncoupled at Consett. In exceptional circumstances (*e.g.* a hot box) the locomotive could be removed from the train and the locking levers would hold the doors closed.(2)

Until 1956, the locomotives of Class O1 were mainly used as train locomotives, with the Q7s banking, although there are photographs of WDs being used. By 1956, ten new (although they were borrowed by the London Midland Region before delivery) Class 9F locomotives fitted with air pumps were available: 92060 - 66 and 92097 - 99. Eventually, these were used as both train locomotive and South Pelaw banker. The banker was detached without stopping.

The air pumps were reputed to be those removed from WD 2-8-0s when purchased from the War Department. The pumps were not removed from the Q7s until 1957-9 and the O1s not withdrawn until late 1962. The 9Fs were loaded up to nine wagons, made into three sets with three spare wagons at Tyne Dock. If two 9Fs were not available, the last (ninth) wagon ran empty.(2) When trains were lengthened to nine wagons no changes to the loading facilities were needed as the extra loading-out hoppers were put in place when the facility was constructed. This suggests that the introduction of more powerful locomotives was planned during the original negotiations.

Steam operation was prolonged by the simple fact that without air pumps diesels could not operate the trains. This was despite boiler problems caused by the cycle of an all out uphill effort followed by gently coasting downhill. However in 1963 banking was taken over by diesels, locomotives of Classes 40 and 46 being used. A test run in September 1962 had shown that one of these (No D171) could actually haul the load single-handed in well under the allowed time. The last steam hauled iron ore train – *The Tyne Docker* – ran on 19 November 1966 behind No 92063. This was probably the last steam working from Tyne Dock shed.

Revised instructions covered the dieselised service.(3) Air compressors were fitted to 1160 hp Type 2 diesels Nos D5102 - D5111. Details were changed little from steam days, although the cab equipment had a third 'neutral' position for non-operating cabs. For some reason the valve was now painted yellow. Air was taken from the system at 92 psi. Wagons were still being orientated to keep all the safety levers on the same side – at least in print. Maintenance of the wagons was now undertaken at Simonside Wagon Repair Shops although there are no details of planned maintenance. The C&W examiner had to check that there was 90 psi in the No 1 pipe, and at the standpipe at the rear before propelling the train under the loading bunkers. The incoming locomotive was to place the van on the kip before returning to shed.

There was now provision for trains to be pre-loaded using fixed pressure plant rather than waiting for the train locomotive. The responsibility was placed clearly with the Tyne Improvement Commission to maintain the pressure once wagons were loaded and until a locomotive could be attached. It was then TIC's responsibility to disconnect the plant.

It appears that bankers were to be retained. The document certainly refers to 'locomotive' in the singular throughout although trains of nine specially constructed wagons and guard's brake van are described. Further research is required to ascertain if these trains ever ran regularly in the form described – the standard formation became double-headed trains of eight wagons with no van and no bankers.

Initially, it appears that steam-hauled trains entered the unloading gantry track at Consett locomotive first; later, the locomotive propelled the wagons on to the gantry. Diesel locomotives appear always to have propelled the wagons on to the gantry, because, I was told, the track beyond the gantry was too short to hold two locomotives.(2)

Matters arising. A number of photographs by IS Carr have been published showing these trains hauled by a single diesel locomotive and dated around August 1966. As this was before the end of steam operation these are presumably test trains. The locomotives shown (D5182, D5181 and D5149) are not those described as being fitted with air pumps in the official instructions. This would suggest a temporary installation for the trials. Fortunately I know someone who was on one of these trains although we do not have a date. He reports (4): 'The Type 2 was a Derby 1160 hp effort. We were banked out of the dock by a Q6, and up from South Pelaw by a Class 40. This dropped off very slightly prematurely and the Type 2 nearly blew up. In fact it also staggered from Green Lane to South Pelaw. The Type 2 had air pumps and was no doubt one of those that was joined by further sisters to work in multiple. That arrangement, as you know, carried on until the end of ore workings.'

Plate 4.4. A Class 9F draws its rake of 56 ton wagons on to the unloading gantry at Consett. (DR Wilcock Collection)

Plate 4.5.

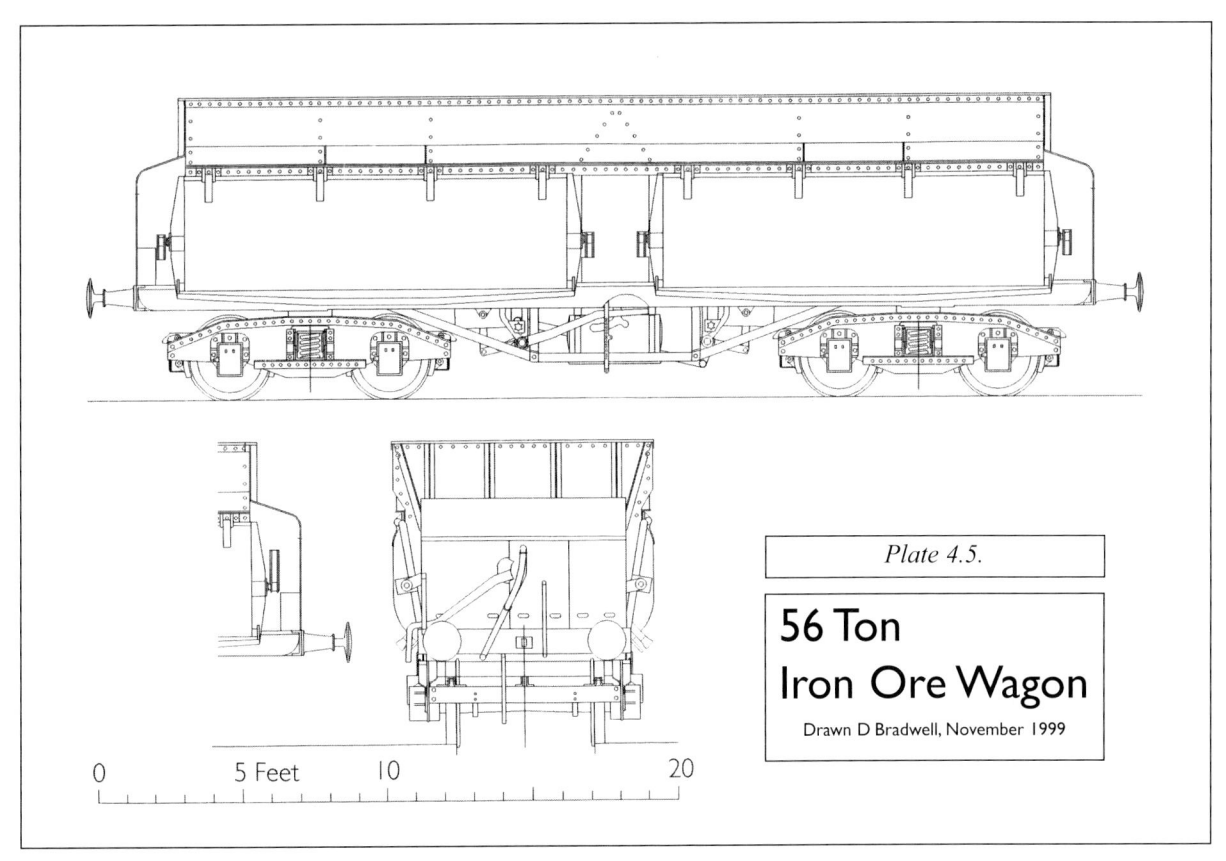

56 Ton Iron Ore Wagon

Drawn D Bradwell, November 1999

Further general notes.

Such was the size of the investment by British Railways, and the importance of the traffic to Consett, that when the new service was introduced in 1953 the trains were given specific times in the Working Time Tables, which had not been the case previously; trains would not fail to run due to lack of a path. There were initially ten timetabled paths per day, increased to fourteen in 1954. Looking at the Working Time Table in effect 18 June to 9 September 1962, we see that the first timetabled train of the day, 8K00, was booked to depart Tyne Dock Bottom at 12.50 am. It was banked from there to Bank Top. At this early hour of the morning when the signal boxes on the Pontop & South Shields were closed, the train was routed via Pelaw and the East Coast Main line as far as Ouston Junction, where the Birtley, Annfield Plain & Consett Branch was joined.(5) En route, a banker buffered up at Birtley for the push up the hill, being detached at Bradley (just short of Consett).

This route was taken by the next two trains, but 8K03 was routed via the Pontop & South Shields, being banked on the Birtley, Annfield Plain & Consett Branch between South Pelaw and South Medomsley. This route was taken by subsequent trains until late in the evening, though such as 8K06 was banked from South Pelaw all the way to Consett Works. Train 8K12, 9.15 pm off Tyne Dock Bottom, reverted to the Pelaw and East Coast Main Line route when the signal boxes on the Pontop & South Shields closed for the night, as did the remaining timetabled train of the day. Most Saturday trains, and any required to run on a Sunday, were also routed via Pelaw and the main line. From 21 November 1966, this became the route for all the trains following the closure of the Pontop & South Shields Branch.

If the Birtley, Annfield Plain & Consett Branch was closed (due to snow or engineering works) trains went via Lanchester. The banker would be attached there.

The trains conveying empty wagons back to Tyne Dock were Class 5. For example, train 8K00, having arrived at Consett Works at 2.52 am, was booked to depart empty as train 5K00 at 3.27 am.

The wagons were restricted initially to 60 mph. However, speed was nowhere near this figure with steam and it was only with diesel power that this speed was achieved on the stretch from Low Fell. Occasional derailments were occurring and following an investigation a speed limit was imposed. Reference (6) gives this as 45 mph but from 8 July 1967 a maximum speed of 25 mph empty or loaded was imposed and the wagons lettered 'max 25 mph'.(7) This may have been for entirely different reasons – the wagon underframes were cracking in their final years. The last version of the GA drawing refers to three changes (dated July 1966, January 1967 and January 1968) covering repairs and reinforcement of the bogie mounting area and an increase in height by $1/2$". Certainly, availability in their final years was poor and a full rake could not be assembled for the planned final trip to empty the bins at Tyne Dock. Incidentally, this became a nightmare with several failures of wagons and locomotives resulting in a very long day for the crews.

The last ore train ran from Tyne Dock to Tyne Yard (for onward staging to Consett) on 26 March 1974. A new service was introduced from Redcar (which could handle 100,000 ton ships) using trains of nine $77\frac{1}{2}$ ton wagons hauled by pairs of Class 37s and emptied by rotary tippler.

From the 1960s, coal and oil as well as iron ore were having to be conveyed 'up the bank' to Consett. A former railwayman, part of the team which has produced this book, was told by a senior manager of the Consett Iron Company that he had done everything in his power to invest so much money in Consett that it could never be closed. However, the cost of conveying raw materials up and finished steel down the bank made Consett steel uncompetitive in the UK and world markets; the steelworks closed in 1980.

Appendices:
1. The MOT wagons were similar to the 21 ton steel coal hoppers with the same type of brakes (four shoes on the same side and a high brake lever) but the bodies were of $5/16$ inch plate rather than $1/4$ inch for coal wagons. One metre diameter wheels and special axleguards and axleboxes were fitted. 2500 were built. After the introduction of the new iron ore facilities they were used as normal coal hoppers

2. Specific details concerning special 56 ton wagons. Length over buffers 36' 5", over headstocks 33' 0". Height 10', width 9', bogie wheelbase 5' 6", centres 21' 0". Wheel diameter 2' 9". Screw couplings were fitted initially, the drawing was changed to show Instanter type on 29 June 1966. The GA drawing gives the minimum radius as 70'. 12" x 6" journals were fitted. The hopper plates were $5/16$ inch thick Corten steel. The underframe carried four air reservoirs. Two 18 inch vacuum cylinders were fitted for braking.

When new, the wagons were tested with coal at Linton Colliery. Written on the back of a pair of photographs is the date 8 October 1952. The full length deflector plates under the doors were added after this test, though they did not effect a total cure; at a conference of Departmental Officers, it was noted that in the first three days of operation of the wagons, no problems had been reported with them apart from a tendency for ore to collect on axle box tops.(8) Other early modifications included: raising the label clip from the solebar; reinforcing the safety levers and increasing the size of the cut-outs in the end boxes; bending down the ends of the safety levers; star plates on Vee hangers.

Initially at least some of the wagons were lettered 'IRON ORE' and 'To work between Tyne Dock and Consett only' on the left hand door, the other carrying the BR totem and tare weight. I am not convinced that all had this full treatment. These embellishments eventually disappeared to leave only number, capacity and tare weight, although a 25 mph speed limit appeared later. After the Tyne Dock - Consett services finished most of the wagons were scrapped at Tyne Dock but the remainder were purchased by British Steel and the underframes used on South Humberside.

Endnotes:
(1) British Railways *Operating Instructions*, probably a first (1953) version.
(2) Personal recollections by BR driver.
(3) British Railways *Operating Instructions,* covering diesel haulage. Although the text is not dated they are annotated 1967 by hand. The text is typed, not printed (as (1)) so they could be a draft copy.
(4) Personal account C Pendlenton.
(5) The signal boxes on the Pontop & South Shields Branch were closed, Monday to Saturday, from 8.45 pm to 6.05 am, and all day Sunday.
(6) *NRM Review*, Autumn 2002. *What goes up must come down*. Harry Reed.
(7) BR (ER) (Northern Area) *Supplementary Operating Instructions*, York, 9 May 1970
(8) NE Region Departmental Officers' Conferences. [National Archives file AN 105/1].

Recommended further reading:
Discharging Iron Ore from Ship to Wagon. Engineering, 13 August 1954.
Railway Wagons for Iron Ore and Other Bulk Materials. Mills, HR, *Engineering*, 18 March 1955.

Plate 4.6.
A pair of Type 2 diesel-electric locomotives run through Beamish en route to Consett on 4 August 1969. (Ken Hoole Study Centre Collection)

Passenger Traffic in the North Eastern Region
John P McCrickard
From Austerity to Modernisation

The Austerity Years

The immediate post-war years were a cheerless time for the railway traveller. Six years of heavy wartime traffic had taken their toll, and with maintenance cut to the bone, the overall image was one of dingy stations served by slow, dirty and often overcrowded trains. With continuing petrol rationing severely limiting car usage, passengers were something of a captive audience. Even Nationalisation and the North Eastern Region's bright new tangerine colour identity could do little to dispel the gloom. The weather, as is often the case, didn't help! The severe winter in early-1947 and national fuel shortage in its aftermath had caused widespread disruption, with the Stainmore route snow-blocked for several weeks in February/March. The following year catastrophic flooding in the Borders during August 1948 forced the closure of the East Coast Main Line between Berwick and Edinburgh from the 12th of that month until re-opening on 1 November (to freight on 25 October) after heroic work by the civil engineers to repair the many wrecked bridges and miles of cuttings and embankments. In the interim, through services were maintained via Kelso, St Boswells and the Waverley route.

As related below, the newly-nationalised British Railways was keen to bring some early cheer for long-suffering travellers and a modest series of timetable improvements were introduced, including restoration of named and Pullman expresses, plus summer holiday trains. However, real improvement was hampered by the lack of much needed renewal and modernisation of motive power and rolling stock, and of the 'way and works'.

Modernisation – at Last!

In 1946, the LNER had issued an illustrated publicity booklet *Forward – The LNER Development Programme*. Widely available (and priced at 4d for sale at bookstalls), it set out an optimistic five year plan to restore pre-war standards and to undertake an ambitious programme of improvements. Of the latter, the main ones effecting passenger traffic in the North Eastern Area (future North Eastern Region) were as follows:

* East Coast Main Line (ECML) colour-light re-signalling: completion of York - Darlington scheme (eventually completed 1961), plus Newcastle (1959).
* Filey: new branch and station to serve Butlin's Holiday Camp (1947).
* Leeds Central station: reconstruction (replaced by enlarged Leeds City, 1967).
* Middlesbrough and Sunderland stations: reconstruction of war-damage (1954/65).

Plate 5.1. Class D20 No 62388 seen near Fulwell with the 12.33 pm Newcastle - Sunderland circa 1951. The train comprises the rostered 'Composition B' set: a Composite flanked by a Brake Third at each end. The van is something of a mystery. Note the branding; it may be conveying locomotive spares to Sunderland shed. (SE Teasdale / NERA T Smeaton Collection)

* Middlesbrough station: conversion of Down platform into an island (not done).
* Newcastle Central station: two additional through platforms, made by connecting existing bay platforms, but reducing concourse area (not done).
* Scarborough station: major remodelling to improve working (not done).

Forward formed part of the LNER's last stand against impending Nationalisation. With the newly-elected Labour Government thus preoccupied, and a continuing dire shortage of men and materials, few inroads were made into the renewals backlog (not cleared until the late-1950s) and little progress was made on the improvement schemes – although many would be executed under the British Transport Commission's 1955 Modernisation Plan (as noted in the above completion dates). The limited resources available were prioritised on new locomotives and rolling stock.

After seemingly years of waiting, the great hope for BR's future came with publication of the BTC's grand £1.24bn, 15-year Modernisation Plan on 25 January 1955. The main proposals for the North Eastern Region are detailed in the introductory Paper of this book.

In June 1959, General Manager HA Short presented an upbeat progress report for the North Eastern Region: *Progress and Aims of the North Eastern Region Traffic Plan 1954-1963*. Marked 'Confidential', it affirmed the need 'to secure and retain at the most remunerative rates the maximum amount of passenger, parcels and freight traffic…at the minimum working costs…and maximum profit return' – a statement which neatly summarised the commercial 'savvy' of the Region.

However, traffic figures were worrying: from a baseline index of 100 in 1948, overall receipts had peaked at 180 in 1952 but then dropped to just under 50 in 1958. This was blamed principally on the 'testing' effects of the trade recession – but could have been much worse were it not from the greatly enhanced receipts from widespread deployment of new Diesel Multiple-Units (DMUs). These and other improvements to passenger services are considered below.

The Modernisation Plan also witnessed major renewal of BR's locomotive-hauled passenger stock with continuing deliveries of large batches of the then-new Mk 1 Standard design coach which had initially entered service in 1951. These comprised many different types, including restaurant, buffet, sleeping and Pullman cars. Pre-Nationalisation vehicles (the last LNER-design stock was built in 1953) remained in use throughout the North Eastern tenure, but in ever decreasing numbers as the BR Mk 1 coach delivery programme proceeded apace. The last Mk 1 hauled stock was built in 1964, the same year that the first of the new successor Mk 2 coaches entered service.(1)

Endnote:

(1) LNER and BR locomotive-hauled stock has been extensively documented elsewhere in the many publications devoted to the subject. Certain details apposite to the development of North Eastern Region passenger services are included below.

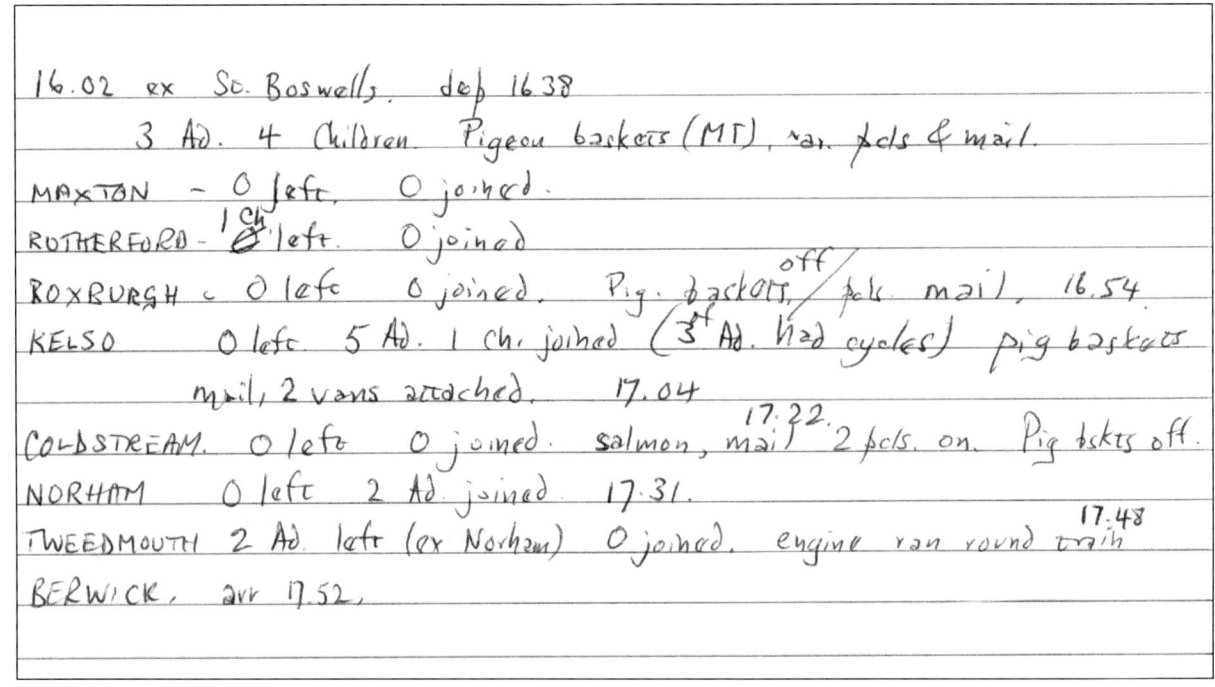

Plate 5.2. This somewhat informal traffic survey was undertaken on the Kelso Branch, in the far north of Northumberland, in the early 1960s. By the time that the survey was made, many of the intermediate stations on the branch had closed (on 4 July 1955). General Manager Short's intention to secure and maintain the maximum amount of passenger traffic – as observed in the June 1959 Traffic Plan – was faced with the reality as exposed by this survey; on such as the Kelso Branch, passenger traffic would never pay its way. The remaining stations on the branch, at Coldstream, Norham and Tweedmouth, would close to passengers on 15 June 1964. (R Davies Collection)

Colour Plate 17. (Above)
Class J39 No 64942 departs Waterhouses with a Durham Miners' Gala special in July 1960. During the BR period, the J39 was the locomotive usually pressed into service for the miners' specials, though such as Class K1 was used occasionally. (C Gammell / Colour-Rail, per CE Williamson)

Colour Plate 18. (Above)
Class V3 No 67684 works empty stock from Newcastle Central station back to Heaton carriage sidings in February 1964. Note the overhead wires in Trafalgar Yard – the workplace of two former North Eastern Railway electric shunters of Class ES1. (DJ Mitchell / Colour-Rail, per CE Williamson)

Colour Plate 19.
A three-car Metropolitan-Cammell DMU stands in the sunshine at Whitby Town station on 31 July 1958 prior to departure as the 10.50 am to Middlesbrough. (JM Boyes / JW Armstrong Trust, per JR Midcalf)

73

Colour Plate 20. An unidentified English Electric Type 4 passes a track re-laying train at Manor House (on the East Coast Main Line south of Northallerton) on 26 July 1964. The carriages are ex-LMSR, so it appears that the train originated in the London Midland Region. (JM Boyes / JW Armstrong Trust, per JR Midcalf)

Colour Plate 21. Metropolitan - Vickers Type 2 No D5707 works the 8.00 am Heads of Ayr - Newcastle Relief through Haydon Bridge on 3 September 1966. These locomotives were particularly unreliable, and it seems unlikely that there was any great sorrow in the North Eastern Region that they were all allocated to the London Midland. (JM Boyes / JW Armstrong Trust, per JR Midcalf)

Colour Plate 22. March 1967, and this '1937 stock' Metro-Cammell electric multiple-unit has just arrived at a gloomy Newcastle Central on a North Tyneside service. Note the red tail lamp built in to the end of the unit; this useful feature was not present on the diesel multiple-units that replaced the electrics, and the DMUs always required the addition of a traditional oil lamp. Note also the BR (NER) tangerine signs in the background. (JF Addyman)

From Sentinels to 'Derby Lightweights' : the Diesel Multiple-Unit Revolution

Railcars were nothing new in the North Eastern Region – the LNER North Eastern Area had introduced a large fleet of Sentinel and Clayton steam-powered examples from the 1920s onwards. Although these enabled economical working of many secondary and branch line services, they were often none too popular with passengers and crews, earning such unenviable nicknames as 'chip vans' and 'sweat boxes'! The last just survived into Nationalisation, appropriately-named *Hope* (Sentinel No 2136) withdrawn at Selby shed on St Valentine's Day, 1948; the services they worked had gradually reverted to conventional steam haulage, including the re-introduction of 'push-pull' working, from the 1930s. During that decade four experimental Armstrong-Whitworth diesel-electric railcars (Nos 25, 224/32/94) were operated, but with only limited success due to mixed reliability, all being withdrawn in 1939. Additionally, a Hungarian design railcar built privately under license by Metro-Cammell/Metro-Vick in 1937 and powered by a Ganz diesel engine was trialled on services around Hull from June 1939 until the outbreak of war when it was returned to the manufacturers.

Post-war, the LNER envisaged a fleet of 59 diesel railcars for the North Eastern Area based on the successful GWR AEC-engined types as replacements for the Sentinels; GWR Nos 6 and 19 had been loaned for services on Tyneside in April-May 1944, the latter also working from Starbeck shed for a spell during that year. However, in the severe economic climate and with Nationalisation looming an order was not pursued.

Following Nationalisation, on 9 August 1951 the Railway Executive appointed the Light Weight Trains Committee to investigate modern alternatives to traditional steam working on main, secondary and branch line services. Based upon the widespread and successful use of diesel railcars in Northern Ireland, Eire and Europe its report, issued in March 1952, recommended 'lightweight' Diesel Multiple-Units (DMUs) as the solution to revamping services and cutting costs – also providing modern rail vehicles to combat growing competition from buses and private cars. Leading light on the committee was Frank Pope, with the North Eastern Region ably represented by Frank Hick, Assistant to Chief Regional Officer (General).(1)(2) Hick's lobbying for a Bradford Exchange - Leeds Central - Harrogate service was successful and this was to become BR's first DMU pilot scheme of those recommended by the committee, followed closely by the London Midland's West Cumberland scheme.

Meanwhile, trials were undertaken in August and September 1952 using ex-GWR railcar No W20W on the Leeds - Harrogate and Wakefield - Doncaster routes. The AEC/ACV experimental lightweight diesel railcar set ran in service on the ex-H&B Hull - South Howden line for a stint in 1953 as part of its national trials; however, the four-wheeled vehicles comprising this set rode badly and were not at all popular with passengers, earning it the unkind sobriquets 'Pup' and 'Flying Bricks'! Based at Springhead it left the area on 10 August 1953, bound for Tyseley shed in the West Midlands.(3)(4)

West Riding

Following Hick's endeavours on the Light Weight Trains Committee his Bradford Exchange - Leeds Central - Harrogate proposal was quickly implemented by the BTC, the required eight two-car DMUs being authorised in August 1952 and ordered from Derby Carriage Works that November. The first two units were out-shopped in March 1954, formed of vehicle Nos E79000+E79500 and E79001+E79501 respectively. Their lightweight design involved extensive use of high-duty aluminium alloys coupled with 'integral' construction to eradicate a separate, heavy underframe; a fully-fuelled two-car unit turned the scales at just 54 tons. In terms of the accommodation provided for passengers, the DMUs were a breath of fresh air and a stark contrast to the existing dingy steam compartment stock, with clean, light and airy open saloons, furnished to standards matching the best in contemporary road coach design; the unobstructed front and rear views recalled those from the Sentinels and were a definite plus point with passengers. Seating was provided for 16 First Class and 114 Third passengers (the latter re-designated Second

Plate 5.3.
In order to reduce operating costs, the LNER introduced steam railcars such as this one: No 273 'Trafalgar'. built by the Sentinel Waggon Works and Cammell Laird & Company in 1928. It is seen here at Darlington (probably bound for the Works) in 1936. The railcar would be withdrawn in March 1946. (JW Armstrong / JW Armstrong Trust, per AR Thompson)

across BR from 3 June 1956), together with a lavatory and guards/luggage accommodation. Because of challenging gradients in the West Riding both cars were powered, each with two road-bus type 125 hp Leyland 6-cylinder horizontal engines, giving a total of 500 hp per two-car unit. (The similar LMR West Cumberland sets had only one vehicle powered.) Coupled with their lightweight design this gave an excellent power/weight ratio, with good performance and accelerative/decelerative capability, the transmission being geared for a maximum speed of 62mph. Up to four of the two-car units could be worked in multiple with one driver. After initial trials both units were shown-off on a London Marylebone - Beaconsfield VIP/press run on 29 April 1954. A demonstration trip a few weeks later between Leeds and Harrogate was unfortunately dogged by engine/transmission failures, but the set made it back to Leeds, proving the safeguards of the multiple-unit concept against individual engine failures – and much to the relief of the senior managers on board! Following crew/staff training, the new DMUs entered service between Bradford Exchange - Leeds Central - Harrogate from the 14 June 1954 summer timetable. Their modern image proved an instant 'hit' with passengers, ridership increasing immediately – with staff morale boosted too. (The weight of passengers at peak times caused problems, the lightweight bodies bowing and making it difficult to close the doors.) An improved half-hourly service was offered between Bradford - Leeds via Stanningley, with some trains routed via Pudsey Greenside; alternate services continued beyond Leeds to Harrogate on an hourly basis, with an extension to Knaresborough on summer Sundays to help cope with heavy day excursion traffic to the popular resort. There was an associated steep 60% rise in train mileage, although steam was not superseded until delivery of all eight DMUs was completed in September 1954. All were allocated to Bradford Hammerton Street (ex-GNR Bowling) shed, although this was a quite unsuitable environment for these modern units in dirty conditions alongside steam; several years were to elapse before it was properly modernised to handle DMUs. This might well have contributed to the mechanical/electrical problems experienced in service, which could also be put down to the units' pioneering nature. However, valuable lessons were learned which were applied to the forthcoming major DMU builds under the BTC's Modernisation Plan.

From 19 September 1955 some Bradford - Harrogate workings were extended to Ripon, set E79000+E79500 officiating on the first day. The DMU's popularity even provoked a campaign in the run-up to the 26 May 1955 General Election to save the ex-GNR Halifax/Bradford - Keighley 'Queensbury' lines which had been posted for closure, but over which the new units were being somewhat tactlessly deployed for crew training! However, this was to no avail, services being axed on 23 May, just days before the election, the Region citing the poor condition of the $1^1/_2$ mile long Queensbury tunnel and other structures. Similar demands for DMU reopening of the Pateley Bridge Branch (closed to passengers on 2 April 1951) fell equally on deaf ears.

Plate 5.4. The North Eastern Railway had operated steam-powered push-pull trains that had been replaced by the LNER with steam and diesel railcars. These latter were in turn replaced by push-pull trains worked by Class G5 0-4-4T steam locomotives as seen here. Note the push-pull control equipment on the buffer beam and on the right-hand side of the smokebox of No 67305. The train is at Ferryhill and is bound for Spennymoor. This train would not be replaced by DMUs; the date is Saturday, 29 March 1952, the last day of passenger services to Spennymoor. (JW Armstrong / JW Armstrong Trust, per AR Thompson)

Newcastle - Middlesbrough

The success of the Bradford - Leeds - Harrogate pilot scheme – which saw fares receipts rise by nearly 120% in two years – proved the springboard for introduction of DMUs across BR. In January 1954, the BTC had already announced a £2m programme embracing all the pilot schemes recommended in the 1952 report. The next North Eastern scheme was Newcastle - Middlesbrough, covering the heavy inter-urban traffics between Tyneside, Wearside and Teesside. Hammerton Street's set E79007+E79507 was recorded on trial runs between Newcastle - Middlesbrough - Saltburn on 20-21 October 1954. However, the new services required greater capacity in the form of four-car DMUs. Of similar 'Derby Lightweight' design to the Leeds - Bradford stock the new units comprised two driving power cars, each equipped with two of the higher-power AEC 150 hp engines now available, plus two intermediate trailers, giving a total of 20 First Class and 206 Second seats. Recognising their longer-distance itineraries, seating was laid out in a spacious '2+2' layout either side of a central gangway, compared with the '2+3' of the West Riding sets. Maximum speed was 70mph – the standard for all subsequent North Eastern Region DMUs. All five four-car units were delivered from Derby Carriage Works to South Gosforth car sheds in September 1955, being trialled on the Ponteland Branch before infiltration into traffic. The new DMU service commenced on Monday, 21 November 1955, replacing seven of the existing, usually Class A8 or V1-hauled hourly steam trains each way, with welcome accelerations of between 12 - 22 minutes. The busy 7.00 am Newcastle - Middlesbrough necessitated an eight-car set, formed from two units coupled together. A trolley refreshment service (complete with tea urn!) was provided on two services each way. Again passengers flocked to the new trains and fares receipts swelled, albeit not as spectacularly as Bradford - Harrogate. Four two-car 'Derby Lightweights' were added in March 1956, giving greater flexibility and allowing six-car formations to be operated.

With Bradford - Harrogate and Newcastle - Middlesbrough under his belt, Hick was to be the driving force behind the vigorous and widespread introduction of DMUs across the North Eastern Region under the BTC's Modernisation Plan, unveiled on 24 January 1955. This envisaged 4,600 new DMU vehicles for BR (including 300 or so already in service or on order) at a cost of some £80m, including maintenance facilities.(5) The sheer scale of the requirement in a relatively short timescale meant it could only be satisfied by extensive contracting with the private rolling stock builders to support BR's own Derby and Swindon Carriage Works. The resulting so-called Modernisation Plan DMUs were highly standardised around an engine/transmission system consisting of two British United Traction (AEC or Leyland type) six-cylinder horizontal 150 hp diesel engines per motor vehicle, each driving the inner axles of the two bogies via a fluid coupling, cardan shaft and a Self-Changing Gears (Wilson type) four-speed gearbox. There were inevitable variations around this basic design, including subsequent higher-power engines, but the object of commonality was writ large by the BTC, who procured the various DMU builds and allocated them to the individual Regions. The more powerful engines compared with the 125 hp type used in the West Riding units enabled relatively expensive light alloys to be dispensed with in favour of steel, saving costs and simplifying construction (although light alloys were used in a further build of DMUs by Derby (subsequently Class 108) some of which were delivered to the North Eastern).(6)

Plate 5.5. Here we see another Class G5, No 67312, a member of the class not fitted with push-pull equipment. It is however doing something that a DMU could not so readily do; it is hauling a mixed train, comprising a cattle wagon, a tank wagon and two carriages. However, the loss of such traffic would mean that, where passenger services were maintained, DMUs would cope. The location is Ainderby, the date July 1953. (JW Armstrong / JW Armstrong Trust, per AR Thompson)

All the North Eastern's DMUs were of 'low density' seating layout, much more spacious and comfortable compared with the 'high density' suburban types delivered en masse to other Regions which were in many respects little different to the obsolete steam stock they supplanted!

'All-out Dieselisation'

In a forward-looking presentation at York on 23 November 1955, Hick revealed details of the Region's ambitious DMU roll-out plan. Over the next three years, 542 vehicles would come into service at a cost of some £6m (see Table 5.1 for dates of introduction of DMU services and Table 5.2 for details of all new DMUs delivered to the North Eastern Region). The policy was to be 'all-out dieselisation' with the prime aims of rapidly reducing working costs, presenting a modern image to the public and raising staff morale. Whilst the initial capital costs of the DMUs, new maintenance depots and re-training of staff were high, these would be quickly recouped, including through the following operating advantages:

* Increased availability due to reduced maintenance requirements (no lengthy 'on shed' preparation and disposal, with much simplified depot working and refuelling).
* Good performance (acceleration and deceleration, over adverse gradients) meant faster schedules; operating experience also led to the concept of differential speed limits whereby DMUs were allowed an extra 5 mph over and above existing speed restrictions on a number of routes.(7)
* A reduction in station movements and platform occupation.
* Quick reversal at termini.
* Cleaner and more attractive environment for passengers and staff.
* Less track wear and damage than with locomotive-hauled trains.

These factors combined to permit more attractive (faster and more frequent) regular-interval services to be offered, which was expected to significantly boost fares revenues – subsequently borne out in practice. Despite the rise in train-mileage associated with improved timetables, the new DMU services were still estimated to cost up to 50% less than steam to operate. All-in-all operating costs would be slashed and working deficits reduced – and the Region's passenger account rendered a lot healthier. Productivity was greatly assisted by an agreement with the trades unions for single-manning of DMU drivers cabs, introduced from 1 January 1958 (albeit with some restrictions).

The new DMUs were energetically promoted via extensive and targeted local press advertising, and the bi-annual passenger timetables even denoted the services booked to be worked by DMUs by a 'D' at the top of the respective train columns.

Despite the progressive aims of the 'DMU-isation' policy, Hick faced stiff opposition from his traditionalist, hidebound 'steam' colleagues, who connived strongly against introduction of the new trains. Notwithstanding these difficulties, his persistent approach secured the backing of Chief Regional Manager HA Short, although even Short had initially wavered and tried to withdraw the Region from the Leeds - Bradford pilot scheme. Also, after a century and more of 'died in the wool' steam working, a perhaps difficult 'culture change' in operating discipline was now required; however, with the welcome simplification of procedures, together with cleaner and up-to-date working conditions, staff were gradually won over. Hick became nicknamed the 'diesel king', surrendering this accolade to George Jones of the operating department when he later took over responsibility for the DMU roll-out.

Hull Area

The Hull area was the first in the North Eastern Region to see mass introduction of DMUs under the Modernisation Plan with the delivery of a large fleet of 31 two-car units (later designated Classes 105/6) from Cravens Limited of Darnall, Sheffield. Of smart appearance, each unit accommodated 12 First Class and 103 Second passengers, the first (E50359+E56114) arriving on 9 August 1956. Following trials and training, the Hull scheme commenced in December 1956 when the first units entered traffic, the New Year seeing introduction of timetabled DMU services from 7 January when they replaced some steam workings from Hull to Beverley, Brough, Goole, Hornsea and Withernsea. This first phase was completed on 4 March 1957 when, two trains excepted, steam was ousted from the Hornsea and Withernsea Branches, each also benefiting from three additional return services, with five more DMU services to and from Beverley; Brough workings also went all-DMU, save for the steam trains for employees at the Blackburn Aircraft plant there. Summer weekends saw the units operated in formations of up to eight cars to Hornsea and Withernsea to cope with the traditional heavy seasonal day-trip demand to these resorts, supported by additional steam reliefs at busy times.

Pending build-up of Hull's own fleet, two four-car Metro-Cammell units (subsequently Class 101) were loaned from South Gosforth for a period. The DMUs were initially allocated to Springhead shed – again enduring unsatisfactory maintenance conditions alongside steam and open to the elements, although half the shed (four roads) was re-roofed for the DMUs, providing at least some protection – awaiting conversion of Botanic Gardens shed as the city's new permanent DMU depot, eventually completed in 1959. The Cravens units incorporated a new standard electro-pneumatic control system, embodied on most Modernisation Plan DMUs, including all those for the North Eastern Region. This enabled similarly-equipped units to be worked together in multiple indiscriminately of class/manufacturer; the control system was designated 'Blue Square' after the small symbols painted above the interconnecting cable plug sockets on the front of each unit. (The earlier 'Derby Lightweight' DMUs were designated 'Red Triangle' (Hammerton Street) and 'Yellow Diamond' (South Gosforth) due to their different control systems, meaning they could not be inter-worked either together or with the 'Blue Square' types.)

Plate 5.6.
A four-car 'Derby Lightweight' newly delivered for the Newcastle - Middlesbrough services is seen here on 27 September 1955. The unit is at the closed West Gosforth station, on the Ponteland Branch, and is in use for driver training. Livery at this time was green with narrow cream bands above and below the windows. (RG Warwick)

Completion of delivery of the 31 Cravens sets in July 1957 enabled their introduction on services between Hull and Bridlington, Scarborough and York (via Market Weighton), and Bridlington - Selby, all from the 29th of that month; York thus received its first regular DMU services. From the 16 September timetable Springhead's DMUs extended their reign to Selby - Goole plus the majority of workings between Hull - Brough - Goole and on the aforementioned routes, with services accelerated accordingly. Continuing deliveries allowed further consolidation of DMU services on the Hull - Scarborough line the following summer.

Newcastle - Carlisle

The next route to see DMUs was Newcastle - Carlisle, commencing 4 February 1957. Many services were converted, again with journey-time reductions – typically 10 - 15 minutes, with a couple 20 - 25 minutes faster. Some traversed the North Wylam route, replacing the Class G5-worked steam 'push-pull' locals. The scheme involved 36 units, including new four-car Metro-Cammell Class 101 sets, supplemented by the earlier two-car 'Derby Lightweights', all based at South Gosforth depot.

Darlington District

The Darlington District was next on Hick's DMU agenda, this major scheme providing for 130 vehicles based at a new purpose-built depot; pending its completion units were accommodated at South Gosforth. Initial deliveries – all of the Metro-Cammell Class 101 type – consisted of 13 four-car units, principally for the Saltburn services and operated as 8-car formations on peak workings, together with 14 two-car 'power-trailers' and 4 two-car 'power-twins'. With the depot complete, DMUs entered service from 19 August 1957 just in advance of the winter timetable commencing on 16 September, with steam replaced on the Darlington - Bishop Auckland - Crook/Durham, Middleton-in-Teesdale, Richmond and Saltburn routes – the latter half-hourly service maintaining that introduced by the LNER back on 1 May 1933. Rosters called for units to be stabled overnight at Middlesbrough, Middleton, Saltburn and West Auckland. Further deliveries allowed dieselisation of Darlington - Penrith services (summer Saturday Blackpool trains and Barnard Castle troop specials excepted) from 3 February 1958 with through journey times accelerated by around 20 minutes to an even 2 hours. The resulting improved train working enabled introduction of an additional Appleby - Penrith service, although some benefits were short lived, the useful 7.34 am Kirkby Stephen - Darlington and 10.34 return being axed from commencement of the winter timetable on 15 September – an early sign of the rundown of the line towards closure. The Darlington scheme swept away swathes of Class A8s – previously the mainstay on Saltburn services – A5 and L1 steam tanks; the entire class of 45 A8s was devoured by the nearby North Road scrap yard. Additionally, the new units were put on the Darlington - Catterick Camp soldiers' leave trains. Tantalisingly, their destination blind displays included 'Keswick' and 'Carlisle' – putative through services from Darlington which never came to fruition.

Extension of Services in the West Riding

Meanwhile, with deliveries of two-car Class 101 Metro-Cammell units to Hammerton Street, West Riding DMU services were extended from 25 February 1957 to cover Bradford Exchange - Dewsbury - Wakefield Westgate, Leeds Central - Wakefield Westgate and Leeds Central - Castleford Central; Hammerton Street's steam passenger turns were cut to just four as a result. With powerful new Metro-Cammell 720 hp Rolls-Royce-engined three-car units available (subsequently Class 111), 3 March 1958 ushered in a new hourly DMU service between Leeds City and Barnsley Exchange via Normanton and Wakefield Kirkgate. From this date some Bradford - Wakefield workings were extended to Goole, via Wakefield Kirkgate and Pontefract Monkhill, with a couple beyond to Hull; many of the Leeds - Castleford trains were projected to Pontefract Monkhill and the units also took over the three Huddersfield - Wakefield Westgate via Wakefield Kirkgate workings which connected with principal King's Cross expresses at Westgate, together with three of the Leeds - Wakefield - Doncaster 'locals'. Later in 1958, the DMUs spread to Leeds - Huddersfield services. The improved services came with an innovative range of value cheap day fares which were given widespread promotion and publicity.

Northumberland

New DMU services in Northumberland from 14 April 1958 saw two-car units deployed on Newcastle - Morpeth - Alnmouth - Alnwick through trains plus some Alnmouth - Alnwick turns (the balance of the latter remained steam worked right up to 18 June 1966, the final such branch passenger service on the North Eastern) and also from 9 June 1958 between Monkseaton - Blyth - Newbiggin.

Save for the intermediate stations stopping trains, most Newcastle - Sunderland services went over to DMUs from the 16 September 1957 timetable utilising Class 101 stock freshly delivered to South Gosforth. These enabled inter-working with similar Darlington-based units, the original 'Derby Lightweights' now banished to self-contained diagrams such as Newcastle - Carlisle. More two-car Class 101s enabled steam to be eradicated from the Newcastle - Sunderland 'stoppers', many Sunderland - South Shields and remaining Sunderland - Durham services from 18 August 1958. Some Class G5-worked Autocar trains persisted on the Sunderland - South Shields service, 28 November being their final day. At the same time DMU operations were further intensified on the Newcastle - Sunderland - West Hartlepool route.

North Yorkshire

The 5 May 1958 saw DMUs introduced on Middlesbrough - Loftus and Middlesbrough - Scarborough services. The former required reversals at Guisborough and Hutton Gate Junction, with the latter entailing no less than four – at Battersby, Whitby Town, Whitby West Cliff and Scarborough (Falsgrave) – all performed with consummate ease by the new units. DMUs displaced steam on both services from the 9 June, Middlesbrough - Scarborough being augmented from six to 12 trains daily with Middlesbrough - Whitby Town average times cut from $1^3/_4$ to $1^1/_4$ hours; services over the Esk Valley route were doubled to 15 southbound and 14 northbound in the summer peak. Summer Sunday services were also provided. Whitby gained as all Scarborough workings now served centrally-sited Town station as well as outlying West Cliff station, albeit with a time penalty for through journeys because of the double-reversal. Outside of the summer timetable period, services reverted to the previous level, with none on the Sabbath. Another benefit of the DMUs was the ability to sell tickets 'on the move' enabling reductions in manning at some little used intermediate stations, for example, Fyling Hall, which became unstaffed the day the diesel services commenced. The boost in workings via the Esk Valley had, of course, been largely due to closure of the precarious coastal route between Loftus and Whitby West Cliff, also effected on 5 May; ironically, the new DMUs had made occasional trial trips over the line during the previous year. Because of the gradients on the Whitby - Scarborough line, Class 101 'power-twins' (both vehicles Driving Motors) were employed on North Yorkshire services – although the occasional sea fret and resulting wet rails could still defeat the units (not equipped with sanding gear) on the steeper sections. Most remaining services went over to DMUs from Monday, 6 April 1959 when they were introduced between Malton and Whitby, save for two steam trains each way daily; new 7.02 am Whitby - York and 10.28 return through DMU workings featured. Services were worked by Darlington-based units on cyclic rosters interlinked with Middlesbrough - Whitby -

Plate 5.7. Two four-car Metro-Cammell DMUs (subsequently Class 101) stand at Middlesbrough en route to Redcar circa 1959. Initially, instead of adopting the four-character headcode designed by British Railways to be used at the front of diesel locomotives, for its DMUs the North Eastern Region continued to use a two-character headcode as seen here. The letter indicates the class of train and the number the route it will take. Note also the small plate bearing the number 23 above the right-hand buffer. This is a local set number, denoting a DMU diagram probably for either Darlington or South Gosforth depot. (R Goult)

Scarborough diagrams. In May, Public Relations unveiled a new colour poster for the summer season. Designed by Gyrth Russell it extolled the virtues of the new DMUs for exploring the Yorkshire coast – 'one of nature's holiday areas' – the attractive painting depicting a Metro-Cammell unit on the scenic stretch south of Robin Hood's Bay.

Further south, on 18 August 1958 most services between York and Harrogate were taken over, initially by four-car Birmingham Railway Carriage & Wagon Company DMUs (subsequently Class 104) recently delivered to Darlington. Ironically, the intermediate stations at Goldsborough, Hessay, Hopperton and Marston Moor were already slated for closure to passengers on 15 September, so enjoyed the new DMUs for just one month. In 1961, summer Sunday services operated over the line for the first time pre-Second World War; six trains ran each way at a two-hourly frequency from 18 June to 10 September, with cheap day tickets available. Initially described as 'experimental', these Sunday services were repeated in subsequent years.

The Tees - Thames Link

The DMUs assumed a more prestigious duty with inauguration of *The Tees - Thames Link* on Monday, 27 October 1958, complete with headboard! Designed to address the perennial problem of giving Teesside an improved early-morning service to the Capital in response to calls from local industry and businesses, this new Monday - Friday 'experimental' train departed Middlesbrough at 6.48 am (with a Saltburn connection) calling at Thornaby, Eaglescliffe and York before arriving at Doncaster at 8.37 to connect neatly into the 7.52 Leeds - King's Cross express. A London arrival of 11.40 gave businessmen a full afternoon for meetings before returning north that evening, as well as assisting onward connections for continental travellers; previously, the earliest practicable daytime London arrival had been 1.06 pm by the 8.00 am ex-Newcastle. *The Tees - Thames Link* had no northbound equivalent, existing evening services sufficing. From 10 November it was made permanent, with the Middlesbrough departure slightly revised to 6.50 and Northallerton added to the calling points; the DMU returned north as the 8.52 am Doncaster - Middlesbrough. *The Tees - Thames Link* was so successful as to require replacement by a through service just a year later. It last ran on Friday, 30 October 1959, the new 7.05 am Saltburn - London *The Tees - Thames* starting with that winter's timetable on Monday, 2 November. Unfortunately this arrived at King's Cross some 35 minutes later (12.15 pm) than the Doncaster connection given by the previous DMU service!

Large-scale Deliveries of DMUs

Continuing large-scale deliveries when more than 140 new DMU vehicles entered traffic – the largest number ever to be introduced by the Region at one time – allowed major consolidation from 5 January 1959 with a big increase in services; at a stroke DMUs replaced over 170 weekday steam trains, with many frequency enhancements and accelerations, virtually completing the North Eastern's conversion programme. The units took over the complex Aire Valley local services (Leeds City - Ilkley (via Guiseley), Bradford Forster Square - Ilkley, Leeds - Bradford and Bradford - Keighley - Skipton) on an accelerated, even-interval hourly clock-face pattern, with good interconnections between each, as at Shipley. Leeds/Bradford - Ilkley was almost doubled in frequency, Ilkley in particular gaining with its previous lengthy timetable gaps plugged. The exception was Arthington - Burley which stubbornly retained a meagre handful of trains. DMUs also displaced steam on a number of Newcastle - York - Leeds semi-fasts, including via the Durham Coast, with additional services and some significant speed-ups. For example, the 5.30 pm Newcastle - York direct had 38 minutes lopped off and was extended to Leeds. Such improvements were assisted by the closure to passengers of sparsely used stations at Alne, Raskelf and Pilmoor from 5 May 1958, and Beningbrough, Sessay, Otterington, Danby Wiske and Cowton from 15 September 1958.

Plate 5.8.
Metro-Cammell Driving Motor Brake Second No E50255 shows off its stylish cab at Whitby in 1960. Note the Blue Square multiple working code above the far buffer, and the tail lamp marking the rear of the train – the built-in marker lamps showed a white aspect when the car was facing forward. (JM Boyes / JW Armstrong Trust, per AR Thompson)

Amongst the myriad of changes from 5 January 1959, DMUs also saw off steam on other services, some of these being shared with Eastern Region-owned units: Doncaster - Hull; Hull - Market Weighton - York, accelerated by nearly 10 minutes with closure to passengers of intermediate stations at Cherry Burton, Fangfoss and Warthill from this date; Hull - Selby - Leeds locals were now all-DMU with some new fast workings; Hull - Scarborough, with 10 - 15 minute journey time savings, steam remaining on just two peak hour trains (usually Class D49-hauled); more York - Harrogate, York - Doncaster and Hull - Sheffield

Plate 5.9. Two Birmingham Railway Carriage & Wagon four-car DMUs (subsequently Class 104) approach Cargo Fleet circa 1960. The working is an extension of the Newcastle - Middlesbrough express service to Saltburn. Note the addition of 'speed whiskers' to the front of the cab; this was a standard embellishment to BR's DMUs, whereas the white cab roof also seen here was not. (R Goult)

(via Doncaster) services went over to the new units, with few steam turns now remaining; with one exception, all Leeds - Northallerton (via Harrogate) locals were now DMUs, which also covered some longer distance workings, for example the 7.45 am to Newcastle and 11.15 am return; York - Sheffield trains were mostly formed of the new units, except the expresses serving destinations further afield, which remained steam hauled for the time being. A further benefit of all the above improvements was the availability of much earlier onward connections, speeding up yet more journeys.

Another feature of this timetable were the complex high mileage cyclic rosters being developed by the North Eastern to eke out maximum productivity from its DMUs, taking advantage of their much greater availability compared with steam and assisted by the units' 350 - 400 mile range between refuellings. They included many ingenious examples lasting over several days with units booked to visit convenient depots (not necessarily their own) en route for refuelling/servicing, maximising revenue earning and minimising unproductive empty stock mileage. A subsidiary passenger benefit were some interesting through services *e.g.* Scarborough - Whitby - Darlington. As mileage accumulated, units were subject to deeper scheduled maintenance by their home depot, but down time was again minimised by 'repair by replacement' of engines and other components. All in all, this was an operating revolution compared with steam. In particular, Hull District DMUs achieved an availability of over 95% – amongst the highest on BR.

The Summer 1959 (15 June) timetable further strengthened the DMUs' stronghold with improvements to Hull - Scarborough workings and introduction of an hourly Manors - Bedlington - Newbiggin high season service on Saturdays. Bradford - Ilkley was boosted from seven to no less than 19 trains each way daily.

Secondary/Branch Dieselisation Completed
The North Eastern Region's secondary/branch line DMU conversion programme reached its conclusion at the turn of the decade (Trans-Pennine services are dealt with separately below):

27 September 1959. Haltwhistle - Alston.

2 November 1959. Huddersfield to Penistone/Clayton West, Bradford (via both Halifax and Cleckheaton) and some Marsden locals; ironically the units concerned included Holmfirth on their destination blinds – abortively, as it turned out, services on this branch being axed from the same date! More DMUs were deployed in the Durham area, between Newcastle and Carlisle, and on an enhanced service over the Alston Branch. All Hull - Scarborough services were DMUs from this date with takeover of the last two remaining steam workings.

4 January 1960. Certain Leeds Central - Pontefract Monkhill services were extended the short distance to Pontefract Baghill, reviving an earlier service (via Garforth) which had ceased back on 1 November 1926; the extension entailed remodelling the junction with the Monkhill curve at Baghill so that DMUs could access the bay platform. Stimulated by housing growth at Baghill, and also to provide connections for York, Sheffield and beyond, in the event it didn't last long, succumbing under the Beeching cuts when the whole Leeds Central - Castleford Central - Pontefract Monkhill service was axed on 2 November 1964.

7 March 1960. York - Scarborough. Though previously appearing on a semi-regular basis, DMU working now commenced 'in force', replacing most weekday and all three Sunday return steam services, with most running through from/to Leeds. Some additional services were introduced, but the DMUs were booked in steam timings until accelerations from the summer timetable (13 June). Also from 7 March, some Leeds - Harrogate via Wetherby services went over to DMUs.

19 April 1960. A new Leeds City - Sheffield Midland hourly through service began, via Wakefield and

Barnsley. This improved facility supplanted the previously separate Leeds - Barnsley Exchange and Barnsley Court House - Sheffield services which required a highly inconvenient change of station for through passengers. The 12 faster weekday through workings each way traversed the Eastern Region's new connecting spur between the ex-GCR and Midland routes at Quarry Junction, Barnsley; this permitted closure of Court House station to passengers from the same date and concentration of services on Exchange (renamed simply 'Barnsley' from 13 June). The move avoided an estimated £200,000 urgent renewal of Court House viaduct, with the new spur costing less than half this sum.

13 June 1960. Keighley - Oxenhope. This had been left 'out in the cold' when Aire Valley services went over to DMUs from 5 January 1959 – allegedly because track curvature was unsuitable for their operation, but more likely because of questions over the branch's future, a passenger withdrawal notice being issued that July. This goaded the locals into action, forcing BR to belatedly introduce DMUs on the line from 13 June 1960. Unfortunately, the much improved timetable of 15 return trains daily with no less than 20 on Saturdays (there were no Sunday services) – supported from 1 September by a new range of cheap day fares – failed to attract passengers. With receipts still flagging, the branch closed to passengers on New Year's Day, 1962. (Later, of course, it was successfully revived as the privately-owned Keighley & Worth Valley Railway, re-opening on 29 June 1968.)

Meanwhile, calls for through Huddersfield - Sheffield services – by extension of the DMUs to Penistone – fell on deaf ears, despite strong lobbying of the Region's senior managers at the first its new public 'open meetings' held in Huddersfield on 29 February 1960.

An unpopular move which attracted much criticism was the rostering of a DMU on the 10.19 am York - Banbury and 3.12 pm return during the winter timetable from 1959 in lieu of the York - Bournemouth express. The units were clearly unsuited to these four-hour plus, 153-miles each way duties, and the year-round express was eventually reinstated from spring 1962. The only 'Inter-City' standard DMUs to be delivered to the North Eastern were the Swindon-built Class 124s in 1960/1 for use on Trans-Pennine services (considered separately).

The last new Metro-Cammell DMU vehicles delivered to the North Eastern (and indeed BR) under the Modernisation Plan were a small batch of six trailer Second buffets in May 1960; numbered E59573-8, these unique TSLRBs were the only ones ever built. Each accommodated 53 Second Class passengers and had a miniature buffet at one end; when not in use, the buffet could be locked-up and the vehicle still used for passengers. As detailed in Table 5.2 (DMU deliveries), the buffet vehicles were inserted in six Class 102 quad sets re-allocated to South Gosforth. These were soon put to use, initially on four return Newcastle - Carlisle trains from the 13 June 1960 timetable, restoring buffet facilities withdrawn in the Second World War. In the winter timetable (12 September) they were additionally deployed on several Newcastle - York - Leeds services and from the following winter (11 September 1961) on five return Newcastle - Middlesbrough workings. These buffet-equipped sets were also rostered on the summer Sunday Newcastle - Keswick return service upon its takeover by DMUs from 1961.

Plate 5.10. A Metro-Cammell DMU, working a Middlesbrough - Loftus passenger train, at Guisborough. This is the rear of the train – note the tail lamp, which will be moved to the other end of the train when reversal takes place for the continuation of the journey to Loftus. (KH Cockerill / JW Armstrong Trust, per AR Thompson)

Plate 5.11. A Metro-Cammell DMU rolls into Scarborough with a train from Whitby on 1 March 1959. Note the cleanliness of the rear power car; it is brand new. (NW Skinner / JW Armstrong Trust, per AR Thompson)

Peak Loadings, Parcels and Excursion Traffic

Although the DMU fleet was sizeable, because it was effectively fixed-formation stock and diagrammed to a premium, there was not the same 'float' of spare vehicles which could be called on to cope with peak/seasonal loadings as was the case with the vast locomotive-hauled coaching pool. Additionally, though the DMUs had the capability (often used) of hauling a tail load of parcels vans, this was limited to a couple of vehicles, and the units themselves were not designed to cater for heavy mails traffic. As a result much conventional passenger and parcels stock was retained to form locomotive-hauled services to meet the aforementioned requirements. The North Eastern had bid to the BTC in 1959/60 for a fleet of nine Gloucester RC&W Company diesel parcels units on the back of a production run of 10 similar vehicles for the London Midland and the Western Regions. However, in light of BR's deteriorating finances and with a re-appraisal of the Modernisation Plan underway this £207,000 pitch was rejected.

Despite their tight diagramming, the DMUs still found gainful marginal use on excursions and other workings, particularly at weekends; for example ramblers' trains to destinations in the Yorkshire Dales and the Scarborough - Whitby scenic specials to name but a couple. On Sunday, 6 September 1959 the Railway Correspondence and Travel Society *Talyllyn Scenic Diesel Railtour* took some 360 passengers from Leeds to Towyn on the Cambrian Coast, running via Chester, Ruabon, Welshpool and Machynlleth. Conversely, the London Midland ran many DMU excursions from various centres to North-East resorts.

DMU Success Story

The North Eastern was keen to trumpet the success of its DMU enterprise, achieved through progress updates in the railway press and presentations by Frank Hick. Typical was his article published in *The Railway Gazette*, 1 January 1960, which reported the substantial increases in fares receipts won by the new trains. The capital cost of the DMU fleet was some £8½ million plus £1¼ million for the servicing depots, although these sums were quickly being offset by a staggering £1m annual saving in operating expenses; also, many ancient and obsolete locomotives and coaches had been condemned to the graveyard. Despite this, the DMUs surprisingly only accounted for some 50% of the Region's coaching train mileage, reflecting their use on mainly semi-fast, secondary and branch services. (See Appendix 6.2 on page 140 for details of DMU depots.)

Hick also sounded a warning note: the use of DMUs was not a solution in itself to the solvency of unremunerative branch lines. In the case of these more 'shaky' routes, though the new trains provided a more economical means of working, evidence showed that there was simply insufficient potential traffic given the mainly rural areas that they served (as demonstrated by Plate 5.2). Though the gap between operating costs and revenues could be narrowed, regrettably this would be insufficient to significantly change their financial fortunes. Even in this generally optimistic period of modernisation, pre-Beeching, it was recognised that replacement bus services might be the only solution to such lines 'beyond redemption'.

The last DMU deployments to be instigated by the North Eastern were, rather ironically, in replacement of the 'Tyneside electric' services, in 1963/7 (see below).

Diesel Railbuses

One of the less successful aspects of the BR DMU story that the North Eastern had not originally been involved with was the saga of the diesel railbuses. Twenty-two of these single-car vehicles – of five different types – were procured under the Modernisation Plan in the late-1950s. However, they failed to save many of the branch lines upon which they had been placed into service, and by 1964 the Eastern Region's five German-built Waggon und Maschinenbau examples had been consigned to store at Cambridge depot. Therefore, it was with some surprise that two of these vehicles were then transferred to the North Eastern the following year for trials usage on the Haltwhistle - Alston branch. Based at South Gosforth depot, No E79964 was the first to arrive, in May 1965, followed by sister E79963 in August; the latter did not stay long, returning to Cambridge the following month, leaving E79964 to soldier on alone. Perhaps not unexpectedly, the experiment was not a total success. As well as their infamous rough riding – a positive discouragement to passengers – difficulties arose in the provision of adequate fuelling arrangements (the railbuses having to travel empty from/to South Gosforth for this purpose), and they were unable to haul a parcels van tail load as could conventional DMUs. The final nail in the coffin was the wintry weather that November/December with which E79964's heating system just could not cope, passengers 'freezing' in the process, and it disgraced itself by stalling on the gradient up to the River Tyne viaduct in the icy conditions! To the great relief of passengers, E79964 was finally withdrawn in December 1965 and returned to Cambridge shortly thereafter, the previous well-accustomed DMUs making a welcome return to the branch.

Non-standard, Life-expired

By 1964 the eight original West Riding 'Derby Lightweight' DMUs had put in a decade's sterling service but were now regarded as non-standard in terms of equipment and spares amongst the vast Modernisation Plan fleet. They were also becoming increasingly unreliable and due to their small number could easily be replaced by the later DMUs, aided by service reductions under Beeching's 'Reshaping Plan'. All were thus withdrawn in February 1964, being closely followed to the scrapman in 1966-8 by their 1955/6 Tyneside cousins.

As regards the Modernisation Plan fleet, modern as the units were when first introduced, by the mid-1960s they were becoming a little tired and 'jaded', comparing unfavourably with the latest main line stock and modern road coaches. In particular, the DMUs' riding worsened alarmingly with speed, not good on lengthy main line turns, and also as mileage accumulated between overhauls; BR was already addressing this issue through technical research, the outcome being the smooth-riding Swindon-design 'B4' type bogie. However, this did not appear in production form until 1963, only just in time to be used in the last Modernisation Plan DMUs, Swindon's build of Class 123 four-car 'InterCity' units for the Western Region. Retrofitting of the new bogies to the earlier DMU fleet was out of the question in BR's adverse financial climate. Large-scale refurbishment of the Modernisation Plan DMUs was finally taken in hand from the mid-1970s, providing a 10-15 year life extension – albeit with the original bogies retained, but fettled to give some ride improvement.

In conclusion, whilst the new DMUs were undoubtedly successful in modernising train working and boosting fare revenues, the resulting reduction in the operating deficit was to prove insufficient to stave off secondary/branch lines closures under Beeching (as related elsewhere). Despite this, Frank Hick will always be remembered for his success in rolling-out DMUs across the North Eastern, in the process raising morale and optimism and redressing the financial imbalance at a time when road competition was becoming an increasing threat. Finally, the heavy reliance on DMUs within the North Eastern Region is exemplified by the Middlesbrough Division, where in a typical four-week period in 1964, out of some 5,159 passenger workings, only 140 were locomotive-hauled, the rest were by DMUs.

Plate 5.12. A Metro-Cammell DMU, by now sporting a yellow warning panel on the cab front, negotiates Hartburn Junction, Stockton, in December 1966 with a Middlesbrough - Newcastle passenger train. (AR Thompson)

Surprisingly, the last North Eastern DMUs (several Class 101s) survived in service for over 45 years, until 2003, based at Longsight depot, Manchester. Some of these and a number of the Region's other DMUs are preserved today on the various heritage railways, happily including one of the rare Metro-Cammell buffet vehicles (No E59575).

Endnotes:
(1) Frank Pope was Chairman of the Ulster Transport Authority and had been instrumental in the post-war deployment of diesel railcars in Northern Ireland.
(2) Frank Hick was appointed Assistant to Chief Regional Officer (General) in 1952; the post was subsequently re-designated Assistant to General Manager (General) and thence (by the North East Area Board meeting 17 May 1957) as Assistant Operating Officer. Hick was promoted to Operating Officer circa September 1960. He served also as chairman of the Region's Diesel Development Committee.
(3) *British Railways Illustrated*, April 1994.
(4) *Railway Bylines*, November 2003.
(5) With ongoing line closures it became possible to redeploy units already in service. This, together with the high fleet availability in practice, meant that the ultimate vehicle total was reduced to 4171, all delivered 1954-63; this included the Southern Region's DEMUs, London Midland/Western Region luxury 'Blue Pullmans', the experimental Battery-Electric 'Derby Lightweight' two-car unit deployed on the Aberdeen - Ballater branch and 22 experimental Railbuses.
(6) The TOPS DMU Class designations were not actually introduced by BR until 1973, but are included here to aid identification of the various unit types, and cross-referencing to the accompanying Table 5.2 (DMU deliveries); the early 'Derby Lightweight' units were withdrawn pre-1973 so did not receive classification.
(7) *British Railways North Eastern Region Supplementary Operating Instructions*, 1 July 1958 (BR.31293).

Plate 5.13. A two-car Metro-Cammell DMU working a Bishop Auckland service has just left Durham on 18 January 1964. The V2 is on a Down freight. Note the yellow warning panel that has replaced the 'speed whiskers' on the DMU's cab front. This panel was to make an approaching DMU or diesel locomotive more conspicuous to staff working on or crossing the track. (AR Thompson)

Plate 5.14. Hull Botanic Gardens motive power depot, as re-built to house DMUs, seen on 5 June 1963. The re-fuelling points are protected by rudimentary concrete canopies. For details of the North Eastern Region's DMU depots, see Appendix 6.2 on page 140. (Ken Hoole Study Centre Collection)

The East Coast Main Line

During the Second World War the East Coast Main Line (ECML) performed a pivotal role as a major traffic artery.(1) The pressures of traffic brought many improvements; in the LNER North Eastern Area these included virtual completion of the York - Northallerton widening with new Up and Down Goods lines between Pilmoor and Thirsk, the latter station being rebuilt for four tracks.(2)

Subsequently, the LNER's 1947 plan to procure 25 1,600 hp diesel-electric locomotives for ECML express services unfortunately fell victim to Nationalisation and the Railway Executive's decision to prolong steam locomotive construction. In the immediate post-war years a fleet of new Class A1 and A2 Pacifics was delivered, giving a welcome boost to the East Coast's war-weary A3s, A4s and V2s.

Wartime schedules had been severely slowed in order to accommodate more traffic, especially freight; Newcastle - King's Cross took some 6 hours (compared with 4 hours by the pre-war Silver Jubilee) and York 4 hours. Early post-war hopes of restoring the LNER's fast streamliners were dashed due to the condition of the track after six years of heavy wartime traffic with maintenance cut to a minimum.(3)

The long-established East Coast Committee continued after Nationalisation in its key role of managing ECML services, the newly-formed North Eastern, Eastern and Scottish Regions now co-operating in place of their LNER Area predecessors.(4) The Committee's main aim was to restore services as quickly as possible, including the war-suspended Pullmans; in the absence of faster schedules, these were seen as valuable brand leaders, their sumptuous ambience having popular appeal in the austere post-war climate. First back, from 4 November 1946, was *The Yorkshire Pullman*, King's Cross - Harrogate (including a Doncaster - Hull portion), with *The Queen of Scots*, King's Cross - Leeds Central - Harrogate - Glasgow Queen Street resuming on 5 July 1948. With great prestige the North-East gained its own new service from the 27 September 1948 winter timetable when *The Tees-Tyne Pullman*, 9.00 am Newcastle - King's Cross and 5.30 pm return, was inaugurated, running to accelerated timings of 5 hours 16 minutes Up (4 minutes longer Down) – 25 minutes faster than the previous best schedules.

Major restorations came with the 23 May 1949 summer timetable. Star turn was the new King's Cross - Edinburgh *The Capitals Limited* which took over the non-stop role from *The Flying Scotsman* during the summer. Also introduced were *The White Rose*, 9.15 am King's Cross - Leeds/Bradford (including a portion for Tyne Commission Quay, detached at Doncaster) and 3.45 pm King's Cross - Leeds *The West Riding*. The 5 June 1950 timetable saw the King's Cross - Tyne Commission Quay boat train, *The Norseman*, and revived the pre-war *Scarborough Flyer*, King's Cross - Scarborough.

More improvements followed through the 1950s as the locomotive fleet and track gradually regained pre-war standards, with 90 mph running re-introduced from 1951. These culminated in the greatly enhanced services of the summer 1956 timetable (11 June): hourly expresses left King's Cross for Newcastle between 8.40 am and 3.40 pm, plus 9.08 am (*The Norseman*), 12.28 pm (*The Northumbrian*), 2.28 pm, 3.00 and 3.08 pm, then 5.00 and 5.40 pm; to Leeds/Bradford services were half-hourly between 8.52 am and 6.18 pm, also the 5.08 pm (*The Yorkshire Pullman*); Hull had four services. An impressive 55 expresses left King's Cross each weekday between 8.00 am and 6.18 pm, with summer Saturday traffic even more intense. The 17 September timetable added a new prestige express, *The Talisman*, which departed the English and Scottish capitals at 4.00 pm (as per the pre-war *Coronation*). Calling only at Newcastle, timing was 6 hours 40 minutes each way, Newcastle - King's Cross achieved in 4 hours 25 minutes. From the 17 June 1957 timetable *The Talisman* also ran as Up and Down morning trains. Momentum continued that winter (16 September) with the use of tighter, limited stock formations permitting further accelerations, for example the 7.30 am ex-Leeds improved by 33 minutes, arriving in London at 11.07.

There were also direct daily return services or through coaches between a wide range of other places and London, such as Halifax, Huddersfield, Middlesbrough, Saltburn, Scarborough, Stockton, Sunderland and West Hartlepool.

Proposed Electrification

Meanwhile, the BTC's Modernisation Plan, published on 24 January 1955, proposed electrification between King's Cross and Leeds, 'and (possibly) York'. After studies by the three Regional Area Boards, electrification to Edinburgh was endorsed by the BTC in April 1957.(5) Bridge-raising works to secure the necessary catenary clearances began in 1957. Maurice Barbey, in the North Eastern Region's Bridge Section, assessed every overbridge between Shaftholme Junction and the Border; Dringhouses (St Helen's Road) and Raskelf station overbridges were but two rebuilt, with Selby Swing Bridge signal cabin bodily raised by 3 feet 6 inches, the latter task completed on Sunday, 1 May 1960. In June 1959, the Eastern and North Eastern Regions issued a joint report recommending 25kV AC electrification between King's Cross and Newcastle at a cost of £105.5m, to be completed by 1970.(6) Of the 268 route miles, 100 mph would be permitted over 150, 90 mph over 54 and 80 mph over 44, with only 7 of the remaining 20 miles restricted to less than 60 mph. Services would be operated with 188 new electric locomotives (79 allocated to the North Eastern) and 62 new 4-car express electric multiple-units. Accelerated, higher frequency services at 70 mph+ average speeds would bring Newcastle and York within 3 hours 45 minutes and 2 hours 31 minutes, respectively, of King's Cross. Doncaster - Leeds and Northallerton - Stockton/Thornaby - Ferryhill would also be wired but Doncaster - Hull was excluded. New electric depots would be at Neville Hill, York, Gateshead and Thornaby – the latter already under reconstruction with appropriate catenary clearances – with Heaton carriage depot also electrified.

Sadly, the report came on the eve of publication of the BTC's wholesale re-appraisal of the Modernisation Plan which, in the event, gave priority to West Coast electrification, deferring work on the ECML scheme until 'after 1964' at the earliest.(7) Electrification of the ECML would not be finally authorised until 1984 and completed in 1991.

Dieselisation

With electrification deferred, the ECML interim dieselisation programme now became permanent. The 21 June 1958 was a historic day when London Hornsey's new English Electric Type 4 D201 (subsequently Class 40 No 40001) hauled the route's first-ever long distance diesel express – the Down *The Flying Scotsman* – as far as Newcastle. Regular workings by the class began on 25 August and they were booked to work all Newcastle - London trains from the 12 September 1960 timetable. However, this was somewhat theoretical as by now the locomotives had gained a questionable reputation as far as their reliability was concerned (their train steam heating boilers were particularly troublesome) and in terms of performance their 2,000 hp proved no match for the Pacifics – now fitted with Kylchap exhausts and at the peak of their own performance – and which were regularly called to cover for failures of the diesels.

Complementing the refreshed motive power was a fleet of 44 new Pullman cars, delivered from Metropolitan-Cammell in 1960-1. Based on the BR Mk 1 coach, they featured traditional appointments in a modern setting and had Commonwealth bogies designed for smooth-riding at speeds up to 100 mph. They entered service on the various East Coast Pullman services in 1960-1, supplanting older wooden-body stock which was due replacement.

The East Coast authorities had always foreseen the need for more powerful locomotives. As is now legendary, English Electric came to the rescue with its mighty 3,300 hp, 105 mph Type 5 'Deltic' (Class 55) design. Twenty-two were delivered, six being allocated to Gateshead with eight each for Finsbury Park and Haymarket, although all operated in a common pool. Delivery was about a year late, thwarting plans for squadron deployment with the 12 June 1961 timetable. However, the winter timetable (11 September) saw the Deltics take over a sprinkling of top-rank duties, notably the Up and the Down *The West Riding*, each speeded-up by 30 minutes. The 7.50 am Newcastle - King's Cross was accelerated by a massive 50 minutes. This was the beginning of the end for East Coast steam, with the fleet increasingly subjugated to lesser duties.

Even more spectacular was the 18 June 1962 timetable when Deltics were rostered on all daytime Anglo-Scottish workings, main Newcastle and West Riding business trains. At last, the King's Cross - Edinburgh pre-war 6 hour timing was regained, but extended to no less than three expresses – *The Flying Scotsman*, *The Talisman* and *The Elizabethan*. Sadly, the latter lost its hallowed non-stop status after Tyneside crews objected to riding in the noise and discomfort of the Deltic's rear cab! A crew-change stop was thus introduced at Newcastle, made public from 16 July. Newcastle was reached from King's Cross just a minute or two shy of the pre-war 4 hour timings.

Further improvements awaited heftier Type 4 power in the shape of Brush's new design (Class 47), the first, D1500, delivered to Finsbury Park on 28 September 1962, followed by D1501-20 into 1963. Their 2,750 hp, 95 mph top speed and performance facilitated interworking with the Deltics. Coupled with use (since 1961) of Neville Hill's BR/Sulzer Type 4s (Class 45) and their Gateshead sisters (Class 46), plus Class 40s on secondary workings, express steam was mostly eliminated from the summer 1963 timetable (17 June),

Plate 5.15. To replace pre-Nationalisation locomotive-hauled stock, BR built the Mark 1 carriage. This is a Corridor Third, No E24472 built at York Works in 1954 as part of the 1951 Carriage Building Programme. It is painted in the carmine and cream livery adopted by BR for corridor stock, replaced (except on the Southern and Western Regions) by maroon in 1956. (BR (NER), per CE Williamson)

Plate 5.16. Class A4 No 60007 'Sir Nigel Gresley' speeds through Northallerton on 6 August 1949 at the head of the Down 'The Flying Scotsman'. The locomotive is still in LNER Garter Blue livery – it would not get the short-lived BR standard blue livery until September 1950. It has though received its BR number, and carries 'BRITISH RAILWAYS' on the tender. Note also that the LNER's 'Flying Scotsman' headboard, lacking the definite article that BR would customarily provide, is still in use. (KH Cockerill / JW Armstrong Trust, per AR Thompson)

King's Cross' famous 'Top Shed' closing. Steam was generally barred south of Peterborough but still occasionally appeared at the London terminus until late-1964.

Also from 17 June 1963 Heaton lost its steam allocation most (including 11 A3 Pacifics) transferring to Gateshead, to which it now became a sub-shed. Gateshead BR Type 2 (Class 24/25) diesels accordingly took on the Heaton depot empty stock turns from the Gresley V3s – but the latter soon resumed these duties! With deliveries of Class 47s to the North Eastern Region in full swing from 1964 the death knell of its Pacific fleet was sounded. Heaton closed completely to steam on 29 August 1964 and diesels worked the majority of passenger services from that winter's timetable (7 September); Gateshead's last A4 (No 60001 *Sir Ronald Matthews*) went in October, the shed closing to steam on 20 March 1965. However, the Pacifics were to have several 'final flings' at the Christmas/New Year, Easter, Whit and August Bank Holidays, helping out with the many extras and reliefs. The North Eastern Region operated its official 'last' East Coast steam working – a York - Newcastle and return relief on New Year's Eve, 1965, hauled by A1 No 60145 *Saint Mungo* – but remaining members of the class still managed to work several trains into 1966 up until their withdrawal! The story in the West Riding was much the same, although Leeds - Bradford Exchange portions of London expresses famously remained steam worked right up to 1 October 1967 – almost to the end of steam traction in this area of the former North Eastern Region.

Road and Air Competition

The North Eastern Region was notable in deploying a very wide range of off-peak reduced fares to encourage traffic. However, with increasing competition from road and air by the early 1960s, new methods were required to retain traffic. Thus, alongside Beeching's remit to develop long-distance Inter-City passenger services came the employment of modern methods of marketing and promoting services. Amongst the market-led decisions was progressive improvement of morning Up services to give businessmen more daytime in London without the need to travel overnight, achieved through earlier departures coupled with journey accelerations. The North Eastern's pioneering fares initiatives were extended, with vigorous promotion, to fill spare off-peak capacity and to boost revenue.

Such improvements came not a moment too soon to ward-off an increasing threat posed by the airlines. On 6 April 1959 BKS Air Transport inaugurated services between Newcastle and London (Heathrow); from 3 October 1960 the West Riding gained its own link with the Capital when BKS commenced operations between Leeds Bradford (Yeadon) airport and Heathrow. From just a few services weekly flights grew in popularity although the North Eastern Region only seriously became perturbed in 1964 when BKS introduced larger and faster aircraft on the Newcastle - London route from 24 April in the shape of the Bristol *Britannia* turbo-props; city-to-city terminal times by air now well undercut those by rail. The opening of Teesside Airport the same year heightened concerns, its own flights to Heathrow starting on 2 November, again by BKS. Such competition was serious enough to disabuse any complacency that a 4 hour fastest schedule from Newcastle (half-an-hour less from Darlington) to London was good enough to sustain rail's market share. In early 1965 the North Eastern Region retaliated with a large billboard beside the Darlington - Saltburn line facing the entrance to Teesside Airport extolling the virtues of rail to London! Services were also being challenged by road coaches,

United Automobile Services gaining licences for several additional services from the North-East via the newly-opened M1 motorway.

Rail fought back with continuing improvements. Summer 1964 (15 June timetable) saw clearance of the ECML's first 100 mph section (Stoke - Lolham on the Eastern Region) enabling the full capability of the Deltics to be at last officially unleashed. BR's Train of the Future – the *XP64* ('Experimental Project 1964') – blue/grey-livery coach set was deployed on the Up Morning and Down Afternoon *The Talisman* for the duration of the summer timetable. Some embarrassment was caused just two days later (17 June) when Deltic D9018 *Ballymoss* failed at Durham on the Up morning *The Talisman*; V3 67628 came to the rescue, hauling the futuristic train to Darlington where standby A3 Pacific 60036 *Colombo* took over as far as York. *The Queen of Scots* Pullman (via Leeds, Harrogate, Ripon) ceased from this timetable, rendered superfluous by acceleration of direct London - Edinburgh services, and cut back to a King's Cross - Harrogate/Bradford return Pullman in similar timings and renamed *The White Rose*, assuming this mantle from the 9.20 am King's Cross - Leeds/3.30 pm return.

The final two years of the North Eastern Region saw enhancements continue: from 14 June 1965 the King's Cross - Edinburgh *The Flying Scotsman* was accelerated by 5 minutes to 5 hours 55 minutes each way, and again from 18 April 1966 to 5 hours 50 minutes. In the latter timetable, King's Cross - Newcastle came down to 3 hours 53 minutes, with Darlington in 3 hours 13 minutes, assisted by clearance of the North Eastern's first 100 mph sections, and not much short of the 1959 electrification proposed timings. New fast business services were introduced on limited load 'Deltic plus eight' (coach) schedules – the 7.25 am Leeds - King's Cross and 3.55 pm return services, both on best-ever 2 hours 40 minutes timings. The 'Deltic plus eight' concept proved successful and was extended to Newcastle from the 6 March 1967 timetable. During this period, the use of locomotive headboards for the named expresses gradually ceased.

These improvements helped BR grow its ECML London traffic; between 1963-7, market share from Newcastle increased from 44 to 48%, albeit now levelling-off; Teesside's rose from 45 to 61% – the latter helped by operator BKS pulling-out of Teesside Airport in 1966 after poor loadings. Road/air competition in the same period pegged rail's share of the Leeds - London market at 46%. Further growth in rail's business would depend on additional journey time improvements which the Eastern Region would pursue vigorously in the years ahead.

One of the more controversial proposals stemming from Beeching's second report *The Development of the Major Railway Trunk Routes* (published 16 February 1965) fortunately did not come to pass. This would have seen downgrading and possible single-tracking of the Newcastle - Edinburgh section in favour of diverting traffic via Newcastle - Carlisle and an electrified West Coast Main Line to Glasgow.

Express Diesel Multiple-Units and Mk 2 Coaches
Finally, one of the North Eastern Region's desires of the mid-1960s was to acquire a fleet of express DMUs to work West Riding - King's Cross services; these would enable regular, portioned workings from both Leeds and Bradford to be more easily provided compared with locomotive-hauled stock. However, this ambition was to remain unfulfilled.(8) BR's preferred option for 'Inter-City' services was the new Mk 2 coach, the initial vehicles of which – a small batch of maroon-liveried Corridor Firsts (E13361-78) – was introduced from June 1964 on East Coast services.(9)

Plate 5.17. Northallerton once again, and un-named Class A1 No 60158 passes through at the head of the Down 'The Flying Scotsman' on 18 September 1950. The locomotive was built at Doncaster Works in November 1949, and would be named 'Aberdonian' in March 1951. Note the BR headboard. (KH Cockerill / JW Armstrong Trust, per AR Thompson)

Colour Plate 23. This is the front cover of the timetable giving information on the new Trans-Pennine service, commencing on 2 January 1961, and formed part of the advertising campaign introducing the new high-powered Trans-Pennine diesel multiple-units to the travelling public. (BR (NER) / JP McCrickard Collection)

Colour Plates 24, 25 and 26. BR (NER) tickets, including the ubiquitous Edmondson. (JG Teasdale Collection)

Endnotes:

(1) ECML post-war history has been fully recounted elsewhere. This section primarily focuses on events concerning the North Eastern Region.

(2) All that was left to do was Alne - Pilmoor, the new Up Slow opening 19 June 1960; Pilmoor - Thirsk wartime goods lines were re-signalled as Slow Lines in 1959.

(3) In the event, the LNER streamliner services were never revived; after storage during the war, the stock was dispersed on other services.

(4) The origins of the East Coast Committee can be traced back to the East Coast Joint Stock scheme, established in 1860; it was renamed the East Coast Management Group following merger of BR's Eastern and North Eastern Regions.

(5) British Transport Commission. *Modernisation of British Railways - Report on Diesel and Electric Traction and the Passenger Services of the future based on proposals of the Area Boards*. April 1957.

(6) British Railways Eastern and North Eastern Regions. *Report on the Modernisation and Electrification of the East Coast Main Line between King's Cross and Newcastle and certain associated lines*. June 1959.

(7) British Transport Commission. *Re-appraisal of the Plan for the Modernisation and Re-equipment of British Railways*. July 1959.

(8) Conversely, an attempt by the BRB to transfer the London Midland Region's two *Blue Pullman* luxury diesel units – made redundant by the 1966 London - Manchester electrification – to the ECML did not come to fruition and they passed instead to the Western Region, although a Leeds Central - King's Cross trial run had been undertaken on 16 October 1965.

(9) Further vehicles were not seen until Autumn 1967 when squadron deliveries of Mk 2a vehicles for ECML services commenced.

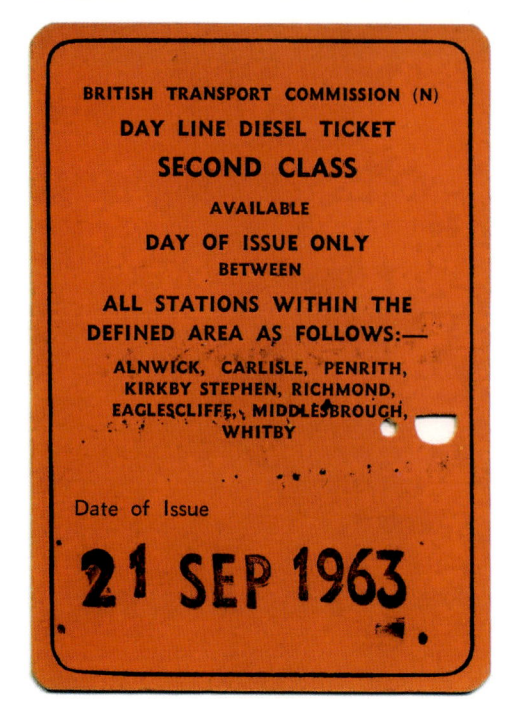

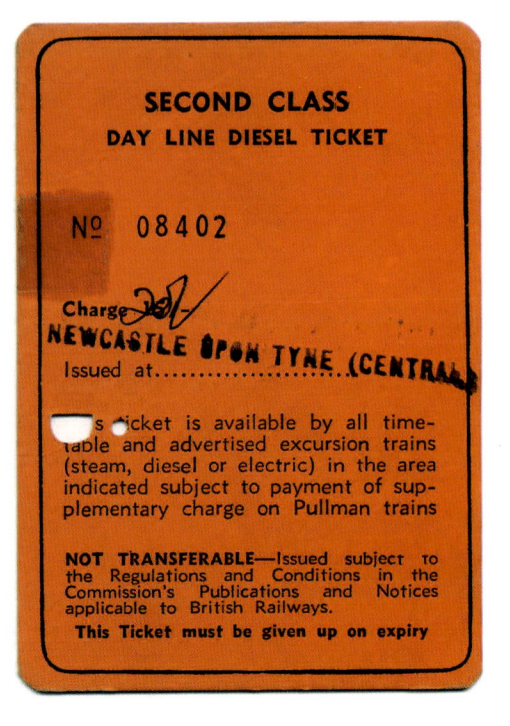

Plate 5.18. Deltic No D9011 works the Up 'The Flying Scotsman' past Little Benton South on 2 June 1962. The locomotive would be named 'The Royal Northumberland Fusiliers' on 28 May 1963. (RG Warwick)

Plate 5.19. Displaying an ominous oil stain on its flank, English Electric Type 5 No D9014 'The Duke of Wellington's Regiment' crosses the viaduct at Plawsworth with the 1.00 pm King's Cross - Newcastle on 28 May 1966. (AR Thompson)

Cross-Country

By the early 20th Century a diverse range of inter-railway 'cross-country' expresses (*i.e.* not serving London) had been established countrywide; the Great Central Railway in particular had vigorously promoted development of such services, using its strategically-placed main line artery as a key north - south link – an oft-forgotten role compared with its prime London focus. Newcastle and York were linked with a wide variety of destinations, including Bournemouth, Cardiff, Southampton and Swindon, with trains formed of stock from the participating companies; Great Central, Great Western and London & South Western Railway vehicles were thus regularly seen in the North-East, although engines usually worked as far as York – which became a colourful 'Mecca' for the enthusiasts of the day. Some overnight services also ran, composed of one or more day coaches attached to mail trains. Services were operated by liaison between the companies concerned, similar arrangements persisting beyond the Grouping and thence Nationalisation under the remit of the respective BR Regions.

Cross-country services were cut significantly in the wartime emergency timetables implemented from September 1939. However, the needs of wartime military personnel movements saw new services between Edinburgh (overnight), Leeds, York and Colchester, plus an Ashford to Newcastle train. Following the end of hostilities many pre-war services were reinstated from the 7 October 1946 timetable although some – such as the daily York - Southampton and the York portion of the Harwich - Liverpool *North Country Continental* – never reappeared. Any optimism was short lived, however, as many cross-country services were suspended again just months later in the nationwide service cuts applied from 9 December (with more from 6 January 1947) due to that winter's chronic fuel shortages, not being fully restored until the summer 1949 timetable. Cross-country workings were hit yet again in service cuts during the 1950/1 fuel and manpower shortages. With regional priorities naturally targeted on prime London services it was to be a long haul back for cross-country, with pre-war schedules not fully regained until dieselisation in the 1960s. Cross-country trains serving the North Eastern Region can be split into two main groupings, as follows.(1)

North East - South West

The most important were the so-called 'NE-SW' services linking the North-East and West Riding with similarly heavily populated industrial centres – South Yorkshire, Derby, the West Midlands – and the western ports of Bristol, Cardiff and Swansea, plus Bournemouth. The following main weekday daily return services ran, as restored from the 7 October 1946 timetable:

* Newcastle - Bristol: two expresses, the second northbound routed via the Durham Coast line, all others running directly between Newcastle and York. These were supplemented by York - Bristol workings. In addition, the overnight Newcastle - Bristol *Midland TPO* conveyed daytime coaches.

* Newcastle (summer)/York (winter) - Bournemouth via the Swinton & Knottingley Joint Line and Sheffield Victoria (reverse), thence the Great Central main line, Banbury, Oxford, Reading and Basingstoke. Suspended early-1947 to 23 May 1949 due to the fuel crisis.

* Newcastle - Swansea (former *Ports-to-Ports* express): routed similarly to the Newcastle/York - Bournemouth as far as Oxford, thence via Swindon. When reintroduced from summer 1949 (23 May), after suspension since early 1947 due to the national fuel emergency, it was cut back to York, although in summers from 1950 the northbound train continued to Newcastle Fridays only, returning from there Saturdays only. Supplemented by the York - Swansea Victoria (SX)/Hereford (SO) overnight TPO (via Leeds, Stockport and Crewe) which included passenger coaches; from the 15 June 1964 timetable this train was cut back to Shrewsbury (SX) upon closure of the direct London & North Western Railway Pontardulais - Swansea Victoria line, but still served Hereford (SO).

* York - Swindon: two overnight mail/passenger services, routed as per the Bournemouth train to Oxford, although the first southbound ran via Doncaster, thence Sheffield Victoria. These trains had continued during the Second World War.

* Bradford Forster Square - Paignton *Devonian*: routed via Sheffield, Derby and Birmingham, summer through coaches ran to Kingswear but in winter the train terminated at Bristol. Augmented by additional Bradford/Leeds - Bristol workings.

North East - East Anglia

* Newcastle - Colchester: generally ran during the summer timetable, serving Lincoln during the rest of the year, except for a period from the 1950s until 7 January 1963 when the train served Colchester all year round. The southbound working ran via the Durham Coast line. Supplemented by an overnight return Glasgow Queen Street - Colchester train (seated accommodation only).

* York - Lowestoft Central: also carried a Yarmouth Vauxhall portion until the winter 1960/1 timetable.

The East Anglian services remained fairly constant throughout the North Eastern Region period, the main developments and improvements taking place on the NE-SW route. As already alluded to, progress was lethargic during the 1950s. However, a useful new 8.05 am Birmingham - Newcastle and 4.05 pm return began from winter 1948 (27 September) and summer 1952 (30 June) saw introduction of through coaches between Newcastle and Cardiff via the direct NE-SW route; conveyed by the 8.15 am SX (7.30 am SO) Newcastle - Bristol, arriving Cardiff at 4.30 pm, with similar return timings. The $8^{1}/_{4}$ hour journey saved a welcome $1^{3}/_{4}$ hours on the *Ports-to-Ports* with its dog-leg itinerary via Oxford/Swindon and signalled the demise of the latter, ultimately reduced to a summer only Friday/Saturday Swansea - York/Newcastle working and dropped at the end of the 1961 season.

Modernisation Plan Progress

Despite some improvement between 1956 and 1960, NE-SW schedules remained little better than pre-war. Real progress came with the deployment of diesel traction under the Modernisation Plan. During 1960-3 a large fleet of 127 BR/Sulzer Type 4 Peak diesel-electrics (later Class 45) was delivered to the London Midland Region for its Midland Division express services, embracing London St Pancras - Leeds - Glasgow St Enoch/Edinburgh Waverley, and the NE-SW route. Numbered D11-137 each locomotive was rated at 2,500 hp with a 90 mph top speed – just what was needed to accelerate services and handle cross-country's often challenging performance requirements! As well as the Midland depots (Cricklewood and Derby) a batch was allocated to the North Eastern's Leeds Holbeck, strategically located at the cross-roads of both routes in whose working it participated. The steam shed had of course to be modified to accept the new traction and whilst this was underway early deliveries went to nearby Neville Hill, recently completed as Leeds' first diesel depot. Peak Nos D11/4 were the first to arrive in December 1960 enabling crew training to commence, soon joined by D12/5/6. An early trial run to Tyneside took place with D14 on 5 February 1961. By July Holbeck's stud comprised 14 locomotives: D11-20/6/9-31. Pre-delivery of the Peaks, Gateshead and York-based English Electric Type 4s had seen some usage on NE-SW turns during 1960/1.

The first NE-SW roster to go over to Peak haulage employed a Derby-based locomotive working: 5.20 pm Derby - Worcester as far as Birmingham, thence shedded overnight at Saltley; 8.05 am Birmingham - Newcastle as far as York; 2.24 pm York - Bristol (12.43 am ex Newcastle) as far as Derby. D19 was an early sighting on this duty on 20 March 1961. Crew training also saw Peaks work the daily Bournemouth service out of Newcastle – for example, D11 on the 25 July and D26 on 27 July. As deliveries built up the locomotives were progressively deployed on more diagrams replacing steam but running in existing timings.

A final 56 Peaks were delivered from Derby works in 1961-3. Later designated Class 46 on account of their Brush electrical equipment (the Class 45s had Crompton Parkinson kit) allocation was split equally, 26 machines each going to Derby (D138-65) and Gateshead (D166-93), the latter's also for Newcastle - Liverpool and East Coast work (although D189-92 were transferred to Holbeck in June 1963).

Chief innovation in the summer 1961 timetable (12 June) was the introduction of a sleeping car on the overnight Newcastle - Bristol *Midland TPO*. This met a long-standing demand for such facilities and honoured the promise made by Assistant General Manager (Traffic) Freddie Margetts to the North Eastern's 'Open Forum' public meeting in Newcastle City Hall on 8 February 1961. Initially experimental it was successful enough to be continued through into the winter timetable – and beyond (lasting until withdrawal from the 7 May 1973 timetable due to poor loadings, although seated accommodation continued).(2)

1962 Diesel Timetable

'Diesel-day' finally arrived on 10 September 1962 when the Midland Lines revamped timetable was introduced upon squadron deployment of the Peak fleet. NE-SW services were completely reorganised in cooperation with the Eastern, London Midland and Western Regions; through trains were speeded-up

Plate 5.20. Brush Type 2 No D5619 is seen here at Sunderland Bridge, Croxdale, with what is thought to be a Colchester - Newcastle train in 1964. Note though that the headcode is incorrect as the 'E' indicates a train bound for the Eastern Region, whereas it is definitely bound for a destination in the North Eastern Region. (AR Thompson)

considerably with the diesels working through rosters between Newcastle/Leeds and Bristol where services dovetailed with the Western's timetable to the South-West. Amongst the many improvements, the best Newcastle - Bristol timing was cut by nearly an hour to 6 hours 40 minutes; the afternoon Newcastle - Birmingham was extended to Bristol and a new return Leeds - Cardiff service introduced.(3) Despite the razzmatazz, however, some schedules remained decidedly disappointing – 2 hours for the 89 mile Birmingham - Bristol section was little faster than Midland Railway days! Steam still persisted on lesser services, reliefs and extras – together with substitutions for failed diesels.

Dieselisation revolutionised traffic working, transforming economics for the better. Single Peaks now worked expresses right through, eradicating the previous locomotive changes with steam. Diesels and crews based on Gateshead, Holbeck, Derby, Saltley and Bristol shared in the working of services, with locomotives diagrammed to visit either of these depots for re-fuelling and turn-round servicing. Locomotive changes still took place at the Western's Bristol diesel-hydraulic 'frontier' (continuing until the 1970s when the Peaks began regular working beyond the city). As well as cross-country duties, North Eastern West Riding-based coach sets and staff inter-worked with those of the Eastern and London Midland – for example to/from London St Pancras. All in all, operating costs were slashed, just as Beeching was to advocate in his imminent 'Reshaping Report'.

Despite the best laid plans, however, problems soon arose. To avoid repeating the mistakes of earlier 'big-bang' dieselisation schemes, the Peaks had been gradually phased into service so that experience could be accrued and, crucially, any emerging problems dealt with. Unfortunately, many defects only came to light under the intensified utilisation from September 1962. Combined with a particularly ill-timed severe winter this had a devastating effect on fleet availability, laying-up many Peaks out of action. Several hundred curative modifications were eventually required but, in the interim, the operators had no alternative but to reduce diagramming of the fleet, instituted from 4 March 1963. The North Eastern was largely able to maintain its diagram commitments albeit with some use of steam traction.

The next major developments came with the summer 1965 (14 June) timetable when the Western Region deployed its new Brush Type 4s (Class 47) on the NE-SW sector. Improvements saw the Penzance - Sheffield *Cornishman* extended to Bradford (via Leeds) with a one hour acceleration each way; the best Newcastle - Bristol times came down to six hours; two new York - Cardiff expresses were provided; York - Sheffield times were cut from a ponderous 70-75 to around 60 minutes each way.(4) That autumn (from 4 October) Bournemouth West station closed and the York (winter)/Newcastle (summer) service diverted to Poole. The train was re-routed again the following year, to the NE-SW route upon closure of the Great Central main line on 5 September; the two York - Swindon overnight services were axed from the same date. A final change under the North Eastern was extension of the 5.20 pm Cardiff - Sheffield to York from 7 November 1966. Just into the Eastern Region era, 1 May 1967 brought the opening of the revamped Leeds City central station; concurrently, as for other NE-SW trains, the *Cornishman* and *Devonian* Bradford terminus switched from Forster Square to Exchange and they ran via the Great Northern route both calling at the recently-opened New Pudsey parkway station, Leeds City (reverse) and Wakefield Westgate, the latter gaining direct trains to and from the West of England.(5)

NE-SW Route Future Development

Meanwhile, the future of the NE-SW route had been assured by Beeching's second report *The Development of the Major Railway Trunk Routes* published 16 February 1965. This conferred developmental status on the route via Sheffield, Derby and Birmingham, with the Great Central main line closed the following year, as previously noted. Spearheading future development would be the new 'NE-SW Committee', set-up in 1966 and headed by the Movements and Passenger Managers of the participating Regions. Based upon the long-standing successful East Coast Committee, it would undertake a similar role giving the NE-SW route a co-ordinated management focus for the first time to develop services, superseding the somewhat piecemeal approach which had prevailed until then; it was sorely needed too, in the face of mounting adverse publicity on the route's timekeeping. The committee was chaired by the Movements Manager of each Region for a two year term, the first incumbent being the Western's Henry Sanderson. One of its early tasks was to study the results of the North Eastern's market surveys which showed, amongst much other useful data, that the NE-SW route share of passenger journeys was only 7%. However, weekday passenger numbers were rising, and there were demands for service improvements. An early move was the spring 1966 addition of cheap weekend tickets to Bristol, Cheltenham and Gloucester. Clearly there was much traffic to go after, and this would shape the development of the route through the remainder of the 1960s and beyond – but that is another story!

Endnotes:

(1) A myriad of services is involved, and only the main developments are described; in the main, this covers weekday services and excludes the many additional 'dated' peak summer holiday trains.

(2) *British Railways North Eastern England Passenger Services*, 12 June to 10 September 1961.

(3) *British Railways Western Region and London Midland – Improved train services between South Wales/Bristol, Birmingham and the North*, from 10 September 1962 until further notice.

(4) *British Rail Western Region Timetable*, 14 June 1965 to 17 April 1966.

(5) *British Rail North Eastern Region Timetable*, 6 March to 3 September 1967.

Trans-Pennine

Six Trans-Pennine routes linked the North Eastern with the London Midland Region. The oldest was the Newcastle & Carlisle, which had improved services from the late-1950s through new Diesel Multiple-Units (DMUs), as did the Darlington/Bishop Auckland - Penrith 'Stainmore Route', although that closed in 1962 after sustaining heavy losses. Next south was Northallerton - Garsdale, axed for similar reasons in 1954. Moving to the West Riding, Leeds - Lancaster/Morecambe underwent some dieselisation in the 1960s. This leaves the two most important to be dealt with, in terms of traffic, and which accordingly received the greatest investment in modernised services – the 'Diggle' (ex-LNWR) and the 'Calder Valley' (ex-LYR) routes.

In the post-war period both retained their status as key express steam routes, with double-heading on the Diggle route due to heavy gradients westwards from Leeds where North Eastern Region locomotives (usually Pacifics) gave way to London Midland Class 5-7 motive power. Services ran from Newcastle/York to both Liverpool Lime Street and Liverpool Exchange, via the ex-LNWR and ex-LYR routes beyond Leeds, respectively. North Eastern Class B1 locomotives also worked through to Liverpool on certain Calder Valley workings. Some service improvements were made during the 1950s but significant enhancement had to await dieselisation.

Trans-Pennine DMUs

In a presentation at York on 23 November 1955, North Eastern DMU 'Supremo' Frank Hick announced plans for 'an inter-city service from Leeds to Manchester with very high-powered diesels'.(1) This was echoed by Lord Rusholme, Chairman of the London Midland Region Area Board during its monthly meeting, held on Merseyside, 6/7 June 1956.(2)(3) The LMR took the lead, out-shopping a two-car prototype DMU from Derby Works that September; converted from LMS BSO coaches Nos M9821/8M, each vehicle was powered by an underfloor Paxman 450 hp six-cylinder horizontal engine, coupled to a generator supplying traction motors on one bogie. Intended to form the traction package for the new Trans-Pennine DMUs, the somewhat ungainly looking prototype underwent exhaustive testing and high speed trials on the LMR and NER/ER, including York – King's Cross, as well as the Trans-Pennine routes. However, as a result of this experience, it was concluded by late-1957 that the unit was too heavy and expensive for production. Fortunately, BR Swindon's Inter-City DMUs had by now been deployed on the Scottish and Western Regions and provided a ready alternative, with further development, to meet the Trans-Pennine requirement.

In the final analysis, the new Hull - Leeds - Huddersfield - Manchester - Liverpool Inter-city express DMUs were sponsored by the North Eastern and would be operated jointly with the London Midland. Taking their place in the DMU investment queue, BTC approval for the 51 vehicles required – formed as eight 6-car 'Trans-Pennine' sets, plus three spare cars (later Class 124, see DMU delivery table) – was granted on 9 April 1959.(4) The North Eastern recognised the considerable traffic potential between the densely populated Trans-Pennine centres, to be targeted with a high quality DMU and improved, accelerated and enhanced frequency services. First Class seats would be sold to the highest possible level to generate maximum receipts.

Four of the six cars in each DMU were each equipped with two 230 hp Leyland Albion engines, giving an impressive 1,840 hp to tackle the Diggle route's gruelling gradients; the units otherwise retained mechanical transmission, 'Blue Square' coupling arrangements and the same 70 mph top speed as most of the other NE Region DMUs. With their BR Design Panel-influenced futuristic wrap-round fibreglass cab ends, these fine-looking DMUs carried excellent appointments for the job in hand: accommodation and amenities to main-line coach standards, in a mixed compartment/open layout – total seating of 292 (60 First Class, 232 Second); buffet car configured to rapidly serve 'cook-as-you-watch' hot 'Griddle' snacks (Aberdeen Angus steak in a toasted bread roll being a particular favourite); enhanced insulation standards; improved bogie suspension for a better ride; double-glazed windows in First Class and buffet car.

Plate 5.21. This hurriedly-taken photograph is not good quality, unfortunately, but is reproduced here because of its interest. Note that there are two Driving Motor Composites at the rear of this Class 124 Trans-Pennine express. The train is westbound from Leeds City station. (R Neate)

1961 timetable

Deliveries of the new DMUs commenced in July 1960 to their Neville Hill home depot, with the first complete 6-car set shown-off to the press at Leeds City on the 12th. Trials and driver training soon got underway but planned inception of the dieselised Trans-Pennine timetable on 7 November had to be abandoned as deliveries of the new units fell behind schedule. This was finally accomplished on 2 January 1961, when the new regular interval, accelerated services were introduced with great aplomb and typical high-profile North Eastern advertising and promotion. The main highlights were as follows:

* Hull - Liverpool. Five return services daily, with through journey times reduced by an average 45 minutes to a fastest $2^3/_4$ hours, the biggest saving being 67 minutes.
* Leeds - Manchester - Liverpool. Hourly service each way, with a best time of 68 minutes on the 'difficult' section between Leeds and Manchester – 15 minutes faster than under steam.
* Newcastle - Liverpool Lime Street. Hauled stock, worked by Gateshead and Edge Hill English Electric Type 4s (Class 40), integrated with the foregoing DMU-operated services. Four return trains replaced the previous steam-worked three. Journey time cuts of 25-83 minutes, with the best Newcastle - Liverpool Lime Street schedule down to 4 hours 4 minutes. Most ran via the Leeds Northern south of Northallerton, with some also routed via Wetherby to avoid reversal at Leeds City; only one now travelled via Sunderland and the Durham coast – the 9.45 am ex-Newcastle. The former Liverpool Exchange - Newcastle daily return 'L&Y express' was now cut-back to York.
* The above were supplemented by revised Leeds - Huddersfield - Manchester stopping DMUs, plus other re-arranged intermediate and connecting services.

Following North Eastern DMU received-wisdom, the new service proved a hit: in the first week passengers from Leeds soared by no less than 45% with 30% each for Huddersfield and Hull. Within months 100% growth was recorded and in the first year a gratifying 30% increase in revenue. However, not everyone was happy! Durham passengers protested at the reduced calls by Newcastle - Liverpool services in pursuit of acceleration. These were belatedly reinstated from the 10 September 1962 timetable change, concurrent with introduction on the route of Gateshead depot's new BR/Sulzer Type 4 Peak diesel-electrics (later Class 46), their 2,500 hp providing a welcome 25% boost compared with the 2000 hp Class 40s.

Calder Valley DMUs

The other main Trans-Pennine service to be dieselised was the complex ex-LYR Calder Valley grouping, for which twenty new 3-car DMUs (later Class 110) were acquired from the Birmingham Railway Carriage & Wagon Company. Due to the relatively frequent stopping nature of these services, the units were to the standard low-density design as per most of the North Eastern fleet, Inter-City units similar to the Class 124s

Plate 5.22. Having travelled via Ripon, Class A3 No 60036 'Colombo' negotiates Dragon Junction, Harrogate, with a Newcastle - Liverpool express circa 1951. The carriages forming the train were built by the LMSR, and are now painted in the BR livery irreverently described by enthusiasts as 'blood and custard'. (JW Armstrong / JW Armstrong Trust, per AR Thompson)

seen as not appropriate – meaning no buffet facilities either. However, the 110s were no sloths, their total 720 hp – provided by two Rolls-Royce 180 hp engines slung under each Driving Motor vehicle – delivering 8.3 hp/ton and outperforming the Class 124's 8.1 hp/ton. The units each seated 24 First and 159 Second Class; the centre trailer was carried on a new design of bogie developed by BR's Stooperdale research department in a further effort to improve riding characteristics. Interestingly, the first six were delivered to Darlington depot from June 1961 and run-in on local services – including, ironically, the threatened Stainmore line workings – before moving to the West Riding later that year. Again, operation was shared with the London Midland, which had their own fleet of ten 3-car Class 110s, based at Newton Heath depot and virtually identical (interior décor apart), delivered immediately after their North Eastern brethren, with which they inter-worked.

The Class 110-based, revised Calder Valley timetable was introduced on New Year's Day, 1962 – a year late, due again to delayed DMU deliveries – consisting of the following improved services:

* Leeds Central - Bradford Exchange - Halifax - Manchester Victoria - Liverpool Exchange. Hourly service to Manchester Victoria, thence two hourly to Liverpool Exchange.
* Harrogate - Manchester Victoria - Liverpool Exchange. Ten of the above services to Manchester Victoria started back at Harrogate, with several running through to Liverpool Exchange.
* York - Normanton - Wakefield Kirkgate - Manchester Victoria. (York - Manchester Victoria through services withdrawn 5 January 1970.)

Accelerations were more modest than on the Diggle route, with Leeds - Manchester typically 86 minutes (10 minutes faster than steam). The timetable finally abandoned the combination and division of Leeds and Bradford portions at Low Moor.

Motive Power Problems

Though the revised Diggle and Calder Valley Trans-Pennine services should have settled down with the modernised motive power, this regrettably proved far from the case, with patchy reliability dogging both throughout the North Eastern Region period. The Class 40s suffered intermittent break-downs, and were also often summoned to replace non-available Class 46s with consequent adverse affects on timekeeping. The Class 124s were not immune either, failures of their motor vehicles being not uncommon, requiring short-notice substitution by standard DMU vehicles; unfortunately, due to the mismatch of gangway inter-connections the latter's passengers were thus deprived access to the buffet car! Things were even worse for the Class 110s, flawed design of the saloon heater and exhausts causing overheating and fires; the worst occurred on (unlucky) Sunday, 13 January 1963, when the 7.31 pm York - Liverpool had just left Sowerby Bridge and entered the nearby tunnel by which time it was alight. Fortunately, the passengers were evacuated, but the damaged unit (E51821/37/59706) was dumped on Sowerby Bridge shed and condemned on 9 November that year. As a result of this serious incident, all Class 110s were temporarily withdrawn on 18 January 1963, with stock from other areas drafted in to help out until remedial action allowed the fleet to be reinstated a short time later.

Fortunately, there was an abundance of steam locomotives which could be called upon in such emergencies! This traction still worked a significant supporting cast of peak, summer holiday and other passenger duties, as well as most freight traffic. The key ex-LMSR steam shed at Farnley Junction clung on until closed 26 November 1966, its Jubilee 4-6-0s surviving nearly to the end, Trans-Pennine celebrity No 45581 *Bihar and Orissa* being the last to be withdrawn, in August that year.

Trans-Pennine Route Development

The inevitable process of eliminating unremunerative lines and stations gathered pace following publication of Beeching's 1963 *Reshaping* and 1965 *Trunk Route* reports, with the latter portending development of the Calder Valley as the route connecting Leeds and Manchester. In the event, both it and the Diggle routes were retained, albeit with intermediate station and connecting branch closures, and reduction of the quadruple sections on the Diggle route to two tracks.(5) Various alternative routes were also dispensed with during this period:

6 January 1964. Harrogate - Wetherby - Cross Gates.

7 September 1964. Leeds (Farnley Junction) - Mirfield (Spen Valley Junction) via Heckmondwike 'New Line'. Ceased to be used as a booked alternative for Trans-Pennine services to the original route via Dewsbury*, most now re-directed via the latter; on 2 August 1965 the New Line closed to all passenger services.

19 December 1966. Leeds - Farnley Junction 'Viaduct Line' closed as through route; Trans-Pennine services diverted via Whitehall Junction.

6 March 1967. Northallerton - Harrogate; all Newcastle - Liverpool services henceforth routed via York.

*Avoiding the congested route section between Thornhill (LNW Junction) and Mirfield (Heaton Lodge Junction).

In the years ahead, the planned new Trans-Pennine motorway would provide the main competition to rail, this eventually opening as the M62 in the early-1970s.

Endnotes:

(1) *British Railways Magazine : North Eastern Region*, January 1956.
(2) *The Railway Gazette*, 15 June 1956.
(3) *The Railway Gazette*, 22 June 1956.
(4) BR(NER) Area Board Minute GPC47 of 7 May 1959. [National Archives file AN117/4]
(5) First section to go was Marsden - Diggle on 31 October 1966, when the two single-line bores of the original Standedge Tunnel were closed.

Plate 5.23. 'Jubilee' No 45698 'Mars' at Chaloner's Whin on 30 August 1952 with the 5.15 pm York - Manchester express. (JW Hague / NERA GM Pierson Collection)

Plate 5.24. English Electric Type 4 No D244 at Darlington on 11 June 1960 with the 2.35 pm Newcastle - Leeds express. Note the platform refreshment trolley and platform number signs, the latter including '1S' denoting the south end of Up Platform No 1. (NW Skinner / JW Armstrong Trust, per AR Thompson)

Sleeper Services, including Car-Sleepers and Car-Carriers

Sleeper Services

With a journey time of 4-5 hours from the North-East to London, overnight travel by sleeper remained essential for one or both legs of a journey if a worthwhile day was to be had in the Capital. Demand accordingly justified several sleepers – weekdays in the summer 1949 timetable these consisted of five Anglo-Scottish trains and two between London and Newcastle, also providing a service for Durham coast line stations.(1) This number stayed fairly constant throughout the North Eastern Region period, with a new service introduced on the Newcastle - Bristol route in 1961 (see above: Cross-Country).

A major boost came with the advent of the new BR Mk 1 sleeping cars in 1957, ushered in as part of a revamp of East Coast Anglo-Scottish overnight services from that winter's (16 September) timetable. The new vehicles provided Second Class passengers with proper beds in twin-occupancy compartments rather than four-berths with just rugs and pillows that had previously prevailed. In fact, apart from single occupancy in First, the compartment facilities provided for both classes were virtually identical – a great step forward. Berth fares were increased accordingly to reflect the enhanced amenities. Over 150 of the new sleepers were delivered to the East Coast coach pool up to the last in 1963.(2) However, these did not completely displace LNER-design sleepers, which lingered on until the 1970s – some even received BR corporate grey/blue livery.

The other major development was acceleration of the overnight timetable from 1961 upon dieselisation, in concert with daytime services, Deltic power being assigned to key sleepers. However, schedules were eased-out again from 1964/5, with a top limit of 80 mph, assisting inter-working with nocturnal freight traffic – and also giving travellers a sounder night's sleep!

Car-Sleepers and Car-Carriers

An innovation introduced by the Eastern Region was the car-sleeper, enabling motorists to take their cars with them on dedicated overnight services, thereby cutting out the lengthy and tedious legs of their journey – and travelling in comfort. King's Cross - Perth *The Car-Sleeper Limited* was the first service, making its inaugural trip on 15 June 1955 and running for that summer. Very much experimental, it quickly proved a sell-out, leading to an immediate expansion of services the following year, the North Eastern doing particularly well with three brand-new workings:

* Newcastle/Stockton - Dover Marine (for Boulogne) *Continental Car-Sleeper* (13 June - 12 September 1956).
* Newcastle/Stockton - Exeter St Davids *West Country Car-Sleeper* (11 June - 10 September 1956).
* York - Inverness *Highlands Car-Sleeper* (17 June - 9 September 1956).

Again very popular, these continued in successive summers, although Stockton was soon replaced by calls at York and Sheffield Midland, respectively, in the first two trains. The Inverness train also called at Newcastle. The North Eastern enthusiastically embraced the car-sleeper, and developed traffic over the following years, growing demand, and expanding the days of operation each week – with some attractive and enticing publicity to match.(3)

Plate 5.25. The Eastern Region's Class A4 No 60003 'Andrew K. McCosh' passes Low Fell station (closed to passengers since 7 April 1952) with a northbound 'Anglo-Scottish Car-Carrier' circa 1962. (RG Warwick)

Daytime services began in 1960 with the new London - Newcastle - Edinburgh *Anglo-Scottish Car-Carrier*, complete with restaurant car, running between 30 May and 1 October. In response to demand, the older four-berth 'rug and pillow' Second Class sleepers were phased out in 1960-3, replaced by new Mk 1 twin-bed equivalents as used on other overnight services. New purpose-designed double-deck car-transporter vehicles were introduced in 1961, enabling a significant increase in capacity to meet continued traffic growth. The East Coast trains were hauled by prime Pacific power, usually A4s, but diesel power allowed significant acceleration of services from the summer 1962 timetable (18 June). From the same year the North Eastern accommodated the 'two-wheel' traveller, with provision for the conveyance of bicycles, mopeds, scooters and motor cycles on its car-sleepers. One of the more notable diesel rosters was the through working of a York Class 40 to/from Inverness.

To meet changed south coast ferry terminal arrangements, the Newcastle - Dover train instead served Newhaven Harbour with effect from 4 June 1964. For the 1965 season, commencing 2 June, it was diverted away from the Great Central main line to run via the Midland route, with Leeds City replacing the York stop. However, this proved to be its swansong as it was replaced in 1966 by the Stirling - Newhaven Harbour car-sleeper now serving Leeds City. The same year saw the Newcastle - Exeter St David's train extended to serve Newton Abbot instead, with the daytime London - Newcastle - Edinburgh car-carrier now running to Perth.

This period was marked by a major upsurge in demand for BR's car-carriers, with the new brand name 'Motorail' adopted from Spring 1966.(4) That year York gained its own Motorail terminal, opened Sunday, 17 July at the south end of the main station, replacing the loading dock at one of former terminus platforms used for the previous decade. Despite continuing good loadings throughout the 1960/70s, Motorail was eventually threatened by an ever-improving trunk road network, which speeded journeys, coupled with the growth of overnight budget 'travel lodge' hotels en route, thus that all car-carrying services (save for the Channel Tunnel 'shuttles') have now disappeared from Britain's railways, the last one – London Paddington - Penzance – withdrawn in September 2005.

Endnotes:
(1) *British Railways North Eastern Region Passenger Services*, 23 May to 25 September 1949.
(2) The new BR Mk 1 vehicles comprised three variants: Sleeper First (designation SLF); Sleeper Second (SLSTP); Sleeper Composite (SLC).
(3) *British Railways Magazine : North Eastern Region* regularly publicised the new facilities offered by the car-sleepers and car-carriers over the years.
(4) *Modern Railways*, April 1966.

Plate 5.26. English Electric prototype Type 4 locomotive DP2, on loan to BR, is seen here at Burnmouth on 1 June 1966 with the Up 'Anglo-Scottish Car-Carrier'. DP2 was built utilising the bodyshell of the Deltic Type 5 locomotives, but had only one engine instead of two (the 2700 hp 16CSVT). DP2 ran successfully on the London Midland, Eastern and North Eastern Regions until it was wrecked in a collision at Thirsk on 31 July 1967. (CJB Sanderson / JW Armstrong Trust, per AR Thompson)

Holidays, Excursions, Events and Special Traffics

The North Eastern Railway helped develop a string of seaside resorts stretching from Northumberland to the Humber. Traffic boomed from Victorian times onwards to the great pre-war peak in 1939. After the Second World War, to satisfy resurgent demand from the public eager for a return of the 'good times', and with continuing petrol rationing, the railway companies and then BR were keen to restore summer services towards pre-war levels as soon as possible. Such traffic was regarded as highly profitable; as previously mentioned, the LNER even provided a branch line to serve Butlin's new Filey holiday camp. However, planned wholesale reconstruction and enlargement of Scarborough station, which would have involved demolition of adjoining properties, fell foul of the severe economic climate and railway Nationalisation.

Major resumption of seasonal holiday services across BR took place progressively from summer 1949 onwards. Return services linking the North Eastern with destinations afar included: Darlington to Blackpool; Leeds/Bradford to Bournemouth/Poole; Leeds to Llandudno, Lowestoft/Yarmouth, Paignton; Newcastle to Blackpool, Heads of Ayr, Keswick, Llandudno, Lowestoft/Yarmouth, Newquay, Paignton, Penzance (the latter train starting out on Friday evenings); Saltburn to Blackpool, Glasgow, Manchester; South Shields to Blackpool; Sunderland to Lowestoft; Whitley Bay - Glasgow.

Alongside was indigenous holiday traffic to the Region's own resorts. Again, demand required high-intensity services during the summer. Main flows included: Teesside to Redcar, Saltburn and Whitby; West Riding to Bridlington and Scarborough.(1)

And then there were the many long-distance holiday trains into the North Eastern, particularly to the popular East Riding resorts. Typical Saturday return workings embraced:
* Bradford, Leeds, Rotherham to Bridlington.
* Bradford, Chesterfield, Derby, Edinburgh, Glasgow, Kings Norton, Leicester, London King's Cross (including *The Scarborough Flyer)*, Manchester, Sheffield and Swindon to Scarborough.

Filey was generally served by the Scarborough trains, whilst Filey Holiday Camp station – normally only open summer Saturdays – received workings from Kings Norton, Bradford, Leeds, Manchester, London King's Cross, Newcastle, Sheffield and York. Additionally, specials ran 'in rotation' from various towns in Lancashire and Yorkshire as each held their annual 'Wakes' (industry shut-down) weeks in turn. Supplementing the above were the many reliefs and day excursions, not to mention the regular, year-round passenger services. The vast amounts of rolling stock involved overflowed even the capacious carriage sidings at Bridlington and Scarborough, with outlying station sidings as far south as Driffield called into use for stabling.

Traffic Demand

The sheer demand necessitated the running of many relief and extra trains, especially on August Bank Holiday. Several hundred reliefs were also necessary at Christmas and the other Bank Holidays – typically, Easter 1962 saw the North Eastern put on no less than 517 such trains.

These were supplemented by numerous excursions, including for the many so-called 'stay-at-home' holidaymakers. Amongst these were seaside day trips and Blackpool/Morecambe illuminations' excursions. The innovative *Northern Venturer* touring train, which first ran on 26 July 1954 from Newcastle and Sunderland, visited various popular resorts daily during the peak holiday weeks, being successfully repeated in succeeding summers; the *Humber Rover*, *Pennine Rambler* and *Tees-side Nomad* excursion trains were later added. Also developed from the late-1950s were day (and longer) tours to a variety of continental destinations such as Paris, Brussels and Ostend, plus Holland for the bulb fields.

Camping Coaches, Cottages and Railway Hotels

As on the other Regions, the North Eastern deployed camping coaches widely. Pioneered by the LNER in the 1930s, they proved highly popular allowing economical holidays for hard-pressed families. After the Second World War, camping coaches were not revived nationally until summer 1952 when the North Eastern was supplied with 15 vehicles converted at York Carriage Works. Ultimately, coaches were provided at 11 sites (1961: Bolton Abbey, Cloughton, Goathland, Grosmont, Hornsea, Newbiggin-by-the-Sea, Ravenscar, Robin Hood's Bay, Ruswarp, Scalby and Stainton Dale). However, all North Eastern coaches were withdrawn at the end of the 1964 season as part of the Beeching economies – and as the lines which served them were mainly slated for closure in any case. Ended at the same time were the last 'camping cottages' of a one-time dozen in present/former station buildings, including such idyllic locations as Allendale, Castle Howard, Hayburn Wyke and Middleton-in-Teesdale. The British Transport Hotels on the Region (at Bradford, Hull, Leeds, Newcastle, Saltburn, West Hartlepool and York) were also popular, the Saltburn establishment usually fully booked during the season.

Sport and Excursions

Post-war saw a resurgence of excursion traffic by special trains for day trips, sports events, *etc.*, the railways securing a major foothold in this traffic long before significant road-coach competition. On the sporting front football and rugby were the main generators, with mass deployment of special trains required to convey the many fans to major fixtures; no fewer than 49 special trains carried 26,507 supporters from York to Sheffield and Sunderland to watch York City's two FA Cup semi-finals on 26 and 30 (replay) March 1955, respectively, whilst 40 extras were put on for the Rugby League Cup Final at Wembley on 14 May 1960 (Hull *v.* Wakefield Trinity). Lesser numbers were run for the more routine weekly matches around the country; sleeping cars were even occasionally included, for example on 22 February 1952 from Newcastle to Swansea for an FA Cup tie.(2) Another major draw was horse racing, Wetherby even having its own station, with the courses at Gosforth Park (race platforms at nearby Killingworth), Redcar (separate race platform) and York also highly popular; the *Tees-Tyne Pullman* set was provided for a Newcastle - Aintree luxury Grand National special on 25 March 1950. Bizarrely, the North Eastern Regions's only two new stations for sports traffic were both in Hull! Boothferry Park served Hull City football ground from 6 January 1951 whilst Hull Speedway stadium saw Hedon Halt opened on 14 August 1948 – although the latter appears to have been in use for just one season.

A full panoply of other events were also catered for. The Durham Miners' Gala, held annually on the second Saturday in July, saw a major operation of special trains swing into action to move thousands of attendees from the surrounding pit villages. Some served stations no longer open to passengers: Durham Elvet (closed 1931, used by trains from the Sunderland area); the Lanchester line (1939); Waterhouses Branch (1951).(3)

The annual cyclists 'Meets' at Barnard Castle and Richmond brought welcome extra traffic as the towns put on fairs and a full range of side-shows, musical entertainment, *etc*., with local services augmented and excursions from as far as Newcastle and Sunderland.

Also of note were the evening tours from Newcastle in the 1950s visiting the attractive, award-winning station gardens on the Tyne Valley and ex-NBR lines. A couple of these excursions ran each summer, a circular routing being followed – via Hexham, Reedsmouth, Scotsgap, Rothbury and Morpeth – up to 1956; closure of the Border Counties line later that year meant an 'out and back' itinerary via Morpeth thereafter.

Add to these regular excursions for ramblers, to admire scenic beauties (including photographers' specials along the North Riding coast lines), theatre and pantomime outings, plus trains to more distant events around the country, and the North Eastern could be seen to be fully committed to this traffic – in 1956 alone it operated over 2,450 excursion trains. A wide range of cheap day and excursion fares, together with holiday rover tickets, were also available for travel on normal services.

In 1960, the Region was still actively seeking and encouraging such leisure traffic, Passenger Assistant to the Commercial Officer Cliff Ayers describing the energetic efforts undertaken. Particularly targeted was so-called 'party travel' for clubs and organisations, plus school and educational outings.(4)

The Slow Decline

The late-1950s saw a post-war boom in holiday and excursion travel on BR, with the sunny summer of 1959 producing record traffics. However, rail was fighting a losing battle; by the following year 47% of holidaymakers travelled by car – up from 34% in 1955 – with rail's share 30%, declining further to 27% in 1961. The emergence of ever-cheaper continental package holidays was also eroding rail's market share.

Additionally, the railway was an unwitting author in its own downfall, as excursions increasingly used connecting road coaches to reach wider destinations, unhelpfully assisted by mounting line closures – soon, most of this trade would transfer completely to road, deserting rail altogether. Notwithstanding these effects, demand for rail remained buoyant on the Region, assisted by the generally lower car ownership in industrial Yorkshire and the North-East.

However, with the onset of the Beeching regime at the BTC the true economics of holiday and excursion traffic came under close scrutiny. North Eastern General Manager Freddie Margetts had already warned that bargain-basement excursions that 'do not make their proper contribution…cannot be expected to survive'.(5) Beeching's 1963 Reshaping Report revealed that the summer, holiday and other peaks in rail travel were continuing to diminish, but that a prodigious amount of rolling stock was needed to handle it, so much so that less than a third of BR's coaching stock – 5,500 of the total 18,500 – were in year-round use, with a staggering 13,000 vehicles largely unproductive, being idle for most of the time. However, this was not for free, requiring extensive siding accommodation for storage, plus maintenance, marshalling, empty stock workings, *etc*. Most of the coaches used for excursions were obsolete, and were often hauled by ancient and decrepit steam locomotives also held in reserve solely for such use; this was not a good advertisement for BR in the new motoring age! The economics of the associated train and engine working were also decidedly unfavourable – with often unproductive rosters and a high proportion of overtime (but good for locomotive crews on bonus pay!). The new DMUs did provide a smart new image and were often used on weekend excursions, but they could only carry a limited amount of the traffic. Steam continued right through to summer 1967 on some West Riding originating holiday trains.

Early rationalisation of holiday/excursion traffic facilities saw elimination of Wetherby Racecourse station (last used 18 May 1959) and Scarborough Londesborough Road station (last trains 24 August 1963; officially closed 4 July 1966), all services thereafter using the main station at both places. Closure of the Stainmore route meant re-routing of the Newcastle - Blackpool trains via Carlisle from 1962, and the Saltburn - Blackpool service last ran the following summer. The Pilmoor - Gilling - Malton section of the 'Ryedale lines' which had lost their regular passenger services still hosted Glasgow/Newcastle - Scarborough summer trains, albeit with an inconvenient double-reversal at Malton, the last running via this routeing on 8 September 1962. This was by accident, not design, as the Gilling line junction at Pilmoor was put out of use by a derailment on 19 March 1963 and never repaired, trains being routed via York from that summer.

Another facility progressively withdrawn was excursions from closed stations; the Ryedale lines again featured here, Gilling, Helmsley, Slingsby and intermediate stations last such use being on 27 July

1964 with a train to Scarborough; Scalby (closed 2 March 1953) was served by some summer trains until 1964 for the occupants of the camping coaches there; Bedlington and Spennymoor were other examples. As part of economies in the Durham Miners' Gala train operation, specials from closed stations on the Waterhouses Branch last ran for the 21 July 1962 event (Durham Elvet's last such use was on 18 July 1953); all trains from the following year originated from open stations only, with higher day return fares levied to offset the cost of the exercise.

Even heavy summer passenger flows could not save some lines, which were sparsely used the rest of the time: the Hornsea and Withernsea Branches, and Scarborough - Whitby all succumbed under Beeching.

Further rationalisation of holiday services and facilities would continue through the 1960s and beyond – this would include the Filey Holiday Camp Branch, closed in 1977 after just 30 years' use!

Endnotes:
(1) *The Railway Magazine*, October 1952 (*Handling the Teesside Holiday Crowds*, PWB Semmens).
(2) *Trains Illustrated*, April 1952.
(3) *Railway World*, April 1964.
(4) *The Railway Gazette*, 5 February 1960 (*Developing the rail travel habit in the North Eastern Region*).
(5) *The Railway Gazette*, 8 December 1961 (*Railway Development in the North East*).

Plate 5.27. Starbeck shed's J39 No 64942 runs through Spofforth with what is thought to be a Wetherby racecourse special. The tablet number '275' indicates that the train started its journey at Leeds City South. (JW Armstrong / JW Armstrong Trust, per AR Thompson)

Plate 5.28. BR Type 4 No D172 arrives at Scarborough past Londesborough Road station with an excursion on 15 July 1962. The locomotive, allocated to Gateshead MPD, was only a week or so old at this time. (NW Skinner / JW Armstrong Trust, per AR Thompson)

Plate 5.29. Darnall shed's brand new Brush Type 3 No D5693 brings an Eastern Region excursion into Scarborough on 20 May 1961. Note that the driver has reproduced the tablet number in the headcode box. (NW Skinner / JW Armstrong Trust, per AR Thompson)

Plate 5.30. It was a long-standing practice to use freight locomotives on weekend excursions. Tinsley MPD's English Electric Type 1 Nos D8055 and D8065 are seen here on Saturday, 13 June 1964 bringing an Eastern Region excursion into Scarborough. Note that the train is running under a four-digit reporting code (displayed via paper labels on the cab front window of the lead locomotive) instead of a tablet number. (NW Skinner / JW Armstrong Trust, per AR Thompson)

Early Line and Station Closures and Economies

The Second World War witnessed a revival in the fortunes of many secondary and branch lines, with increased traffic due the twin effects of petrol rationing and munitions flows. At the end of hostilities, the steady decline of traffic from pre-war days gradually resumed as road and bus competition re-emerged. The gloves really came off with the end of petrol rationing on 26 May 1950; henceforth, the railways would have a fight on their hands to retain traffic. The first North Eastern Region passenger withdrawal was Bedlington - Morpeth on 3 April 1950 (although the initial one in its area after Nationalisation was, perhaps ironically, that on the private Easingwold Railway on 29 November 1948). There were 30 or so service withdrawals in the remainder of the decade (see Table 5.3): amongst these were Hull - South Howden (the last section of the Hull & Barnsley Railway open to passengers), the Weardale and Wensleydale Branches, and the Middlesbrough - Whitby coastal route. However, many lines were retained for goods traffic. As well as embracing some Borders area ex-North British lines, the closure net widened considerably to include ex-LMSR ones in the West Riding as the Regional boundary expanded in the 1950s.

The 1959 Traffic Plan report recorded 186 station closures in the period 1950-8, but envisaged further drastic surgery: a map therein depicted abandonment of services by 1962 on most lines west of the ECML north of York (save for the Leeds Northern, Darlington - Crook and Newcastle - Carlisle), together with others in the Yorkshire Ridings – although some would be retained for freight. These proposals were kept under wraps at the time – no doubt due to the outcry they would have caused – not being revealed in a published report the following year on the 'streamlining' of the Region's railways by RW Hall of the Traffic Headquarters, York. This stated that withdrawals between 1950-9 had generated improved net annual revenues of £511,318. Elimination of sparsely-used wayside stations on retained routes also produced valuable savings; in 1958 alone, 21 stations on the ECML between Shaftholme Junction and the Border were closed.(1)

Various operational economies were made. In 1954/5, 'Conductor-guard' working – in which passengers purchased tickets on the train, with staffing of intermediate stations thereby reduced – was introduced on the Haltwhistle - Alston and Keighley - Oxenhope branches. Similar conversion of the Hull - Hornsea/Withernsea services on 4 January 1960 enabled 15 intermediate stations to be made unstaffed halts (although both branches still required a sizeable contingent of staff to attend to the many level crossings). Huddersfield - Penistone followed on 2 January 1961, joined on 14 August by Durham - Sunderland (Cox Green, Pallion and Penshaw partially de-staffed). These apart, and continuing occasional downgrading of rural stations to unstaffed halts (*e.g.* Great Ayton on 1 January 1962), Conductor-guard working was not deployed more widely until the late 1960s when DMU-operated lines were converted by the Eastern Region under its *Paytrain* branding. The latter was now possible following excision of goods and mail traffics at most of these stations.

Plate 5.31. An unidentified Class A8 departs Sandsend with a Whitby-bound train. The railway through Sandsend – the Saltburn & Whitby Branch – would close on 5 May 1958. (JW Armstrong / JW Armstrong Trust, per AR Thompson)

In 1955 the Alston Branch and its five stations were placed under the supervision of the stationmaster at Alston, and from 1962 the Riverside Branch, on Tyneside, came under the Walker stationmaster. Many lightly-loaded winter services were withdrawn and certain lesser-used stations closed on Sundays from the 11 September 1961 timetable, for example on Tyneside and in the West Riding. Similar cuts the following year (10 September 1962 timetable) saw closure of Leeds Central and Wakefield Westgate on winter Sundays from 11 November, traffic being re-routed to serve Leeds City and Wakefield Kirkgate, respectively.

The most significant closure in this period was the Stainmore route in 1962 (see Closure Case 1 below).

The Beeching Report

Though it had been trailed for months beforehand Beeching's 1963 Report *The Reshaping of British Railways*, published on 27 March, still shocked in the extent of closures it proposed. However, it is a common fallacy that mass rail closures began with the 'Beeching Report' (as it came to be known); whilst it recommended closure of some 5,000 route miles, 4,236 had already been closed between 1950 and 1962.(2) Beeching merely accelerated the process. For the North Eastern Region some 55 passenger service withdrawals were proposed (including two already under consideration), plus a further six to be modified, with 228 stations to be closed to passengers (including eight already tabled).(3) Main line stopping services were particularly unprofitable and slated for eradication, together with the stations served, as were unremunerative peak holiday and excursion trains. However, Beeching recommended the development of fast and frequent 'Inter-City' express services, which could profitably compete with air and road. Interestingly, ex-North Eastern Region General Manager FC Margetts, by now BRB member for Operations, had a major role in preparing the report, and endorsed his master's tough line at the unveiling press conference on 27 March 1963, stating: 'it means contraction. But it also means survival'.(4)

The first North Eastern Region Beeching withdrawal was Newcastle - Washington (9 September 1963), to be followed by many others in subsequent years (see Table 5.3); included were most of those foreseen in the 1959 Traffic Plan report. Astonishingly, closure proposals would completely isolate Whitby, with all rail services axed. Naturally, there was fierce opposition, and with a General Election looming the Ministry of Transport announced on 11 September 1964 the retention of the Esk Valley route to Middlesbrough. (That part of the Whitby - Malton line between Grosmont and Pickering was later saved by the preservationists and re-opened from 1973 as the highly-successful North Yorkshire Moors Railway.) Darlington - Bishop Auckland and the Riverside Branch were also reprieved on 11 September 1964, although the latter succumbed in 1973.(5)(6)

These closures bore-out North Eastern DMU-chief Frank Hick's warning back in the 1950s that this method of traction was not a panacea for rescuing loss-making services. Though the popularity of the DMUs increased receipts, this was not enough to significantly alter the fortunes of such lines – particularly when put under Beeching's financial scrutiny. The first DMU service axed was Middlesbrough - Loftus; the surprise withdrawal of most trains from 2 March 1959 after less than a year's DMU operation was not enough to stem losses and Guisborough - Loftus services followed on 2 May 1960, with Middlesbrough - Guisborough following under Beeching on 2 March 1964. Though the Darlington District DMU fleet had generated £245,206 operating savings plus £54,526 increased revenue annually by 1962, this impressive record was still insufficient to save loss-making lines in the area, and despite the success of the new trains passenger numbers on the Region were in decline. In 1957 receipts from the Darlington - Saltburn, Northallerton - Newcastle and Middlesbrough - Loftus services topped £1.4m; by 1964 passenger revenue for the whole of the Middlesbrough Division was just £1.5m!(7)

The dense network of bus services that had built-up since the 1920s, especially by United Automobile Services, offered a cheaper, more frequent alterative, as well as serving many more communities than the railway. BR even encouraged their use by including details in its timetables of destinations that could be reached by bus, together with through ticketing facilities and helpful contact information for the operators! Most railway stations remained un-modernised, dirty and dingy Victorian edifices, contrasting unfavourably with the swish new bus stations and their attractive facilities, that opened by United at Darlington in 1963 being a good example. These factors assisted in the rout of many urban stations which had little hope of competing with passing buses which directly served town and other centres.

Despite noises to the contrary, closures continued largely unabated after Labour returned to power in the 1964 General Election.(8) However, the new administration did take a more sympathetic view, with a number of proposals ultimately refused by the Minister of Transport – in the North Eastern Region this saved Leeds City/Bradford Forster Square - Ilkley (via Guiseley), York - Harrogate, Middlesbrough - Whitby (via Battersby) and Darlington - Bishop Auckland.

With passenger traffic in general decline for most of the period under consideration, few new stations were opened, but these did include New Pudsey, a 'Parkway' type station to lure the motorist onto rail – a North Eastern Region pioneering concept later adopted across BR. (See also Table 5.3.)

Rationalisation and the 'Basic Railway'

One of the key outcomes of the Beeching Report was the process of 'Rationalisation' – the elimination of costly infrastructure no longer required to meet modern traffic requirements: for example, reduction in running lines (including singling of branches), signalling, station facilities, *etc*. The main lines excepted, most routes remained Victorian time-warps – with manpower-intense operating practices to match.

Colour Plate 27.
In an apparently idyllic setting, this camping coach stands behind Ruswarp station. The photograph was taken on 4 May 1964, in the last season for the North Eastern Region's camping coaches. (JM Boyes / JW Armstrong Trust, per JR Midcalf)

Colour Plate 28.
This is the front cover of a 1950 brochure extolling the scenic virtues of Teesdale. Inside the rear cover is a map of the dale and the railways serving it, and on the outer rear are details of the diverse tickets – Cheap Day, Circular Tour etc. – of which travellers by rail can take advantage. (BR (NER) / DJ Williamson Collection) (Reproduced at 75% of original size.)

Colour Plate 29.
These folded-card timetables date from 1954 (yellow) and 1956 (pink). The rear of each promotes the new diesel multiple-units: 'HOURLY THROUGH SERVICE ON SUNDAYS by DIESEL CAR TRAINS' and 'INTERVAL SERVICE BY DIESEL CAR TRAINS' respectively. (BR (NER) / DJ Williamson Collection) (Reproduced at 75% of original size.)

109

Colour Plate 30. Class K1 No 62021 passes Hendon Junction signal box on 10 August 1966 with coal from Vane Tempest colliery bound for the staiths in Hudson Dock, Sunderland. The signalling arrangements here have been modernised by BR; the installation of Westinghouse theatre-type route indicators has allowed a significant reduction in the number of semaphore signals, particularly on the gantry. (JM Boyes / JW Armstrong Trust, per JR Midcalf)

Colour Plate 31. This mechanically-operated colour-light signal was installed at Eaglescliffe. The mechanical to electrical conversion takes place at the post with balance weights and rotary boxes in the right foreground. The view dates from 13 May 1966. (JM Boyes / JW Armstrong Trust, per JR Midcalf)

Colour Plate 32. Wilton Works was a private signal box, built on behalf of ICI, designed by BR, and operated and maintained by BR staff. Opened in 1954, it was based on the LNER Style 15 design boxes, as seen at Filey Holiday Camp and Harrogate (North), the latter still extant. Taken on the occasion of the SLS Brake Van Tour of 8 June 1963, this view clearly shows the characteristic overhanging roof and chamfered front corners.

On Christmas Eve, 1970, errant runaway wagons would derail in front of the box, demolishing it and killing the signalman on duty. (JM Boyes / JW Armstrong Trust, per JR Midcalf)

The North Eastern Region was an early proponent of rationalisation, notably the Modernisation Plan scheme to close Leeds Central and concentrate the city's rail services on a modernised Leeds City station, effected on 1 May 1967. With Dr Beeching in attendance, the 19/20 July 1962 Area Board even discussed proposals to dispense with Bradford Forster Square in favour of Exchange, ultimately not proceeded with.(9) The York - Market Weighton - Beverley Centralised Traffic Control (CTC) scheme, which would have slashed costs by automating the many manned level crossings, dispensing with most signal boxes and singling of the line, was halted for 're-assessment' in February 1962, regrettably never revived. CTC may well have saved the line, which eventually succumbed on 29 November 1965. (The 1959 Traffic Plan report additionally envisaged conversion of Knaresborough - York - Scarborough - Hull and the Hornsea/Withernsea branches, controlled from CTC panels at York and Hull.)

Ironically, it was only Beeching's wholesale elimination of slow-moving, unremunerative goods traffic, combined with simplification of timetables, which enabled much uneconomic infrastructure to be cut out. Early examples were the Alnmouth - Alnwick branch, singled on 14 February 1965, and reduction of Malton station to a single platform on 22 May 1966 with abolition of its island platform and curious 'trolley bridge' link. Bizarrely, closure of Ferryhill station (6 March 1967, postponed from 18 April 1966) was apparently justified by the savings that would thereby be realised by simplifying the complex track layout in the area, despite the station having a relatively healthy usage!

Cost-cutting rationalisation would be carried out much more vigorously in the years ahead under the 'Basic Railway' concept following the unveiling of Minister of Transport Barbara Castle's 'Network for Development' on 15 March 1967; this largely safeguarded the rail system as we know it today, with Government 'Grant Aid' support for unremunerative lines. Beeching's second report, *The Development of the Major Railway Trunk Routes*, published on 16 February 1965, was already being implemented, its implications already referred to above.

Case Studies
Closure Case 1 : Darlington - Penrith

A particularly contentious pre-Beeching closure. Whilst the introduction of DMUs in 1958 brought some increase in traffic, mainly during the summer months – in which the popular North-East - Blackpool holiday trains also ran – and there was still a modicum of freight, the line's glory days were well and truly over. By 1960, passenger services were running at an annual loss of £25,000 and freight was a fraction of that which had justified building the route a century earlier. BR proposed that the main remaining flows – limestone from Merrygill and Warcop to Teesside, and Durham coke to Furness – could easily be re-routed via Carlisle and Newcastle, which was instituted from 4 July 1960. Objectors marshalled a strong attack on the closure proposals, enjoying cross-party support from local MPs in a long drawn-out and often bitter fight. Allegations were made that the line had been deliberately run down through lack of promotion, inefficient train working, unattractive timetables, indulgence in unnecessary civil and signalling renewals, *etc*. But all to no avail – the line closed on 22 January 1962 and passengers needs thereafter were served by a daily return coach via the A66, augmented by other services in the summer to cater for holidaymakers.(10)

Closure Case 2 : Darlington - Richmond

The intermediate station of Catterick Bridge was the junction for the important Catterick Camp Military Railway serving the major Army base (renamed Catterick Garrison 1 January 1973). In the 1950s soldiers' weekend leave trains ran directly from Camp Centre station to Birmingham, King's Cross and

Plate 5.32. Winston was the passing place on the single line Darlington & Tebay Branch between Piercebridge (Up) and Broomielaw (Down). The Down DMU seen here in 1961 is bound for Penrith (displayed on the indicator blind). Note the new signal box steps, used also as a token exchange platform. (JW Armstrong / JW Armstrong Trust, per CJ Woolstenholmes)

Newcastle, supported by a Richmond - Glasgow Friday working, with many other troop specials and military freight traffic. Despite this healthy traffic, the Richmond Branch was tabled for closure in the 1963 Beeching Report. The first closure notice, posted 10 October 1963 to take effect 6 January 1964, was deferred after objections over alleged underestimation of revenue from camp traffic. The long distance trains already discontinued, the last Darlington - Camp Centre service (latterly DMUs) ran on 26 October 1964 – terminating thereafter at Catterick Bridge, which became the passenger railhead for the camp. A second notice (26 January 1968, effective 6 May 1968) failed due to inadequacy of the proposed replacement bus service. This rectified, on 11 December 1968 the Ministry of Transport finally consented to closure, which duly took place on 3 March 1969; the military railway and Catterick Bridge - Eryholme Junction remained open for freight until 9 February 1970. This must go down as one of the more crass and short-sighted closure decisions. The branch was said to be losing over £15,000 annually – but this overlooked the valuable income from military traffic, no less than £96,000 in 1963. Incredibly, the Ministry stipulated that the latter revenues were not to count towards those of the branch – surely a case of 'underhand accounting' if ever there was one! So the branch was lost – but the camp missed its rail link, so much so that the nearby Northallerton - Redmire branch was reopened on 4 April 1996 to enable trains of military vehicles to be transported to southern England.

Closure Case 3 : Haltwhistle - Alston

Closure of this unremunerative branch had been contemplated in the late 1950s. However, the North Eastern chose it for an experiment in which cheap day fares were abolished commensurate with the deployment of DMUs in 1959 – to test whether users were prepared to pay the full ordinary fares for the improved services thereby introduced. Unfortunately, passenger numbers dropped by 11%, although revenue jumped by 30%.(11) Regrettably, this was insufficient to avert closure, tabled on 26 January 1962 and later subsumed by the 1963 Beeching Report.(12) The line then notably became the first Ministerial refusal of a Beeching closure proposal; before this could go ahead, local roads had to be upgraded so that replacement buses could run. On 9 October 1966 the branch was converted to 'One Train Working' with all remaining signal boxes dispensed with and level crossings downgraded to 'open' status; intermediate stations had been de-staffed back in 1954/5, Alston following in 1969. The branch clung on, finally closing on 3 May 1976 with opening of a new 'all weather' road (subsequently blocked by snow!).

Endnotes:
(1) *The Railway Gazette*, 4 March 1960: *Streamlining the Railways in North Eastern England* by RW Hall, Head of Traffic Facilities Investigation Sub-section, Traffic Headquarters, York.
(2) White, HP. *Forgotten Railways*. David St John Thomas, 1986.
(3) Of these 228 station closure proposals, 171 (75%) were effected, with no less than 57 (25%) reprieved and still open; of those closed 18 have since reopened, two of these being on the Tyne & Wear Metro and five on preserved lines.
(4) *The Daily Express*, 28 March 1963.
(5) Darlington - Bishop Auckland was retained to cater for worker's traffic, especially to Newton Aycliffe 'New Town' industrial growth area.
(6) The Riverside Branch was reprieved because of the inadequacy of other transport to convey the large number of shipyard workers in the area. *Railway Magazine*, November 1964.
(7) BR (NER) Area Board Minute GPC456 of 15 February 1962 [National Archives file AN117/7].
(8) Labour Party General Election Manifesto: *The New Britain*. September 1964.
(9) BR (NER) Area Board Minute NE1652 of 19/20 July 1962 [National Archives file AN117/7].
(10) Central Transport Consultative Committee for Great Britain. Annual Report for the year ended 31 December 1961. HMSO, 1962 (pp.8,9).
(11) BR (NER) Area Board Minute NE1285 of 19 February 1960 [National Archives file AN117/5].
(12) BR(NER) Area Board Minute GPC391 of 20 July 1961 [National Archives file AN117/6].

Plate 5.33.
BR Standard 4MT No 76024 at Alston – the terminus of the branch from Haltwhistle – in June 1954. Note that the turntable has been removed by this date, so the locomotive will have to return tender-first. (IL Gray-Jones)

The End of the 'Tyneside Electrics'

The 'North Tyneside' (Newcastle - Tynemouth and Manors - Percy Main Riverside Branch) and 'South Tyneside' (Newcastle - South Shields) 3rd rail 630V DC electrified lines led a fairly uneventful life in the first few years after Nationalisation; their 42 route miles hosted the North Eastern Region's only electrified passenger services.(1) However, by the early-1950s the reconditioned ex-NER electric units employed on the South Shields line were life expired. Replacement stock in the form of 15 new 2-car Electric Multiple Units (EMUs) was accordingly ordered from Eastleigh Works. Similar to the Southern Region '1951 Stock' 2-EPB EMUs, they entered service from 10 February 1955, joined the following year by a solitary Motor Parcels Van (No E68000) of similar parentage. On the infrastructure side, modern replacement remote supervisory equipment at the Wallsend electric control room for the system was commissioned on 1 May 1956. The electrified lines seemed set for a secure future.

However, the arrival on Tyneside from the 1950s of new versatile, 'go anywhere' Diesel Multiple-Units (DMUs) were to spell the beginning of the end for the Tyneside Electrics. By this time, the electrified services were suffering drastic loss of traffic – on the South Shields line passengers drained away from 3.5m in 1956 to 2.5m in 1961 – due to intense road competition and relocation of population away from the railway. (The 1955 EMUs probably did not help, having cramped compartments which contrasted most unfavourably with the spacious open saloons of their NER predecessors, and proving very unpopular with passengers.) On the Riverside Branch, Byker closed 5 April 1954 with St Anthonys following on 12 September 1960, both stations suffering from the nearby bus services. First Class accommodation was abolished on the North Tyneside electrics from 4 May 1959.

Plates 5.34 and 5.35. Two views of electric trains working on the lines north of the Tyne. Right, departing Newcastle Central on 10 August 1953; below, at Cullercoats, 31 March 1962. The basic unit comprised an articulated twin-set, built by Metro-Cammell in 1937/8. Units were coupled to give the required length of train for the particular time of day.

The four lamps arranged in a square on the front of each car were used to display a route code. (RG Warwick).

Combined with poor off-peak traffic, rising electricity costs and looming further essential renewals of the electrified infrastructure/equipment and ageing LNER North Tyneside stock, the future looked increasingly bleak. By the early-1960s the North Eastern was seriously mulling over what to for the best to stem the losses. The issue came to a head in a high-profile way on 15 March 1962 when Dr Beeching, guest at a Newcastle business lunch, decreed 'off the cuff' that heavy losses on both the North and South Tyneside lines might mean their closure. Thus goaded into cost-cutting action, the North Eastern Area Board agreed at its 19 October 1962 meeting that the South Tyneside service would go DMU – implemented from the 7 January 1963 timetable change – with the North Tyneside lines to follow suit in due course; DMUs had already been trialled, with minimal extension of schedules (due to their lower acceleration compared with the electrics), and offered a ready economic alternative.(2)(3) The electric lines thus escaped inclusion in the 1963 Beeching closure list – save for the Riverside Branch (eventually closed 1973).

Experimental cut-price fares introduced 1 October 1962 on both the North and South Tyneside electrics off-peak weekdays and all day on Sundays (giving 25% reduction on existing cheap day returns) were withdrawn after less than a year after proving unsuccessful in encouraging significant additional custom.

Hopes of early conversion of the North Tyneside lines were dashed by lack of additional DMUs units to bolster the South Gosforth fleet, 7 September 1964 having been pencilled-in as an intended date. However, further economies were effected from the 9 September 1963 timetable whereupon off-peak workings were restricted to two cars only; this enabled a cull of the electric fleet, 15 twin-units being condemned in June 1964. In the event, the electrics were to eke out several more years service, suitable DMUs finally not becoming available until late-1966, initially Derby Class 116 DMUs from the Western Region, joined by ex-Scottish Region Gloucester RC&W Company Class 100 units from June 1967, with South Gosforth depot going 'all diesel' in the process. Changeover thus commenced from the 6 March 1967 timetable with the last electric service on 17 June, the 6.15 pm Newcastle Central return service via Wallsend and Tynemouth. (All electric stock was subsequently scrapped, save for NER 1904 Motor Parcels Van No 3267, happily preserved today.)

Interestingly, the decline of the electric services was matched in an almost identical timescale (1963-6) by the Newcastle Transport trolleybuses – due to similar factors of electrical infrastructure costs, inflexibility, ageing equipment, *etc.* – abolished in favour of a fleet of new generation Leyland *Atlantean* 'go-anywhere', more economical diesel omnibuses.

Back on rail, in a matter of just 13 years electric trains returned to North Tyneside with the opening of the first stage of the Tyne & Wear Metro light rail system – extended to the South Shields line in 1984 – proving that the NER had got it right 80 years previously!

Endnotes:
(1) Hoole, K. *The North Eastern Electrics*. Oakwood Press, 1987.
(2) BR(NER) Area Board Minute NE1698 of 19 October 1962 [National Archives file AN117/7].
(3) The 15 South Shields EMUs were transferred to their native Southern Region (and later designated Class 416/2), with MPV E68000 sent to Merseyside.

Plate 5.36. An Eastleigh-built two-car EMU waits at South Shields for the return to Newcastle Central in May 1959. (NERA T Smeaton Collection)

Fares, Marketing and Tickets

Passenger fares policy on the North Eastern Region broadly followed that on the rest of BR. However, the BTC delegated certain commercial freedoms to the Regions which allowed, for example, development of reduced price tickets; the North Eastern will always be remembered for its energetic promotion of cheap fares. The 'trick' was to generate extra revenue without significant loss (abstraction) of full-fares traffic; this was largely achieved, contributing significantly to the balance sheet. The North Eastern very much led the way, and was an early pioneer of what is now known as Yield Management through Selective Pricing. For example, reduced midweek returns introduced in 1953 were adopted nationally by BR from summer 1955. Cheap weekend returns were also made available. An increasing range of off peak cheap day fares were rolled-out during the 1950s, including on the new Diesel Multiple Unit (DMU) services from 1954 onwards. These were accompanied by vigorous local promotion and press advertisements, and significantly contributed to the revenue improvements generated by the new trains. In 1956 alone, the Region issued no less than 19,250,000 cheap day tickets.(1) However, their deployment on unremunerative rural/branch services usually failed to significantly boost revenues, assisting management's cause in 'proving' that such lines were unprofitable. The reductions of fares on the Hornsea and Withernsea Branches to levels similar to those on the parallel bus services from 9 July 1962 may be taken as examples; both branches were axed a couple of years later.

'Day-Line Diesel' Ticket

Another North Eastern innovation was the 'Day-Line Diesel' leisure ticket, introduced on 12 May 1958. Designed to promote the new DMU services (but also valid on steam and electric), and with particular appeal to the enthusiast market, it offered a day's unlimited off-peak travel, and was issued in an attractive folder, complete with souvenir medallion badge depicting a DMU. Available for two areas (Northern and Southern) these were a bargain at 15s (75p) each, proving highly popular and were offered for several years.(2)

Holding the 'Bottom Line'

Coupled with active promotion of holiday, tourist and excursion travel, these measures enabled the Region to hold its own against the ever-pervading road and air alternatives, with a gradual increase in traffic/revenue to a peak of some 54m passenger journeys in 1958. (The 1957 figure of 58m was discounted as it had been inflated due to the Suez fuel crisis and a provincial bus strike.) Thereafter, there was a slow but inexorable decline, not helped by the 1959 trade depression and pan-BR above-inflation rises in ordinary/season tickets, which for years had lagged well behind the retail price index, instituted from the late-1950s in an effort to counter BR's mounting deficits.(3)(4) A new 'Five-Day Ticket' introduced from 29 February 1960 on a number of short-distance journeys eased the fares burden for commuters, giving a return journey each day, Monday-Friday, but costing less than a Weekly Season ticket.

The Impact of the Market

The advent of the Beeching-era saw the introduction on BR of modern market research techniques to help shape future service improvements and, combined with powerful advertising, to retain and capture new traffics 'favourable to rail'. The North Eastern was in the vanguard of these developments, assisted by its progressive and modern commercial outlook. Back in 1959, for example, one minute adverts had been taken out on the new Tyne-Tees Independent TV channel for holiday travel by train.(5)

In April 1963 the North Eastern's Marketing Department was established, headed by Eric Jones.(6)(7) This soon got down to work, and in the following year a major survey of travel patterns at every booking point in the Region was undertaken – the most extensive yet on BR. Market research work in 1964/5 addressed East Coast and cross-country services.

Amongst other things, the results of these surveys revealed large scale public ignorance of the improving services under modernisation, and a widespread view that rail travel was too complex and expensive. There was a potentially large, untapped market of passengers, beyond the existing 'captive audience' – which, of course, had worryingly diminished since the 1950s – to be enticed from road to rail, particularly for 'random' and leisure journeys including 'visiting friends and relatives' (VFR) travel. It was concluded that future developments should encourage such a market to use rail by making the whole travel experience easier, through simpler train information, ticketing, *etc*. Also a high proportion of existing bookings were for a limited distance.

The North Eastern responded with a big cheap fares campaign in 1964 to drum-up new business, backed by some ingenious publicity, supermarket-style to emphasise the cost savings possible. This produced a welcome increase in revenue – much more than a simple recovery from the adverse effects of the 1963 industrial recession, and especially as summer holiday rail travel continued to fall. Importantly, this was not at the expense of full fares receipts, which also rose.(8)

London services were experimentally included in the cheap fares scheme. This produced an anomaly with the neighbouring Eastern Region, which believed that improved and faster services should be priced appropriately, not at 'bargain basement' rates, and thus did not provide similar facilities in the reverse direction from the Capital! Though this was partially resolved later with introduction of a limited range of cheaper fares from London to the North-East, the Eastern Region approach on pricing largely prevailed following the 1967 merger with the North Eastern.

The increasing dominance of market-led decision making caused some friction with the Operating Department who had traditionally been 'King' in designing the passenger timetable. However, understanding the market and its requirements increasingly proved to be a crucial input to timetabling, so that trains could be scheduled to attract the greatest number of passengers, supported by controlled availability of the various fares to obtain the best yields.(9) The North Eastern's pioneering work in market-driven selling of cheap fares to fill empty off peak seats and boost revenues can be seen in the employment of such methods on Britain's railways in the present day.

Ticketing

As on the rest of BR, at Nationalisation the Edmondson card-type ticket reigned largely supreme on the North Eastern. An AEG *Multiprinter* automated ticket machine (a type popular on other Regions) was experimentally trialled at Durham station booking office from January 1958.(10) However, large scale mechanisation of ticketing on the North Eastern did not take place until after merger with the Eastern Region. Remaining wayside ticket offices were closed with the large-scale de-staffing of stations from the late-1960s consequent upon introduction of Conductor-Guard *Paytrain* DMU operation. Principal booking offices went over to the ubiquitous National Cash Register NCR51 type ticket machines by the early-1970s. On lesser-used rural branches, stocks of LNER tickets lasted into the 1960s, or closure, with even NER ones surviving on some! The last NER ticket is believed to have been sold from Newton Kyme on 6 December 1963.(11)

Finally, just after its abolition, Newcastle and Leeds represented the former North Eastern amongst the select group of BR's first stations to accept the new *Barclaycard* credit card from 6 March 1967 – another pointer to the future.

Endnotes:

(1) *British Railways Magazine : North Eastern Region*, April 1957.
(2) *North Eastern Express*, February 2001 (No 161) (*All for fifteen bob!* by 'Enthusiast' – the late Ken Hoole).
(3) *The Railway Gazette*, 5 February 1960 (*Developing the rail travel habit in the North Eastern Region* by C Ayers, MBE, Passenger Assistant to Commercial Officer, York).
(4) *The Railway Gazette*, 16 December 1960 (*The future of the North Eastern Region* by F C Margetts, MBE, Assistant General Manager (Traffic)).
(5) BR(NER) Area Board Minute NE1098 of 16 January 1959 [National Archives file AN117/4].
(6) BR(NER) Area Board Minute GPC1/32 of 21 March 1963 [National Archives file AN117/8].
(7) BR(NER) Area Board Minute NE2/285 of 5/6 November 1964 [National Archives file AN117/9].
(8) BR(NER) Area Board Minute NE2/70 of 5/6 March 1964 [National Archives file AN117/9].
(9) Notes of interview with the late Norman Blackstock (formerly of the Marketing Department, BR(NER)) conducted by the late Patrick Howat, 30 April 2002.
(10) *British Railways Magazine : North Eastern Region*, February 1958.
(11) Foster, Colin et al. *North Eastern Record : Volume 1*. North Eastern Railway Association, 1988.

Plate 5.37. Class K1 No 62022 with the 11.10 am Newcastle - Hawick near Humshaugh on 13 October 1956, the last day of passenger services on the line. The wreath on the smokebox door is just visible. RG Warwick)

Conclusions

As in so many other areas of its jurisdiction, the North Eastern Region was highly progressive and innovative in the development of its passenger services – providing a lead which can be followed through to today's railway. Notable amongst these were:

* The widespread deployment of Diesel Multiple-Unit trains to provide enhanced, faster and more frequent services, whilst significantly reducing operating costs.
* The use of yield management techniques coupled with vigorous promotion to sell reduced price tickets, filling empty seats and successfully generating additional passengers and revenue without significantly harming full-fare traffic.
* The employment of market research techniques to identify passenger requirements and thereby design the timetable to attract the maximum usage.
* The first 'parkway' type station on BR (New Pudsey).

All of these initiatives helped the Region to retain traffic in an era of wholesale road competition. The relatively compact nature of the North Eastern compared with the other BR Regions no doubt assisted management in bringing these concepts to successful fruition in the relatively short time-span of just 19 years.

Table 5.1 : Principle Dates of the Introduction of DMU Services on BR (NER)

Introduced	Service
14 June 1954	Bradford Exchange - Leeds Central - Harrogate - Knaresborough
19 September 1955	Harrogate - Ripon
21 November 1955	Newcastle - Middlesbrough (Newcastle - Sunderland locals steam-worked until 18 August 1958)
1957	Sunderland - Durham
7 January 1957	Hull - Hornsea
7 January 1957	Hull - Withernsea
4 February 1957	Newcastle - Carlisle (including via Scotswood)
25 February 1957	Bradford Exchange - Dewsbury - Wakefield Westgate
25 February 1957	Leeds Central - Castleford Central
25 February 1957	Leeds Central - Wakefield Westgate
29 July 1957	Hull - Market Weighton - York (partial; some loco-hauled workings until closure of line)
19 August 1957	Darlington - Richmond
19 August 1957	Darlington - Saltburn
16 September 1957	Darlington - Crook
16 September 1957	Darlington - Middleton-in-Teesdale
16 September 1957	Bishop Auckland - Durham
16 September 1957	Selby - Goole
3 February 1958	Darlington - Penrith
3 March 1958	Bradford Exchange - Leeds Central - Wakefield Westgate - Hull via Wakefield Kirkgate, Pontefract Monkhill and Goole
3 March 1958	Leeds City - Barnsley Exchange via Wakefield Kirkgate
3 March 1958	Castleford Central - Pontefract Monkhill (extension of service from Leeds Central)
14 April 1958	Newcastle - Morpeth - Alnmouth - Alnwick (some branch-only services steam worked until 18 June 1966)
5 May 1958	Middlesbrough - Battersby - Whitby - Scarborough
5 May 1958	Middlesbrough - Guisborough - Loftus
9 June 1958	Monkseaton - Blyth - Newbiggin
18 August 1958	Sunderland - South Shields
18 August 1958	York - Harrogate
5 January 1959	Leeds - Bradford - Keighley - Ilkley - Skipton
5 January 1959	Sheffield Midland - York
6 April 1959	Malton - Whitby
27 September 1959	Haltwhistle - Alston
4 January 1960	Pontefract Monkhill - Pontefract Baghill (extension of some services from Leeds Central)
7 March 1960	York - Scarborough
19 April 1960	Leeds City - Sheffield via Wakefield and Barnsley (extension of Leeds City - Barnsley Exchange service)
13 June 1960	Keighley - Oxenhope
2 January 1961	Hull - Liverpool (*Trans-Pennine* services)
1 January 1962	York/Harrogate/Leeds - Bradford - Manchester - Liverpool (*Calder Valley* services)
7 January 1963	Newcastle - South Shields (replacement of electric services)
18 June 1967	North Tyneside (replacement of electric services)

NB. These are the dates when DMU services officially commenced; units were usually infiltrated into traffic on existing services in the period immediately preceding. (Despite extensive research, the full date for introduction of DMU services between Sunderland and Durham has not yet been established; only the year, 1957, is known thus far.)

Table 5.2 : Deliveries of New DMUs, BR (NER), 1954 - 1961

Date	Vehicle	Quantity	Numbers	Depot(s) to which delivered

BR Derby/Leyland 'Lightweight' : 8 power-twins, DMBS + DMCL (16 vehicles), Bradford - Leeds - Harrogate - Knaresborough.

Date	Vehicle	Quantity	Numbers	Depot
April - September 1954	DMBS	8	E79000-7	56G
April - September 1954	DMCL	8	E79500-7	56G

BR Derby/AEC 'Lightweight' : 5 quads, DMS + TBSL + TSL + DMC (20 vehicles), Newcastle - Middlesbrough.

Date	Vehicle	Quantity	Numbers	Depot
September 1955	DMS	5	E79150-4	52J
September 1955	TBSL	5	E79325-9	52J
September 1955	TSL	5	E79400-4	52J
September 1955	DMC	5	E79508-12	52J

BR Derby/AEC 'Lightweight' : 4 power-trailers, DMBS + DTCL (8 vehicles), Newcastle - Middlesbrough.

Date	Vehicle	Quantity	Numbers	Depot
March 1956	DMBS	4	E79137-40	52J
March 1956	DTCL	4	E79658-61	52J

Class 106 (Cravens/Leyland) : 14 power-trailers, DMBS + DTCL (28 vehicles), Hull Area.

Date	Vehicle	Quantity	Numbers	Depot
August 1956 - February 1957	DMBS	14	E50359-72	53C
August 1956 - February 1957	DTCL	14	E56114-27	53C

Class 101 (Metro-Cammell/AEC) : 7 quads, DMCL + TSL + TBSL + DMCL (28 vehicles), Tyneside (initially Newcastle - Carlisle).

Date	Vehicle	Quantity	Numbers	Depot
October - November 1956	DMCL	14	E50138-51	52J
October - November 1956	TSL	7	E59042-8	52J
October - November 1956	TBSL	7	E59049-55	52J

Class 101 (Metro-Cammell/AEC) : 6 power-twins, DMBS + DMCL (12 vehicles), West Riding.

Date	Vehicle	Quantity	Numbers	Depot
December 1956 - January 1957	DMBS	6	E50152-7	56G
December 1956 - January 1957	DMCL	6	E50158-63	56G

Class 101 (Metro-Cammell/AEC) : 4 power-twins, DMBS + DMCL (8 vehicles), West Riding.

Date	Vehicle	Quantity	Numbers	Depot
January 1957	DMBS	4	E50164-7	56G
January 1957	DMCL	4	E50168-71	56G

Class 101 (Metro-Cammell/AEC) : 13 quads, DMCL + TSL + TBSL + DMCL (52 vehicles), Darlington District (Darlington - Saltburn).

Date	Vehicle	Quantity	Numbers	Depot
January - April 1957	DMCL	26	E50172-97	51A
January - April 1957	TSL	13	E59060-72	51A
January - April 1957	TBSL	13	E59073-85	51A

Class 105 (Cravens/AEC) : 17 power-trailers, DMBS + DTCL (34 vehicles), Hull Area.

Date	Vehicle	Quantity	Numbers	Depot
February - July 1957	DMBS	17	E50373-89	53C
February - July 1957	DTCL	17	E56128-44	53C

Class 101 (Metro-Cammell/AEC) : 12 power-trailers, DMBS + DTCL (24 vehicles), Darlington District.

Date	Vehicle	Quantity	Numbers	Depot
April - May 1957	DMBS	12	E50198-209	51A
April - May 1957	DTCL	12	E56050-61	51A

Class 101 (Metro-Cammell/AEC) : 27 power-trailers, DMBS + DTCL (54 vehicles), Tyneside.

Date	Vehicle	Quantity	Numbers	Depot
May - September 1957	DMBS	27	E50210-33/46-8	52J
May - September 1957	DTCL	27	E56062-85/218-20	52J

Class 101 (Metro-Cammell/AEC) : 10 power-twins, DMBS + DMCL (20 vehicles), Darlington District.

Date	Vehicle	Quantity	Numbers	Depot
June - October 1957	DMBS	10	E50250-9	51A
June - October 1957	DMCL	10	E50260-9	51A

Class 101 (Metro-Cammell/AEC) : 6 quads, DMCL + TSL + TBSL + DMCL (24 vehicles), Tyneside.

Date	Vehicle	Quantity	Numbers	Depot
September - October 1957	DMCL	12	E50234-45	52J
September - October 1957	TSL	6	E59086-91	52J
September - October 1957	TBSL	6	E59092-7	52J

Class 111 (Metro-Cammell/Rolls-Royce) : 10 triples, DMCL + TSL + DMBS (30 vehicles), West Riding.
October 1957 - January 1958	DMCL	10	E50270-9	56G
October 1957 - January 1958	TSL	10	E59100-9	56G
October 1957 - January 1958	DMBS	10	E50280-9	56G

Class 101 (Metro-Cammell/AEC) : 3 triples, DMCL + TSL + DMBS (9 vehicles), West Riding/Darlington District.
November 1957	DMBS	3	E50290-2	56G/51A
November 1957	TSL	3	E59302-4	56G/51A
November 1957	DMCL	3	E50745-7	56G/51A

Class 101 (Metro-Cammell/AEC) : 2 quads, DMCL + TSL + TBSL + DMCL (8 vehicles), Darlington District.
November 1957	DMCL	4	E50748-51	51A
November 1957	TBSL	2	E59112/3	51A
November 1957	TSL	2	E59305/6	51A

Class 101 (Metro-Cammell/AEC) : 4 power-trailers, DMBS + DTCL (8 vehicles), Darlington District.
| December 1957 | DMBS | 4 | E50293-6 | 51A |
| December 1957 | DTCL | 4 | E56086-9 | 51A |

Class 104 (Birmingham RC&WC/Leyland) : 5 power-trailers, DMBS + DTCL (10 vehicles), West Riding.
| May 1958 | DMBS | 5 | E50594-8 | 56G |
| May 1958 | DTCL | 5 | E56185-9 | 56G |

Class 108 (BR Derby/Leyland) : 21 power-trailers, DMBS + DTCL (42 vehicles), Darlington District/Hull Area/West Riding.
| May - September 1958 | DMBS | 21 | E50599-619 | 51A/53C/56G |
| May - September 1958 | DTCL | 21 | E56190-210 | 51A/53C/56G |

Class 104 (Birmingham RC&WC/Leyland) : 21 quads, DMCL + TSL + TBSL + DMCL (84 vehicles), Darlington District/Hull Area/Tyneside.
June - December 1958	DMCL	42	E50542-83	51A/53B/53C/52J
June - December 1958	TSL	21	E59188-208	51A/53B/53C/52J
June - December 1958	TBSL	21	E59209-29	51A/53B/53C/52J

Class 101 (Metro-Cammell/AEC) : 20 power-trailers, DMBS + DTCL (40 vehicles), West Riding/Hull Area/Tyneside.
| July - October 1958 | DMBS | 20 | E51204-23 | 56G/53C/52J |
| July - October 1958 | DTCL | 20 | E56362-81 | 56G/53C/52J |

Class 108 (BR Derby/Leyland) : 5 triples, DMCL + TSL + DMBS (15 vehicles), Hull Area.
October - November 1958	DMBS	5	E50620-4	53B/53C
October - November 1958	TSL	5	E59386-90	53B/53C
October - November 1958	DMCL	5	E50642-6	53B/53C

Class 108 (BR Derby/Leyland) : 6 quads, DMCL + TSL + TBSL + DMCL (24 vehicles), Hull Area/Tyneside.
October 1958	DMCL	12	E50630-41	53C/52J
October 1958	TBSL	6	E59245-50	53C/52J
October 1958	TSL	6	E59380-5	53C/52J

Class 104 (Birmingham RC&WC/Leyland) : 5 quads, DMCL + TSL + TBSL + DMCL (20 vehicles), York/Hull Area/Tyneside.
December 1958 - March 1959	DMCL	10	E50584-93	50A/53B/52J
December 1958 - March 1959	TSL	5	E59230-4	50A/53B/52J
December 1958 - March 1959	TBSL	5	E59240-4	50A/53B/52J

**Class 102 (Metro-Cammell/Leyland) : 10 power-twins, DMBS + DMCL (20 vehicles), Darlington District/West Riding.
| February - May 1959 | DMBS | 10 | E51425-34 | 51A/56G |
| February - May 1959 | DMCL | 10 | E51495-504 | 51A/56G |

**Class 102 (Metro-Cammell/Leyland) : 10 quads, DMBS + TCL + TCL + DMCL (40 vehicles), Darlington District/Hull Area/Tyneside/West Riding.
February - May 1959	DMBS	10	E51435-44	51A/53B/56G/52J
February - May 1959	TCL	20	E59523-42	51A/53B/56G/52J
February - May 1959	DMCL	10	E51505-14	51A/53B/56G/52J

**These 60 vehicles were originally ordered as 20 triples but delivered as 10 power-twins and 10 quads (as shown).*

Class 105 (Cravens/AEC) : accident replacement (1 vehicle), Darlington District.

September 1959	DMBS	1	E50249	51A

Replacement for Metro-Cammell Class 101 DMCL E50173 written-off in an accident at Hexham on 1 July 1957, when it was run into by Class K1 No 62029 (hauling a coal train) around noon; E50173 was the rear vehicle of a four-car DMU which had just terminated at Hexham in the Down Main platform, but, fortunately, was empty at the time of the collision.

Class 111 (Metro-Cammell/Rolls-Royce) : 4 triples, DMCL + TSL + DMBS (12 vehicles), West Riding.

December 1959 - January 1960	DMBS	4	E51541-4	56G
December 1959	TSL	4	E59569-72	56G
December 1959 - January 1960	DMCL	4	E51551-4	56G

Class 111 (Metro-Cammell/Rolls-Royce) : 6 power-twins, DMBS + DMCL (12 vehicles), West Riding.

February - March 1960	DMBS	6	E51545-50	56G
February 1960	DMCL	6	E51555-60	56G

Class 111 (Metro-Cammell) : 6 trailer buffet vehicles.

May 1960	TSLRB	6	E59573-8	53B

Six Metro-Cammell Class 102 quads (DMBS + TCL + TCL + DMCL) delivered to Hull Botanic Gardens February 1959 - May 1959 (see above) were transferred to Leeds Neville Hill in early-1960. That summer the newly-delivered buffet vehicles were substituted for one of the intermediate trailers in each set (which thus became DMBS + TCL + TSLRB + DMCL) which were thence re-allocated to South Gosforth for use on the buffet-equipped services as described in the text. (The displaced TCL vehicles at Neville Hill were used to increase three other two-car sets to four cars.)

Class 124 (BR Swindon/Albion) 'Trans-Pennine' : 8 six-car units, DMC + MBSK + TSL + TFKRB + MBSK + DMC (48 vehicles plus 3 spares).

July 1960 - January 1961	DMC	17	E51951-67	55H
July 1960 - January 1961	MBSK	17	E51968-84	55H
July - December 1960	TSL	9	E59765-73	55H
July - December 1960	TFKRB	8	E59774-81	55H

Includes one spare DMC, MBSK and TSL for maintenance cover.

Class 110 (Birmingham RC&WC/Rolls-Royce) 'Calder Valley' : 20 triples, DMCL + TSL + DMBC (60 vehicles).

June - November 1961	DMBC	20	E51809-28	51A/56G
June - November 1961	TSL	20	E59693-712	51A/56G
June - November 1961	DMCL	20	E51829-48	51A/56G

The first six sets were delivered to Darlington pending completion (Summer 1961) of improvement work to their home depot of Bradford Hammerton Street, to which they were then subsequently transferred. 10 similar triple sets (M52066-75, M59808-17, M52076-85) were delivered to BR (LMR) November 1961 - January 1962, 26A Newton Heath, which shared the Calder Valley Trans-Pennine services with BR (NER).

Notes:

Delivery. Total number of DMUs delivered to BR (NER) : 293 units comprising 816 vehicles, plus three spares and one accident replacement. The units were delivered from the manufacturers in the formations shown. Not included are the many subsequent unit reformations and depot re-allocations to meet traffic and maintenance requirements which reflected the high degree of operating flexibility possible with the DMUs. Later transfers of DMUs from other BR Regions are excluded.

Class Numbers. For convenience and ease of identification, the BR TOPS class numbers are provided, although these were not introduced until 1973; however, the early 'Derby Lightweight' DMUs did not receive classification as they had all been withdrawn by this date.

Vehicle designations:

DMBC : Driving Motor Brake Composite	TBSL : Trailer Brake Second Lavatory
DMBS : Driving Motor Brake Second	TCL : Trailer Composite Lavatory
DMC : Driving Motor Composite	TFKRB : Trailer Buffet First Corridor Lavatory
DMCL : Driving Motor Composite Lavatory	TSL : Trailer Second Lavatory
DMS : Driving Motor Second	TSLRB : Trailer Second Buffet Lavatory
DTCL : Driving Trailer Composite Lavatory	

MBSK : Motor Brake Second Corridor Lavatory (non-driving)

Depot (shed) codes: See Motive Power Depot Paper.

TABLE 5.3

New Stations

Billingham-on-Tees	7 November 1966(1)
Boothferry Park	6 January 1951(2)
Hedon Halt	14 August 1948(3)
New Pudsey	6 March 1967(4)

Notes:
(1) Replaced old station about $3/4$ mile to the west; relocated to serve Billingham New Town.
(2) For Hull City Football Club ground; closed by 1986.
(3) For Hull Motor Cycle Speedway stadium; closed 23 October 1948 (only used for one season).
(4) 'Parkway' type station.

Passenger Services Withdrawn

The dates below refers to withdrawal of advertised passenger services. Included are cross-boundary services into the Eastern, London Midland and Scottish Regions. Excluded is any subsequent use (in whole or part) of the lines concerned by other services, seasonal, special and excursion traffic.

Bedlington - Morpeth	3 April 1950	Barnard Castle - Penrith	22 January 1962
Malton - Driffield	5 June 1950	Barnard Castle - Bishop Auckland	18 June 1962
Pickering - Seamer	5 June 1950	Newcastle - Washington	9 September 1963
Knaresborough - Pilmoor	25 September 1950	Church Fenton - Harrogate	6 January 1964
Garforth - Castleford	22 January 1951	Cross Gates - Wetherby - Harrogate	6 January 1964
Harrogate - Pateley Bridge	2 April 1951	Nunthorpe - Guisborough	2 March 1964
Saltburn - Brotton	10 September 1951	Bishop Auckland - Durham	4 May 1964
Wakefield Kirkgate - Edlington	10 September 1951	Durham - Sunderland	4 May 1964
Durham - Waterhouses	29 October 1951	Bramley - Laisterdyke (via Pudsey)	15 June 1964
Beeston - Batley (via Tingley)	29 October 1951	Selby - Goole	15 June 1964
Ferryhill - Spennymoor	31 March 1952	Tweedmouth - St Boswells	15 June 1964
Stockton - Ferryhill	31 March 1952	Bradford Exchange -	
West Hartlepool - Murton	9 June 1952	Wakefield Westgate (via Batley)	7 September 1964
West Hartlepool - Ferryhill	9 June 1952	Leeds City -	
Morpeth - Reedsmouth/Rothbury	15 September 1952	Sheffield Midland (via Chapeltown)	7 September 1964
Kirkby Stephen East - Tebay	1 December 1952	Hull - Hornsea	19 October 1964
Pittington - Sunderland	5 January 1953	Hull - Withernsea	19 October 1964
York - Pickering (via Helmsley)	2 February 1953	Leeds Central - Pontefract Baghill	
Etherley - Wearhead	29 June 1953	(via Castleford Central)	2 November 1964
Scotswood - Blackhill	1 February 1954	Backworth - Hartley - Newbiggin	2 November 1964
Northallerton - Hawes	26 April 1954	Monkseaton - Hartley	2 November 1964
Picton - Battersby	14 June 1954	Newsham - Blyth	2 November 1964
Billingham - Haverton Hill	14 June 1954	Darlington North Road -	
Birtley - Blackhill	23 May 1955	Middleton-in-Teesdale	30 November 1964
Bradford Exchange -		Bishop Auckland - Crook	8 March 1965
Halifax/Keighley (via Queensbury)	23 May 1955	Scarborough - Whitby	8 March 1965
Hull - South Howden	1 August 1955	Malton - Grosmont	8 March 1965
Crook - Tow Law	11 June 1956	Leeds City/Bradford Forster Square -	
Hexham - Riccarton Junction	15 October 1956	Skipton (local services)	22 March 1965
Bradford Forster Square -		Arthington - Skipton	22 March 1965
Harrogate (via Otley)	25 February 1957(1)	Selby - Driffield (via Market Weighton)	14 June 1965(2)
Whitby West Cliff - Loftus	5 May 1958	Sunderland - South Shields	14 June 1965
Hawes - Garsdale	16 March 1959	Bradford Exchange - Huddersfield	
Thirsk - Melmerby	14 September 1959	(via Mirfield and via Halifax)	14 June 1965
Brockholes - Holmfirth	2 November 1959	Leeds - Huddersfield (via	
Guisborough - Loftus	2 May 1960	Spen Valley 'Leeds New' line)	2 August 1965(3)
Halifax - Sheffield Midland		York - Beverley	29 November 1965(4)
(via Thornhill and Royston)	13 June 1960	Bradford Exchange -	
Heckmondwike - Thornhill	1 January 1962	Wakefield Westgate (via Gildersome)	4 July 1966
Keighley - Oxenhope	1 January 1962		

Independent Railway Passenger Services Withdrawn in the Area Encompassed by BR (NER)

Easingwold: Alne - Easingwold	29 November 1948
North Sunderland: Chathill - Seahouses	29 October 1951
Thorp Arch (Royal Ordnance Factory) 'Circular' Railway	15 August 1958(5)
Catterick Military Railway: Catterick Bridge - Catterick Camp	26 October 1964(6)

Notes:
(1) Excluding Arthington - Skipton services (these withdrawn 22 March 1965).
(2) Local services withdrawn and intermediate stations (except Market Weighton) closed 20 September 1954.
(3) Local services withdrawn and intermediate stations closed 5 October 1953.
(4) York - Hull trains superseded by through services via Selby.
(5) Private railway for workmen and women only; date is of last passenger train.
(6) Private railway for military personnel only; date is of last passenger train.

The North Eastern Region's Locomotives and their Maintenance
James Rogers
Locomotives of the North Eastern Region

At Nationalisation the North Eastern Region inherited 1744 steam locomotives and 13 electric locomotives from the London and North Eastern Railway.(1) The steam locomotives comprised 61 different classes, 33 of them unique to the Region. (See Appendix 6.1.) The electric locomotives comprised three different classes but only one, ES1, was active. The two locomotives forming this class worked the Quayside Branch in Newcastle. The other two classes, EE1 and EB1, were in store, most at South Gosforth.

New locomotives designed by the LNER continued to be delivered after Nationalisation. In 1942 Edward Thompson had introduced his B1 4-6-0. At the end of 1947, 56 out of 274 then in service were allocated to the North Eastern Area of the LNER. The first to be delivered to the North Eastern Region was No 1274, which was allocated to Darlington on 2 January 1948. Seventeen more followed, the last being 61339 on 8 September 1948.

On 13 May 1948 the Region received its first new L1 2-6-4T, No 67719, delivered to Hull Botanic Gardens. A further ten followed, the last being 67766 delivered to Darlington on 26 September 1948. Six of the locomotives delivered had Westinghouse air brakes, the others vacuum brakes. In 1949 it was decided to concentrate those with Westinghouse brakes at Stratford on the Eastern Region. As a result the North Eastern examples were transferred in exchange for vacuum-braked examples.

In 1946 Arthur H Peppercorn had succeeded Thompson as the LNER's Chief Mechanical Engineer, and the following year had produced his A2 Pacific. The first, No 525, was the only one delivered in LNER days. The second, 526 *Sugar Palm*, was delivered on 9 January 1948 and allocated to York. Of the fifteen built, eight were allocated to the Region when new. Four went to Gateshead, three more to York, and one to Heaton. In 1949, six A2 locomotives were transferred to the Scottish Region, leaving only 60526 *Sugar Palm* at York, 60538 *Velocity* at Gateshead, and 60539 *Bronzino* at Heaton. In return York received three A2/2 locomotives: 60501 *Cock o' the North*, 60502 *Earl Marischal*, 60503 *Lord President*.

On 3 September 1948 the Region received its first Peppercorn A1 4-6-2, No 60115. This was allocated to Gateshead, and on 27 September was used to haul the first up Tees-Tyne Pullman from Newcastle to King's Cross. Of the 49 A1 locomotives built, 22 were delivered new to the Region, the last being 60155 on 29 September 1949. Gateshead received twelve, York six, and Heaton four.

Plate 6.1. As a temporary expedient, from 1 January 1948 British Railways began to re-number its ex-LNER locomotives by adding a letter E prefix. Starbeck shed's D49/2 No E2773 'The South Durham' is seen here at York on 1 August 1949 so re-numbered. From March 1948, the prefix was dropped and 60,000 added to the LNER number. However, not all locomotives were re-numbered; some were scrapped without ever receiving their British Railways identity. (TJ Edgington)

Plate 6.2. Evolution of the LNER's Pacifics reached its peak in 1948 (i.e. after Nationalisation) with the introduction of AH Peppercorn's A1. The North Eastern Region's No 60126 'Sir Vincent Raven' is seen here southbound from York at the head of a Newcastle - King's Cross express on 30 June 1961. (RG Warwick)

The A1 locomotives were all allocated names, but it was some time before they all received their nameplates. Most nameplates were fixed without ceremony at the works or motive power depot, but seven locomotives, four on the Eastern and three on the North Eastern were the subject of naming ceremonies. On 3 August 1950, No 60126 was named *Sir Vincent Raven* by the Mayor of Darlington, Councillor Doughill, at a ceremony at Darlington North Road Works. On 30 October 1950, 60127 and 60142 were named *Wilson Worsdell* and *Edward Fletcher* respectively at a joint ceremony at Newcastle Central station. The Lord Mayor of Newcastle, Alderman Chapman, named 60142 and the Mayor of Gateshead, Alderman Tyrell, named 60127.

The last LNER-designed locomotive class delivered new to the Region was the K1 2-6-0. The first, No 62001, was delivered to Darlington on 30 May 1949. Of the 70 examples built, 40 were allocated to the Region, and were split between just two motive power depots : 30 at Darlington, and ten at Blaydon. The last to be delivered to the Region was 62065 on 23 January 1950.

Perhaps the most surprising new locomotives were 28 examples of the J72 0-6-0T, a North Eastern Railway design dating back to 1898. Although authorised in 1946 the first, No 69001, did not appear until October 1949. Twenty-four were allocated to the Region; the last delivered, 69028, went to Heaton in May 1951.

Nationalisation allowed locomotives of LMSR design to be allocated to the Region. The first of 36 new Ivatt 4MT 2-6-0 locomotives, No 43050, arrived in July 1950. Deliveries continued until November 1951, with 17 going to Hull Dairycoates, eleven to Darlington, five to Selby, two to Heaton, and one to Scarborough. These however were not the first ex-LMSR locomotives to be based at a North Eastern Region motive power depot. In the summer of 1948 two ex-LMSR 2MT 2-6-0 locomotives, 46418 and 46419, had arrived at Darlington motive power depot on loan from Newton Heath for trials on the Darlington - Kirkby Stephen - Penrith line. This line was currently worked by ageing ex-North Eastern Railway 0-6-0 locomotives. More modern locomotives were needed but weight restrictions on some of the line's viaducts restricted the locomotives that could be used. The two 2MT locomotives soon returned to Newton Heath, but from July 1951 the Region received its own allocation when 46470 was delivered new to West Auckland. By November twelve more had been delivered. When new they were spread over three motive power depots : five at Kirkby Stephen, four at Darlington, and four at West Auckland.

The first BR Standard locomotive delivered to the Region was a 4MT 2-6-0, No 76020, delivered new to Darlington in December 1952. In total, 13 locomotives of this class came new to the Region. A year later, in December 1953, the first of ten new Standard 2MT 2-6-0 locomotives arrived. The first nine, 78010 to 78018, went to West Auckland, while the last, 78019, went to Kirkby Stephen.

BR introduced its Standard 3MT 2-6-0 in February 1954. Twenty were built and divided equally between the Scottish and North Eastern Regions. The ten delivered new to the North Eastern between February and July 1954 were 77000 to 77004 and 77010 to 77014. All were allocated new to Darlington.

The Standard 3MT 2-6-2T locomotives were introduced in 1952. Nos 82020 and 82021 were allocated new to Hull Botanic Gardens in September and October 1954 but were immediately transferred to Nuneaton on the London Midland Region. The next batch intended for the North Eastern Region, 82022 to 82025, went instead to the Southern. The North Eastern eventually received four: 82026 and 82027 in November 1954, and 82028 and 82029 in December. The first two went to Kirkby Stephen and the second two to Darlington.

Three new Standard 4MT 2-6-4T locomotives, Nos 80031 to 80033, were to have been allocated to the Region in 1952, but went instead to the Southern in exchange for three ex-LMSR 2-6-4T Fairburn tanks. As a result the North Eastern did not receive its first Standard 4MT 2-6-4T, 80116, until May 1955. This was allocated to York. Four others, 80117 to 80120, were allocated to Whitby, and within a month had been joined by 80116.

In 1951/52 five O1 2-8-0 locomotives and five Q7 0-8-0 locomotives were fitted with Westinghouse air pumps to operate the doors on the new wagons due to be introduced to work the iron ore traffic between Tyne Dock and Consett. In June 1955, Standard 9F 2-10-0 No 92037 arrived on loan from the Eastern Region for trials on the iron ore trains prior to Tyne Dock receiving its own allocation. The seven 9F locomotives destined for Tyne Dock, 92060 to 92066, were built in late 1955, but were first loaned to the London Midland Region. It was not until June 1956 that all seven were working from Tyne Dock. In June and July 1956 they were joined by three more of the same class : 92097 to 92099. All were fitted with Westinghouse pumps to work the doors on the iron ore trains.

Between January and May 1957 twelve Standard 5MT 4-6-0 locomotives came new to the Region. The first two, Nos 73160 and 73161, were allocated to Blaydon, whilst the remaining ten, 73162 to 73171, went to York. No 73171 was the last new steam locomotive allocated to the North Eastern Region.

Two Standard classes came to the Region after use elsewhere. No 84009, a 2MT 2-6-2T, was allocated to Royston when that motive power depot came under the control of the North Eastern Region in 1957. In 1958, three 4-6-2 Britannia Class locomotives, 70044 *Earl Haigh*, 70053 *Moray Firth*, and 70054 *Dornoch Firth*, were received from the London Midland and the Scottish Regions in exchange for three of Holbeck's Royal Scot locomotives, 46103 *Royal Scots Fusilier*, 46108 *Seaforth Highlander*, and 46133 *The Green Howards*.

A proposal that the Region would receive 20 Clan Class Pacifics under the 1956 building programme was cancelled in favour of diesels when the Modernisation Plan was adopted.(2)

New Diesel Locomotives

The first diesel locomotive allocated to the Region was a new four-wheeled diesel-mechanical shunter built by FC Hibberd and Company and delivered in June 1950. It replaced Y11 No 15097, a petrol-driven 0-4-0 of 1922 vintage, at West Hartlepool sleeper depot. It was given the number 11104, which was a number in the sequence of running numbers allocated to ordinary shunters. The Hibberd was from the first a departmental locomotive, and was re-numbered 52 in the departmental series in May 1953.

The first diesel shunter allocated to the Region for other than departmental service was No 12113, a diesel-electric built by BR's Darlington Works to an LMSR/English Electric design (subsequently designated a member of TOPS Class 11). It was allocated to Hull Dairycoates on 9 July 1952. Between that date and 24 September 1952, the Region received a further nine shunters of the same class, all of which were allocated to Dairycoates.(3)

Plate 6.3 Colonel KMW Leather with the crew of V2 No 60964 on the occasion of its being named 'The Durham Light Infantry' on 29 April 1958. Both of the enginemen had served with the regiment, and are being presented with regimental badges as souvenirs of the day. The regiment's buglers are recognisable by the distinctive wings on their shoulders. (K Hoole / Ken Hoole Study Centre)

In March 1953 three new Drewry diesel-mechanical shunters, Nos 11105 to 11107 (Class 04) were allocated to West Hartlepool. Between then and 27 October 1961, 64 came new to the Region, the last being D2339 allocated to Heaton. In addition D2340 was taken into British Railways stock in March 1962 after being on loan to West Hartlepool since being built in 1956. Hartlepool also received three new North British diesel-hydraulic shunters, 11700 to 11702, between 13 July 1953 and 9 August 1954. On 12 November 1953 the Region received the first of what would become the Class 08 diesel-electric shunter. This was 13070, which was allocated to Hull Springhead. Deliveries continued until 2 April 1960 when the Region received its last, D3946 allocated to York. In total, 100 were delivered, and twelve motive power depots received them new.

The Region also received 92 new BR-built diesel-mechanical shunters (Class 03) between 29 November 1958 and 31 December 1960. The first, D2044, was allocated to North Blyth.

The final class of diesel shunter to be delivered to the Region was the Hunslet-built diesel-mechanical subsequently designated Class 05. The first, D2586, was delivered to Ardsley on 5 November 1959. Thirty-three came new to the Region. One delivered in January 1960, D2612, was immediately transferred to departmental stock at Faverdale wagon works and renumbered 88.

On 21 June 1958, English Electric Type 4 diesel-electric locomotive D201, based at Hornsey on the Eastern Region, worked the Down *The Flying Scotsman* between King's Cross and Newcastle, and the 5.05pm return. This was the first time a main line diesel-electric locomotive had been seen working a train on the North Eastern Region. The first regular diesel main line working to Tyneside commenced on 25 August 1958 when D207 worked the Down *The Talisman* and returned the same night with the Up *The Aberdonian*. D201 and D206 to D209, also based at Hornsey, became regular sights on the North Eastern Region, but the Region did not receive its first example of the class until 20 October 1959 when D237 was allocated new to Gateshead. Construction of the class, subsequently designated Class 40, continued until September 1962 when the last, D399, was delivered to Gateshead. Sixty-six of the 200 built came new to the Region, and went new to only three motive power depots: 31 to Gateshead, 31 to York, and four to Neville Hill.

The English Electric Type 4 locomotives were soon displaced on the more important main line passenger trains by the Deltics, and later by the Brush Type 4 locomotives. The English Electric Company had produced the prototype Deltic locomotive in 1955. After running trials on the London Midland Region it was transferred to the Eastern Region in 1959. In March of that year it ran trials on the North Eastern Region. It proved to be slightly out of gauge – for example, it had not to travel past Platform 9 at York, nor Platform 4 at Darlington, at a speed in excess of 10 mph. This resulted in the locomotive spending its time on the Eastern Region confined to the line between King's Cross and Doncaster. Nevertheless, the Eastern Region was so impressed that 22 were ordered, the design of the production models being altered to eliminate the gauging problems. The North Eastern Region received an allocation of six. The first, D9002, arrived on 9 March 1961, the last, D9017, on 10 November 1961. All six were allocated to Gateshead.

Although the Region did not receive any Sulzer Type 4 diesel-electric locomotives (Class 45) new, some were transferred from the London Midland Region shortly after their introduction in 1961. By June of that year eight, D11 to D18, were at Neville Hill, working Holbeck turns pending part of Holbeck shed being converted into a diesel depot. The last 56 built were fitted with Brush traction motors instead of Crompton Parkinson, and were later designated Class 46. Between May 1962 and January 1963, 28 of these were delivered new to the Region. Numbered D166 to D193, all were allocated to Gateshead.

In 1963 the prototype Type 4 diesel-electric locomotive *Lion*, built by the Birmingham Railway Carriage & Wagon Company the previous year, ran trials on the Region, hauling such trains as *The Yorkshire Pullman* between Leeds Central and King's Cross. British Railways however decided not to adopt the design, and instead 512 Brush Type 4 locomotives (Class 47) were built. Although the first, D1500, appeared in September 1962, it was not until March 1964 that the Region received its first example. This was D1570, allocated to Holbeck. In total 48 were received new, the last four being delivered after the merger with the Eastern Region. Twenty-two went to Gateshead, 22 to York, and four to Holbeck. The last locomotive delivered new to the North Eastern Region was Class 47 number D1107, allocated to York on 23 December 1966.

In 1958 the Durham Light Infantry celebrated its bi-centenary, and to mark the occasion Gateshead's V2 number No 60964 was named *The Durham Light Infantry* by Colonel KMW Leather at a ceremony at Durham station on 29 April. Unlike the Western and the London Midland Regions, the North Eastern chose not to name its diesel locomotives. An exception, however, was made with the Deltics, all of which were eventually named. The six allocated to the Region were named as follows :

D9002 *The King's Own Yorkshire Light Infantry* at York station on 4 April 1963.

D9005 *The Prince of Wales' Own Regiment of Yorkshire* at York station on 8 October 1963.

D9008 *The Green Howards* at Darlington station on 30 September 1963.

D9011 *The Royal Northumberland Fusiliers* at Newcastle Central station on 28 May 1963.

D9014 *The Duke of Wellington's Regiment* at Darlington station on 22 October 1963.

D9017 *The Durham Light Infantry* at Durham station on 29 October 1963.

Between April 1960 and May 1961 the Region received 22 new Sulzer Type 2 locomotives (Class 24). Numbered D5096 to D5113 and D5147 to D5150, all were allocated to Gateshead. Thirty-two Sulzer Type 2 locomotives (Class 25) were also delivered new to the Region between April 1961 and March 1963. These were numbered D5151 to D5182. Twenty-five went to Thornaby, four to Gateshead, and three to Holbeck.

1961 saw the arrival of the Region's first English Electric Type 3 locomotive (Class 37), D6730, allocated new to Hull Dairycoates in October. Between then and March 1963, 52 more were delivered new to the Region. Thornaby received 24, Hull Dairycoates 18, and Gateshead eleven.

Nine Birmingham Railway Carriage & Wagon Company Type 2 locomotives (Class 27) were delivered new to the Region between 17 January and 7 March 1962. These were numbered D5370 to D5378, and were allocated to Thornaby. By February 1966 all had left the Region.

Sixteen Clayton Type 1 locomotives (Class 17) were delivered between 20 March and 7 September 1964. Numbered D8588 to D8603, twelve went to Gateshead and four to Thornaby. They were not a successful design, and by July 1971 all had left the Region – some had even been withdrawn. Another short-lived class was the BR Type 1 diesel-hydraulic locomotive (Class 14). When new in 1964/5 all 56 were allocated to the Western Region, but in December 1966, 20 were transferred to Hull Dairycoates. Twelve more followed in 1967. All 32 were withdrawn in 1968.

The Decline of Steam

At Nationalisation some locomotive classes were on the verge of extinction, none more so than the Sentinel steam railcars. Only one, No 2136 *Hope*, survived to become British Railways property. It was withdrawn in February 1948 from Selby. Also withdrawn that month were the last two D17/4 4-4-0 locomotives, both from York. 1948 also saw the withdrawal of the last of the former North Eastern Railway Atlantics. The last two C6 locomotives went in March, and the last C7, 2970, was withdrawn from Hull Dairycoates in December.

In August 1950, after fifteen years in store, all the EB1 and EE1 1500 volt electric locomotives built by the North Eastern Railway were withdrawn, except 26510 which had been rebuilt by Sir Nigel Gresley in 1942 and transferred to the Eastern Region in 1949.

An early benefit of Nationalisation was seen in the autumn of 1948 when an ex-Lancashire and Yorkshire Railway 0-4-0ST, No 11217, arrived at Tweedmouth on loan from Burton on Trent. The loaned locomotive was required to work the North Sunderland Railway while Y7 No 68089, which normally worked the line, underwent repair at Darlington works.

Mention has already been made of the three ex-LMSR Fairburn 2-6-4T locomotives transferred from the Southern Region in place of new Standard 2-6-4T locomotives in 1952. In late 1954, four more, 42072, 42073, 42093 and 42094, were transferred from the Southern. In June 1955 four were at Gateshead and three at Darlington. Also in 1954, two Fowler 2-6-2T locomotives, 40059 and 40061, were transferred from Lees on the London Midland Region to Hull Botanic Gardens to work local push and pull trains. By June 1955, the North Eastern Region had eight, all allocated to Botanic Gardens. All were returned to the London Midland Region in late 1956 in exchange for eight J10 0-6-0 locomotives which were allocated to Darlington but almost immediately withdrawn.

The North Eastern Region acquired over 400 former LMSR locomotives when it took over the London Midland Region motive power depots in the West Riding in 1956/7. These ranged from Royal Scot and Jubilee 4-6-0 locomotives to ancient ex-Midland and ex-Lancashire & Yorkshire Railway tank and tender locomotives. The absorption of London Midland and Eastern Region motive power depots allowed ex-LMSR locomotives to be transferred more freely to former LNER sheds, and vice versa. For example, ex-LMSR 0-6-0T locomotives replaced former North Eastern Railway 0-6-0T locomotives at such sheds as Starbeck, Scarborough, and York. Locomotives of Class B1 went to Wakefield and Low Moor, and Mirfield acquired locomotives of Class B16.

In 1954 the first British Railways diesel multiple-unit (DMU) service began, between Bradford and Harrogate via Leeds Central. By the end of the decade DMUs had replaced the steam passenger services on most of the Region's branch lines, resulting in the withdrawal of those steam locomotives that had previously worked the services. A notable withdrawal from Neville Hill in October 1956 was of N13 0-6-2T number No 69114. This was the last Hull & Barnsley Railway locomotive. The 4-4-0 locomotives of Class D20 were rendered extinct in November 1957 when the last three, 62381, 62395 and 62396, were withdrawn from Alnmouth. In December 1958, the G5 0-4-4T, the mainstay of many a North Eastern branch passenger service since 1894, was rendered extinct. Less than two years later, in June 1960, the last A8 locomotives were withdrawn, rendering the former North Eastern Railway and LNER 4-6-2T locomotive classes extinct.

The Region's monopoly of the locomotives of Class D49/2, the *Hunts*, had been broken in January 1951 when No 62743 *The Cleveland* was transferred to the Scottish Region in connection with tests involving cast steel axleboxes for the coupled wheels. No 62744 *The Holderness* followed in March 1952. In return the Scottish Region transferred 62717 *Banffshire* and 62702 *Oxfordshire*. None of the locomotives returned to their original Regions. In November 1952 62768 *The Morpeth*, the unique D49 rebuilt as a two-cylinder locomotive in 1942, was withdrawn following a collision at Dragon Junction near Harrogate. Planned withdrawals commenced in 1957 and continued until January 1961 when the Region withdrew its last members of the class.

In May 1960, two locomotives of Class J72, Nos 68723 and 68736, which acted as station pilots at Newcastle and York respectively, were painted in North Eastern Railway green livery; both carried the NER and the BR crests. The two ES1 electric shunters were similarly painted, 26500 in 1961 and 26501 in 1962. Both, however, were withdrawn in 1964.

*Colour Plate 33.
North Road Works in 1965, still repairing steam locomotives. (JF Addyman)*

*Colour Plate 34.
Withdrawn locomotives of Class J27, including Nos 65811, 85855 and 65882 at Tyne Dock MPD on the Monday after the cessation of steam locomotion in the Division, September 1967. (MC Crawley)*

*Colour Plate 35.
York shed's diesel-electric shunter No D3235, complete with steam-era 50A shedplate, at work with a Taylor & Hubbard twin-jib track-laying crane in October 1962. (JF Addyman)*

Colour Plate 36.
Rail ends prior to thermite welding of a length of Continuous Welded Rail; the 4 inch piece of rail that has been cut off to allow for expansion can be seen below the gap. The white-painted steel bars are part of the tool used to stretch the rails to their optimum length before welding. (JM Wild)

Colour Plate 37.
Fitting hydraulic tensors prior to welding – a very necessary task, given the snow on the ground. (JM Wild)

Colour Plate 38.
Thermite welding in progress. Note the joints are staggered to allow both rails to be welded simultaneously. (JM Wild)

Colour Plate 39.
'STEAM FOREVER!' it says, chalked on to the motion of a withdrawn steam locomotive at Tyne Dock. This might have seemed a plaintive call in 1967. But strange things comes to pass; during 2008 / 2009, a brand new Class A1 was commissioned for service on the main line. (MC Crawley)

Plate 6.4. British Railways' initial replacement for ageing ex North Eastern Railway locomotive classes such as J21 was the LMSR-designed 2MT 2-6-0. Two such locomotives (one banking at the rear) are seen here negotiating Stainmore with a freight train. The BR Standard 2MT was based upon this design of locomotive; the North Eastern Region was allocated ten of them. (JW Armstrong / JW Armstrong Trust, per AR Thompson)

Plate 6.5. In turn, British Railways replaced such as the Standard 2MT with Type 1 diesel locomotives. The English Electric Type 1 (Class 20) was very reliable, and a fleet of them would have been a wonderful thing for railwaymen and for the accountants in the Treasury so worried about BR's accumulating deficit. So it was unfortunate to say the least that instead of standardising on the English Electric Type 1, the fleet was augmented from 1962 with Clayton Type 1 locomotives. These looked well enough, and unlike the English Electrics offered crews a good view both forwards and backwards from the centrally-located cab. However, the twin engines of the Clayton locomotives were particularly unreliable. The North Eastern Region was allocated 16 of the locomotives; no tears were shed when they were re-allocated elsewhere. An unidentified example, apparently running properly for the moment at least, is seen here at Penshaw North on 31 August 1964. (IS Carr / JW Armstrong Trust, per AR Thompson)

The introduction of new diesel shunters meant that the days of the steam shunter were also numbered. The older North Eastern Railway types also faced competition from the more modern ex-LMSR 0-6-0T shunters acquired upon the take over of the London Midland Region motive power depots. By March 1961, Classes J71, J73 and J77 were extinct. The specially-painted J72s served as station pilots at Newcastle until 20 September 1963 when they were replaced by 204 hp diesel shunters. The last two J72s, 69005 and 69023, survived in normal service until October 1964, then continuing in departmental use until final withdrawal in October 1967 and September 1966 respectively. The only 0-6-0T locomotives allocated to the Region after 1964 were those of Class J94. The last ten of these were withdrawn from Darlington in May 1965.

At Nationalisation only three of the Region's motive power depots, Gateshead, Heaton and York, had an allocation of Pacifics. In December 1948, two A3 locomotives were transferred from Gateshead to Darlington to act as standby locomotives in the event of a failure on the main line. The following year five locomotives of the same class were transferred from Gateshead to Neville Hill to work trains between Leeds and Newcastle. Both Copley Hill and Ardsley motive power depots had an allocation of Pacifics when transferred to the North Eastern Region in 1956.

From 1959 main line diesel locomotives began to displace the Pacifics. In November of that year the North Eastern Region withdrew its first Pacific, A2 *60503 Lord President*. *60501 Cock o' the North* followed in February 1960, and *60502 Earl Marischal* in July 1961. The withdrawal of the latter rendered the class extinct, the Eastern Region having withdrawn its own three members of the class in the meantime.

On 21 February 1960, two surplus A3 locomotives, 60038 *Firdaussi* and 60077 *The White Knight*, were transferred from Gateshead and Heaton respectively to Holbeck. By the end of the year Holbeck had an allocation of nine. They were used to work express passenger trains on the former Midland line from Leeds to Carlisle. They were too large for the roundhouses at Holbeck, and had to turn on the Whitehall triangle. They also had to go to Neville Hill for boiler washouts. The introduction of Class 45 diesel-electric locomotives made their reign at Holbeck a short one. In June and July 1961 all were transferred away, with the exception of 60038 *Firdaussi* which remained for another two years before being transferred to Neville Hill in June 1963.

By the end of the 1962 summer timetable the Region had sufficient diesel locomotives to start a mass withdrawal of steam locomotives. By the year's end Classes A2, A2/3 and Royal Scot had been rendered extinct in the Region. Five locomotives of Class A1 and five of A3 were also withdrawn.

1963 saw steam in full retreat. In June of that year steam was prohibited on the main line south of Peterborough, thus ending booked steam-hauled trains between King's Cross and the North. The same month the North Eastern Region withdrew its first A4 locomotive, 60018 *Sparrow Hawk*. The failure of the Scottish Region's North British Type 2 diesel-electric locomotives to live up to expectations saw four A4 locomotives, 60005 *Sir Charles Newton*, 60016 *Silver King*, 60019 *Bittern*, and 60023 *Golden Eagle*, transferred from Gateshead to St Margarets in the Scottish Region in October 1963. The three remaining A4 locomotives at Gateshead were withdrawn in 1964. The last to go was 60001 *Sir Ronald Matthews* in October. 1964 also saw the elimination of the A3 from the North Eastern Region. The last four, 60036 *Colombo*, 60045 *Lemberg*, 60051 *Blink Bonny*, and 60084 *Trigo*, being withdrawn in November.

At the start of 1965 the only Pacifics remaining on the Region were 24 locomotives of Class A1. By the year's end only two, 60124 *Kenilworth* and 60145 *St Mungo*, remained. On the last day of 1965, *St Mungo* worked a special return train from York to Newcastle to mark the end of steam on the East Coast Main Line. Both locomotives were withdrawn from Darlington in March 1966. *St Mungo* was, however, reinstated and re-allocated to York before being finally withdrawn in June 1966.

By 1965 only two classes of Standard locomotive remained on the Region: 3MT 2-6-0, and 9F 2-10-0. The number of locomotives of the latter class on the Region had increased from 1963 onwards with the transfer of redundant locomotives from the Western Region. The three Britannias at Holbeck had been transferred to Crewe North on the London Midland Region in August 1962. Also transferred to the London Midland, in December 1962, was the North Eastern's solitary 2MT 2-6-0T, No 84009. The four Standard 3MT 2-6-2T locomotives on the North Eastern Region, 82026 to 82029, were transferred to the Southern in September 1963.

In December 1962, six Standard 4MT 2-6-4T locomotives, 80071, 80073 to 80077, redundant on the Eastern Region, had been transferred to Ardsley. In October 1963 all were transferred to the Scottish Region, along with the North Eastern Region's original five, in exchange for eleven Fairburn tanks. The last nine Standard 4MT 2-6-0 locomotives on the North Eastern Region were also transferred to the Scottish Region the same month. The following year the last Standard 5MT 4-6-0 and 2MT 2-6-0 locomotives on the Region were transferred to the London Midland, in November and December respectively.

By April 1965 only 18 classes of steam locomotive remained on the Region. These were: Fairburn 2-6-4T; Fowler 2-6-4T; Stanier two-cylinder 2-6-4T; Ivatt 4MT 2-6-0; 4F 0-6-0; 5MT 4-6-0; Jubilee 4-6-0; 8F 2-8-0; A1 4-6-2; V2 2-6-2; B1 4-6-0; K1 2-6-0; Q6 0-8-0; J27 0-6-0; J94 0-6-0T; Standard 3MT 2-6-0; WD 2-8-0; Standard 9F 2-10-0.

Steam was rendered extinct in the former North Eastern Region in 1967. The last Standard locomotive classes, 3MT and 9F, were withdrawn in May. Steam came to an end in the north-east in September when the last J27 and Q6 locomotives were withdrawn. J27 No 65882 was the last North Eastern Railway locomotive, and the last pre-Grouping standard gauge locomotive, to remain in service in the entire country.

The same month the last Fairburn and Stanier tanks, Ivatt 4MT 2-6-0, B1 and WD locomotives on the Region were withdrawn. Also withdrawn was the last locomotive of Class J72, from departmental service. The last ex-LMSR 5MT locomotives, the Black 5s, followed in October, and the last Jubilee and 8F locomotives in November. The last steam locomotive on the former North Eastern Region was K1 number 62005, which was withdrawn on 30 December 1967.

Endnotes:

(1) The figure of 1744 steam locomotives is calculated from the shed allocations as listed in WB Yeadon's *LNER Locomotive Allocations. The Last Day 1947.*

(2) See Atkins, CP. *The 36 'Britannias' that never were. The Railway Magazine*, December 1996.

(3) The LMSR had built its examples of this diesel-electric shunter with a 350 hp engine. RA Riddles ordered that for BR the engine was to be up-rated to 400 hp. However, this proved to be too much, and an instruction was issued on 2 February 1954 that the engine be de-rated to 350 hp. De-rating was effected by adjusting the fuel injectors – maximum engine revolutions remained unchanged at 680 rpm.

Plate 6.6. When it came to hauling rakes of unfitted wagons, British Railways' new diesel locomotives suffered in comparison with the steam locomotives that they had replaced in the matter of weight. The diesels, being lighter, could not exert as much brake force. Between 1962 and 1964 therefore, a fleet of 122 Diesel Brake Tenders was constructed using materials recovered from scrapped coaching stock. The tenders, ballasted to an overall weight of 35^1/$_2$ tons (or in six instances, 37^1/$_2$ tons) were intended to be either towed or propelled in front of the train locomotive. By the end of the 1960s, towing was preferred, and this was made mandatory in the 1970 'General Appendix'. A 35^1/$_2$ ton Diesel Brake Tender is seen here being towed behind Type 2 No D5148 at Low Fell in 1962. (RG Warwick)

Appendix 6.1
Locomotive Classes Allocated to the North Eastern Region at Nationalisation

4-6-2 : A2/3, A3, A4.
4-6-2T : A5/2*, A6*, A7*, A8*.
4-6-0 : B1, B13* (counter-pressure service locomotive), B16*, B16/1*, B16/2*.
4-4-2 : C6*, C7*.
4-4-2T : C12.
4-4-0 : D17/2*, D20*, D20/2*, D32, D49/1, D49/2*,, D49/4*.
2-4-2T : F4.
0-4-4T : G5.
0-6-0 : J21, J24, J25*, J26*, J27*, J36, J39.
0-6-0T : J71*, J72, J73*, J77*, J94.

2-6-0 : K3.
0-6-2T : N8*, N9*, N10*, N12, N13*.
2-8-0 : O1, O4, O4/5, O4/8, O7 (later WD Class).
0-8-0 : Q1, Q5*, Q5/2*, Q6*, Q7*.
4-8-0T : T1*.
2-6-2 : V2.
2-6-2T : V1, V3.
0-4-0T : Y1, Y3, Y7*, Y8*.
Electric shunter : ES1*.

* Indicates class unique to the North Eastern Region.

131

Motive Power Depots

At Nationalisation the North Eastern Region had 1740 traffic locomotives allocated to 51 motive power depots.(1) In addition there were three locomotives stationed at North Road Works, and service locomotives at Faverdale Wagon Works, York Engineer's Yard, West Hartlepool sleeper depot and Geneva Permanent Way yard. The largest motive power depot in the Region was Hull Dairycoates but the depot with the largest allocation was York with 168 locomotives, although five were out-stationed at the former LMSR depot at Normanton. Five other motive power depots, Heaton, Gateshead, Newport, Darlington and Hull Dairycoates had allocations of over 100 locomotives. At the other end of the scale (not including Normanton), 18 depots had an allocation of less than 10 locomotives. These smaller depots were mainly sub-sheds situated on branch lines where for operational reasons it was more convenient to house the locomotive working the branch.

Years of under investment had left many motive power depots in a dilapidated state. At Scarborough the walls at the east end of the straight shed had to be shored up because of subsidence, and eventually half of the building had to be demolished. A new wall was provided on the south side of the remaining portion converting the shed into a four-road building with the four southerly roads remaining in place but open to the elements.

Thornaby

The motive power depot in the worst condition however was Middlesbrough where war-time bomb damage had caused one of the three roundhouses to be demolished and the locomotives stood around the turntable in the open. The depot also occupied a very cramped position. In 1953 it was decided to replace this depot, and the one at Newport, which stood in the way of the redevelopment of the vast Newport marshalling yard, with a new motive power depot to be built at Thornaby. The depot was to have two roundhouses, each with a 70 foot electrically-driven turntable. A third roundhouse was to have been added later if necessary. Part of the depot was set aside for the maintenance and servicing of diesel shunters. As it turned out only one roundhouse was built, and the depot so designed that it could easily be converted to service diesel locomotives. Externally the roundhouse was octagonal and had 22 stalls with two inlet/outlet roads. In addition Number 22 stall could be used as an outlet road if required. There was another electrically-driven 70 foot turntable in the depot's yard as well as a 350 ton coaling plant capable of coaling four locomotives simultaneously. As well as the roundhouse there was a double-ended straight shed with six roads. Under the same roof, but separated from it by a wall, was a repair shop with five roads, plus one giving access to wheel dropping facilities. Adjoining this building was a diesel maintenance shop for diesel shunters. On the north side of the depot were four covered preparation pits and four covered inspection pits. At the west end of the inspection pits were wet ash pits which could accommodate 16 locomotives. At the east end of the depot, the access tracks to the running shed and to the preparation pits was spanned by a gantry carrying water and sand mains. Water supply pipes, suspended from the gantry, could be controlled by locomotive firemen from the top of the locomotive tenders.

The new depot opened on 1 June 1958 and was coded 51L. The same day Middlesbrough and Newport motive power depots closed and their locomotives transferred to Thornaby. An official opening ceremony was held four days later on 5 June. It had been intended the Minister of Transport, Harold Watkinson, would perform the ceremony by driving a new diesel-electric loco, D5510, through a banner stretched across one of the depot's entrances. The Minister however was unable to leave London and so his Parliamentary Secretary came north by air. Unfortunately fog caused his plane to be diverted and he arrived too late.

Plate 6.7. Thornaby motive power depot in the early stages of construction, 28 November 1956. Overhead clearances were designed such that electric locomotives could be accommodated in the future if the proposed electrification of the East Coast Main Line and selected branches off it went ahead as planned. (BR (NER) / Ken Hoole Study Centre)

The ceremony was therefore performed by TH Summerson, chairman of the North Eastern Region Area Board. At this time the North Eastern Region had no main line diesel locomotives, D5510 was a 30A (Stratford) locomotive. It arrived on a special train but was not used to break the banner. It later worked the special to Saltburn where a VIP lunch was provided.

Thornaby was designed to handle up to 220 locomotives, 80 of which could be accommodated under cover.(2) At the depot's opening 151 steam locomotives were allocated there; 88 came from Newport and 63 from Middlesbrough. Thirteen diesel-electric shunters which worked in Newport yards, but had been allocated to Darlington pending the opening of the new depot, were transferred to Thornaby in the week after opening.

Re-Roofing

In 1952 the North Eastern Region began a programme of re-roofing its more dilapidated motive power depots. Those selected for re-roofing or partial re-roofing included Starbeck, Sunderland, Hull Springhead, Ardsley, Wakefield, Goole, and Sowerby Bridge. In many cases the work involved more than just replacing the old roof, or what was left of it. With the exception of the side walls and outbuildings, the entire shed was demolished. The side walls were increased in height and a new flat roof and smoke ducts provided. New roofs consisted partly of pre-cast concrete beams supported by brick walls and reinforced concrete columns. Longitudinal secondary pre-stressed beams of channel section placed in pairs carried the roof cladding, smoke ducts and walkway slabs, and also acted as rainwater gutters. When the time came to replace steam with diesel or electric traction the hopper portion of the smoke ducts could easily be replaced to leave natural ventilation, or some other form of extraction. Also a headroom of 18 feet from rail level to the undersides of the main beams allowed overhead electric catenary to be installed should it be required.

Plates 6.8 and 6.9. The completed Thornaby roundhouse. (BR (NER) / Ken Hoole Study Centre)

133

Plate 6.10. This view is of the repair shop at Thornaby. Beyond the wheel drop an unidentified locomotive of Class Q6 receives attention. The label on the 12 ton van on the right indicates that it has conveyed loco parts from Darlington North Road Works. (BR (NER) / Ken Hoole Study Centre)

Plate 6.11. The coaling plant at Thornaby motive power depot on 21 May 1958; workmen add the finishing touches. (BR (NER) / Ken Hoole Study Centre)

Plate 6.12. As bequeathed to the North Eastern Region, Hull Botanic Gardens comprised a large shed enclosing two turntables. Part re-newal of the roof was authorised in 1955. The work that was done can be seen here – note the new roof girders in the centre span of the remaining half of the shed. The other half has been demolished and the turntable removed. In their place, work is underway in the foreground on new straight servicing roads. See also Plate 5.14. (BR (NER) / Ken Hoole Study Centre Collection)

At some depots more substantial work was undertaken. At Bowes Bridge the shed, which had been roofless since a fire during the war, was rebuilt, whilst at York in 1957/8 two roundhouses were demolished and replaced by a straight shed. The remaining two roundhouses were re-roofed.

Diesel Multiple-Units

In 1954 the first British Railways diesel multiple-unit (DMU) service began between Bradford, Leeds, and Harrogate. The DMUs working this service were stabled at Bradford Hammerton Street, then in the Eastern Region but transferred to the North Eastern Region in June 1956. Hammerton Street continued to house steam locomotives, as well as the DMUs, until 12 January 1958 when its steam locomotives were transferred away, mainly to Low Moor. Thus Hammerton Street became the first motive power depot in the North Eastern Region to eliminate the steam locomotive. The depot consisted of a straight shed and, and because of its interior layout and proximity to Bradford Exchange station, was particularly suited for conversion to diesel maintenance. The track layout inside the depot required little modification and the special facilities required for servicing and maintaining diesels could be provided with a minimum of alteration and new construction. However, it was not until 1961 that the depot was fully converted to service and maintain DMUs and shunting locomotives. There were then 85 diesel cars and 19 diesel shunters, maintained there, with a further 60 diesel cars due to be delivered. Facilities for heavy maintenance and interior cleaning were set up within the main shed and a new servicing shed, fuelling siding and stabling sidings were the only external additions necessary. The offices, stores and staff amenities were extensively modernised. Three of the 11 roads in the main shed were partitioned off to provide a repair shop for heavy maintenance, fully equipped to undertake all stages of engine overhaul as well as engine replacement. Two of the roads were 260 feet and one 245 feet long. They had illuminated centre pits and could accommodate 12 diesel cars.

The remaining roads within the shed were equipped to clean the interiors of the coaches. Hot water mains to provide water for carriage cleaning purposes, and power points for battery charging and vacuum cleaning were installed. The former lifting shop, once used for heavy repairs of steam locomotives, was converted for maintenance of diesel shunting locomotives; it could also accommodate diesel railcar repair work when necessary. The new servicing shed was 80 feet in length, and had been erected over a track with a 190 feet long pit which was already in existence. The building was open at both ends to enable diesel railcars to progress through it for regular routine inspections, minor adjustments and repairs. The fuelling road to which the DMUs ran after leaving the servicing shed was equipped with five dispensing points each with a 20 gallon per minute fuel pump. There were also ten watering points alongside the road to refill overhead lavatory tanks and engine cooling systems, and there was concrete runaway troughing and drainage between the tracks to facilitate the cleaning of DMU toilets. A new carriage washing machine operated by push button control was provided.

Another steam depot converted to house diesels was Hull Botanic Gardens. This depot had been substantially rebuilt in 1956/7, but on 14 June 1959 it closed to steam. The remaining shed turntable was removed, and the depot converted to a straight shed to house DMUs.

At Darlington a completely new depot was built to provide maintenance and servicing facilities for the 130 diesel cars scheduled to operate in the Darlington and Teesside districts. It was situated north of Darlington station, adjacent to the main line on the Down side, and was connected to the steam depot on the opposite side of the main line by a footbridge. The new depot comprised a running shed with three through roads and a repair shop with two dead-end roads, all capable of holding a four-car set Both buildings had reinforced concrete frames carrying pre-stressed concrete main roof beams with patent glazing and brick apron walls.

Twenty-seven 12 inch diameter extractor fans ensured freedom from diesel fumes. Full length inspection pits to all the tracks in the running depot and repair shop were equipped with bulkhead lighting and panel heating, and were supplied with compressed air. The rails were carried on elevated beams, giving access beneath as well as to the sides of the vehicles. There were four fuelling points, two at the extreme north end of the depot yard so spaced that front and rear tanks of DMUs could be fuelled simultaneously, and two at the north entrance to the running depot. Fuel was supplied from four 7000 gallon storage tanks situated at ground level. There was also a carriage washing plant used not only by the DMUs but also by the remaining steam-hauled stock. A paved and drained area at the south end of the depot had five open roads equipped with water hydrants for exterior cleaning, whilst electric power points enabled car interiors to be vacuum-cleaned. Thirty-six cars could be cleaned simultaneously. There was also an accommodation block for approximately 130 staff. The depot was officially opened on 17 September 1957 by George RH Nugent MP, Parliamentary Secretary to the Minister of Transport and Civil Aviation.

Three years later, on 17 June 1960, Sir Linton Andrews, the editor of *The Yorkshire Post*, officially opened a new diesel depot at Leeds Neville Hill when he drove a DMU through a ribbon placed across the entrance. The completely new 290 feet long DMU running shed stood somewhat apart from the depot's other buildings and was open at both ends. It had three roads 12 feet apart. Each road could stand a four-car train for daily fuelling and servicing. Full length pits under each road, and a floor 15 inches below rail level, permitted easy access to the DMU's underfloor equipment. The new depot was equipped to service DMUs operating in the Leeds and York areas.

As well as a new running shed, a new DMU repair shop was provided. It too was 290 feet long, having five roads each 15 feet 3 inches apart, all equipped with full length centre and side inspection pits. It was only open at its west end, but total enclosure was possible if desired. The existing stores accommodation was extended and modernised to provide a combined store for steam and diesel parts. Amenities for the staff employed at the depot were centralised and were of a high modern standard in rebuilt accommodation. The track layout had been redesigned to keep the diesels separate from the steam side of the depot, but a central machine shop and stores was provided. Unfortunately, DMUs returning to service had to cross the main line to the Waterloo carriage shed and sidings for cleaning, until 1969, when a carriage washing plant was erected adjacent to the shed, and the old one abandoned.

The steam shed was also rebuilt. Two of the four roundhouses were demolished, and the remaining two rebuilt. Of the two rebuilt roundhouses, one had a 70 foot turntable, the other one of 55 feet. Seven of the roads and pits radiating from the longer turntable had been lengthened to accommodate larger locomotives.

At opening, Neville Hill diesel depot's allocation of DMUs numbered 121 cars, comprising 22 four-car sets and 3 triple and 12 twin units. (Not quite all had yet been delivered.)

An English Electric Type 4, D278, and a Sulzer Type 2, D5099, on loan from Gateshead for crew training, shared the one-time steam repair depot with an English Electric 350 hp shunter and the depot's four Drewry 204 hp locomotives. This shed, renamed the diesel shunting locomotive shop, was equipped with a 40 foot inspection pit, battery charging points, water hydrants, and an oil fuel supply, and had had its heating and lighting modernised.

In opening the diesel depot, Sir Linton said he was sure that 'in a few years we would think of these nippy diesel trains with just as much affection as the old steam engines'. TH Summerson replying, said 'the new section of the depot would make its contribution to bring BR right back into public esteem after their years in the wilderness. In a few years time if we are left reasonably alone BR will be generally recognised as being among the most efficient undertakings in the country.' (See also Appendix 6.2 on page 140.)

Holbeck

Another Leeds depot to be partly converted to maintain diesels was Holbeck, although in this case the diesels were locomotives not DMUs. In 1962 two machine shops in the steam shed were converted to diesel repair shops. Their high-pitched roofs, which had been in need of renewal, were replaced by new concrete and glazed roofs at a lower level. Machines in the shops were re-sited so three 200 feet long roads with pits could be laid on steel supports 2 feet 6 inches above floor level. Elevated concrete platforms on both sides of the roads gave access to the engines and other equipment at footplate level. A 7 ton overhead crane was installed, and a lean-to building erected outside to provide accommodation for battery charging, locomotive air filter cleaning, and re-oiling and cleaning of engine parts. Three 25,000 gallon capacity fuel storage tanks fed dispensers at a concreted and drained locomotive fuelling gantry under a canopy roof. The new shop, which was dead-ended, was entered from the south over newly-constructed approach lines. The two roundhouses of the steam shed were left untouched, and were demolished in 1970 after the end of steam.

Gateshead

Gateshead depot was rebuilt in 1956. Two of the roundhouses were re-roofed and the other two abandoned. A 70 foot turntable was provided in one of the re-roofed roundhouses allowing Pacifics to be housed in the main shed for the first time. Further improvements were made in 1961. A new building was provided housing modern offices, staff amenities, a machine shop and stores, as well as a central heating and water softening plant. While steam locomotives continued to occupy the main part of the shed, maintenance and repair facilities for diesel locomotives were provided in a temporary self-contained and screened-off enclave within the main shed. This enclave included two roads, one 230 feet long the other 160 feet, with room for five Type 4 locomotives, and platforms and pits to allow maintenance at three levels.

In 1964/5 further work was undertaken. The main aim was to separate work on diesels from that on the remaining steam locomotives and to provide separate facilities for daily inspection, servicing, and fuelling as distinct from maintenance. The turntables and radial pits were removed from the shed and replaced by five straight roads with pits, each approximately 160 feet long. Extensive alterations were made to the east gable of the shed to give access to these new roads. A new two-storey office building was also erected. A new inspection and servicing shed 800 feet long and 25 feet wide with one pitted road and canopied fuelling road was also provided. It was reached by a new connection from the Down main line at the west end of the depot. Fuel and water points were installed in openings in the south wall, and could be utilised either inside or outside the shed so that locomotives requiring only fuel or water could be dealt with on a road which bypassed the shed on the south side. To facilitate inspection and servicing the floor was set 15 inches below rail level, and a fixed platform was provided at footplate level.

Healey Mills

On 27 June 1966 the North Eastern Region opened a new diesel locomotive depot at Healey Mills. It was coded 56B at first and was the only depot opened by the Region not associated with a former steam shed. Built in conjunction with Healey Mills marshalling yard, which had opened in 1963, it consisted of a two-road double-ended servicing shed and a maintenance shed with three through-roads and one dead-ended. At the west end of the depot, an automatic washer was provided to wash the sides of locomotives. On opening the depot's allocation consisted mainly of English Electric Type 4 locomotives and 350 hp shunters transferred from York and from Bradford Hammerton Street respectively.

Depot Codes

In LNER days the motive power depot to which a locomotive was allocated was painted on the locomotive's bufferbeam, either in full or in an abbreviated form. In 1949 BR decided to adopt the LMSR practice of giving locomotive depots a code which was shown on a small oval plate fixed to the smokebox door. The codes given to depots in the North Eastern Region were as given in Table 6.1.

Table 6.1 : BR (NER) Depot Codes, 1949

50A	York	51A	Darlington	52A	Gateshead
	Normanton		Middleton in Teesdale		Bowes Bridge
50B	Neville Hill	51B	Newport	52B	Heaton
	Ilkley	51C	West Hartlepool	52C	Blaydon
50C	Selby	51D	Middlesbrough		Alston
50D	Starbeck		Guisborough		Hexham
	Pateley Bridge	51E	Stockton		Reedsmouth
50E	Scarborough	51F	West Auckland	52D	Tweedmouth
50F	Malton		Wearhead		Alnmouth
	Pickering	51G	Haverton Hill	52E	Percy Main
50G	Whitby	51H	Kirkby Stephen	52F	North Blyth
		51J	Northallerton		South Blyth
			Leyburn		Rothbury
		51K	Saltburn		
53A	Hull Dairycoates	54A	Sunderland		
53B	Hull Botanic Gardens		Durham		
53C	Hull Springhead	54B	Tyne Dock		
	Alexandra Dock		Pelton Level		
53D	Bridlington	54C	Borough Gardens		
53E	Cudworth	54D	Consett		

Plate 6.13. On shed at Darlington, 28 April 1962. Part – but only a rather small part – of the reliability problems that BR suffered with its diesel locomotives was due to their having to share shed accommodation with steam locomotives. (RG Warwick)

The smaller sub-sheds did not receive a code, and locomotives stationed there carried the code of the parent depot.

In 1956/7 two new districts, Leeds and Wakefield, were added to the North Eastern Region. These comprised depots formerly in the Eastern and the London Midland Regions. Their dates of transfer were :
17 June 1956: Ardsley; Copley Hill; Bradford Hammerton Street.
17 September 1956: Goole; Wakefield; Low Moor; Mirfield; Sowerby Bridge; Farnley Junction.
1 January 1957: Holbeck; Stourton; Royston; Normanton; Manningham; Huddersfield.
New codes were provided as shown in Table 6.2. (The former code is shown in brackets.)

Table 6.2 : BR (NER) Leeds and Wakefield District Depot Codes		
55A	Holbeck (20A)	
55B	Stourton (20B)	
55C	Farnley Junction (25G)	
55D	Royston (20C)	
55E	Normanton (20D)	
55F	Manningham (20E)	
55G	Huddersfield (25B)	
56A	Wakefield (25A)	
56B	Ardsley (37A)	
56C	Copley Hill (37B)	
56D	Mirfield (25B)	
56E	Sowerby Bridge (25E)	
56F	Low Moor (25F)	
56G	Bradford Hammerton Street (37C)	

In addition Goole (25C) was transferred from the London Midland Region to the Hull District and became 53E.

Shortly after Nationalisation, on 13 June 1948, the small sub-shed at Duns was transferred to the Scottish Region and became a sub-shed of Hawick, and consequently is not shown in the above. It also made sense after Nationalisation that the York locomotives sub-sheded at the former LMSR depot at Normanton be transferred there, but it was not until January 1952 that this was done.

Following regional boundary adjustments Kirkby Stephen motive power depot was transferred to the London Midland Region, on 1 February 1958, and was re-coded 12E. Also, from 15 September 1958, the Sunderland motive power district was incorporated into the Gateshead district, and its depots re-coded from the 54 series to the 52.

From 4 January 1960 the Hull motive power district was absorbed into the York district, and Neville Hill transferred from the York motive power district to the Leeds. Some depots were re-coded, the codes of some depots which had closed being reused. From 4 January 1960, the Region's depot codes were as shown in Table 6.3.

The introduction of diesel traction, along with the closure of lines and goods yards resulted in the closure of many depots, especially from 1963 onwards. Only 12 depots survived the extinction of the steam locomotive in the North Eastern Region in 1967 and continued to have an allocation of diesel locomotives. Depots in the Region were closed as follows, D indicates the depot continued to house diesel locomotives:
13 June 1948: Duns transferred to the Scottish Region.
1 April 1951: Pateley Bridge.
30 July 1951: Cudworth.
15 September 1952: Reedsmouth; Rothbury.
29 June 1953: Wearhead.
2 May 1954: Leyburn.
20 September 1954: Guisborough.
16 September 1957: Middleton in Teesdale.
12 January 1958: Bradford Hammerton Street (D).
26 January 1958: Saltburn.
1 February 1958: Kirkby Stephen transferred to LMR.
1 June 1958: Middlesbrough; Newport.
1 December 1958: Bridlington (last locomotives transferred away 8 June 1958).
8 December 1958: Durham.
15 December 1958: Hull Springhead (steam locomotives transferred away 30 November 1958; remained as a diesel servicing point until July 1961).
5 January 1959: Ilkley (became a sub-shed of Manningham in April 1954).

Table 6.3 : BR (NER) Depot Codes, 1960					
50A	York	51A	Darlington	52A	Gateshead
50B	Hull Dairycoates	51B	West Hartlepool	52B	Heaton
50C	Hull Botanic Gardens	51F	West Auckland	52C	Blaydon
50D	Goole	51J	Northallerton	52D	Tweedmouth
50E	Scarborough	51L	Thornaby		Alnmouth
50F	Malton			52E	Percy Main
				52F	North and South Blyth
				52G	Sunderland
				52H	Tyne Dock
					Pelton Level
				52J	South Gosforth
55A	Holbeck	56A	Wakefield	52K	Consett
55B	Stourton	56B	Ardsley		
55C	Farnley Junction	56C	Copley Hill		
55D	Royston	56D	Mirfield		
55E	Normanton	56E	Sowerby Bridge		
55F	Manningham	56F	Low Moor		
	Keighley	56G	Bradford Hammerton Street		
55G	Huddersfield				
55H	Neville Hill				

6 April 1959: Hexham (last locomotive transferred away 25 January 1959); Pickering; Whitby.
13 June 1959: Borough Gardens; Haverton Hill.
14 June 1959: Hull Botanic Gardens (converted to house DMUs); Stockton.
13 September 1959: Selby; Starbeck.
27 September 1959: Alston.
18 June 1962: Keighley.
10 September 1962: Bowes Bridge.
March 1963: Blaydon (became a sub-shed of Gateshead; steam locomotives transferred away on 16 June 1963, and closed completely on 15 March 1965).
3 March 1963: Northallerton.
15 April 1963: Malton.
20 May 1963: Scarborough.
16 June 1963: Heaton (became a sub-shed of Gateshead until closed to steam 29 August 1964).
27 October 1963: Hull Alexandra Dock.
November 1963: Pelton Level.
11 January 1964: Sowerby Bridge.
1 February 1964: West Auckland.
9 September 1964: Copley Hill.
13 December 1964: Thornaby (D).
28 February 1965: Percy Main (D).
20 March 1965: Gateshead (D).
24 May 1965: Consett.
31 October 1965: Ardsley.
27 February 1966: Percy Main.
27 March 1966: Darlington (D).
12 June 1966: Neville Hill (D).
19 June 1966: Alnmouth; Tweedmouth (D).
2 January 1967: Huddersfield; Mirfield.
15 January 1967: Stourton (D, became a sub-depot of Holbeck August 1967).
29 April 1967: Manningham.
28 May 1967: South Blyth.
3 June 1967: Wakefield.

6 June 1967: York (D).
25 June 1967: Hull Dairycoates (D); Goole (D).
9 September 1967: Sunderland; Tyne Dock; North Blyth; West Hartlepool.
30 September 1967: Normanton.
2 October 1967: Low Moor.
4 November 1967: Royston (D).
26 November 1967: Farnley Junction.
1 December 1967: Holbeck (D).

Depots which survived the elimination of the steam locomotive in 1967 and continued to have an allocation of diesel locomotives: 50A York; 50B Hull Dairycoates; 50C Goole; 51A Darlington; 51L Thornaby; 52A Gateshead; 52D Tweedmouth; 55A Holbeck; 55D Royston; 55H Neville Hill; 56G Bradford Hammerton Street; HM Healey Mills. In addition, a new diesel depot was opened at Knottingley on 6 March 1967.

Endnotes:

(1) The figure of 1740 traffic locomotives is calculated from the shed allocations as listed in WB Yeadon's *LNER Locomotive Allocations. The Last Day 1947*.

(2) The figure of 220 locomotives at Thornaby MPD comes from *Trains Illustrated*, November 1958.

Plate 6.14. 6 September 1966, and work is underway on the construction of a new motive power depot, specifically for diesel locomotives, at Knottingley. When opened in 1967 the depot will provide locomotives, initially of Brush Type 4 (Class 47), and crews primarily for the working of Merry-Go-Round coal trains to Thorpe Marsh, Ferrybridge, Eggborough and Drax power stations. (E Sanderson / RA Smith Collection)

Appendix 6.2
DMU Servicing Depots

Apart from the West Riding, the scheme for the allocation and maintenance of the DMUs required one major depot in each Traffic Manager's area plus supporting locations, as follows:

Teesside

Darlington. Estimated cost: £341,000. Approved by the BTC on 15 March 1956. Located on the west side of the East Coast Main Line opposite the existing engine shed, to which it was linked by a new metal footbridge. Construction began 1956, the depot coming into use into use August 1957, with a formal opening ceremony on 17 September 1957.

Middlesbrough station carriage sidings. Fuelling, light maintenance and stabling facilities. Estimated cost: £12,409, approved by the North Eastern Area Board on 22 June 1956.

Tyneside / Wearside

South Gosforth. Estimated cost: £73,522. Approved by the North Eastern Area Board 21 October and the BTC on 24 November 1955. Work began in 1956 to extend and equip the existing electric car sheds to handle a planned 134 DMU vehicles. This consisted of four additional servicing roads on the south side of the shed – these actually to hold the EMUs displaced outside by the new DMUs, which had to be stabled under cover – plus requisite cleaning/refuelling facilities. In late 1960 a state-of-the-art, German-manufactured carriage washer was installed, a similar one being provided at nearby Heaton depot.

Blaydon. Fuelling and light maintenance facilities. Estimated cost: £19,553. Approved by the North East Area Board on 22 March 1957. Blaydon shed was closed 15 March 1965 (to steam 16 June 1963), DMUs thereafter being dealt with at South Gosforth.

Sunderland. A sub-depot was approved by the North East Area Board on 16 September 1957 at an estimated cost of £28,002. However, the depot was cancelled by the Board's meeting of 20 February 1959. South Gosforth proved able to fully handle the area's requirements, and DMUs were merely stabled at Sunderland (in the sidings south of the station); cancellation could also have been influenced by the impending merger of the Sunderland and Gateshead motive power districts. It is believed that no significant construction work on the proposed Sunderland DMU depot ever took place; despite extensive research, its precise location has not been established.

West Riding

Bradford (Hammerton Street). Estimated cost: £44,537. Approved by the North Eastern Area Board on 18 July 1958 and the BTC shortly thereafter. Completed Summer 1961, this scheme substantially upgraded the depot to accommodate a fleet of 145 DMU vehicles, with conditions much improved compared to the pioneering days of the 'Derby Lightweights'; this was assisted by the depot going 'all-diesel' upon banishment of its steam allocation to Low Moor shed from 11 January 1958.

Leeds (Neville Hill). Estimated cost: £344,382. Approved by the North Eastern Area Board on 18 August and the BTC on 18 September 1958; this sum included £35,000 preliminary works, approved by the board on 17 January and BTC on 20 February 1958. Completed in mid-March 1960, the new self-contained depot was built as part of the modernisation/dieselisation of Neville Hill shed. It provided facilities for 250 DMU vehicles, 117 already in service by the time of the depot's formal opening on 17 June 1960.

Manningham. Fuelling and light maintenance facilities. Estimated cost: £34,841, approved by the North East Area Board on 20 February 1959. This two road sub-depot, completed Spring 1960, was provided for the DMUs on the network of services based on nearby Bradford Forster Square.

York and Hull

Hull (Botanic Gardens). Estimated cost: £228,363; first stage (£97,832) approved by the North Eastern Area Board on 19 October and the BTC on 15 November 1956 with the second stage (£130,531), including conversion of No 2 roundhouse authorised by the board on 13 December 1957 and BTC on 23 January 1958. This major rebuilding transformed Botanic Gardens from a double-roundhouse shed to modern five-road diesel depot, work beginning in 1956 and completed in 1959; it closed to steam on 14 June 1959 with transfer of its remaining locomotives to Dairycoates the same day. The modernised depot was designed to service 140 DMU vehicles. Springhead had served as a temporary depot in the interim, but on 30 November 1958 its DMUs were re-allocated en bloc to Botanic Gardens to which all new deliveries went, but some units continued to be serviced at Springhead, which closed to steam on 15 December but remained a crew signing-on point until final closure in July 1961.

Darlington Works

The DMU depots were backed by a repair and overhaul facility for the engines/transmission equipment, established at Darlington Works under sanction of the North East Area Board on 18 January 1957 at an estimated cost of £45,056; the same meeting approved spares cover of 44 diesel engines and gearboxes, plus 16 final drives.

Workshops

Traditionally the larger railway companies of Britain, and many of the smaller ones, built and repaired their rolling stock in their own workshops. At Nationalisation British Railways inherited 29 main railway workshops. In the North Eastern Region there were locomotive workshops at Darlington and Gateshead, carriage and wagon works at York and Walker Gate, and wagon works at Shildon and Faverdale. There were also smaller wagon works outside the management of the main workshops at Simonside on Tyneside and Springhead in Hull.

The locomotive works at Gateshead was a comparatively small affair. At the end of 1957 it had a staff of only 235 compared to 3543 employed at Darlington Locomotive Works. No locomotives had been built there since 1910. It had been closed in 1932 but had reopened during the Second World War. It closed again, this time permanently, in 1959.

Darlington Locomotive Works opened in 1863. It had built locomotives for the NER and the LNER and continued to do so for British Railways. Steam locomotives built there after nationalisation were:
37 Ivatt 2-6-0 4MT, Nos 43070 - 43106;
38 Ivatt 2-6-0 2MT, Nos 46465 - 46502;
23 A1 4-6-2, Nos 60130 - 60152;
20 B1 4-6-0, Nos 61350 - 61359 and 61400 - 61409;
29 L1 2-6-4T, Nos 9001 - 9003, E9004 - E9012, 69013 - 69015, 67717 - 67730. The first 15 were later renumbered 67702 to 67716.
28 J72 0-6-0T, Nos 69001 - 28;
65 BR Standard 2-6-0 2MT, Nos 78000 - 78064;
10 BR Standard 2-6-2T 2MT, Nos 84020 - 84029.
The last steam locomotive built at Darlington was 84029, which left the works on 11 June 1957.

In 1952 Darlington began to turn out new diesel-electric shunting locomotives, and from 1960 main line diesel-electric locomotives. In total 250 steam and 506 diesel-electric locomotives were built at Darlington between 1948 and 1964. Darlington, however, in common with the other BR workshops, did not design and manufacture the diesel engines, transmissions or electrical traction equipment, this was done by private industry. The locomotives, however, once built were maintained in BR works.

Diesel-electric locomotives built at Darlington:
LMSR/English Electric 350 bhp (Class 11) Nos 12103 - 12138;
Blackstone 350 bhp (Class 10) Nos 13137 - 13151, D3439 - D3453, D3473 - D3496, D3612 - D3651, D4049 - D4094;
Blackstone 350 bhp (unclassified under TOPS) Nos 13152 - 13166;
English-Electric 350 bhp (Class 08) Nos 13060 - 13081, 13127- 13136, 13217- 13244, 13298 – 13336, D3454 - D3472, D3665 - D3679, D3687 - D3727, D4028 - D4048, D4158 - D4192;
Sulzer Type2 (Class 24) Nos D5094 - D5113;
Sulzer Type2 (Class 25) Nos D5151 - D5185, D5223 - D5232, D7578 - D7597.

Darlington turned out is first new main line diesel-electric locomotive, D5094, at a special ceremony at the works on 21 January 1960. The Railway Queen, (1) Hazel Dobinson, drove it through a ceremonial tangerine ribbon stretched across the exit of the assembly shop and handed it over to KA Kindon, Area Traffic Manager, Teesside. The locomotive carried a large rectangular headboard bearing the words 'BR North Eastern Region. The first main line diesel-electric locomotive built at North Road Works, Darlington, January 1960.' On entering traffic D5094 was allocated to March on the Eastern Region and later numbered 24 094. It was withdrawn in December 1976.

Plate 6.15. BR Standard 2MT 2-6-0 locomotives in build at Darlington in March 1954. These locomotives were in essence HG Ivatt's 1947 design of 2-6-0 for the LMSR, 4MT examples of which had been built at Darlington in the early years of British Railways. (R Goult)

The works went on to build 84 more Type 2s. The last locomotive built at the works was one of these, D7597, in August 1964.

Both the carriage works and the wagon works at York dated from NER days. The carriage works had built new carriages for the NER and the LNER and continued to do so for BR. From 1951 it began to build all-steel coaches. Two years later in 1953 electric stock for the Liverpool Street - Shenfield services was built, and from 1958 electric stock for the London Tilbury & Southend and Enfield - Chingford services. From 1948 to the end of 1966 the works built a total of 3091 new vehicles. The carriage works also carried out repairs to coaching stock. In 1962 approximately ten coaches a week were thoroughly overhauled and forty a week given light repairs. The building of new wagons at York ceased in LNER days leaving the wagon works to deal only with repairs.

Walker Gate Carriage & Wagon works, situated in Newcastle on Tyne, was approximately a quarter the size of York carriage works and covered an area of 12.5 acres of which 5 were under cover. The works were built in the latter half of the Nineteenth Century to replace the repair shops of the Newcastle & Carlisle and the Blyth & Tyne Railways. They covered the repair of carriages and wagons in the area from Berwick on Tweed in the north to Durham in the south and Carlisle in the west. They also repaired the Tyneside electric stock and railway barrows. In the mid 1950s they repaired approximately 850 carriages, 10,500 wagons and 1,000 barrows a year.

Plate 6.16. Class J21 No 65099 at Darlington Works on 28 April 1962. The locomotive had been withdrawn in October 1961, and was set aside for possible preservation. Eventually it was decided to preserve No 65033 instead, and 65099 was cut up circa February 1966. (RG Warwick)

Plate 6.17. Having assisted in its erection, apprentices and their instructors pose in front of Type 2 No D5096 in April 1960. The locomotive was allocated to Gateshead MPD. (BR (NER, per CE Williamson)

Shildon Wagon Works originated with the Stockton & Darlington Railway and became NER property after the S&D was taken over by the NER in 1863. The works was extended over the years and in 1954 covered 40 acres, of which 11.5 were covered by roofed buildings. In 1953 Shildon built approximately 9,500 wagons. This figure included 2,250 frames and sets of iron work which were sent to Faverdale wagon works to have wooden bodies fitted. If the wagons had steel bodies they were completed at Shildon. Shildon also repaired approximately 43,000 wagons. In addition the greater part of the drop stamping requirements for the Locomotive, Carriage and Wagon Departments of the Eastern and North Eastern Regions were supplied by the forge at Shildon.

Faverdale Wagon Works, in Darlington, was opened by the LNER in 1923 and was BR's newest workshop. In the mid 1950s it occupied 60 acres, of which 9.5 were under cover. The works was designed for the construction of 10,000 timber-framed wagons a year using iron work supplied by Shildon wagon works nine miles away. By the mid 1950s new wagon frames were made from steel and as already mentioned these were manufactured at Shildon and travelled to Faverdale on their own wheels to have wooden bodies fitted. Wagons built at Faverdale included BR's standard goods brake vans. As well as building and repairing wagons Faverdale also built and repaired rail/road containers.

From the time of nationalisation the workshops were under the tight control of the Railway Executive (RE), as were all aspects of the railway. RA Riddles, the Member for Mechanical and Electrical Engineering, thought the traditional arrangement whereby the Chief

Mechanical Engineer (CME) was in change of locomotives, as well as carriage and wagon matters, led to a relative lack of interest in the latter. Therefore at RE HQ there were separate officers reporting to him on these matters: Chief Officer (Loco Construction and Maintenance); Chief Officer (Carriage & Wagon Construction and Maintenance); Chief Officer (Electrical Engineering). This separation was undone in September 1953 when Riddles retired and RC Bond was appointed Chief Mechanical Engineer and took over responsibilities for both locomotives and Carriage & Wagon work. In 1954 the functions were again separated, not being rejoined in one office until 1958, when JF Harrison was appointed CME.

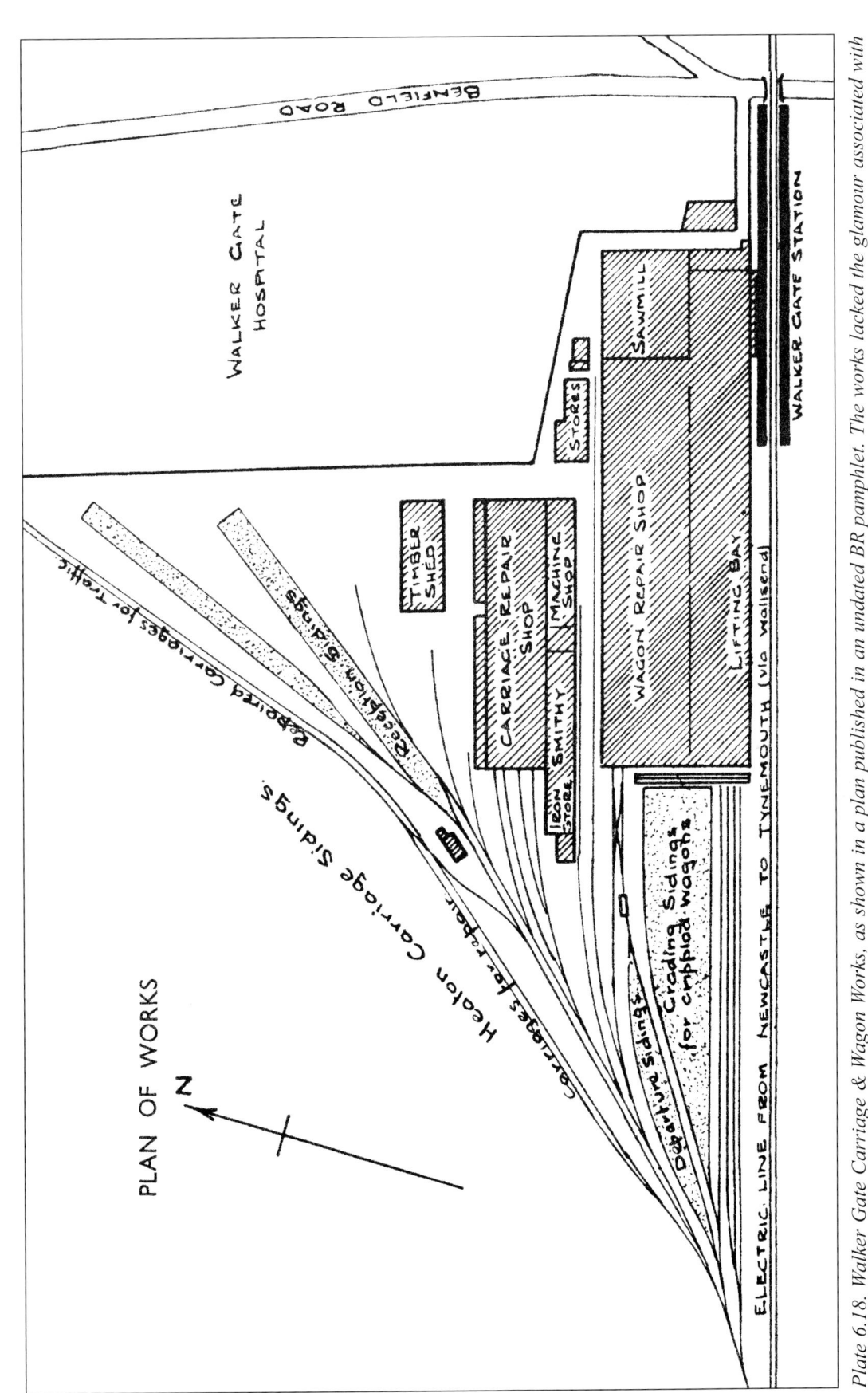

Plate 6.18. Walker Gate Carriage & Wagon Works, as shown in a plan published in an undated BR pamphlet. The works lacked the glamour associated with such as Darlington Locomotive Works, and its history has been difficult to trace. So much so that the date of final closure is still unknown to us. (NERA Collection)

Central control was loosened as a consequence of the passing of the Transport Act 1953 which abolished the RE and set in train the devolution of power to the Regions. In the case of the North Eastern Region's workshops power devolved to the Chief Mechanical and Electrical Engineer (ER & NER) KJ Cook, and the Carriage & Wagon Engineer (ER and NER) L Reeves. The ER and the NER did not get their own Mechanical Engineers, combining both locomotive and Carriage & Wagon responsibilities in one office, until 1959. The man appointed the NER's CME was MG Burrows, succeeded by J Sinclair in 1965.

Workshops Division

In early 1962 it was considered the railway workshops should be run for the benefit of BR as a whole and this could best be achieved by removing them from the management of the Regions. Consequently, in June 1962, the workshops were removed from the control of their regional chief mechanical and electrical engineers and a Workshops Division, governed from the centre, was set up. Its first General Manager was HO Hochen, previously a BOAC engineer. He was succeeded in 1966 by RC Bond.

When D5094 was handed over at Darlington Locomotive Works in January 1960, Area Traffic Manager Kindon spoke of the railway's bright future. However, the future of some BR's workshops was already in doubt. Diesel and electric locomotives could do the work of a greater number of steam locomotives, and needed less maintenance. More modern rolling stock was also replacing a greater number of older types. *The Reappraisal of the Plan for the Modernisation and Re-equipment of British Railways*, published the previous year, in July 1959, had made it clear the activities of the railway workshops would both alter in character and diminish in the years 1959 – 1963. Workshop activities would be concentrated at fewer places with the consequent closure of certain establishments whose capacity had become surplus to requirements. Of the 22 BR works then engaged in the repair of locomotives only twelve were likely to remain in use at the end of 1963. The report however did not name the workshops likely to be closed. Three years later on 19 September Sir Steuart Mitchell, the member of the BTC with responsibility for the workshops, announced 12 of the 29 main works would close in the next three years.

It was planned that Darlington Locomotive Works would close in the second half of 1965. The works then had a staff of 2,543. York Carriage Works, which had a staff of 2180, would continue with an increased labour force of approximately 600 men. The wagon shops would close but container repairs would continue in part of the carriage works. Walker Gate, which had a staff of 365, was to close as a main works. The carriage shop was to close at the end of 1963 and the wagon shop by mid 1964. It was thought the NE Region would take over the works as a running maintenance depot. Faverdale Wagon Works would close in mid 1963; 366 staff were employed there. Shildon, which had a staff of 2261, was to continue as a wagon works, although there was to be a gradual reduction in its labour force.

By 1966 it was planned the staff at Shildon would have been reduced to approximately 1,800 by natural wastage.

The National Union of Railwaymen as a protest against the closures called a one day strike for 3 October 1962. The closures, however, went ahead. Faverdale closed in 1963. Darlington Locomotive Works closed on 2 April 1966, although no locomotives had been repaired there since February. In 1963 Darlington had begun to repair steam locomotives formerly repaired at Doncaster and Derby, leaving those works to concentrate on repairs to diesel locomotives. The last locomotive to be dealt with at Darlington works was BR Standard Class 4 No 76040. This left the works on 3 February 1966 for repairs to be completed at Crewe.

Under the 1962 Transport Act the railway workshops were permitted only to build and maintain equipment for the British Railways Board and other Boards, *i.e.* London Transport, British Transport Docks and British Waterways. This was at the behest of private companies concerned about the implications of competing for work against a state owned concern. This restriction was resented by those running the workshops as undertaking work for outside companies would be a useful way of making the most of available workshop capacity. The Transport Act of 1968 gave the workshops the right to undertake such work. This was not popular with private industry who lobbied for a separate company to be formed to operate the workshops in order that the financial performance, and therefore the fairness of competition with the existing private companies, could be monitored. Bond was very much against this as he was worried a new workshop company would become divorced from the interests of BR by undertaking more lucrative work. However, on 1 January 1970 a new company, British Rail Engineering Limited (BREL), was formed to operate BR's then existing 14 main works. Bond had by then retired and had been succeeded by AE Robson who became the first managing director of BREL.

By this time the only former North Eastern Region workshops still open were York Carriage Works and Shildon Wagon Works. Both had benefited from a programme of modernisation and re-equipment in the mid 1960s, £200,000 being spent on York and £943,000 on Shildon. A lack of orders lead to the closure of Shildon Wagon Works in 1984. In 1989 York Carriage Works was privatised and was bought by a consortium which included Asea Brown-Boveri. From 1967 to 1995 the works turned out 5032 new vehicles but new orders dried up and the works closed in 1996. It was reopened in 1998 by Thrall Europa to build railway wagons but again new orders dried up and after five years the works closed again, this time permanently, in 2003.

Endnotes:
(1) The Railway Queen was the winner of a national beauty contest held each year for the daughters of railway employees. The contest ceased in 1975.

Civil Engineering
John F Addyman

Background

In 1948 the new regional Civil Engineers of British Railways inherited a large backlog in maintenance and renewals caused by the war, and post-war shortages. Many miles of track, numerous bridges and buildings were still in dire need of repair or replacement, and the rationing of steel, until May 1953, did not help. Labour, even to do basic track maintenance, was soon to become impossible to recruit within the major conurbations. Ironically, in rural areas, with lower volumes of traffic, maintenance gangs remained at full strength. The recruitment problems and escalating labour costs meant that the pioneering of mechanised maintenance was essential; the North Eastern Region would take a leading part in its development.

The first Chief Civil Engineer (CCE) of the new North Eastern Region was a dyed in the wool North Eastern Railway man, John Taylor Thompson. He left to head the larger London Midland's civil engineers department and was succeeded at York in 1951 by the dynamic Arthur Dean, who had formerly worked on the Southern Railway. In 1960 Dean moved 'across the road' to further his career towards becoming, in 1962, the North Eastern's last General Manager. Edwin Triffitt took over as CCE from 1960 until his retirement in 1965. Harold Ormiston became acting CCE for a year until Archibald William McMurdo was available to become the last CCE of the Region; he continued as the first of the new Eastern Region.

The size of the Region was increased in 1950 and 1956 by taking over former LMS and LNER (Southern Area) lines covering virtually the whole of the West Riding of Yorkshire. Even the former Midland main line from Cudworth almost to Skipton, and the GNR Leeds - Doncaster came into the Region. Also the unremunerative lines built by the North British in Northumberland came fully under the Region's control.

Organisation

The early regional organisation called for a CCE's head office at York and District Engineers' offices at Bradford, Leeds, Hull, York, Darlington and Newcastle. In 1954 Leeds and Bradford were merged to form West Riding District with rented offices in Leeds. The railways around Hull almost disappeared in the mid-1960s following the Beeching cuts, and what was left was added to York District. The District Engineers supervised the routine maintenance and renewals of the track and structures, and were described by one CCE as 'The people who do all the work'. Arthur Dean introduced an extra level into the District Engineers' technical staff – the Area Assistant. These posts were intended as training posts for newly qualified civil engineers and usurped the role of Chief Permanent Way Inspector. Initially, the posts were much resented by some Permanent Way Inspectors and District Engineers, but they soon became accepted as a valuable part of the organisation.

The CCE's head office at York was situated in the old station buildings where large drawing offices housed the architects, bridges, construction, new works, and permanent way design teams. There was a clerical office to support each drawing office plus a general section, staff section, the engineer's accountant and, later, the work-study office. The typing pool, plan room, printing and photographic sections provided ancillary services. The offices were to expand considerably to provide additional functions. For example, the permanent way drawing office had 20 staff in 1950 but by the time the merger with the Eastern Region was completed in 1967 there were 100

Plate 7.1. This posed publicity shot, in York Old Station, was taken circa 1955 for a brochure to aid recruitment to the Region's Student and Graduate Training Scheme. Graduate John Thompson is seen 'working' the Hallade track recorder, while student, John F Addyman, is 'recording the mileposts' with the electro-magnetic control in his hands. (BR (NER))

technical staff. In the early 1950s the 'soil mechanics department' comprised of an auger that usually reposed under a junior assistant's desk, but soon a complete laboratory had to be set up in Leeman Road to deal with earthworks questions posed by the backlog of maintenance and the start of major new works. Likewise, sections had to be inaugurated to cover the design, development and procurement of the large amount of plant necessary to maintain and renew the track; in the early BR days this was covered as *part* of the duties of one senior assistant.

The Region took an active part in the BR student and graduate scheme for civil engineers, which aided recruitment for the drawing offices. Under this scheme the Chief Civil Engineers undertook to give school leavers or university graduates the training and experience necessary for them to become chartered civil engineers. (See Plate 7.1.) The school leavers needed either to pass the Institution of Civil Engineers' Part I and II examinations, or gain exemptions from them to reach graduate status. Initially, day release courses were set up at local technical colleges for the students, but, later, six or nine months 'sandwich courses' were started at Bradford, Salford and Constantine College, Middlesbrough. As part of their agreed training the students and graduates were moved round the offices to gain experience in each section. Graduates were also employed for six months as lengthmen with an ordinary track maintenance gang, and many of them felt it was the best part of their training.

It was fortunate that this scheme was well under way when the funding arising from the Government's 1955 Modernisation Plan became available. Most of the design and supervision of works arising from the Plan could be tackled 'in house' with only a small amount of structural work being let to consultants. Many young men were given major projects that had not been available to railway engineers for several decades, achieving valuable experience and rapid promotion as a reward. Some ended their careers as Chief Civil Engineers or General Managers of the Regions and two or three reached even higher positions in the BRB hierarchy.

Rails and Fastenings

In the seven years prior to the 1955 Modernisation Plan some progress was being made by the civil engineers to return the track to acceptable standards to allow the acceleration of train services from their abysmal post-war timings. The 'Big Four' had experimented with flat bottom rails before the war, and in 1949 the Railway Executive made an early, and sensible, decision to introduce this type of rail as standard, realising that the more rigid section should provide better track with lower maintenance costs. A section weighing 109 lbs per yard was chosen for main lines and 98 lbs for the more important branch lines that justified relaying with new, rather than second-hand, material. The first 1,000 yards of 109 lb rails were laid between Tollerton and Alne on 6 June 1949, and reasonable strides were made as, by the end of 1950, nearly 1600 miles of flat bottom track had been laid throughout BR. Other difficulties needed to be addressed; the low quality of the softwood sleepers now available meant that they had very limited lives, and the shortage of maintenance staff meant that rail joints were becoming a real problem. The search for suitable pre-stressed concrete sleepers with simple and effective rail fastenings, and the elimination of rail joints by the development of long welded and, later, continuous welded rails were to present a worthy challenge to design staff both within BR and its supply industry.

When AN Butland became Chief Civil Engineer at BR Headquarters in 1962 he made it a priority to decide which of the 20 types of fastenings being developed for concrete sleepers should be accepted as standard. The North Eastern Region's contribution was a Heath Robinson affair thought up by Arthur Dean. No less than 26 components were required to fasten the rails to a sleeper, but his ego was satisfied when he proudly named it the 'AD type'. (See Plate 7.2.) In Butland's search for a maintenance-free 'fit and forget' fastening it did not stand a chance! In 1963, the Western Region's SHC (Spring Hoop Clip) fastening and the independently-developed Pandrol clip were selected, but from 1966 the latter was to gain almost universal acceptance as the ideal fastening for flat bottom rails on concrete or timber sleepers.(1) Concrete sleepers had been introduced during the war, and after experimenting with sleepers with between 22 and 34 pre-stressing wires BR accepted 26 as standard. The new concrete sleepers were manufactured by either Costain or Dowmac, and their overall cost proved to be slightly less than chaired or baseplated timber ones. Another advantage was that they were anticipated to have a life of 50 years.

Plate 7.2. An 'A.D.' type sleeper. The bolt laid loose on top of the sleeper shows how it was secured – by means of a locking pin passed through the sleeper and the hole visible at the bottom of the bolt. (BR (NER))

The Development of Continuous Welded Rails

The fishplated rail joint and the sleepers on either side of it required a high proportion of the maintenance gangs' time to keep the track up to standard; also most rail breakages occurred through the bolt holes at their ends. Jointless track could give increased safety, a better and quieter ride for the passenger, reduced maintenance and fuel costs. The problem is that a 60 feet rail varies in length by as much as half-an-inch (13 mm) due to temperature fluctuations over the seasons. If several lengths of rail are to be welded together this must be taken into account to prevent the track from buckling in hot weather. The use of the more rigid flat bottom rail and the much heavier concrete sleeper helped, but some method of 'de-stressing' (now called 'stressing') the track must be found. If long welded rail was laid on an 'average summer day' the track was unlikely to buckle on very hot days, and the fastenings were capable of resisting the tension in the rails caused by low temperatures in the following winters. 'Adjustment' or 'breather' switches at their extremities took up any movement that did occur towards the ends of the long welded sections. When there was only a very small mileage of welded rails it was practical to de-stress the track that had been laid on a colder day, when the *rail* temperature rose to the required 75°F (later 80°F, 27°C). This needed a possession as the rails had to be unclipped and raised on small rollers to be allowed to 'breath' or 'adjust' to the correct temperature before being refastened. However, the necessity of booking possessions and arranging manpower in advance did not always fit in with the vagaries of the British weather on the appointed day. With nearly 90 miles of welded rails in the Region, by the end of 1961, obviously an 'all weather' system must be found.

In the North Eastern Region the rails were flash-butt welded into 300 ft (later 600 ft) lengths at the Rail Welding Depot at Dinsdale, which had opened in 1957-8. They were taken to site on a dedicated train of 11 'Salmon' bogie wagons. When the ends of the new welded rails had been anchored, by wire ropes, to the existing track they were off-loaded by means of a special gantry fixed to the end wagon. (See Plate 7.3.) The sleepers had been renewed in a previous possession with 30 ft 'service rails'. These service rails were removed as the gantry wagon of the long welded rail train moved clear of them, allowing the new rails, to drop on to their correct seating on the sleepers. The first pair of welded rails was fastened to the sleepers by a number of clips being inserted from where they were fishplated to the existing track. The remainder, and largest part, of the rails was supported on rollers on top of every tenth sleeper. Tables were available to the site staff showing how much a given length of rail needed to expand from its current temperature to be 'stress free' at 80° F. If, for example, the table suggested from the temperature and the length of the first two rails to be site welded that they would be 4 inches longer at 80°F, then this amount, plus an allowance for the site weld, was cut off one rail to form a gap where it had abutted the second rail. (See the colour plates on page 128.) Initially, an artificial heat source was tried, and propane burners, which were supplied from gas bottles,

Plate 7.3. Laying continuous welded rails at an unidentified location circa 1960. (BR (NER))

on platelayers' bogies were pushed along the rails. The idea was to warm the rails on either side of the site weld enough to close the gap, and to maintain it during welding, but their use was quite futile on a very cold day. Norman Macleod developed the now almost universally accepted idea in the North Eastern Region's Permanent Way Development Section. This used hydraulic pullers with rail clamps to close and maintain the gap for site welding. Some difficulty was experienced with the rail clamps which had to grip the rails firmly, with a load up to 40 tons, without indenting the rails. No movement could be permitted during the site weld and the critical period during its cooling, as this could result in a torn weld.(2) Long welded rails were generally only half to three-quarters of a mile long, but with better means of 'de-stressing', and growing confidence, 'continuous welded rails' several miles long were used together with specially strengthened switch and crossing work.

Switch and Crossing Design and Manufacture

The new standard drawings for switches and crossings (S&C) in flat bottom rail were produced at the Railway Executive and, later, BR headquarters. However, little imagination was used to increase turnout speeds from the extremely limiting range of the 1920s bull head designs until 'vertical S&C' was introduced towards the end of the Region's independent existence. Parts of switches and crossings obviously require the rails to be vertical instead of the normal inclination of 1 in 20. The bull head rail was flexible enough to return from vertical to inclined over a short length, but the more rigid flat bottom rail required to be permanently set or twisted, in the space between two sleepers, at every switch and crossing. In complex layouts this became a little ludicrous and a decision was made for a new series of turnouts, with a range of speeds up to 70 mph, to be vertical throughout their length. Standard designs were also produced at BR headquarters for many items ranging from track tools to bridges.

Mechanised Maintenance

The maintenance of the level (top) and alignment (line) of the track was carried out by well established, but labour intensive, hand methods. 'Measured shovel packing', when done correctly, produced long lasting high quality track 'top' but it was very slow. Measurements of the dips in the track were recorded on each sleeper between high spots by means of sighting boards, and the movement of the rails under traffic was read with void meters. The ballast was then removed for 15 inches on either side of the rails to allow measured quantities of chippings, based on the sighting board and void meter readings, to be spread over these bearing areas with the track jacked up. A cruder and quicker method was 'beater packing' where the track was jacked up to allow an estimated amount of ballast to be beaten under each side of the low sleepers with a specially shaped tool. Mechanical tamping machines were to follow the second method, but the first machines required considerable skill and judgement by their operators to improve the quality of the track. The first very basic 'on track' tamping machines were manufactured by Matisa (Matériel Industriel SA) of Switzerland and introduced on BR in the early 1950s (the Region had five in 1953). The early machines were capable of tackling up to ten times more track per hour than was achievable by measured shovel packing, but tended to reproduce existing errors in top and cross level. However, they were of great utility in packing newly relayed or re-ballasted track. It was, of course, necessary for the machines to work under a track possession, or 'between trains'. (See Plates 7.4, 7.5 and 7.6.)

The North Eastern Region was highly critical of the lasting quality of the top produced by tamping, and monitored a number of test sites by reading the levels of the rails on every sleeper at frequent time intervals. In 1963 courses were even given for every permanent way inspector and main line ganger in the Region in order to reintroduce measured shovel packing if necessary. However, the manufacturers got the message, and considerable improvements were soon made to tampers both by Matisa and their rivals Plasser & Theurer. Automatic controls were introduced to ensure precise lifting by means of wires or infrared beams extending ahead of the machine to target boards placed on high points on the track. Tamping speeds during this decade doubled to 400 yards per hour, and track lining machines were introduced to correct the errors in alignment caused by tamping. Inevitably both functions were soon incorporated in one machine. The final development was a tamper that could pack two sleepers at once.(3)

The earlier tampers required an adequate depth of 'stone' ballast to work correctly. The 'stone' ballast could be either crushed and graded slag or limestone, but on many lines it was only a cosmetic covering over ash ballast. In the mid-1950s an average of 140,000 tons of new ballast had to be used each year

Plate 7.4. A Matisa tamper at Selby, circa 1962. (LM West)

Plates 7.5 and 7.6. Having proved the principle, tamping machines steadily increased in size. In the photograph below, the gentleman on the right holding the brochure is the late Brian Hollingsworth, a well-known railway enthusiast and author. (BR (NER), per A Dow)

within the Region. On the main lines good depths of stone ballast were being achieved by lifting the track to the limits permitted by overbridge heights and formation widths. However, even where stone ballast was used it eventually became fouled with detritus or reduced to pulp, and it needed to be removed and replaced. Immediately before Nationalisation the LNER had investigated the use of a Matisa ballast-cleaning machine, which allowed the ballast to be cleaned or totally excavated without removing the track. The track was jacked up and a cutter bar on the machine was inserted under the sleepers and, as the machine moved forward, the dirty ballast was conveyed to screens and sieves and the clean stone returned to the track. Alternatively, all the ballast could be discharged to wagons or, more usually, merely tipped to the outside of the formation. (See Plates 7.7 and 7.8.) The North Eastern Region acquired two of these machines, and in 1958 developed a prototype, which the Hunslet Engine Company built, to clean the ballast clear of the sleeper ends *i.e.* in the six-foot and shoulder of the track.

Plate 7.7. A Matisa ballast-cleaning machine at work at Tollerton on 28 September 1952. Note the winch drum and steel wire by means of which the cleaner is being drawn along the track. (BR (NER), per A Dow)

Plate 7.8. As with tampers, so ballast-cleaning machines also increased in size. This Matisa ballast cleaner is working near Harrogate in August 1956 (thought to be between Starbeck North Junction and Dragon Junction, looking towards Starbeck). Again note the steel wire by means of which the cleaner is drawn along the track. (HC Whitby / ST Askew Collection)

Drainage

Good track drainage is essential to avoid deterioration of the formation, which could make it almost impossible to maintain the top and, in the worst cases, cause landslides. Traditional methods using earthenware pipes and brick manholes had been giving way to pre-cast concrete for manholes and other materials for pipes. Corrugated galvanised steel 'Armco' pipes had gained favour with some engineers, but the early 1960s saw the introduction of the lightweight plain or perforated pitch fibre ones. These were three times as long as the old earthenware pipes and very easy to handle and lay. At the same time the Region started to replace the bottom sections of the pre-cast concrete manholes with fibre-glass sumps, which were made in its own concrete depot at Leeman Road, York. A rail-mounted trenching machine, also built by the Hunslet Engine Company to the Region's requirements, was brought into use in 1963, to supplement an earlier, 1956, version by Auto Mowers Limited of Bath. Together these innovations speeded up the drainage work to a rate of 50 yards per hour.

Other Plant Developments

A plant exhibition organised at Ponteland by the Chief Civil Engineer in 1961 had no less than 60 items on show ranging from off the peg power tools to the weed spray train complete with spray coach, tank wagons and living accommodation for the crew. The weed spraying train, designed by JM Wild under the direction of AC (Sandy) Layhe, operated during the spring growing season, and it eliminated much of the costly hand weeding done by the lengthmen. Its operating speed was such that, after the Beeching cuts of the mid-1960s, it had the capacity to treat much of the Scottish Region's tracks as well as its own.

Powerful mechanical excavators, like the modern JCB and Hymac, were just being introduced in the mid-1960s, but a decade earlier the Region had purchased a fleet of six gutsy American-built Gradall lorry-mounted hydraulic excavators for around £15,000 each. These had a telescopic boom that was capable of tilting and slewing, and were ideal for re-profiling cuttings or embankments, as well as for general excavating with their $^1/_2$ cubic yard bucket. (See Plate 7.20) The author recalls carrying out a trial between a Gradall and a brand new specimen of the first generation of modern excavators in 1966. This was during the demolition of the island platform at Copmanthorpe, where the Gradall was capable of removing chunks of the very substantial walls and footings whereas the new machine only produced a few sparks and a bit of dust!

Depots and Workshops

Each District Engineer had his own depot where his maintenance staffs *e.g.* plumbers, bricklayers, joiners and their supervisors, were based. The cynic might say that the main job for the joiners' shop was the replacement of damaged level crossing gates! There was also a sizable area where his permanent way relaying gangs pre-assembled the track necessary for the next weekend's renewals. Plain line was built up into 30 or 60 feet track panels and loaded straight on to wagons, but the switch and crossing work had to be broken down after pre-assembly in order to remain within, or near, the permitted loading gauge to travel to its destination. In 1958 it was decided to concentrate the work of several small permanent way depots within the West Riding in a new one at Crofton, near Wakefield; it was opened in 1960 at an approximate cost of £160,000.

Every district had its own cranes, ranging from 3 to 15 tons capacity, to assist in handling track and equipment at its depots and to carry out renewals; these were supplemented by breakdown cranes at the weekends, and the 75 ton ones were especially useful for structural work. (See Plate 7.9.) The increased weight of concrete sleepers and the decrepitude and slow speed of some of the steam cranes suggested more new plant was needed. Twin-jib tracklayers had been introduced soon after the war, but they had limited lifting capacity and needed a locomotive to propel them. Self-propelled twin-jib tracklayers, capable of lifting 60 feet track panels with concrete sleepers, were introduced in 1965. (See Colour Plate 35 on page 127.)

The small tank locomotives or Sentinel shunters, used within the engineers' depots, were also being replaced by 88 hp diesels from 1958.

Plate 7.9.
Steam Travelling Crane No 325, based at York, lifts at track panel during work at Dragon Junction in March 1955. (HC Whitby / ST Askew Collection)

The Region inherited its own switch and crossing manufacturing depot at Park Lane, Gateshead, but, as it needed considerable investment to handle the new flat bottom designs, it was decided to close it and have all S&C manufactured by Messrs Taylor Brothers (Sandiacre) Limited. The sleeper depot at West Hartlepool was closed on 30 November 1964; this was partly brought about by the inability of the District Outdoor Machinery Engineer to repair the seal of the loading door of the high pressure creosoting cylinder. The concrete depot at York was modernised and continued to produce many pre-cast concrete items of LNER designs, but its main output was the new three feet long 'S92' cable ducts and lids. A fibre-glass workshop was set up initially to make moulds for the smaller concrete items, but its later productions were as diverse as manhole sumps and 'bonnets' for Scammell Scarab tractors. Until 1966 the central reclamation depot at Darlington sorted material recovered from each weekend's renewals; the serviceable being saved for re-use in minor branch lines or sidings.

Plate 7.10. 30 feet pre-stressed cable ducts and their lids. (BR (NER))

Switch Heaters

In wintry weather the larger stations had employed scores of men assisted by steam locomotives, using steam lances attached to their train heating connections, to clear ice and snow from the switch blades of turnouts and slips. With the imminent demise of steam and rising labour costs a new way had to be found. Again the North Eastern Region was in the forefront of this development with an experimental switch heater installations being brought into use at York (electric) and Newcastle Central (gas) in 1959. Each gas heater unit comprised five propane-fed radiant elements attached to both stock rails of each switch. The elements were fed from remote propane storage tanks, or gas bottles, by means of plastic pipe runs. Their success was such that in July 1961 the Area Board authorised major installations at York, Darlington and Newcastle, totalling 460 Mills 'Arma' heaters at a cost of £39,000. It was estimated that only 24 men would be required, at these three centres to cover an emergency, compared with the 200-240 men formerly drafted in to do the work to the detriment of other duties. Small installations were also provided at important junctions throughout the Region. Ultimately electric heaters were found to be the most satisfactory.(4)

Modernisation Plan

The 1955 Modernisation Plan was supposed to assist the railway industry to move away from its Nineteenth Century working methods imposed, in some ways, by its aging infrastructure. However, a number of very bad decisions were made, and a lot of the finance was squandered by still pandering to outdated traditional ideas. The civil engineer was faced with large expenditure on repairing existing, or building new, facilities for steam locomotives whose life expectancy turned out to be less than ten years. The new motive power depot and coaling plant at Thornaby was a prime example. The new marshalling yards at Lamesley (Tyne), Thornaby (Tees) and Healey Mills cost around £4 million each but never worked to anything like capacity. A fourth one at Stourton, outside Leeds, was cancelled. The existing yards at York were modernised, and a new freight depot was provided at Gateshead. They were all intended to replace numerous outdated and inefficient smaller yards, but customers often changed to road haulage when their local yard closed. The expected upsurge in heavy industry with its additional freight traffic just did not occur, and, after the 'Beeching Plan', general wagonload traffic plummeted. The expensive, well-designed modern yards, instead of handling extra business well into the future, had a declining use over a 20 year span.

The engineering work for the major new yards was demanding and each had different problems. Tyne Yard occupied a site in the Team Valley beside the East Coast Main Line four miles south of Newcastle; it was to replace nine old shunting yards. The whole 135 acre site had to be raised by an average of over 10 feet, and required 2,250,000 cubic yards of fill. Over two thirds of the material came from colliery tips, but the remainder came from new railway cuttings near Corbridge and Durham. The cutting at Corbridge was to allow the diversion of the tracks to avoid a life-expired tunnel built by the Newcastle & Carlisle Railway in the 1830s. (See Plate 7.11.) At Newton Hall, north of Durham, a new cutting was formed to allow for the future realignment of the main line following the anticipated closure of the branch to Sunderland, whose junction with the Team Valley route restricted main line speeds. Both these cuttings produced around 300,000 cubic yards of fill for the new yard, and much needed improvements to their respective railways.

Tees Yard was to be built over the site of four well-used yards, so its construction had to be phased to cause minimum disruption to the heavy traffic passing through them from the steelworks and chemical plants on both sides of the River Tees. The main line from Darlington to Middlesbrough needed to be diverted to clear the southern boundary of the yard. (See Plate 7.12.) The marshy area next to the Tees had to be consolidated to accommodate the northern groups of sidings, and Stainsby Beck required bridging seven times as it crossed the site.

The yard to serve the West Riding was set in the Calder Valley four miles west of Wakefield, but any suitably large level area within a densely populated district was bound to have problems. The site chosen for Healey Mills Yard needed half-a-mile of the River Calder to be diverted southwards into a new cut, and the main Manchester to Leeds railway to be re-routed.

It was decided that the two Up (Manchester) lines should follow the southern boundary of the site, and that the two Down (Leeds) lines should be diverted northwards between the Calder Bridge and Horbury and Ossett station. The new embankment for the Up lines also served as a flood bank to protect the yard. High voltage electric lines and high pressure gas mains also needed to be diverted. The salubrious nature of the location was not improved by part of the site being occupied by the almost defunct Ossett sewage works, which was due to be replaced by a large modern plant further up the valley. Where the River Calder crossed the site only the reception sidings were to the west of it, but the low lying area for these sidings needed to be raised an average of 17 feet. The fill for the yard came from the river diversion, a new cutting at Stourton and burnt red shale from nearby collieries.

Plate 7.11. On 8 February 1960, work proceeds on the excavation of a new cutting to by-pass the life-expired Farnley tunnel on the former Newcastle & Carlisle Railway near Corbridge. (BR (NER), per Ken Hoole Study Centre)

Plate 7.12. A view of Tees Yard under construction. The Up Reception sidings, not yet complete, are partially obscured by the exhaust of a train passing along the diverted Up Main. (BR (NER), per A Dow)

153

Each yard had several groups of sidings, each with a dedicated function. Trains arrived at the reception sidings, and were then shunted over the hump to gravitate into the primary sorting sidings. Tyne and Healey Mills each had one group of hump sidings equipped with two primary and eight secondary retarders, but Tees had an Up and a Down hump yard with one primary and six secondary retarders for each. Further conventional shunting could be carried out in the secondary sorting sidings, as necessary, before the new train went to the departure sidings to await a path to its destination. The size of these yards can be indicated by the fact that they had at least 120 sidings and required up to 70 miles of track. A safety feature was the increase of the 'sixfoot' between the sidings to 7 feet $5^{1}/_{2}$ inches. All the yards opened in 1963.(5)

The provision of Up and Down slow lines between York and Northallerton had started as far back as 1899, but the last section, of the Up slow, between Pilmoor and Alne, was only approved by the British Transport Commission on 20 June 1957 at a cost of £560,069. It opened to traffic on 19 June 1960, and was one of the better ways of using the Modernisation Plan money.

Leeds City Modernisation

In 1950 with the take over of the 'penetrating lines' in the West Riding both Leeds City and Leeds Central came totally under the control of the North Eastern Region. In the 1955 Modernisation Plan the proposal to close Leeds Central and divert all traffic into Leeds City was considered. The two stations were a quarter of a mile apart and presented considerable inconvenience to passengers who had to carry heavy luggage between them. From the Region's point of view economies in maintenance, operating and staff costs could be realised by combining the two stations, and a budget sum of £2 millions was put into the Modernisation Plan for the project. A formal case was finalised in 1957 and put to the Area Board in September, by Arthur Dean. With the introduction of the DMUs on local services, three years earlier, passenger traffic had grown considerably, with a significant share being handled by the smaller Leeds Central. Ticket sales at Central had risen from just over one million in 1952 to almost 2.4 millions in 1956, and City's from 2.9 to 3.8 millions over the same period.

In order to accommodate these numbers of passengers the scheme was not going to be cheap; this led to hard battles to get authorisation. The arguments in favour included: the need to renew the roofs of Central and the older parts of City; the credit for the sale of the land occupied by Central; the operating advantages of new signalling covering the whole immediate area (Leeds West had been re-signalled in the 1930s). The BTC was not convinced by the financial arguments and twice asked for the project to be reconsidered, but eventually gave their consent, in January 1959, to a scheme now estimated at £4.6 millions. The Ministry of Transport added its approval to the first phase of the track alterations, and the new Platform 17 outside the trainshed at City. Bridge No 1, at the west end of the station, over the Leeds - Liverpool Canal was renewed and widened for additional tracks in the first half of 1960. The remainder was halted by the Tory Transport Minister, Ernest Marples, and in 1961 the alterations above track level virtually ceased.

Beeching came into the picture, and was invited to the North East in 1962 to consider the Board's rationalisation plan for the West Riding. This plan envisaged closing all unremunerative local services together with Bradford Forster Square, thus enabling the Leeds City scheme to be scaled down to take account of the reduced train movements. In one of his brighter decisions, Beeching backed the new Leeds proposals, and got Ministerial approval in July 1962. (See Plate 7.13.)

Plate 7.13. Leeds City Modernisation: cutting up for scrap the roof trusses of the old trainshed, 2 October 1960. (BR (NER), per A Dow)

Bridge Renewals and Repairs

With the tracks clear of overbridges being lifted during re-ballasting, often by as much as a foot, pronounced (in railway terms) hog and sag curves could occur under the bridges. The limited vertical clearances of the majority of old bridges over the railway meant it was not possible to lift the tracks to get any increase of ballast under the sleepers. On the main lines the desire to get good depths of ballast throughout, a return to the original even longitudinal gradient profile, and the clearances necessary for future electrification, meant that many bridge superstructures must be raised. Obviously this would mean raising the road levels where they crossed over the railway, and steepening the approach gradients to the bridge. With the BTC reiterating its intention, in 1960, to electrify between King's Cross and Newcastle, at a cost of £105.5 million, and most of the original overbridges on the main lines being unsuitable for electrification, plans went ahead to replace many of them. Delicate negotiations were often necessary with the highway authorities to allow a bridge renewal to take place with the raised road profiles. Beams made of rolled steel joists embedded in concrete provided a minimum depth of construction for the superstructure, and were often used to reduce the problems with the road levels. (See Plates 7.14 and 7.16.) The work on the main line bridges and the essential renewal of others elsewhere meant an average of one bridge per week was being replaced in the Region in the early 1960s. Design work was helped by adapting BR standard bridge types for many locations.

Bridges were inspected at regular intervals and repairs to masonry, brick, iron and steelwork were programmed as required. In 1953 £322,000 was spent on repairs and another £45,000 on repainting; the total annual budget for bridges and tunnels was one tenth of that spent on permanent way. In order to allow the inspection of high bridges and viaducts, without the use of scaffolding, a rail-mounted Viaduct Inspection Unit was introduced in 1960. (See Plate 7.19)

Colliery Subsidence

Colliery subsidence, often of several feet, particularly in the South Yorkshire and Durham Coalfields, caused severe problems for the Region. It totally ruined the longitudinal profile of the track, damaged bridges and buildings and, unless very severe speed restrictions were imposed, it endangered trains using the affected lines. Provided that the National Coal Board served proper notice of their intended workings BR could not even recover the full cost of the remedial works. BR had the option of purchasing the coal under the railway, to protect their lines and structures, but the expense was such that this only happened in exceptional cases. Obviously, the number and sequence of the coal seams being worked, their thickness and depth below the surface affected the severity of the subsidence and the speed with which it occurred. The effects could be such that long speed restrictions of 15 mph had to remain in force for several years, and timetables had to be adjusted to accommodate them. On freight only lines the drain on manpower was such that it was an achievement just to keep the trains on the track!

Many damaged arch bridges had to be shored up, where clearances allowed, while one seam after another was worked. Ultimately, the decision had to be made to replace a bridge, which had been ruined in both structural integrity and appearance, thus causing another drain on resources that the Region could have done without. (See Plate 7.15.)

Gauging and Standard Cross Sections

When permanent way, structures or signals were renewed every attempt had to be made to meet the latest desirable 'structure gauge' profile laid down by the Ministry of Transport. With a number of the early lines in the North East having been built to 'waggonway' rather than 'railway' standards they suffered from inadequate sixfoots and very limited structural clearances. It was obviously impossible to rebuild, for example, parts of the Newcastle & Carlisle to allow modern coaching stock to pass in safety, but it was essential to know exactly where the most limiting clearances occurred.

Plate 7.14. Overbridge renewal between York and Northallerton. (BR (NER))

Plate 7.15. Marshall Hill bridge on the Midland Main Line near Normanton, having suffered significantly from colliery subsidence, is to be replaced by a new steel girder bridge erected adjacent to it. (BR (NER))

A gauging section, within the department, carried out measurements of all trackside structures by using a special wagon equipped with measuring rods fixed to a frame. (See Plate 7.17.) Sixfoots and platform clearances were measured manually. The heavy industries within the Region provided a commercial reason for 'out of gauge loads' to be transported long distances by rail, and the data collected on clearances allowed the selection of the best route. Conditions had to be imposed for the safe progress of the load; closing adjacent lines to traffic, running 'wrong line', and even temporarily removing signals were often necessary to get a very large load through. Some loads were even carried on special wagons which allowed them to be moved sideways to clear obstructions. The weights imposed on under-line structures by extreme loads were monitored in the bridge assessment office, and again special wagons with numerous wheels helped to spread the load.

Increased depths and widths of ballast meant that it took over the level 'cess' along the track sides, and tipping spent ballast on to the sides of cuttings or embankments gave the main lines an untidy appearance. New ideal cross-sections were drawn up for embankments, cuttings and level territory, and some attempt was made to implement them. The railway signal engineer has always been averse to burying his cables, and they were liable to be on or just outside the cesses. One of Arthur Dean's less successful ideas, for the standard cross-sections, was that cables should be enclosed in large pre-stressed concrete ducts, 30 feet long. (See Plate 7.10.) Where they were on embankments it was decided that their ends should be supported on special concrete piles, driven in by a purpose built, rail-mounted, machine. The ducts turned out to be badly designed and badly manufactured, and were liable to revert to aggregate and wires within a short time. A new design of duct was then made only 27 feet 6 inches long and therefore did not fit on the existing piles!

Bonus Incentives and Monitoring Track Quality
1950 saw the introduction of work-study and 'payment by results' schemes intended to increase productivity, reduce the workforce, but enhance wages of those remaining by earned bonus payments. Initially, American consultants were employed to do the studies necessary to find the standard times required to complete most tasks. It was one of the maxims of work-study that the 'observer' did not need to know anything about the task that he was timing. At one depot, where a consultant had implemented a scheme, it was claimed that he had increased the efficiency by 60%. Management did not realise that the same amount of work was done each week, as before, with the same number of men who were now being paid bonus for it! Because the work-study observer did not know the best way of doing a job, he often timed the most laborious way that the men could devise, and there were cases

156

where the bonus times in depots were six times those required for the task. Eventually all routine track maintenance work came within the bonus scheme, but it was claimed that it was easier to earn money by pulling out weeds than by repairing the track!

A target was to reduce the total manpower to almost one third with the aid of the bonus scheme, larger mobile gangs to do special tasks, and increased mechanised maintenance. However, it seemed that the overall standards were deteriorating both where manning was still at full strength and when mechanisation had taken over. Derailments of freight trains became common; these arose partly from track defects, and partly from wagon defects which were exacerbated by the higher speeds being achieved by diesel haulage. The notorious BR-designed Palvans were liable to jump off the track at the slightest provocation. It was found that derailments were most likely to occur where the track was 'twisted', *i.e.* where one rail climbed or dropped relative to the other; if a difference in level of one inch occurred over a distance of 12 feet a Palvan derailment was almost inevitable.

Since the 1920s track quality on passenger lines had been monitored up to three times a year by the Hallade track recording machine. This was a portable machine which could sit on the floor of a coach and give a permanent record of the alignment and top of the track. (See Plate 7.1.) Copies of the record were sent to the District Engineers with the faults highlighted. In the 1950s Matisa developed a track recording trolley which was capable of running at 20 mph and giving the amount of twist, variations in gauge, curvature, cant, and high and low spots on each running rail. (See Plate 7.18.) All but the cant were reproduced on a roll of paper at full size. As with the Hallade recording only a visual assessment of the data was possible, but the more complex information made it a lengthy process. It was also difficult to determine whether the overall quality of the track was improving or deteriorating.

By 1965 Neptune (North Eastern Electronic Peak Tracing Unit and Numerical Evaluator) was developed jointly by the Region and Derwent Electronics Limited for use in the Matisa trolley. It used a computer which took the data directly from the recording pens' mechanism, and produced a summation of numbers related to the amount of movement of each pen. These totals became known as 'penalty points', and the lower the number, obviously, the better was the track. The machine was capable of squirting red or yellow paint on to the track where severe faults occurred, and the dreaded 'red twist faults' had to be dealt with immediately by the maintenance staff. The amount of bonus paid to the permanent way inspectors was related to the 'penalty points', but where mechanised maintenance was predominant their earnings obviously depended on the quality of work produced by the machine operators. Having reduced manning levels, and achieved the transition to mechanised maintenance, average bonus earnings were incorporated into the wages, and a large bureaucracy was dispensed with in the early 1970s.

Plate 7.16. Replacing a life-expired underbridge near Bishopthorpe on the York - Doncaster stretch of the East Coast Main Line. The new steel girder bridge has been erected on steel supports adjacent to the original bridge. Over a weekend possession, the old bridge will be slid out on to supports set up on the far side of the bridge, and the new bridge slid in. (BR (NER))

Track Abandonments

The Reshaping of British Railways or the 'Beeching Report' came out in 1963, and, like the curate's egg, it was only good in parts. No one could disagree that there was a considerable amount of hopelessly unproductive railway throughout BR, but the report achieved little to improve the fortunes of the remainder. The Civil Engineer was saddled with the task of removing hundreds of miles of redundant branch lines and sidings. The operation was carried out under the auspices of the Supplies and Contracts Manager. Two types of contract were used; one for small groups of sidings on lines that were to remain open, and the other for complete branch lines or large marshalling yards. Serviceable rails and sleepers could be retained for use on BR or sold to other users; for example, a large tonnage of 98 lb flat bottom rails from the Market Weighton to Driffield line went to the Republic of Ireland. Older rails were cut up into furnace lengths and sent to the steelworks, together with the cast-iron chairs, for re-cycling. Surplus wooden sleepers were sold in situ to various timber or firewood merchants. Each District Engineer had to set up a small section to deal with the work, often employing permanent way inspectors for the sad task of supervising the removal of branches that they had once maintained.

During the very difficult 19 years of its existence the Region's Civil Engineers Department carried out a phenomenal amount of work, and made some extremely valuable contributions to railway civil engineering. With more effective management at national level and less government interference it could have done even better.

Endnotes:

(1) Permanent Way Institution Journal, 1964, pages 39-40.
(2) Permanent Way Institution Journal, 1970 Part 1 pages 50-60.
(3) Permanent Way Institution Journal, 1973 Part 1 page 44.
(4) *The Railway Magazine*, December 1961, page 829.
(5) *British Marshalling Yards*, pages 133-175.

Plate 7.17. The North Eastern Region's Gauging Van (DE46891) seen at Heaton in 1957. Numerous horizontal and vertical measuring rods slotted into the frames at each end of the wagon to give accurate profiles of the signals or structures within 'gauging limits'. The van was built on an ex-North Eastern Railway plate wagon and a former Officers' Saloon of the same railway (by now DE900268) was used as 'living quarters'. (D Hebditch)

Plate 7.18. In 1961, in connection with a Newcastle meeting of the Permanent Way Institution, BR (NER) put on a large display of track machinery at Ponteland station. To the left we see a Matisa track recording trolley, set up as if it was about to commence recording. (RA Smith)

Plate 7.19. To the right is the Viaduct Inspection Unit (known as the 'Gozunda'), seen here stowed for travel. The Gozunda comprised an inspection platform mounted at the end of an hydraulic arm; the arm could reach over a bridge parapet, and under an arch below. An inspection of a bridge made using the Gozunda was effected much more cheaply than one done from the traditional scaffolding. (RA Smith)

Plate 7.20. A Gradall lorry-mounted excavator – expensive, but very capable. (RA Smith)

Notes on North Eastern Region Architecture
Bill Fawcett

At Nationalisation, all Regions established a common management structure with a Regional Architect operating within the Department of the Regional Chief Civil Engineer. In the case of the North Eastern, this meant a continuation of the LNER North Eastern Area regime, with an office headed by Albert Newton Thorpe (1900 - 1960) and responsible to J Taylor Thompson, as CCE. Under the LNER the design responsibility for new buildings had become divided between engineering and architectural staff, and this continued under the new regime. Thus, for example, the major structural design of the new engine sheds was carried out by the engineers, with the architect's office handling such elements as the staff amenity blocks. In fact, there was some shortage of expertise in structural engineering and the Region called on outside consultants in a number of cases. The most common choice was John Dossor's, a long-established York consulting firm, who, for instance, carried out design work for the re-roofing of Middlesbrough station in 1954 and the relay room for the Newcastle re-signalling, while SW Milburn & Partners of Sunderland were called in to design the structure for the offices ingeniously inserted above the portico of Newcastle Central Station in 1959-60.

During the nineteen-fifties, most of the new building work was concerned with making good war damage and general dilapidations. The two stations most in need of attention were Middlesbrough, where the remains of the trainshed were replaced by concrete platform roofs with an interesting vault over the circulating area, and Sunderland, whose roof was replaced by low-level cantilevered steel awnings while a bland but better substitute was provided for the dingy south entrance in 1953. Arrears of maintenance also began to make inroads on the trainsheds of the country-town stations designed by GT Andrews in the eighteen-forties. The first to go was Market Weighton, in 1949, followed by Rillington in 1952, Whitby in 1953, and then Driffield and Pickering, followed by Bridlington in 1961. Their roofs were replaced by cantilevered platform awnings, welded up from standard steel sections and providing a functional if inelegant alternative. In each case the station buildings and trainshed walls survived unaltered, and indeed throughout the fifties the passenger station continued to fulfil a traditional role, little altered for a hundred years.

BR also set about rationalising its district offices, and this resulted in new office blocks at Hull (completed 1962) and Middlesbrough, to concentrate staff hitherto dispersed among several locations. Both were squeezed into the station sites. Zetland House at Middlesbrough was by far the better; fitted largely into the gap created by bomb damage, it was an honest if not exactly likeable design, given some interest by the use of concrete mullions and aggregate cladding panels. Paragon House, slapped crudely in front of Hull station in place of its cab shelter and therefore perched up on piloti, was an unmitigated eyesore. Ironically, in later years both became regarded as unsuitable for modern office needs, and both have been demolished.

The main infrastructure project carried out by the Region was the concentration of the three principal Leeds stations – Central and City North and South – into one. The driving force behind this was Arthur Dean, and most of the design was carried out by the civil engineering staff. John Poulson designed the speculative office block, City House, which helped finance the scheme, and the railway architects were left with the much smaller block housing railway offices and the signal box, together with a new entrance concourse. The rebuilding, which lasted from 1960 to 1967, gave Leeds City a much better layout for passenger movement, but a drastic paring down of the budget led to unfortunate economies. These included a more constricted track layout at the west end and abandonment of the original scheme for the station roof. That would have resembled some German

Plate 8.1. The semi-subterranean nature of Sunderland station was not conducive to a light and airy feeling. This view – admittedly taken on a dull day in 1963 – shows the platform awnings installed in the 1950s. (BR (NER), per J Kearney)

examples in combining low platform awnings with raised roofs over the tracks, equipped with clerestory openings for light and ventilation. In the event the budget only ran to a pair of low, dark portal-framed sheds, like a cheap and cheerless factory building. A bizarre, and to passengers unexpected, outcome was the virtual abandonment of the light and spacious LMS north concourse, dating from 1938. The latest reconstruction at Leeds has retained the best features of the sixties development but reinstated the north concourse, increased track and platform capacity and provided a light, new trainshed.

Although Leeds was on the drawing board during Thorpe's term, he died at the end of 1960 and was succeeded the following March by Syd Hardy (born 1923), who had been in the office since 1953 and had been involved with the new signal boxes at Newcastle and Huddersfield and the amenity block at Thornaby engine shed. During his time at the head several important station schemes came through, notably the long-promised new station at Sunderland, alterations at Durham and unfortunate re-buildings of Wakefield Westgate and Harrogate.

Sunderland was the first substantial new station building in the Region, completed in 1965 and reflecting the design themes of BR's new Corporate Identity, launched at the start of that year. In layout it echoed the original NER building, in being planned around an overtrack clerestory-lit central hall. Its appearance was, however, very different from its once-handsome Gothic predecessor. Instead, there was a flat roof with a prominent fascia, and large expanses of glazed and white-panelled wall. Things were not so happy at platform level, where a gloomy cave was created so that the tracks could be decked over for the commercial development required to finance the scheme. Until its recent renovation, for the extension of the Tyne & Wear Metro, Sunderland was looking much the worse for wear, as was the Up platform office range at Durham. This latter was built in 1966-7 on a prefabricated system, with panels slotted into a light steel frame, obviously not intended for a forty-year life. The original Tudor-Revival station buildings, of 1856, were fortunately retained as the parcels office – not out of sentiment but because this was cheaper. Ironically, the BR building has now been demolished, with passenger facilities transferred back into the renovated 1856 block.

Wakefield Westgate was one of the rare instances where the Great Northern Railway had been persuaded to build ambitiously, providing a large station with a prominent and vigorously-detailed clocktower. In the nineteen-sixties the authorities regarded such things as a conspicuous embarrassment, and so the main station buildings were demolished in 1966-7 as part of a scheme to make Wakefield a 'park & ride' station for travellers to London. The result is a neat, low, white building with a flat roof with a bold box fascia – ideal for sticking signs on – floating above a shallow clerestory. It is perfectly inoffensive, and has a clever, compact plan, but makes no contribution to the townscape. The same cannot be said of Harrogate, where an attractive and generally satisfactory station was sacrificed to a commercial development which brutalises its surroundings.

During 1963-5, Harrogate station's best features were destroyed to permit the construction of a speculative office block, with the station offices cowering beneath. Some of the platform roofing was renewed, using materials recovered from Sunderland, and the rest was left to deteriorate and to gradually be removed. Despite the provision of a light and spacious entrance/booking hall, the overall effect was a messy patchwork of ill-related elements. Intended as an advertisement for the modern railway, Harrogate simply became a bleak warning of the worst that might happen.

Syd Hardy fostered a new design ethos in the Region, reflecting the new image encouraged by the BR Design Panel. Unfortunately the outcome was fairly banal in the case of the stations described so far; it was certainly much less striking than the work done on the Eastern Region at Potters Bar (1955) and Broxbourne (1960), or on the London Midland at Coventry (1962). Potters Bar did produce some north-east progeny, however; its iconic signal box being echoed in such new ones as Tweedmouth and Belford.

Plate 8.2. Leeds City Modernisation, 1960 - 1967. A view of the west end of the train shed under demolition, May 1963. (RA Smith)

161

Plate 8.3.
City House, still clad in scaffolding, towers above Leeds City station. The more elegant rear profile of the Queen's Hotel is to the left of the photograph. (BR (NER), per A Dow)

Plate 8.4.
The view over the west end of the station looking west from City House. (BR (NER), per RA Smith)

Plate 8.5.
An interior view of Leeds City station, showing the inelegant steel girders supporting the roof cladding. (BR (NER), per RA Smith)

The sixties also brought a change in the role of the smaller station, with the concentration of sundries traffic and coal traffic at selected railheads paving the way for having unmanned stations. This reduced staff costs considerably but meant that there was no-one on site to look after the station facilities, and soon led to the abandonment of all those features once deemed essential, such as toilets and waiting rooms. This was only beginning as the North Eastern Region ended its independent life, and in 1967 the main casualties among station buildings were those brought about by line closures and the withdrawal of stopping services from the main line. By then the need had also emerged for a new type of station, handling passengers who wanted a long-distance railhead accessible by car and with plentiful parking. Arthur Dean's response was a scheme for a new station serving the Leeds-Bradford area, which opened in 1967 as New Pudsey. This had a neat office building, but the platforms were bleak and inhospitable.

Arguably the most satisfying buildings constructed by the Region were those provided for motive power: engine sheds and diesel multiple-unit stabling and maintenance depots. Unfortunately, most of these have since become redundant and been demolished, though there are survivors at Leeds Neville Hill (the most extensive), Thornaby and Hull Botanic Gardens. The Second World War had brought a halt to the heavy repairs routinely required by steam locomotive sheds, accompanied by bomb damage which included the destruction of a large part of York North shed. Thus British Railways inherited a serious backlog of maintenance, while the social ethos of the new organisation meant they would also need to provide much-improved facilities for locomotive men in the form of messrooms and amenity blocks.

Most of this work had to wait until the 1955 authorisation of the BR Modernisation Plan, and was then carried out with thoroughness and enthusiasm. The most ambitious individual project was the engine shed and workshop at Thornaby, opened in 1958, which replaced a number of facilities on Teesside including the near-derelict Middlesbrough sheds. More typical was the reconstruction of old North Eastern Railway 'square roundhouses' as at York North, Gateshead and Leeds Neville Hill. For these the Region provided a 'nave and aisles' form of roof, with a high middle span over the turntable. The 'nave' got a pitched roof on concrete beams with an attractive and distinctive arched soffit, while the flanking 'aisles' were spanned by concrete beams bearing shallow ridge and furrow roofs, in which spans of patent glazing alternated with concrete channels which doubled as valley gutters and maintenance walkways. The latter construction was adopted also for DMU repair sheds, such as the one at Neville Hill, opened in 1960 and still in use. Responsibility for these structures lay with the engineering staff, while the architects got on with the amenity and office blocks, but it is noteworthy that John Dossor was called on to provide the structural expertise for York North, rebuilt in 1957-8.

The merger with the Eastern Region was symbolised by the building of Hudson House at York, designed by one of Syd Hardy's senior architects, Dave Kellett, to accommodate the combined engineering headquarters staff. Formally opened in November 1968, it comprises three office blocks ranged around a large courtyard, and is a surprisingly good design for the time. The offices are faced by boldly-modelled, aggregate-faced concrete modules and the ranges are joined by glazed links containing staircases, which are exploited to provide vertical accents. The site is a sensitive one, just inside the city walls, yet the building, which has worn very well, fits in without making any egregious stylistic references. Its quality can be judged by comparing it with some of the more recent developments nearby.

Further information on post-nationalisation railway architecture in the north-east of England is contained in Volume 3 of my *A History of North Eastern Railway Architecture* (NERA, 2005).

Plate 8.6. Thornaby MPD from the air, looking west. The 22-stall roundhouse is very distinctive. Closer to the camera is the rectangular block housing left, the two road diesel repair shop, centre the main repair shop (note the lack of smoke outlets in the roof) and right the 6-road running shed. Separate buildings house the covered preparation and inspection pits. To the right again is part of Tees Yard. (BR (NER, per J Kearney)

At the Leading Edge of the New Technologies :
Signal and Telecommunications Engineering in the North Eastern Region
Chris Woolstenholmes

At the beginning of its relatively short life, as compared with other Regions, the North Eastern Region (NE Region) was at the forefront of signalling development in Britain. Indeed, for a time, it led the country in the exploration of new initiatives for the control of single lines, the supervision and control of level crossings, and the application of new technology to telecommunications. This is not really as surprising as it might at first seem, given the history of Signal and Telegraph Engineering during the period when most of the Region had been part of the LNER's North Eastern Area. The achievements in the 1930s of the Area's first Signal & Telegraph Engineer, the dynamic Arthur Ewart Tattersall,(1) in re-signalling the main line between York and Northallerton, at Goole Bridge, at Hull (New Inward Goods Yard), and at Leeds, plus those of his successor Charles Carslake, in re-signalling the main line between Northallerton and Darlington and at Hull (Paragon), are already well-chronicled.(2) At the time, the men led the world in technical development and they ensured that the NE Region's claim to pre-eminence in Signal and Telecommunications Engineering, despite the ravages of the Second World War, was no idle boast. To sum up, therefore, it is fair to say that, of the six Regions, the North Eastern at its formation had in service the greatest proportion of the latest power signalling, controlled by leading edge equipment, housed in the most modern signal boxes.

Prior to 1948, the three Signal & Telegraph Departments of the LNER's three Areas had been part of the much larger corresponding Civil Engineer's Departments. Each Signal & Telegraph Engineer reported to his respective Civil Engineer. But the increasing importance of the Signal Engineering and Communications functions, as disciplines in their own right, was recognised in 1948 by the creation of a Signal and Telecommunications (S&T) Department, with its own head of department, as a completely separate entity from the Civil Engineer's. John Holden Fraser was the NE Region's first S&T Engineer. He was no stranger to the north-east of England, having been Assistant S&T Engineer, LNER (NE Area), York, for thirteen years from 1931, returning in 1946 as Assistant to Engineer (Signals), York. He remained at York until the end of 1951, when he was promoted to the Railway Executive as Chief Signal Engineering Officer. He was succeeded by Arthur Frederic Wigram, who served in the post until the Region was absorbed into the Eastern. (See Appendix 9.1.)

Signalling Schemes

Apart from dealing with considerable arrears of maintenance, which occupied almost a decade, Fraser's priority was to complete the re-signalling of York, originally planned by Tattersall fifteen years earlier, and halted because of the Second World War. Like most of the LNER (NE Area) major signalling contracts, York had been awarded to the Westinghouse Brake & Signal Company. The company's patented One Control Switch (OCS) panel route relay interlocking had first used been used at Hull (Paragon) in 1938. As installed at York, with a total of 825 routes, it was at the time of commissioning in May 1951 the largest in the world. The success of the new signalling was apparent almost overnight. A congested area which had been an operator's nightmare, where it was said that freight trains could stand for up to eight hours without even turning a wheel, became a dream in which all traffic flowed smoothly throughout each 24-hour period. Addressing the NER York Literary and Debating Society in May 1953, York's District Operating Superintendent HM Lattimer, in reviewing a full year's operation, said that freight train speed in the York District rose by 16%, and that freight train hours decreased by 20% between 1950 and 1952. Further economies of £22,000 per annum had been achieved in the wages of signalmen no longer needed.

It was therefore no surprise that in July 1951 it was announced that authority had been received from the BTC to proceed with another of Tattersall's aborted schemes, the Newcastle re-signalling, at a total cost of £780,000. Again, Westinghouse was the principal contractor, and a 641 route OCS panel, of similar design to that installed at York, was supplied. Replacing worn-out Westinghouse electro-pneumatic equipment installed by the North Eastern Railway between 1906 and 1909, the signal box, situated immediately east of the footbridge between Platforms 9 and 10, also housed the station announcer. The panel was extended twice, eastwards in 1965 to fringe with South Gosforth (East), and westwards to Scotswood in 1966, resulting eventually in the closure of fourteen signal boxes.

The Region's first major new re-signalling scheme was centred on Huddersfield, where traffic density was high and outdated assets made renewal imperative. The proposed amalgamation of Nos 1 and 2 signal boxes, and the construction of a new power box at the end of No 7 bay platform, had been under discussion as early as 1954.(3) In May 1956, the BTC approved the acceptance of the tender submitted by the Siemens and General Electric Railway Signal Company (SGE) for a relay interlocking on the company's own Individual Function Switch (IFS) principle, costing £176,650. Compared with the OCS system, operating this kind of control panel took slightly longer, but it was a cheaper option in terms of initial outlay. It was authorised partly to gain comparative data in terms of operating costs and reliability between itself and OCS; it was not duplicated elsewhere in the Region. However, extension of its control area westwards to encompass the work of Springwood and of Gledholt Junction signal boxes, as was foreseen when it was planned, was completed in due course.

But the impetus for modernisation throughout BR, on a scale never previously dreamt of, came early in 1955 with the publication of the BTC's *Modernisation and Re-Equipment of British Railways*. One of the plan's basic components was the improvement of the track and signalling equipment to make higher speeds possible in greater safety. This was to be achieved by extending the use of colour-light signalling and the automatic warning system of train control – then known as Automatic Train Control (ATC) – and installing technically more advanced systems of telecommunications. Following the publication of the BTC's Modernisation Plan, in October 1956 the White Paper *Proposals for the Railways* was published. This White Paper was a re-examination of the 1955 Modernisation Plan, and gave a much more detailed account of the proposed modernisation. The construction of new mechanised marshalling yards and an extensive programme of re-signalling related to other aspects of modernisation also featured prominently. In the NE Region, therefore, plans for the provision of colour-light signalling were concentrated on the major artery – the East Coast Main Line – and the large centres of industry on Tyneside, on Teesside, and in the West Riding. The effects of the plan were first seen in the construction of the Up Slow line between Pilmoor and Alne, which, with the existing Down Slow line, had 3-aspect colour-light signalling fitted. Almost 30 miles of continuous quadruple track between York and Northallerton could now comfortably accommodate all types of traffic from fast-moving passenger trains to slow-moving freight trains.(4) Major schemes, shown in Appendix 9.2, mainly using 4-aspect colour-light signalling (sometimes an unnecessarily extravagant expense), with continuous track circuiting – an essential ingredient for modern signalling – were completed on Tyneside, on the North Main Line from Benton to Burnmouth (just north of the Scottish Border), on Teesside, at Leeds and in the West Riding. Marking a departure from previous philosophy towards the design of control panels, many of the smaller power boxes, exemplified best perhaps by Tweedmouth, were arranged so that the signalmen could operate their consoles from a sitting position, and simultaneously keep a watchful eye on traffic movements outside.

However, while these schemes were being developed, a confidential report had been prepared by the General Managers of the Eastern and the North Eastern Regions.(5) This report pertained to the modernisation and electrification of the East Coast Main Line as far north as Newcastle, plus certain feeder lines. It proposed that: the lines be re-equipped with colour-light signals, which would allow for improved headways; that continuous track circuiting be provided; that power-operated or 'hybrid' signal boxes be provided, each such to replace several manual boxes.(6) In the NE Region's electrified area, the report envisaged that there would be a spectacular decrease from 149 to 48 signal boxes, 21 of which would be new power boxes. The decrease would make possible a significant reduction in the number of signalmen employed, from 550 to 250. The plan as described in the report had wide-spread implications for the S&T Engineer, because the immunisation of 25 kV 50 cps overhead electrification required the provision of special facilities on line relays, track circuits, signal mechanisms, and point operation circuits that would

Plate 9.1. Photographs of the large OCS panels at York and Newcastle have been published widely. So, by contrast, here is Huddersfield on 27 November 1958, three days before commissioning. In appearance the individual switch console and illuminated diagram were virtually indistinguishable from their OCS rivals. The horizontal desk at the front of the console displayed the nomenclatures of the signal switches. On the sloping part, the top row of black switches operated the points, while the two lower rows of white switches operated the signals. In the centre of the vertical portion is the clock, showing 11.30. To either side are the Earth Leakage and Power Supply indicators.

Next are the Absolute Block indicators and bell tappers to Hillhouse No 1 signal box and Springwood Junction signal box, both quadruple-track block sections, hence an instrument for Fast and Slow lines in each direction. The telephone concentrator for the east end is housed at the left-hand end, while that for the west end to Springwood is nearer the camera. When the area of control was enlarged in 1961, the space below the diagram accommodated an additional console. Still open, albeit with completely new equipment, the signal box is situated at right angles to the tracks, at the end of the then Bay Platform 7. (BR (NER), per CJ Woolstenholmes)

provide protection against false operation by extraneous feeds from traction circuits. Special cabling would also be necessary for telecommunications circuits. In the NE Region, the estimated S&T costs associated with electrification amounted to some £22.1 million at 1958 prices. In addition, an increase in S&T staff from 100 to 150 was expected. However, although some preliminary work in connection with electrification was authorised and undertaken, the actual task of installing overhead wiring on the East Coast Main Line had to wait for almost three decades.

The contracts for all the signalling schemes as listed in Appendix 9.2 were, except for those marked †, awarded to the Westinghouse Brake & Signal Company, which had had close ties with the north-east of England since the earliest part of the Twentieth Century. At Tollerton (and at Pilmoor where the new panel was installed in 1960 in the 1933-built structure), the NE Region decided to try out one of the last of Tattersall's pioneering innovations, the so-called 'sequence switch' type of interlocking panel. Supplied by Standard Telephones and Cables Limited (STC) of London, these two panels were improved versions of those commissioned at Doncaster North and South signal boxes in 1949.(7) The signalling console featured specially-designed rotary switches, placed on the track diagram in the true geographical position of each set of facing points. The switches, similar in size and appearance to cotton bobbins, could be turned to one of up to seven positions corresponding to the different routes to which the points concerned could read. Then, by depressing a plunger built into each rotary switch, a route could be set up. Interlocking between conflicting routes was achieved by the fact that the rotary switches could not be in two positions simultaneously. This ingenious idea, developed from telephone technology, considerably reduced the number of relays and associated free wiring needed in the relay room and consequently saved money. It was not deployed subsequently on the North Eastern or the other Regions.

The panel and associated internal equipment at York Yard South, however, supplied by Henry Williams Limited, Watford, agent for the Swiss company Integra AG, embodied the latest of geographical circuit techniques as applied to BR requirements. Making considerable use of miniature equipment, which was being successfully used by the railway administrations in Germany and Switzerland, York Yard South was in the nature of a large-scale experiment. It provided an ideal location – a busy freight-only line, literally within sight of Regional Headquarters offices – for testing the apparatus with a view to its ultimate adoption on passenger lines at a cost well below that of conventional power signalling. It was the first of its kind in the UK and the only one of its type on the NE Region. Unlike York Yard South, where a route could be set up by the simultaneous pressing of the push-buttons at the commencement and termination of the route, most of the subsequent power boxes employed the entrance – exit (N – X) principle of route signalling. In this system, first installed in the UK in 1937 at Brunswick (8) on the Cheshire Lines Railway, a joint LNER/LMSR concern, the entrance button was depressed first and followed by the exit button. The large power boxes at Tyne, Tees and Healey Mills also housed, in a room adjacent to that occupied by the signalling panel, a separate control console for the adjoining marshalling yard. This practice was unique to the Region. By combining signalling and marshalling yard contracts, and thereby employing the same company on the schemes, the astute regional management was able to secure very advantageous contract prices as well as relatively quick completion dates.(9)

Plate 9.2. To some extent, it seems likely that the design of Tollerton signal box, and its three cousins, was influenced by that of Potters Bar, opened by the Eastern Region in 1955. Nevertheless, it is a striking statement of incipient modernisation, although the LNER-style nameboard appears to have been rescued from its predecessor. Photographs of the pioneer, Pelaw, are well-known, so this previously unpublished rear view looking South shows the entrance to Tollerton box, which was situated on the Up side of the ECML. Access to the operating room was via an internal staircase. The approach roadway had yet to be constructed when this photograph was taken on 19 January 1961. The box would open on 31 January. After closure on 10 December 1989, it would be demolished; ironically only the LNER 1933 electricity sub-station building, seen in the background, remains. (BR (NER), per CJ Woolstenholmes)

While Wigram dealt mainly with the North Eastern Area Board, with the Ministry of Transport, and with the general direction of policy and strategic planning, his assistant GC Thew, very much a moderniser and forward thinker in the same mould as Tattersall whose department he had joined in 1929, concentrated on the detail and implementation of schemes.(10) Some involved the amalgamation of adjacent signal boxes in association with the modernisation of traditional mechanical signalling, where the cost of replacing life-expired assets made sense economically. A typical example was at West Hartlepool, where the work of two neighbouring NER bridge signal boxes was taken over by the new Cliff House box in 1959. Changing operating requirements, often caused by the withdrawal of passenger services and by industrial decline such as the closure of a colliery, spelt the end for many signal boxes, in some cases without the need for and added expense of signalling alterations at adjacent boxes.

Comprehensive descriptions of these schemes appeared in both the lay and technical press. What received little attention in these journals, however, were the difficulties Wigram (and his colleagues on other Regions) were encountering in recruiting suitably qualified staff to plan, install, test and commission the considerable amount of new work required. Nor indeed was this problem solely confined to BR.(11) It had been foreseen in the 1955 Modernisation Plan (12), but ten years later the effects of the shortage of qualified signal engineers nationally had become 'very serious'. Twice, in 1956 and 1959, it had led to particular concern at North Eastern Area Board level about possible delay in the implementation of a number of the Region's signalling projects. Wigram explained to the Board his inability to recruit and train suitable candidates was due to the limited scope for promotion because of the specialised nature of the work, and the relatively low rate of remuneration compared with that offered by outside companies. In 1959, for example, he said the shortage 'amounted to at least 30'.(13)

ATC and AWS

The concept of ATC had exercised the minds of locomotive and signal engineers since the latter part of the Nineteenth Century. It had developed from the need to ensure that drivers had observed those signals which were applicable to their trains, had registered the signals' messages, and had reacted correctly to their indications. Its purpose therefore was to improve safety by reducing or even eliminating drivers' errors, particularly, in the early days, during fog or falling snow when visibility was at its poorest. On the North Eastern Railway, Vincent Raven and Charles Baister had devised a form of mechanical cab signalling; this had been tested in 1894 at Merrybent Junction, between Darlington and Barnard Castle.(14) It was later installed on the East Coast Main Line north of York.

In 1907, successful trials of Raven's more sophisticated electro-mechanical version of cab signalling had been conducted between Durham and Bensham.(15) Three years later, an improved system had been tested on the Richmond Branch. By the mid 1930s, these installations had been discontinued by the LNER, which had instead decided to adopt the Strowger-Hudd magnetic, non-contact method of transmission between track and train, following the disastrous rear-end collision at Castlecary (on the Edinburgh - Glasgow line) on 10 December 1937. However, little installation work had been done before the Second World War killed off the scheme. Although the LNER management was interested in the idea, no further work was authorised by the company after 1945.

Commendably early in its life, the Railway Executive took the decision to adopt an improved version of the Strowger-Hudd system of ATC, which was tested between New Barnet and Huntingdon in 1949. It had the approval of the Chief Inspector of Railways, Lieutenant-Colonel GRS Wilson, but it was not until early December 1956, after further refinements and extensive trials, that final approval was forthcoming from Harold Watkinson, Minister of Transport and Civil Aviation (MoT&CA). The scheme envisaged the extension of ATC to all important routes in the country, which were almost universally mechanically signalled, but including multiple-aspect colour-light signalling areas, such as York – Darlington, where the warning would be given at the approach to any signal showing anything but green. Lengthy discussions then took place at BTC Headquarters. These culminated in the Commission's decision, at its meeting on 19 September 1957, to approve in principle a long-term plan for the installation of ATC equipment on all BR main passenger lines, and an initial five-year plan for the equipping of certain main lines, of which the NE Region's was one.(16)

It was now up to the Regions to submit their detailed proposals. Accordingly, plans were finalised by the North Eastern. At its meeting on 17 January 1958, the North Eastern Area Board recommended for approval by the BTC the installation of ATC apparatus between Shaftholme Junction and Marshall Meadows, and on locomotives and multiple-units operating over the Region's portion of the East Coast Main Line, at an estimated net cost of £1,287,703.(17) A further £118,038, of which the NE Region's portion was £68,454, was sought for the fitting of ATC to 256 locomotives (belonging to the Eastern, North Eastern and Scottish Regions) which were required to work express passenger trains over the East Coast Main Line between King's Cross and Grantham. (ATC equipment was already installed on this section of the main line.) The BTC approved the proposed expenditure on 20 February, and work on the installation of ground equipment south of York had commenced by July.

In 1959, ATC was officially re-named Automatic Warning System (AWS). On 25 October 1959, the track equipment was brought into use between York and Darlington. *British Railways Magazine: North Eastern Region* of July 1960 reported that installation of AWS track equipment had been completed between Durham and Newcastle, which meant that the 268 miles between King's Cross and Newcastle was now fully operational. Work continued north of Newcastle; by January 1963, apart from the platform lines at

Darlington and Newcastle, where speeds were low, the whole of the 393 miles between London and Edinburgh had been commissioned.

Secondary lines, such as the Leeds Northern between Northallerton and Teesside, and other centres where re-signalling was being undertaken, were next dealt with, as were mechanical distant signals at key locations. However, the NE Region was unable to complete the programme in its lifetime. The task was ultimately brought to fruition by Network Rail, but from authorisation it had taken about forty years so to do.

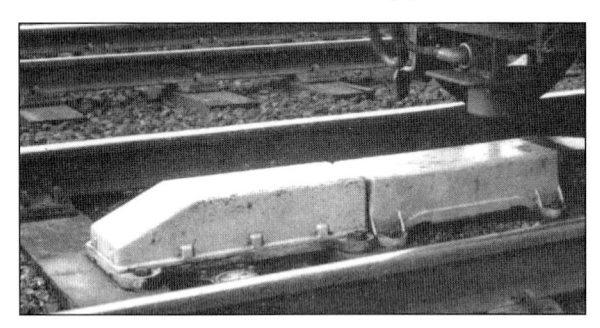

Plate 9.3. This photographs shows an AWS twin-magnet installation. On the locomotive looming over it can be seen the AWS receiver in its round housing. (BR, per J Kearney)

Centralised Traffic Control (CTC)

The 1955 Modernisation Plan envisaged the introduction to this country for the first time of CTC on certain sections of line where conditions were considered to be favourable.(18) Already extensively used in the USA, Africa and elsewhere, it enabled the operation of remote signals and points by power from a central control. Seen in Britain as a solution to the problem of escalating staff costs on lightly-used secondary lines, where its development could eliminate the need for intermediate signal and gate boxes, the concept was however fatally flawed. Laudable though the objective was, it failed to take into account the fundamentally different operating conditions in this country. Compared, for example, with the States, where hundreds of route-miles of main line were controlled from one CTC machine and used chiefly by lengthy freight trains earning considerable revenue, here the length and number of trains simply failed to earn sufficient income to justify the high capital costs of installing CTC on much shorter sections of less important line. At the time, in a spirit of optimism following the publication of the 1955 Plan, where investment had to be undertaken and was sometimes misplaced, these differences failed to be perceived.

The catalyst for the development of a scheme of CTC in the NE Region was Frederick Chilton Margetts, at that time Assistant General Manager (Traffic). Conscious of the continuing losses being made by passenger services on secondary lines for which he was responsible, he had, in 1958, initiated a study of financial and traffic developments which had convinced him that the $31\frac{1}{2}$ miles route between York (Bootham Junction) and Beverley (North Junction) was a suitable candidate for CTC. The scheme, however, would be an economic proposition only if singling of the line was undertaken.(19) It was proposed therefore to provide double line connections some 1,000 yards long approaching the two junctions, and passing loops $\frac{3}{4}$ mile long at Pocklington and $1\frac{1}{4}$ miles long at Market Weighton; and to equip 19 of the 23 level crossings with automatic half-barriers.(20) Seven of the ten intermediate signal boxes would be abolished, leaving only Pocklington to supervise its passing loop, and Market Weighton East and West to work traffic for the Selby – Driffield line. (As authorisation for this latter closure might not have been received by the time the CTC was commissioned, it was thought prudent to plan for the possibility of the line remaining open.) The provisional net cost of the scheme was £165,732. Sought by the North Eastern Area Board from the BTC, approval in principle for the scheme came in March 1959, subject to a further report when firm estimates became available and negotiations had taken place with the MoT&CA about the scheme as a whole, and with the Local Authorities concerned in regard to the conversion of the 19 level crossings. After lengthy consultations and further refinements, the scheme received approval on 20 December 1960, an additional expenditure of £78,739 being authorised to cover minor variations and under-estimation. The following month, at a cost of £212,900, the tender of the Westinghouse Brake & Signal Company for the supply, delivery, installation and commissioning of colour-light signalling by CTC, from a panel to be housed in York signal box, was accepted by the North Eastern Area Board.(21)

Work outside now started in earnest. On 4 May 1961, the Signal Sighting Committee met to agree the profile and exact location of each signal. By September, detailed surveys of the 19 level crossings to be modernised had been completed; and, with a view to obtaining informal approval of the proposals for each crossing before applying formally for an Order under Section 66 of the BTC Act, 1957, site meetings with all interested parties had been arranged. The sites for the eleven field stations, housing wayside interlocking apparatus, had been fixed and details of the buildings required finalised. Material for the work was being assembled on site. It was planned to commission the scheme in three stages, but, on 24 February 1962, came the decision to place it in abeyance.(22)

Had the scheme been successfully completed, it would have yielded valuable technical information, enabling a more accurate appraisal to be made about the future of CTC projects in this country. Indeed, so confident was the Region in the early stages of the scheme that consideration had been given to further installations between York and Harrogate, to be controlled from York signal box, and York - Scarborough, Hull (Cottingham South) - Seamer, Hull (Wilmington) - Hornsea, Hull (Hedon) - Withernsea, for remote control from Hull. But, in the end, high capital costs and recurring maintenance charges outweighed the savings to be gained from CTC and British operating conditions led to the demise of this interesting experiment, both in the Region and on BR as a whole.

Signal Box Design

Signal box design on the NE Region was the responsibility of the Regional Architect, whose department was a small sub-section of the large hierarchy which was the Civil Engineer's department. Construction of new cabins from 1948 was invariably undertaken by outside contractors, a practice, in the case of the north-east of England, dating back at least to the early 1870s. After completion, the maintenance of the fabric of the buildings themselves became a matter for the Regional Civil Engineer. Installation and maintenance of the signalling and communications equipment was carried out by the S&T Engineer's staff, while the Operating Department provided the signalmen to work the equipment. Strictly speaking therefore, signal box design belongs in the Paper on Civil Engineering, but has been covered here for the convenience of readers.

Designs can be divided into two principal groups, mechanical and power signal boxes, each of which had three distinct phases. The earliest mechanical signal boxes opened by the Region owed their origins to the Architect of the LNER (NE Area), Albert Newton Thorpe; typical examples were Copmanthorpe (1950) and Grangetown (1954) (near Redcar and still open). However, in their detailed designs for new signal boxes, the Architects of the Regions were guided by directives and plans from the Architect of the Railway Executive, Dr Frederick Francis Charles Curtis, ARIBA. Indeed, early in 1953, his department would prepare four standard signal box designs, classified as Types A, B, C and D.(23) The aim was to facilitate the mass production of articles of good appearance and the various designs covered the general layout and such aspects as floor arrangements, cooking, heating and sanitary equipment, natural and artificial lighting, and nameplates. Therefore, in his early signal box designs for the NE Region, Thorpe, who had been appointed Regional Architect in 1948, followed this guidance. Over a dozen examples appeared to this first design between 1952 and 1958. All featured brick construction, and a flat roof overhanging each elevation. The first was Ferryhill No 2, which can still be seen today. It was constructed to replace a life-expired North Eastern Railway building and to control also the functions of its near neighbour, Ferryhill Sidings box; and was in fact the forerunner of a number of signal box amalgamation schemes.

Freed from the shackles of central direction imposed by the Railway Executive, the Region's General Manager made arrangements late in 1956 for two outside architects to prepare contemporary standard designs for new mechanical and power signal boxes. With Dr Curtis, the North Eastern Area Board considered the competition entry designs in May the following year, but deferred a decision until June. The Board stipulated that proper regard should be paid to cost, that maximum use should be made of prefabrication, that the materials used should not readily deteriorate, that window space on both floors should be broken to relieve the design, and that some sort of canopy should be provided.(24) Shaftholme was the first example of the new styles. The only one to be built to the revised Number 1 design and opened in 1958, it incorporated a steel frame to counteract the effects of possible mining subsidence and a wooden superstructure. Then, following the disastrous fire in Cannon Street signal box, Southern Region, on 5 April 1957, the Board decided that timber-framed cabins presented too great a fire risk and that future designs would feature a steel frame, a gently-pitched gable roof and a range of pre-fabricated parts. In 1960 and 1961, a clutch of these types, exemplified by Sudforth Lane (east of Knottingley) and West Sleekburn (north of Bedlington), appeared in areas prone to subsidence. A few others were built elsewhere when speed of construction became paramount. The first similar brick-built versions, authorised as a result of the competition, were opened in 1959 at Cliff House (south of West Hartlepool) and Rillington.

Plate 9.4. This model of the proposed North Eastern Region standard design for a mechanical signal box was made in October 1950. With one exception, it shows all the architectural elements associated with the Region's early boxes: a brick base, a pre-cast concrete lead-out for point rodding and signal wires, pre-cast concrete locking room window surrounds, a flat roof overhanging the operating floor windows, and a chimney at the front, the lever frame being placed at the back of the box. (See Plate 9.5 and Colour Plate 32.) The exception was the operating room windows, inclined outwards to eliminate glare and extraneous light. This feature was incorporated into the later 'Pelaw' style power boxes. (BR (NER), per CJ Woolstenholmes)

The Region's earliest power signal boxes were built within the train sheds of Huddersfield and Newcastle and were not standardised in design. However, the next generation of power boxes, at Pelaw, Tollerton, Tweedmouth and Belford, opened between 1960 and 1962, were perhaps among the most aesthetically-exciting, innovative and functional designs ever produced by BR. Of steel-framed construction, a cuboid-shaped mess and relay room, faced with prefabricated units, was surmounted at one end by a flat-roofed, glass-encased control room, whose walls were inclined outwards at an angle of $8\frac{1}{2}$ degrees, in order to minimise glare and reflection. Today only Tweedmouth survives in operation.

Thorpe died in office on 31 December 1960 and was succeeded by Sydney Hardy, who presided over the Region's final design of power boxes. Opened from 1962, these much larger buildings were designed individually, although all had similar characteristics such as a concrete framework, with a brick exterior, and a flat roof. Those at Tyne, Tees and Healey Mills also housed the control rooms for the adjacent marshalling yards. In all, the Region was responsible for the construction of 38 mechanical and 18 power boxes.

Plate 9.5. A significant proportion of the signal boxes opened by the North Eastern Region had short lives; Backworth was no exception and survived a mere six years. As usual, the contract to construct the signal box and relay room was awarded to a local firm, in this case, RA Gofton (Monkseaton), Whitley Bay, in September 1955. Situated in the vee of the junction immediately east of Backworth station – see Ken Hoole's photograph on page 62 of 'Rail Centres, Newcastle' – it was built to what is now known as the NER Style 16b design, with the 30-lever frame positioned at the back. It was brought into use on 16 November 1958. After closure on 1 March 1964, as part of the Benton power signal box scheme, the relay room was retained to house the 'Westronic' remote control apparatus for the new colour-light signalling. (BR (NER), per CJ Woolstenholmes)

Plate 9.6. Benton power box was built in the vee formed by the South West Curve (foreground) and the East Coast Main Line. The architecture was typical of the design of second generation medium-sized power boxes, such as Heaton, York Yard South and Hessle Road. The relay room and the S&T technicians' mess room occupy the ground floor. On the left is the building housing the emergency standby power plant. The box was commissioned on Sunday, 1 March 1964, although this view was taken on 18 February 1963, before fitting out. (BR (NER), per CJ Woolstenholmes)

Plate 9.7. Low Gates was the prototype of a number of signal box amalgamation schemes which the North Eastern Region completed. When it was decided to close Northallerton East signal box and re-control the junction and provide colour-light signalling, Individual Function Switches, enclosed in a modular frame which replaced the block shelf, were employed. Electrically interlocked, these thumb switches operated power-worked points and colour-light signals in the same manner as mechanical levers. The three units at the left-hand end are the block indicators and bell tapper unit for the Absolute Block section to Brompton. At the other end, as Track Circuit Block regulations were worked to Northallerton (locally known as 'top box') and Boroughbridge Road signal box, only two tapper units and their associated block bells concealed below, were provided. The power signalling was commissioned on 6 March 1960, while the signal box and lever frame replaced their predecessors in 1956. (BR (NER), per CJ Woolstenholmes)

Plate 9.8. This previously unpublished photograph, dated 25 January 1960, shows the panel constructed by STC for Pilmoor signal box. Replacing the hybrid equipment provided for the 1933 colour-light signalling, it was positioned at the back of the cabin and controlled, in addition, the new Up Slow line from Pilmoor to Alne. It was brought into use on 15 May 1960. At the top of the panel is a group of four detonator switches, next to which are seven point switches. Further along is the Down Siding ground frame release switch. At the right-hand end is the Shunt Signals switch. This could be turned to any of three positions: Day/Off/Night, depending on circumstances. In their correct geographical positions on the diagram are the red 'cotton bobbin' switches for main running signals and white for position light shunt signals.

In the near bottom corner is the gradient diagram for the Transient Track single line to Coxwold, next to which is the 'Branch Control' switch and associated push button 'Release', respectively from and to Coxwold signal box. Next is the 'Signal Post Telephones' switch for Up and Down lines, and their 'Reset' push buttons below. The five black push buttons are to operate the block bells to Coxwold, Tollerton (Slow and Fast lines), and Thirsk (Fast and Slow lines). When commissioned, however, the proposed closure of Sunbeck signal box did not take place, and an overlay was fixed over the Coxwold Branch. This can clearly be seen on later photographs, and lasted until the derailment of a Sunderland to York parcels train on 19 March 1963. The junction was destroyed and the branch and Sunbeck signal box were closed subsequently. The wings for the Signal Post Telephone Concentrator (nearer the camera) and for the signalman's desk have yet to be fitted. Pilmoor signal box closed on 28 July 1985. (BR (NER), per CJ Woolstenholmes)

Plate 9.9. Replacing a gantry-type box of 1901, a new signal box at Belford was commissioned on Sunday, 25 February 1962. The control panel in the new box was the first North Eastern Region installation to employ the N – X principle of route relay interlocking. The panel was positioned at the back of the box, giving the operator an unimpeded view of the line and adjacent level crossing. The Tweedmouth end is nearer the camera. Note that the windows are angled at 8.5 degrees. (Westinghouse Rail Systems Limited, per CJ Woolstenholmes)

Level Crossings

In Britain, safety legislation designed to protect the general public from the dangers of the railway has been a regular feature of Parliamentary proceedings since early Victorian times. Politicians of the day took a keen interest in railway development (25) and were concerned to ensure that adequate safety precautions were established, for example, at road and railway intersections. Section 1 of the Railway Level Crossings Act, 1839, made it necessary for railway companies to install gates at level crossings of public roads and to provide a suitable person to attend to them. The Railway Regulation Act, 1842, stipulated, *inter alia*, that level crossing gates were to be kept constantly closed across the public road when not required to be opened for road traffic, unless the Board of Trade ordered otherwise, and that they be so constructed as to fence in the railway at both ends of the roadway. In addition, Section 13 of the Act empowered the Board of Trade, where it thought appropriate, to authorise railway companies to construct bridges in place of level crossings at their own expense. Twenty-one years later, the Railway Clauses Act, 1863, required railway companies to erect and maintain a lodge at each level crossing. These requirements set the very rigorous standards for level crossings, which remained unchallenged for the next ninety years.

It was not until 1927 that serious consideration was given to means of improving the control of level crossings in Britain. In his paper before the Institution of Railway Signal Engineers on level crossings, Frank Horler (26) sought to test the reaction of expert opinion to the proposal to experiment with the provision of lifting barriers instead of conventional gates at level crossings.(27) The object of the proposal was to provide a form of protection for the crossing, which was adequate and simultaneously easier and less expensive to maintain. It was also intended that the arrangements might be the prototype for other similar crossings. However, it was not until 1945 that the proposal was submitted by the Divisional General Manager of the LNER (North Eastern Area) to the Ministry for approval. Provisional sanction was received in April 1946. Subsequently, the question of the legality of the proposal under Sections 47 and 48 of the Railway Clauses Act, 1845, arose. The LNER's solicitors decided therefore to legalise the use of lifting barriers beyond all doubt by Section 72 of the LNER Act, 1947. In 1952, some twenty-five years after Horler's paper, the experimental installation of mechanical lifting barriers at Warthill, on the York to Market Weighton Branch, was brought into use.(28) It aroused considerable interest both amongst railway managers and in the technical press of the time.

The arrangements generally were similar to crossings on the continent of Europe. Consisting of substantially-constructed booms of tubular steel, 30 feet long, with folding skirts, the barriers replaced four 15 feet gates and were operated via channel rodding from a conventional 3' 4" diameter 'Quadruple Purchase' geared wheel in the signal box. To counteract the effects of wind pressure, they worked in opposite directions, the effort needed to work them comparing favourably with that of working a normal four gate layout. Controlled by a lever in the signal box, two 3' diameter 'Stop' boards, with white 9" letters, illuminated at night, were placed on each side of the crossing facing road traffic. When the barriers were about to be lowered, operation of this lever rotated the 'Stop' boards on a vertical axis through 90 degrees, so that they faced road vehicles.

The installation was over-engineered; so, in the light of practical experience, modifications suggested by the MoT&CA were introduced in December 1954. These included twin red road flashing lights in each direction, with black backing boards, a single red fixed light on each barrier, and a circular group of reflectors placed on a red target in the centre of each boom. The flashing lights were operated by alternately heating and cooling mercury contained in a U-shaped glass tube. The heating and cooling caused a rise and fall of mercury within the tube, which in turn made and broke the electrical circuit connected to the lights. The tube was mounted on a wooden board attached to the front centre brick pillar inside the signal box. The original flood lighting was replaced by two 100 watt distributing reflectors.

Plate 9.10. Following the relaxation of certain requirements for manned controlled barriers in 1957 by the MoT&CA, Warthill was modified in 1959. Taken on 31 August, this view shows the simplified arrangements. It looks south-west towards the village of Stockton on the Forest. The signal box is situated on the left and the line to York is on the right. (BR (NER), per CJ Woolstenholmes)

By Section 40 of the British Transport Commission Act, 1954, the Commission was empowered 'with the written consent of the Minister [to] replace level crossing gates with lifting barriers'. It was hoped that this Act would stimulate development of level crossing control techniques, but few economies resulted because the Act provided no opportunity of operating the barriers from a remote location.

In the meantime, the NE Region management, conscious of the escalating costs of operating the large number of level crossings in its charge, was urgently seeking ways in which to ease the financial burden by withdrawing attendance at those level crossings which were lightly used. Under Section 9 of the 1954 Act, all rights of way over the minor level crossings at Harlthorpe, Balkholme and Green Lane in East Yorkshire and Coanwood, on the Alston Branch, were 'extinguished to all except persons on foot'. At Coanwood, for example, the existing 40 feet gates, hand-worked by the signalman since the removal of the gate wheel in the signal box a few years earlier, were replaced by padlocked field gates, keys being issued to persons with vehicular rights over the level crossing. 'Stop! Look! Listen!' notice boards, anti-trespass guards and a telephone to Lambley signal box were provided, these alterations enabling the closure of Coanwood signal box on 21 August 1955.

But it was the British Transport Commission Act, 1957, (29) which provided the necessary stimulus for the development of new techniques of level crossing control. Earlier that year, the Committee of Ministry of Transport and BTC officials, who had been deputed by the Minister, Harold Watkinson, to study modern Continental level crossing protection systems and practice, had presented its report. Subtitled *Report on Level Crossing Protection based on a visit to the Netherlands, Belgian and French Railways by Officers of the MoT&CA and of the BTC*, the report was dated 14 March 1957, and was published the following month. Its recommendations were designed to reduce delays to road traffic at level crossings and to reduce the spiralling cost of crossings, both in terms of staffing and physical maintenance without compromising standards of safety.(30) These included the introduction of automatically-operated half-barriers, remotely-operated barriers and the application of open crossings without gates or barriers on public roads.(31) To give effect to these revolutionary proposals, new legislation was necessary. As a result, the Act gave the Minister power 'to authorise special safety arrangements at public level crossings'. An Order, made under Section 66, permitted 'the BTC to maintain and operate such barriers, lights, traffic signs and automatic and other devices and may lay down conditions and requirements which . . . are necessary for the safety and convenience of the public'.

The way was now clear for a full-scale programme of modernisation of suitable level crossings. At first, efforts were directed to the replacement of gates with full-length lifting barriers, worked by channel rodding from conventional gate wheels in signal boxes adjacent to level crossings. Based on the experience with the apparatus installed at Warthill, these were to an improved design, developed to a large extent by Denis George Parker, of the Chief Signal & Telegraph Engineer's level crossing section.

Following extensive tests, the first production model was installed at Oxmardyke in 1961, on the quadruple track main line between Hull and Staddlethorpe, where eight gates were replaced by a pair of manually operated mechanical barriers. Inside the barrier pedestal, which was enclosed in sheet metal, the movement of the rodding (about 7$\frac{1}{2}$ inches) rotated a cross shaft, via a vertical crank and a rack and pinion. The shaft revolved through 265 degrees in moving the barrier the required 85 degrees, giving a slow, powerful start and finish to the boom movement, in addition to locking it both up and down. Constructed in timber, the boom was fitted with a folding light alloy curtain which extended to reach almost to the ground when in the horizontal position. Steel fixed weights behind the boom fulcrum, aided by an ingenious system of sliding trimming weights balanced the boom in all positions, thereby reducing the physical effort needed to raise or lower the booms. Two 12 volt, 6 watt double-sided warning lamps placed on the top of the booms in the centre of the carriageway and controlled by a micro-switch, were illuminated automatically when the barriers were moved a few degrees from their fully raised position.

Some 16 installations were commissioned by the NE Region, with a further four following after 1966, the last being placed in service at Hessle Haven as late as 1975. All consisted of two barriers only, a typical length being 24 feet, as at Rigton, (32) which survives today along with examples at Barton Hill, Norton on Tees and Nunthorpe. A re-conditioned set, removed when redundant from How Mill, has been re-assembled for use at Alston on the South Tynedale Railway.

While the barriers were economical to manufacture and an efficient and initially cheap alternative to power-operated equipment at crossings where road traffic was insufficient to justify a powered installation, they did not significantly reduce maintenance costs; nor did they eliminate staff.

The next stage was to deploy more expensive electrically-operated barriers. The first location to be completed was Teams level crossing, where, after an abortive attempt begun in 1954, it was decided eventually to widen the busy A6081 Gateshead - Blaydon road (at an approximate cost of £2750), and install four lifting barriers and flashing pairs of red lights on either side of the crossing to warn road traffic. Installation of barriers and lights cost approximately £3500.(33) Conforming to Ministry of Transport requirements, the barriers were designed and constructed by the Westinghouse Brake & Signal Company and installed by the staff of the Chief Signal & Telegraph Engineer. The modernised crossing came into operation on Monday 5 June 1961 and was inspected on the 29th.

But at Hillam Gates, where a minor road with a low level of traffic crossed the busy quadruple track main line between Milford and Burton Salmon Junction, road traffic lights were not deemed necessary when the crossing was re-equipped with two electric barriers on 17 December 1961. Of a new design, the barriers were constructed of light alloy booms derived from aluminium extrusion used on sailing dinghies. Fringed skirts were suspended from the booms. Because of their light weight, the power required to raise them was only about half that used for operating conventional lifting barriers of similar size. A special feature was the incorporation of pre-designed 'fracture points' so that the booms would break from their seating if struck by a road vehicle. This reduced the risk of damage to the barrier mechanism, and enabled the quick and easy replacement of the barriers themselves.(34)

Plate 9.11. The modernisation of the busy and complicated crossing at Teams in Gateshead was an early example of the Region's policy of installing electrically-operated barriers. The four barriers (two of which are seen here) are in the process of being installed and will protect railway lines running both sides of the box. This view looks west towards Blaydon. (BR (NER), per CJ Woolstenholmes)

Concurrently with the development of the mechanical lifting barrier, the innovative Denis Parker and a colleague, Don Peverley, were working on another design proposal which ultimately reached maturity in the form of the boom gate. Initially, it was decided to fit an electric motor to each 'toe' of the existing mechanical gates at Bootham level crossing, just outside York on the Scarborough line. Each toe motor, as it was known, drove a small solid rubber wheel, which enabled the gates to be moved through the requisite arc to close off the road from the railway. While this equipment did not eliminate staff, it was nevertheless important in that it speeded up the operation of the gates at this awkward and busy crossing; it thus eased the work of the signalman and showed substantial economies in maintenance costs.(35) In the case of Belford level crossing, it was possible to fit the existing gates with toe motors and control them from a separate small panel overlooking the level crossing. In all, some five crossings were equipped until in November 1962, the first set of motorised boom gates made an appearance at North Ormesby level crossing, on the double track branch to Whitby, just east of Middlesbrough station.

Constructed of timber throughout, with pairs of vertical bars painted alternately red and white, each boom gate was powered by a small 30 volt DC compound-wound motor, attached below the boom and directly coupled to a gearbox, incorporating a 24 volt electro-magnetic brake. Its purpose was to hold the boom gate in its fully Normal or Reverse position (*i.e.* across the road or the railway), while dynamic braking brought the gate itself to a standstill. A short cardan shaft connected the motor to the drive wheel, whose rubber tyre required 50 to 60 lbs/sq inch pressure, depending on the length of the boom. In the signal box, the control unit, consisting of a pressed steel galvanised case mounted on a pedestal, contained a three-position switch. This governed the movement of the gates, which were interlocked with the signalling.

Toe motor gates and boom gates were especially useful at crossings where the road crossed the railway at an acute angle or where nearby buildings and fences made the provision of barriers difficult. To accommodate these special conditions, the gates were often of different lengths; for example, at Coxlodge, the gates on the Down (south) side were 15' 6" and 21' 6", while those on the Up were 18' 3" and 13' 6".(36) Generally speaking, installations comprised two gates, although three and four gates varieties could be found, such as at North Ormesby (37) and Billingham on Tees. At Blaydon and Tile Shed signal boxes, both of which controlled junctions and where minor roads crossed both diverging lines, a set of boom gates was installed at each crossing. Even the Eastern Region borrowed the technology and installed a set at the difficult crossing at Parkeston West in Harwich.

Plate 9.12. When the two sets of power-worked gates installed by the LNER in 1929 at Blaydon began to fail more frequently in the early 1960s, it was decided to replace them with boom gates. This is Factory Road level crossing on the former main line from Scotswood, looking west to Carlisle on 9 September 1963. Because this busy and difficult crossing was on the skew, the gates were of unequal lengths, and the arcs of the paths of the rubber-tyred wheels can clearly be seen on the road surface. (BR (NER), per CJ Woolstenholmes)

By the end of 1966, some 28 crossings sported boom gates, while another two proposals were actively being considered. Another six lightly-used crossings were fitted with the cheaper alternative, which were hand-worked by signalmen, gate keepers or trainmen. Installation of both types continued after 1966. Ten power-operated examples remained in use on Network Rail in January 2007.

The NE Region was also responsible for the introduction into Britain of what is now known as the automatic open level crossing (locally monitored), or AOCL. Again, the development of this apparatus was propelled by a desire to reduce costs by withdrawing attendance by crossing keepers at locations where road and rail traffic levels were low. Yafforth level crossing, on the single line between Northallerton and Ainderby, was the first to be tackled, when HA Short proposed its conversion to an open crossing in a letter to the MoT&CA, dated 13 January 1959. A reply from Colonel Dennis McMullen, one of the Ministry's Railway Inspecting Officers, stated that a visual warning to road users, initiated by the train itself, was considered necessary although no audible warning need be provided. Detailed design work then ensued and the crossing, having been authorised by the British Railways Board (Bedale Branch Railway) (Yafforth Crossing) Order, 1963, made 19 July 1963, came into operation on Tuesday 10 September that year.

The crossing had neither gates nor barriers, and was unattended. Road traffic was controlled by double-sided twin red flashing light road signals positioned in line with the fences on each side of the railway. The aspects of these road signals were actuated by an approaching train occupying one of the 100 yard long track circuits, situated on each side of the crossing. Two notice boards for train drivers were placed alongside the railway in each direction and were worded 'Ungated level crossing 250 yards ahead' and 'Whistle', the latter at 200 yards from the crossing. The train's speed was limited to 10 mph from passing the Whistle board until it had passed completely clear of the crossing. In addition to the notice boards, a white indicator lamp, fixed adjacent to each flashing light unit, was focussed to shine along the railway in each direction. It gave one of three indications to the train driver:

No indication: Power supply on – Red lights lit and flashing;

White flashing light: Power supply failed – Red lights lit and flashing;

White steady light: Power supply failed – Red lights failed.

Should the second indication be displayed, a driver had merely to report the circumstances immediately on arrival at the next signal box. If however a white steady light appeared, a driver had to bring his train to a stand short of the crossing and proceed over it only when satisfied that the crossing was clear and that it was safe to do so. Yafforth was followed by installations at Ham Hall (between Ainderby and Leeming Bar) on 23 October 1966, and Battersby Road (between Battersby and Castleton) on 6 November 1966, while development work on a further three crossings continued.

On the lightly-used roads at Morpeth North and Wooden Gate (south of Alnmouth), another new type of level crossing protection, known as 'on call' barriers, was installed in 1964. It was interlocked with the signalling system. Beside each barrier pivot post, a bell, together with a telephone and a call plunger linked to the controlling signal box, was provided. Depression of the plunger by an intending road user caused an annunciator to sound in the signal box. When there were no trains in the vicinity of the crossing, the signalman raised the barriers by remote control. After a pre-determined time, usually 45 or 60 seconds, although in certain circumstances this could be longer, audible and visual warnings were given to road users to indicate that the barriers were about to descend automatically. In case of emergency, another plunger, situated within the crossing and by each barrier pivot post, could be depressed. This action disengaged the barrier mechanisms, enabling the

Plate 9.13. The 'on-call' barriers at Wooden Gate, commissioned on Sunday, 31 January 1964, were controlled from Alnmouth signal box. This detail view looks east – Newcastle is to the right – and shows the instructional notice boards for users, the metal box housing the phone to the signalbox, below which the plunger to call the signalman was situated. Similar equipment was fixed on the other approach to the crossing. The wicket gates remained unlocked at all times. Maximum speed through the crossing was 80 mph. (BR (NER), per CJ Woolstenholmes)

road user to raise the barriers by hand and leave the crossing. While the North Eastern Region was keen to modernise a number of minor road crossings by this method, including for example Newham and Mill Lane (near Staddlethorpe) (38), the concept never gained universal acceptance, the number of crossings installed barely reaching double figures on the whole of BR. The MoT declared 'on call' barrier crossings obsolete early in 1968, although an example at Ashwell (near Oakham) survives.

On the single line Alston Branch, the NE Region was successful in gaining Ministry approval for two 'Open Crossings with St Andrew Crosses', as they were then known. Unlike the pioneer AOCL, no lights of any sort were provided. Instead, a St Andrews Cross was erected on each road approach, while illuminated Stop boards, two yards on each rail approach displayed 'Stop. Whistle before proceeding'. A driver had to bring his train to a stand at the Stop board, sound the horn and proceed cautiously over the crossing only if it was clear. Any failure of the equipment, such as the lighting of the Stop boards, had to be reported as soon as possible to the station master or person in charge at Alston or Haltwhistle. The new arrangements at Featherstone Park were brought into use on Sunday 4 September 1966 and at Slaggyford a week later. Both gate boxes were closed and all signalling was dispensed with except the four distant signals, which were fixed at caution.

British Railways-designed Mark I automatic half-barriers were proposed for installation at 19 locations on the York - Beverley line in connection with the CTC scheme, and at a number of other places, including Cayton*, Clifton (near Morpeth), Hepscott*, Denton School* (west of Haltwhistle), Dalton Gates and Straggleton Gates (Richmond Branch), Scruton, New Lane (Earswick) and Sandhill Lane (Selby). For various reasons, however, none of these schemes came to fruition during the life of the NE Region; only those with an asterisk were completed quite some years later. It was not until 1964 that the NE Region commissioned its first examples of the new BR standard Mark II design automatic half-barriers at Follingsby (near Pelaw) and Naworth on 5 and 19 July respectively. By the end of 1966, a further seven sets had been brought into use, and work was progressing on another twelve, which were commissioned during 1967.

Plate 9.14. Ancient (in the form of a Q6) meets modern (the new BR standard Mark II design automatic half-barriers – AHB) at Follingsby, on the Leamside line. Supervised by the signalman at Wardley signal box (similar in design to Wilton Works), 1470 yards away or Pelaw power box when Wardley was switched out, the crossing was the first AHB to be commissioned in the Region, on 5 July 1964. Twin-red double-sided flashing lights and loud-sounding warning bells were provided on each barrier pedestal. Nearby there were two different notice boards which read: 'In emergency or before crossing with exceptional or heavy loads or with cattle, telephone signalman' and 'Another train is coming if lights continue to flash.' The telephones were housed in the sides of the barrier pedestals and were not at all conspicuous to intending road users. Note the cattle-cum-trespass guards. Line speed was 60 mph. (BR (NER), per CJ Woolstenholmes)

Developments in Telecommunications Engineering

To gain experience with short-wave radio telephone communication between fixed and moving points, the NE Region conducted experiments in the adjacent yards at Newport in 1957. Known locally as No 1 Up and No 1 Down, the yards were separately controlled by their own hump ground frames. The equipment in each ground frame comprised a transmitter/receiver, re-entrant horn loudspeaker, microphone and foot-operated send/receive switch. Additionally in each ground frame, a special foot-operated emergency stop switch was installed. When depressed, it transmitted a high-pitched warning note, instructing the driver to stop immediately and await instructions over the radio telephone. Each locomotive was equipped with a mobile set consisting of a transmitter/receiver, an extension control unit with a hand micro-telephone, and re-entrant horn loudspeaker. Supplied and installed by British Communications Corporation Limited, of Wembley, the equipment in each yard operated on adjacent channels 100 kilocycles per second apart. Although the locomotives fitted with the radio telephones could work in either yard, a special Yale lock on each ensured that the driver communicated only with the pointsman in the yard in which he was working. Aimed at speeding up the work of marshalling freight trains, the system was of particular value during foggy weather and the hours of darkness, when communication by fixed and hand signals, and by word of mouth became difficult and led to inefficient operation.

Using equipment supplied by Pye Telecommunications Limited, of Cambridge, further experiments were undertaken early in 1958 to establish the feasibility of employing VHF radio communication to maintain telephone contact with a moving train engaged in snow clearing operations between Bowes and Kirkby Stephen over Stainmore Summit. A transmitter/receiver was installed at Bank Top station, Darlington, with directional aerials mounted on the roof of the clock tower, at a height of 90 feet above sea level. Directional aerials at an approximate height of 950 feet above sea level were erected at Bowes station, which was used as a link-through point between Darlington and the moving train. On the western side of the summit, at Kirkby Stephen station, another transmitter/receiver was provided, with an aerial mounted on the roof, about 750 feet above sea level, while in the grounds of The New Inn public house, Great Musgrave, a fourth transmitter/receiver, with an aerial about 500 feet above sea level, was established as a link-through point between the moving train and Kirkby Stephen.

Representing a snow plough, a brake composite coach was fitted out with a transmitter/receiver and horizontal polarised aerials mounted transversely across its roof. Inside the coach, a control unit, powered from the coach lighting batteries, was provided in a sound-proof cubicle. All fixed equipment was operated from a 240 volt 50 cycle ac supply, that at Bowes being powered by a petrol engine standby set. Except for a dead spot at Winston station, and a momentary loss in one of the cuttings, the tests proved that loud and clear signals could be maintained throughout the length of the route between the moving train and the control points at Darlington and Kirkby Stephen.

By 1963, the system, unique on BR, had been refined for use in Tyne, Tees and Healey Mill Yards.(39) Radio telephone transmissions to the locomotives from fixed locations, such as the Yardmaster's and Yard Inspectors' offices, were made via an inductive loop; the driver replied by an UHF radio link. The system now also incorporated cab-signalling. Inside the locomotive cab, a repetition in miniature of one of the hump signal aspects was given, affording visual indication to the driver. The indications were 'hump slow', 'hump fast', 'stop' or 'emergency stop'. Between each change of signals, an audible indication was given. Although the 'emergency stop' signal was visually the same as 'stop', the audible signal was different.

The mobile equipment fitted in the locomotives consisted of a control unit with which was mounted the telephone handset; a cab signal indicator; a low frequency receiver; an UHF transmitter and ancillary equipment. Installed in the control tower buildings at each marshalling yard, rack-mounted fixed station equipment consisted of relay switching apparatus; a modulator; a low frequency transmitter; a tone generator; an UHF receiver for incoming calls from drivers. By operating a lever key on the panel, the control tower operator could bring the cab signalling into use. The signals would be extended, under the control of the hump signal switch, to the locomotive selected. Similarly, the operation of a lever key on the control tower panel, and at switchboards in the various yard offices, would effect radio communication with the locomotives. This caused an audible signal to be given in the cab, enabling conversation as in a normal telephone call.

All the outstation switchboards, panel switch boards and switching apparatus were manufactured by the CS&TE workshops at York. Associated Electrical Industries-GRS Limited was awarded the contract for the manufacture and supply of the low frequency and UHF transmitting and receiving equipment for the three yards.

Like the other Regions at Nationalisation, the North Eastern inherited a largely out-moded network of telegraph and telephone equipment, which was of limited capacity and in urgent need of renewal. It was expensive to operate both in terms of staffing and maintenance. All the existing telephone exchanges needed switchboard operators, and all centres were connected by means of open-pole routes alongside the railway lines, which due to the effects of sun, wind, rain, snow and ice, were difficult to maintain in good working order.

Little progress in replacing this aging equipment had been achieved in the first decade of the Region's life. The catalyst for investment in new equipment was the Modernisation Plan. By the time of its publication in 1955, significant advances in telecommunications engineering had been made. For example, in 1950, the world's first permanent railroad operated microwave system had been installed on the Chicago, Rock Island & Pacific Railroad. By 1955, over 30,000 route miles of microwave had been installed in the USA by communication companies, industrial and transport concerns, and the military agencies.

In following the general policy, stipulated by the Chief Signal Engineering Officer, BTC, for the development of a telecommunications network throughout BR, Charles C Ellison, Assistant to the S & TE, Telecommunications, BR (NER), was aiming to establish a modern railway telephone network giving 'on demand' subscriber dialling facilities throughout the region, while simultaneously taking into account the telephone facilities which would ultimately be needed to integrate such a system with those being developed by other regions. It required automatic telephone exchanges at principal centres and adequate trunk facilities. The NE Region was quick to get off the mark; the first automatic exchange to be completed under the Modernisation Plan was York (in March 1959). Planning had begun in 1955 at an estimated cost of £66,702 but an extra outlay of £16,472 was authorised in 1957 to cover additional work and the increased cost of labour and materials.(40) York was followed by similar exchanges at Middlesbrough, Newcastle (March 1961), Leeds (1962), Darlington and Hull.

Impressive as these schemes were, in terms of improved performance and extra capacity, they were overshadowed (almost literally) by a highly innovative scheme, which was unique on BR and regarded at the time as something of an experiment. It was discussed formally on 16 May 1958, at a meeting of the North Eastern Area Board, which recommended, for approval in principle by the BTC, the provision of a microwave telephone system between York, Darlington and Newcastle, a distance of 80 miles, at an estimated cost of £237,378; and the inclusion of the item in the BTC's 1958/9 Parliamentary Bill. The scheme was given approval in principle by the BTC at its meeting on 19 June, 1958. By the time it had been developed fully for approval by the BTC Works & Equipment Committee on 25 October, 1960, the net cost had risen to £248,860. At that meeting, the reasons for the early introduction of the scheme were explained. It was calculated that it would lead to an annual saving of some £10,800 in day to day maintenance. In addition, to continue with the renewal of the pole route as essential maintenance would cost £171,000, and increase over the next five or six years. If the introduction of the microwave link were postponed, the existing sub-standard and restrictive factors, particularly relating to the trunk telephone circuits, would be perpetuated. On technical grounds, it was considered to be unsound practice to seek to increase the existing inadequate number of trunk telephone circuits by adding more wires to the already overloaded open pole route. Such circuits would also be subject to intermittent faults caused by the weather. Neither would they be compatible for use with the automatic exchanges at Newcastle, Darlington, Middlesbrough and York, which had already been authorised. To replace the pole route by cabling could not be justified on the grounds of cost. Not only was the link cheaper than cabling but also its great advantage was that it was capable of extension to 720 channels, if required, at the cost only of the extra terminal equipment. Cable would be restricted to 300 channels. The comparative estimates for cable and microwave showed first costs and annual outlays of a radio system to be approximately half the cost of a cable system. (41) Following the granting of parliamentary powers to purchase land and erect towers of varying defined heights (42), the NE Region invited tenders for the scheme. In a letter dated 6 April 1961, from the Secretary-General, BTC, the Region was informed that the Works & Equipment Committee had approved the acceptance of the tender of Marconi's Wireless Telegraph Company Limited in the sum of £196,047 12s 6d, including import duty, for the supply, delivery, installation and commissioning of the scheme. The contract was signed on 18 April.

In a microwave radio system, communication is achieved by a series of transmitters and receivers working into paraboloidal aerials, with diameters ranging from 6 feet to 12 feet, positioned along the route. Since microwaves do not follow the curvature of the earth, but travel in straight lines, it was necessary to mount the dish aerials on towers or high buildings, or site them on high ground, or a combination of all three. A condition of the contract was that the contractor should carry out over the whole of the route a propagation survey in order to establish by actual radio tests the suitability of the route chosen.

The plan therefore envisaged terminal stations at the three main centres with two unattended repeater stations on intervening high ground. At York, the dish aerial was positioned on a 46 feet high tower on the roof of the Regional Headquarters offices, the terminal radio apparatus being housed in a room at the top of the building. At Darlington, an 80 feet tower was mounted on the roof of Bank Top station. To support the additional weight, part of the building which would accommodate the microwave multiplex and automatic telephone exchange equipment was reconstructed by fitting a special steel frame. Intermediately, Woolmoor, a hill 830 feet above sea level, situated just outside the North York Moors National Park boundary about five miles north-north east of Thirsk and about 24 miles from York, provided 'line of sight' conditions; it had the added advantages of good road access and a power supply available about half a mile from the site. North of Darlington, a tower was erected on a hill near an old disused windmill at Dean Bank, just to the west of Ferryhill. At Newcastle, it was intended to erect a 191 feet high tower on top of the telecommunications apparatus room. When however it became known that a multi-storey block of flats was to be built directly in the line of sight (at Gateshead), it was decided to increase the height of the tower to 275 feet. Powers for this alteration were sought in a clause of the BTC 1961/62 Bill. But by April 1962, the authorised scheme had had to be changed yet again because planning permission for such a large tower in the centre of Newcastle had been refused. The solution was to erect a 366 feet tower in Tyne Marshalling Yard, then under construction, four miles to the south, with the link into Newcastle being completed by two co-axial cables. This variation cost a further £10,731, bringing the total for the scheme to £259,951, still considerably cheaper than cabling, and only £22,213 more than the cost estimated in 1958, an overspend of less than 10%.(43) The clauses dealing with the acquisition of powers for the increase in height of the Newcastle tower were deleted from the 1961/62 Bill.

On 31 May 1964, the NE Region successfully brought into use Britain's first privately owned and operated microwave radio telephone link. Initially the system catered for 159 speech channels, which were later expanded to 300. Apart from accommodating normal telephone traffic, the high channelling capacity enabled transmission of other data such as seat reservations, stores requisitions and train and wagon movements. As sub-contractors to Marconi, the BIC Construction Company Limited supplied the five lattice steel towers, while the Automatic Telephone & Electric Company Limited, Marconi's trading associate, was responsible for the carrier multiplex part of the contract.

Conclusion

At the end of the Region's independent existence, its S&T engineers and staff could reflect with not a little pride and justification on their considerable achievements. Not only had they managed to continue and complete their predecessors' pioneering work, but they had also succeeded in developing and fructifying several significant innovative ideas of their own, some of which had been adopted subsequently for system-wide use. *Multum in parvo* is perhaps a fitting tribute and suitable epitaph to the spirit, vision and dedication of the staff of the Region's S&T Department, who were at the leading edge of the new technologies in the Modernisation era.

Endnotes:

(1) AE Tattersall was once described to the author as being 'a small man with big ideas'.
(2) For details of this and other re-signalling schemes, see *The Railway Gazette*, various issues 1937 - 1965.
(3) BTC Works & Equipment Committee Minute 328 (Item N° 42) of 15 December 1954. [National Archives file AN97/207]
(4) The work also paved the way for the closure of the Leeds Northern line between Northallerton and Starbeck. Used predominantly by freight trains, this route proved difficult to operate owing to the fearsome gradients especially between Leeds and Harrogate.
(5) *Report on the Modernisation and Electrification of the ECML between King's Cross and Newcastle and Certain Associated Lines*, BR (ER) and (NER), June 1959.
(6) A 'hybrid' signal box generally comprised a mechanical lever frame for the operation of points close to the signal box, and a switch panel for the operation of signals, and points remote from the signal box, such as Low Gates.
(7) The panel from Doncaster South is preserved at the National Railway Museum, York.

(8) This panel is preserved at the National Railway Museum, York.
(9) In his book *British Railway Signalling*, published by George Allen and Unwin in 1969, OS Nock recounts the same story from the point of view of a signalling contractor.
(10) Letter from GC Thew to author, 1975.
(11) *Report from the Select Committee on Nationalised Industries together with the Proceedings of the Committee: British Railways*, 11 July 1960, paragraph 297.
(12) *Modernisation and Re-Equipment of British Railways*, paragraph 106 et seq.
(13) North Eastern Area Board Minutes, Minute NE1176 of 19 June 1959 [National Archives file AN117/4].
(14) Patent number 23384/6.1.1895.
(15) Patent numbers 10507/4.5.1906 and 14089/19.6.1906.
(16) North Eastern Area Board Minutes, Minute NE676 of 18 October 1957 which refers to BTC Minute 10/402 of 19 September 1957 [National Archives file AN117/2].
(17) North Eastern Area Board Minutes, Minute NE748 of 17 January 1958 [National Archives file AN117/3].
(18) Paragraph 22.
(19) This was the standard practice abroad with CTC schemes, which typically featured long stretches of single line, punctuated by strategically placed loops, where trains could be crossed.
(20) The first automatic half-barrier crossing in Britain was commissioned at Spath, near Uttoxeter, BR (London Midland Region) on 5 February 1961.
(21) North Eastern Area Board Minutes, Minute GPC310 of 19 January 1961 [National Archives file AN117/6].
(22) Conversation with WL Cartwright, Assistant S&T Engineer, BR (ER), York, 1976.
(23) *The Railway Gazette*, 6 February 1953, page 151.
(24) North Eastern Area Board Minutes, Minute NE578 of 17 May 1957 [National Archives file AN117/2].
(25) Between 1840 and 1900, there were some 31 Acts of Parliament relating to the regulation of railways.
(26) Assistant Signal & Telegraph Engineer, North Eastern Area, LNER.
(27) It should not be thought, however, that the concept of barriers was an innovative development of that time; the first lifting barriers in Europe had been installed near Montreux in Switzerland as long ago as 1909, while in Britain, 'drop gates', as they were sometimes known, had been brought into use at a minor road level crossing on a colliery railway system in Northumberland in 1922.
(28) Warthill had been selected for a number of sound reasons: it was close to the York HQ offices, and the existing crossing gates were difficult to maintain and were in need of renewal anyway.
(29) 5 & 6 Eliz 2 Ch xxxiii. Royal Assent 1 October 1957.
(30) Annual costs system-wide in 1956 were estimated at over £1m.
(31) Open crossings on Light Railways were already authorised.
(32) BR (NER) drawing No YS385095, dated 11 August 1966.
(33) National Archives file MT114/242.
(34) National Archives file MT114/245.
(35) North Eastern Area Board, Minute GPC 485, Thursday 12 April, 1962. [National Archives file AN117/7]
(36) BR (NER) drawing No YS385007, dated 17 April 1963.

(37) *A Pictorial Survey of Railway Signalling*, Allen and Woolstenholmes, OPC, 1991, plate 127.
(38) National Archives files MT114/3888 and MT114/3923.
(39) *Healey Mills Marshalling Yard*, BR (NER), July 1963 [BR35028/4]
(40) BTC, Works & Equipment Committee, List 85, August 1957.
(41) In July 1958, the estimated cost for installation of telecommunications cables between Newcastle and Burnmouth (70 miles) had been £757,008. A microwave link for this section had been considered too, but had been rejected by September 1959 in favour of a carrier cable because of the type of terrain over the route. BTC, Works & Equipment Committee, Minute 1558/9, 1959.
(42) BTC Act 1959, 7 & 8 Eliz. 2 ch. xliv.
(43) North Eastern Area Board, Minute GPC 503(a), 14 June 1962. [National Archives file AN117/7]

Appendix 9.1
Principal Officers, BR (NER), S&T Department

Signal & Telecommunications Engineer
John Holden Fraser, 1948 – 1951 (promoted);
Arthur Frederic Wigram, 1952 – 1966. *

Assistant S&T Engineer
Robert James Purves, 1948 – 1951 (retired);
George Charlton Thew, 1951 – 1966. #

* Re-designated Chief Signal & Telecommunications Engineer, with effect from 1 January 1961, by order of the Secretary-General of the BTC.
# GC Thew was Acting S&T Engineer in the first two months of 1952 until AF Wigram arrived in York to take up his new post.

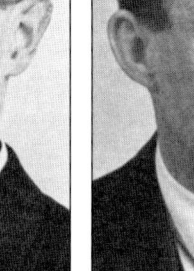

John Holden Fraser — *Arthur Frederic Wigram* — *Robert James Purves* — *George Charlton Thew*
(Railway Gazette International Limited, per CJ Woolstenholmes)

Appendix 9.2
Major Power-Operated Signal Boxes Opened and Planned by the North Eastern Region

Date	Place	Type of Panel / Number of Routes	Number of Boxes Displaced	Cost (£000s)
1951	York	OCS / 825	7	
1958	Huddersfield †	IFS	2	177
1959	Newcastle	OCS / 641	4	780
1960	Pelaw	OCS / 45	2	264
1961	Tollerton †	STC / 30	1	
1961	Tweedmouth	OCS / 90	4	
1962	Belford	N – X / 31	2	
1962	Tees (first stage) #	N – X / 315 *	4 *	
1962	York Yard South †	N – X / 188	1	128
1962	Hessle Road	N – X / 75	1	
1962	Gateshead	N – X / 234	5	619
1963	Tyne #	N – X / 523	10	1,213
1963	Healey Mills #	N – X / 464	7	853
1964	Benton	N – X / 39	9	
1964	Heaton	N – X / 138	3	
1965	Sunderland †	IFS / 33	2	
1967	Leeds	N – X / 520	17	

The building also incorporated a Hump Yard Control Tower.
* By 1963.
Note: All the signal boxes except for those marked † were equipped by the Westinghouse Brake & Signal Company. Details are correct at opening date; in many cases, the area of control was extended subsequently, although not necessarily by the North Eastern Region.

Ships, Shipping, and the North Eastern Region
John G Teasdale
with contributions by John Edgington

Plate 10.1. SS 'Selby' moored at Goole on 29 October 1957. She was built in 1922 for Wilson's and North Eastern Railway Shipping Company Limited, and operated from Goole and Hull to the continent until withdrawal in June 1958. Typical of the ships acquired at nationalisation, she was propelled by a three-cylinder triple-expansion steam engine. (TJ Edgington Collection)

The Transport Act, 1947, nationalised all those companies which were in the business of inland transport. By definition then, shipping companies in the business of maritime transport were not, for the most part, affected by the new Act. However, the British Transport Commission did nevertheless acquire fleets of ships. These ships were those that had been owned by subsidiary companies of the Big Four.

In May 1935, two of those Big Four companies, the LNER and the LMSR, had formed jointly the Humber Steamship Lines Control Committee (AHL). This organisation had been charged with the management of: the shipping services of the LNER's Great Central Section; the shipping services of the LMSR's Goole Section; the Hull and Netherlands Steam Shipping Company Limited; Wilson's and North Eastern Railway Shipping Company Limited. The Second World War put paid to the activities of the LNER's Great Central Section. When the Big Four were nationalised, the BTC took control of the nine ships of the LMSR's Goole Section, and allocated them to the North Eastern Region of British Railways. The four ships belonging to the Hull and Netherlands Steam Shipping Company Limited and to Wilson's and North Eastern Railway Shipping Company Limited remained under the names of those companies – which, as former subsidiary companies of the LNER, were now themselves the property of the BTC. (In the case of the latter company, the BTC was only part-owner, as a private company that was not nationalised, Ellerman's Wilson Line Limited, owned fifty percent of the company's shares.) Despite the hiatus of nationalisation, the ships continued to be managed by AHL, and continued to operate out of ports on the River Humber or, in the case of Goole, on the River Ouse, to diverse European ports.

Plate 10.2. SS 'Blyth' moored at Goole on 29 October 1957. This ship was built in 1930 to operate the LMSR's traffic out of Goole. However, she suffered collision damage while on her trials, and did not enter service until January 1931. She was withdrawn from service in May 1959. (TJ Edgington Collection)

182

In the early years of British Railways, the North Eastern Region's senior officers exercised the same strategic management of AHL as they did of their railway – none whatsoever. However, this began to change as the BTC began to devolve power to the Regions. When the North Eastern Area Board was formed on 1 January 1955, its members assumed responsibility for the management of AHL as well as of the Region's railways. General Manager HA Short, who had developed considerable expertise in matters marine during his service on the Southern Railway, was appointed Chairman of AHL. Deploying that expertise, Short drew up a re-organisation scheme for AHL that would fully incorporate the operation into the Region as its Shipping and Continental Department. This scheme did not find favour with either the BTC or the Ministry of Transport – the latter regarded railway-owned shipping as an anachronism not to be further encouraged. In February 1957 however, AHL was indeed re-organised, though not as envisaged by Short. The Hull and Netherlands Steam Shipping Company was re-named Associated Humber Lines Limited (AHL Limited). Most of the shares in Wilson's and North Eastern Railway Shipping Company Limited owned by Ellerman's Wilson Line Limited were bought up by the BTC, and the company absorbed by AHL Limited. Unlike AHL, which had managed ships but not owned them, AHL Limited actually owned ships. All but two of the ships the new company acquired were old steam ships however, so an extensive modernisation programme was instituted; in total, eight new motor ships were ordered in addition to the two that had been ordered prior to the formation of the new company. The old steam ships that had been operated by the LMSR's Goole Section remained the property of the North Eastern Region. Two motor ships ordered by the BTC were also allocated to the Region: *Kirkham Abbey* and *Byland Abbey*. These ships were specifically designed to work the route Goole – Copenhagen, and had refrigerated holds to accommodate such as butter and bacon. All of the Region's ships continued to be managed by AHL Limited in the same way as they had previously been managed by AHL. The Region's fleet steadily shrunk in size however, as ships were sold or scrapped.

The North Eastern Area Board lost its strategic management of AHL Limited as a consequence of the passing of the Transport Act, 1962 – on 1 January 1963, the responsibility was given instead to the Transport Holding Company. The successor to the Area Board, the North Eastern Railway Board, decided early in 1965 that it would get out of the shipping business altogether. In March the BTC approved the sale of the Region's two remaining ships to Ellerman's Wilson Line Limited, along with the sole rights to trade on the route Goole – Copenhagen. When this sale went through in September 1965, the railways in the north-east of England severed a link with the sea that had been in place since the middle of the Nineteenth Century when the Hartlepool Dock & Railway Company had bought three steam ships in order to extend its reach to continental Europe.

Plate 10.3.
MV 'Melrose Abbey', built for AHL Limited to operate the company's Hull - Rotterdam service. She began her maiden voyage on 17 January 1959. Typical of the post-war ships, she was propelled by two eight-cylinder diesel engines. (TJ Edgington Collection)

Plate 10.4.
MV 'Selby', moored at Heysham on 28 July 1970. She began her maiden voyage for AHL Limited, from Goole to Amsterdam, on 8 July 1959. In March 1965 she was sold to the London Midland Region, for which she conveyed traffic across the Irish Sea. (TJ Edgington)

The North Eastern Region : A Personal View
Illtyd Lloyd Gray-Jones

How did it come about that a Welshman found himself beginning his railway career on Tyneside? The answer lies in the policy of the LNER in sending its Traffic Apprentices (Management Trainees) as far away from home as possible. When I joined British Railways in December 1949, graduate recruitment to the Eastern and North Eastern Regions was still in the hands of the former LNER organisation based in London. My home at the time was Abergavenny and so Tyneside was an obvious destination. Hence the letter of appointment from York told me I was to begin my training at Stocksfield, after first reporting to the Regional Staff Officer at York.

Stocksfield was completely new to me but I soon found myself at home. The infectious vigour of the Geordie accent was no problem, its rhythms reminiscent of South Wales. The industrial areas had their attractions but the Tyne Valley was delightful. For a historian there was the Roman Wall and combining this with an expedition to look at the stations along the West Line was an ideal way to spend leisure time. There was a timeless quality about both the Wall and the stations, with their fine architecture – both seemed eternal. The Wall is still there, going from strength to strength, but the stations . . .

Plate 11.1. I took this photograph of the station house at Stocksfield in June 1955. However, there had been no changes made at the station since I had begun my career there in 1949. (IL Gray-Jones)

That, however, is hindsight and Stocksfield station was a vigorous, well-established community in 1949. It had a long tradition of starting the training of traffic apprentices including a pre-war trainee, John Bonham Carter, who had ended up as a General Manager. The staff took a relaxed attitude to the inevitable errors of an over-enthusiastic and inexperienced trainee. My own mini disaster was to confuse the different parts of an invoice for government traffic dispatched by the local RAF station. The invoice was supposed to be simple and foolproof, but it was neither. However, there was no permanent damage to Stocksfield's freight receipts.

The pride of the station staff in their place of work was reflected in the care taken of the buildings. Although the station had not been painted since the 1930s the interiors of, for example, the signal box and waiting rooms were immaculate. The station garden was outstanding and Stocksfield regularly gained a first prize. There was great rivalry with Riding Mill next down the line which also had a famous garden, but this did not prevent the two station masters from cooperating fully in other respects.

The station itself was still an important part of village life and the booking office a regular meeting place, not only for passengers. The ticket window was rarely used and most transactions took place in the office whether collecting papers, dispatching parcels or using the telephone. Security was not a priority in those days!

There was a great contrast between the informal atmosphere at Stocksfield and that at my next two stations, South Shields and Sunderland Goods Depots. They were large stations, organised in departments with definite functions. At South Shields, I became acquainted with the complex world of goods rating and charging which needed a lifetime study to become expert. At Sunderland I spent more time outside on the handling side. A new technique to me was what was known as 'perambulation' of forwarded (outgoing) sundries traffic. Instead of being unloaded on to a deck and barrowed over to wagons alongside the deck, the goods were taken around to a pre-set rake of wagons in the yard and loaded direct from road vehicle to wagon. It was a technique which came in handy later in my career, in another Region.

The next stage of training was the District Goods Manager's office at Newcastle, more formal still with much time spent in reading bulky files of correspondence. Some light relief came in one section where the head of section welcomed me with the news that they were a little behind with correspondence, but that I could rescue him from his problem. He produced some of the files of the outstanding correspondence, rattled off a stream of instructions about how to deal with them and rang for a typist. I had never previously dictated a letter but fortunately the typist was capable and experienced and my halting words came back as lucid script. Unfortunately, I got one of the addresses wrong and a letter came back saying my letter had been redirected, ending, 'kindly note for the future'.

In the North-East, passenger traffic was inevitably regarded as less important than goods and the period of training less intense. A spell in the booking office at Sunderland gave an insight into passenger accountancy and a spell in the Station Master's office an idea of the complex task of running a large organisation. The District Passenger Manager's office at Newcastle was concerned with things like excursion traffic, seat and sleeper reservations, parcels traffic, accountancy and publicity.

The final stage of the commercial part of training came with a spell in the Commercial Superintendent's office at York Regional Headquarters. Here there were wider perspectives and more understanding of issues like the setting of exceptional goods rates and the policies dictating the shape of passenger services. There was contact too with senior officers who decided these things.

At the end of each stage of training one had to submit a written report to the Divisional Training Committee on one's impressions. Each department was represented on the Committee by a senior officer, and Traffic Apprentices were interviewed and questioned about their progress. One of my reports had made some mildly critical comments about the cost of special measures to deal with 'vulnerable' goods, *e.g.* tobacco, wines and spirits, clothing *etc*. As a result I received a two page memorandum justifying the special measures, signed by no less than the Assistant Commercial Superintendent! It was a reminder of the interest taken by senior management in the progress of trainees.

In March 1951 at the end of my commercial training I returned to Tyneside, to the Sunderland District, for Operating and Motive Power training. This began with a period of sixteen weeks with the District Inspectors attached to the District Operating Superintendent's office at Sunderland. It was a most instructive experience – the District Inspectors were the backbone of the Operating Department. Their duties included examining operating staff on knowledge of rules and regulations, investigating any operating problems and general supervision of any special working. They were highly experienced and anxious to share their knowledge and experience and I hope that some of this rubbed off on me.

One of the major events in the Sunderland District was the Durham Miners' Gala. On this day virtually all the members of the National Union of Mineworkers in County Durham converged on Durham for a day of celebration, of parades through the city and a grand meeting addressed by a leading politician. The railway's part in this was to lay on an intensive programme of special trains to get the crowds to Durham and home again. Closed branches were opened for the one day, the most important of which was the Durham Elvet Branch, closed since 1930 but on this day carrying its most intensive service ever. Months of planning went into this event and the smooth running of the service depended on the supervisors on the spot. Taking part in the planning and being out on the day was great experience.

The next stage of training was to get experience of working in a marshalling yard. Because the Sunderland District no longer had a main yard, I went to Heaton, north of Newcastle, and then on to Blaydon to the west. The main impression I got from this period was the amount of time wagons spent in being transferred from one yard to another without being any further towards their eventual destination. It was also dangerous work for the shunting staff – the design of the yards in the Newcastle area was primitive.

Plate 11.2. This photograph is dated 26 July 1952, when I was on duty in connection with the working of trains for the Durham Miners' Gala. The view is of Durham Elvet station; the signal box at the end of the platform is prominent. (IL Gray-Jones)

The same could be said of my next port of call, Tyne Dock Motive Power Depot. The facilities for maintaining, coaling and watering the large stock of locomotives here were primitive and so were the staff amenities. Despite this, traffic was kept moving and the raw materials for Consett steelworks were never held up. This meant a good deal of work dealing with incidents such as derailments, and the tool vans were out quite frequently. One sign of hope for the future was the development of the well-known Tyne Dock – Consett ore trains. The first of the special wagons for this traffic arrived at Tyne Dock during my time there and the specially-fitted locomotives were also on hand. (There is more about this subject elsewhere in this History.)

A final period of twenty-six weeks in the Sunderland District Operating Superintendent's office was spent going around the various sections. Time in the Freight Trains section was most interesting because of the planning of the timetable for the Consett ore trains. The District Control office was a very lively place whatever the hour as the traffic was kept moving. The Mineral Leading office looked after the supply of empty wagons to the local collieries and the movement away of the loaded wagons. The controllers had a better idea of the potential output of the pits than the NCB staff and any exaggerated requests for empties were quickly rejected!

The final stage of training was a return to the Regional Headquarters at York to see the head office view of operating. It has to be said that this was not the most exciting period and I was not sorry when it came to an end in September 1952. After formal training, it was usual for Traffic Apprentices to spend a year or so on special inquiry work and I was allocated to the Transit Investigation Committee.

The Committee was a small body consisting of an experienced former Yard Master and two Traffic Apprentices. All kinds of delays in transit were investigated and the work meant lots of time spent trudging around marshalling yards and goods depots investigating working methods, often at night and usually in bad weather. It was hard on the feet – railway ballast is uncomfortable to walk on and remarkably destructive of boots! For all that it was fascinating and one example will be enough to show the detective work involved.

There was a complaint that sundries traffic from Stockton to Leeds was being delayed. According to the timetable of transits prepared by head office it should have been delivered the day after collection and I was told to find the reason for the delay. I suspected Stockton and went down to follow the traffic through. All went well at Stockton goods depot and the local traffic engine which took the wagons round to the local marshalling yard was on time. At the marshalling yard it was soon clear where the delay was occurring. The booked service to Leeds (Neville Hill) was the 12.55 am Class C express goods and there was ample time to make the connection. However, the wagons were being put on the 1.20 am Class H goods. When challenged about this the inspector at Stockton said that the 12.55 am was a special service not to be delayed on any account so it was made ready as early as possible, 'and in any case twenty-five minutes would not matter'. But the 1.20 was a slow train and did not reach the Leeds marshalling yard until long after the local trip to the goods depot had left. So the wagons from Stockton were not unloaded until later in the day – too late for that day's delivery.

Plate 11.3. This February 1952 photograph shows the Tyne Dock MPD Tool Van crew re-railing double bolster wagon No M725050 at Jarrow yard. Note the rather primitive methods that had to be employed. Tyne Dock did have a crane, but it was hand-operated and had a capacity of, I think, 6 tons only. It was taken out on calls but I never heard of it being used. Anything serious called for the steam crane from South Dock. (IL Gray-Jones)

Plate 11.4. While at Tyne Dock I made several footplate trips with Driver J Imrie and Fireman E Todd. (I regret to say that I did not record the name of the guard.) This photograph was taken at Consett on 14 February 1952. (IL Gray-Jones)

It was usual for the first minuted appointment of a Traffic Apprentice after training to be a spell of outdoor work as Assistant Yard Master or Assistant Goods Agent, to get management experience 'on the ground'. I was looking forward to this, but things turned out differently. The Divisional Training Committee decided that too many Traffic Apprentices were going into the Operating Department and that the next few should go to the Commercial Department. I was sent to a post in the District Passenger Manager's office at Newcastle, described as Deputy Head of Development Section, though it was in fact a purely clerical post. I spent a rather wasted year looking after routine matters like seating and sleeper reservations, excursions and other special travel arrangements.

My next post offered more promise. In 1955 I was appointed Leader of the Detailed Analysis Committee, which was charged with improving working methods at goods depots. In spite of the neutral-sounding name, the handling staff soon re-christened us 'The Razor Gang' and regarded us with suspicion. As it turned out, our chief assignment was gathering information for a major reshaping of freight facilities on Tyneside, which led to the building of the new Tyneside Central Freight Depot. However, getting together the statistics on which to base the design of the new depot did mean an awful lot of time spent going through traffic returns and not enough spent outside examining what was really happening there.

In February 1957, I moved to York for my last period in the North Eastern Region and the most exciting. I joined the General Manager's office, described by Frank Hick in *This Was My Railway* as 'The Holy of Holies' – a very apt description. The General Section dealt with virtually everything not covered by the Works Section so there was a good deal of variety. Highlights included preparing and organising Area Board tours of inspection, dealing with VIP visitors to the Region, scrutinising traffic returns, co-ordinating the preparation of the Regional Revenue Budget and high level correspondence on behalf of the General Manager. The VIPs included a delegation railwaymen and civil servants from the Soviet Union's Ministry of Ways of Communication, the Minister of Transport and the Central Transport Users Consultative Committee. The hours were long, but I lived in walking distance of the office and York was a pleasant place to be, especially during the York Festival.

Towards the end of my time at York a reorganisation meant that my job became rather less interesting, but another door opened. I was 'head-hunted' to join an even 'Holier Holy of Holies', in the Secretary General's office of the British Transport Commission and moved to London in November 1958. My new post was to administer the Modernisation Plan, but that is another story!

At the end of this stage of my career some stocktaking is appropriate. First, a look at the Traffic Apprentice Training scheme. For its period, it was a good scheme, with a long history in the North-East, which gave it acceptance and a good reputation. One of its strengths was that it was not solely a graduate training scheme.

From the very beginning, half the places on the scheme were reserved for existing members of staff who qualified for consideration by passing competitive examinations. For university graduates, the scheme gave a good appreciation of what really happened at ground level. Another of its strengths was the personal interest taken in it by senior management, formally by the Divisional Training Committee at York and informally by local managers as a matter of routine. Some Traffic Apprentices might at times have felt that they were under excessive scrutiny!

Plate 11.5. Q6 No 63437 in which I travelled to Consett in 1952 had been built in June 1920. In contrast, when I photographed BR Standard 4MT No 80119 at Malton in June 1957, it was not quite two years old. It was allocated to Whitby shed. (IL Gray-Jones)

187

Plate 11.6. When I first came to the North Eastern Region at the end of 1949, sundries traffic was dealt with in a multiplicity of small goods sheds. Here is Durham, the former Belmont passenger station, photographed in February 1956. This way of working would not persist; sadly, neither would the traffic. (IL Gray-Jones)

There were weaknesses. The timetable was rather rigid and someone who had experience as a booking clerk still went through the standard rota of station booking offices. There was too much of the traditional practice of sitting beside someone and watching what he did. Some managers tried to devise special tasks to stimulate trainees, but not enough was done in this way. There was a lack of formal instruction, though there were good quality evening classes of university standard which trainees were expected to attend. All in all, there was too much emphasis on existing practice and on operating the existing system. Finally, the transition from training to regular post could be difficult and depended too much on what posts were available to be filled rather than how appropriate they were for the development of the individual. In the end the scheme produced good railwaymen but not necessarily good managers.

Any organisation depends in the last resort on the quality of its staff, and the North Eastern Region was fortunate in this respect. I was impressed from the start with the calibre of those who worked for the railways in the North-East in all grades and later experience in other places and Regions confirmed that early feeling. There was a strong community spirit, indeed a family feeling since many had parents or grandparents who had been in the railway service. This community feeling was enhanced by out of work activities, office trips, staff dances, the Railway Institute and the Lecture and Debating Societies.

Another feature of the Region was the persistence of the influence of the North Eastern Railway. Much of the infrastructure of course dated back to before 1923 but so did attitudes of mind. There was a proud tradition but it had good and less good consequences. Less good was the tendency to regard new ideas with suspicion. 'That's not railway work' was the phrase which I heard too often. But the tradition of service was strong and kept things going in the face of outdated equipment well past renewal date. At times one felt in a time warp where things had come to a stand in 1914! The humour and resilience of railway staff triumphed over these difficulties.

It was almost chance that took me to Tyneside to begin my railway career, but I regard myself as very lucky to have had the experience. When I was looking to join a graduate training scheme in 1949 there was no national British Railways scheme and of the pre-nationalised companies that of the LNER was most recommended. This took me to Tyneside into the company of some very fine people and I am extremely grateful to those railway men and women of all grades for the willing help they gave me during my training and early career.

Plate 11.7. This formal portrait was taken when I was appointed Freight Commercial Officer of the Southern Region's Central Division. (per IL Gray-Jones)

References:
Personal file of letters of appointment and training programmes.
British Railways Traffic Apprentices. The Railway Magazine, Volume 98 (1952), page 847.
Hick, FL. *That Was My Railway: From Ploughman's Kid to Railway Boss, 1922 - 1969*. Silver Link Publishing Limited, 1991.

A Brief Postscript

The history of the railways in the north-east of England did not, of course, end with the demise of the North Eastern Region. The most dramatic event in the railways' post 1966 history was the demise of British Railways itself following the passing of the Railways Act, 1993. The various passenger and freight traffic flows were parceled up and franchised to private operators, with mixed results. For good or ill, this is a situation which will endure for the foreseeable future.

Plate 12.1
The most popular of the passenger train franchise holders was Great North Eastern Railway, which operated the InterCity East Coast franchise between King's Cross and Scotland. GNER did not, however, invest in new rolling stock. Virgin Trains did so invest, and here we see a Yoyager diesel-electric multiple-unit departing northwards from Newcastle with a cross-country working on 19 February 2003. Neither popularity nor heavy investment were enough to maintain the respective franchises in the hands of GNER and Virgin Trains.

Note, by the way, the overhead electrified wires; British Rail completed the electrification of the East Coast Main Line in 1991. (JG Teasdale)

Plate 12.2. Privatisation of BR's freight traffic has, arguably, been much more successful than that of the passenger. The largest of the new private freight train operators was English, Welsh & Scottish Railway (EWS). This company initially used inherited equipment such as the MGR wagons seen here on 14 February 2002. However, the company also invested hugely in such as locomotives and wagons; General Motors diesel-electric No 66205 is at Milford drawing the rake of MGR wagons out of the sidings en route to Gascoigne Wood Mine. (JG Teasdale)
STOP PRESS! EWS was purchased by Deutsche Bahn in 2007. As this book was going to print, the news broke that from 1 January 2009 EWS will be known as DB Schenker. The history of the railways in the north-east of England continues to unfold...

Bibliography
(Supplementary list to the references in the diverse Endnotes)

Officially-published Documents and Reports
Annual Reports and Accounts. British Transport Commission / British Railways Board.
British Railways Carriage and Wagon Works, Doncaster. GA drawing 18764N. (56 ton iron ore wagon, 2 issues.)
British Railways North Eastern Region Magazine.
Freight: The North Eastern Region of British Railways in the service of industry. 1961.
London & North Eastern Railway Magazine.
Re-appraisal of the Plan for the Modernisation and Re-equipment of British Railways. White Paper, July 1959.
Report of the Light Weight Trains Committee. Railway Executive, March 1952.
The Development of the Major Railway Trunk Routes. BRB, February 1965.
The Reshaping of British Railways. BRB, 1963.

Privately-published Books
A Detailed History of BR Standard Steam Locomotives: Volume 3, the Tank Engine Classes. RCTS, 1997.
Locomotives of the LNER. RCTS, various dates.
Locoshed Book. Ian Allan Limited, annually.
Allen, GF. *British Railways After Beeching.* Ian Allan Limited, 1966.
Allen, GF. *The Eastern Since 1948.* Ian Allan Limited, 1981.
Allen, GF. *The Southern Since 1948.* Ian Allan Limited, 1987.
Bagwell, PS. *The Railwaymen: the History of the NUR, Volume 2.* George Allen & Unwin, 1982.
Bonavia, MR. *A History of the LNER : III. The Last Years, 1939-48.* George Allen & Unwin, 1983.
Bonavia, MR. *The Birth of British Rail.* George Allen & Unwin, 1979.
Bonavia, MR. *British Rail - The First 25 Years.* David & Charles (Publishers) Limited, 1981.
Bonavia, MR. *The Nationalisation of British Transport: The Early History of the British Transport Commission 1948 - 53.* The Macmillan Press Limited, 1987.
Bonavia, MR. *The Organisation of British Railways.* Ian Allan Limited, 1971.
Bonavia, MR. *The Organisation of British Railways 1948/64.* PhD Thesis. University of London.
Clegg, P, and Styring, J. *British Nationalised Shipping.* David and Charles (Publishers) Limited, 1968.
Collins, MJ. *Freightliner.* Haynes Publishing Group, 1991.
Dean, CH. *The Operation of the Tyne Dock – Consett Iron Ore Traffic, NER.* Trains Annual 1964.
Derry, R. *The Book of the BR Standards.* Irwell Press Limited, 1997.
Duckworth, CLD, and Langmuir, GE. *Railway and Other Steamers.* T Stephenson and Sons, 1968.
Fawcett, WA. *History of North Eastern Railway Architecture, Volume 3: Bell and Beyond.* North Eastern Railway Association, 2005.

Fiennes, GF. *I Tried to Run a Railway.* Ian Allan Limited, 1967.
Golding, B. *A Pictorial Record of British Railways Diesel Multiple Units.* Cheona Publications, 1995.
Gourvish, TR. *British Railways 1948 - 73: A Business History.* Cambridge University Press, 1986.
Haresnape, B. *British Rail Fleet Survey. 8 - Diesel Multiple-Units: The First Generation.* Ian Allan, 1985.
Harris, M. *British Main Line Services in the Age of Steam 1900 – 1968.* Oxford Publishing Company (Haynes Publishing), 1996.
Harris, M. *Decades of Steam 1920-1969.* Ian Allan Limited, 1999.
Harris, R. *The Allocation History of BR Diesels and Electrics.* 1985.
Hick, FL. *That Was My Railway: From Ploughman's Kid to Railway Boss, 1922 - 1969.* Silver Link Publishing Limited, 1991.
Hinde, DW, and Hinde, M. *Electric and Diesel-Electric Locomotives.* MacMillan and Company Limited, 1948.
Hoole, K. *Darlington North Road Locomotive Works, 1863 – 1966.* Roundhouse, 1966.
Hoole, K. *North Eastern Branch Lines Since 1925.* Ian Allan Limited, 1978.
Hoole, K. *North Eastern Locomotive Sheds.* David and Charles (Publishers) Limited, 1972.
Hoole, K. *The East Coast Main Line Since 1925.* Ian Allan Limited, 1977.
Jenkinson, D and Lane, BC. *British Railcars 1900 to 1950.* Atlantic Transport Publishers, 1996.
Johnson, J and Long, RA. *British Railways Engineering 1948 - 1980.* Mechanical Engineering Publications Limited, 1981.
Morrison, B. *British Rail DMUs and Diesel Railcars : Origins and First Generation Stock.* Ian Allan Limited, 1998.
Munns, RT. *Milk Churns to Merry-Go-Round.* David and Charles Publishers plc, 1986.
Quick, ME. *Railway Passenger Stations in England, Scotland and Wales : A Chronology.* R&CHS, 3rd Edition, 2005
Rowland, D. *British Railways Wagons: the first half million.* David and Charles (Publishers) Limited, 1985.
Rhodes, M. *The Illustrated History of British Marshalling Yards.* Oxford Publishing Company (Haynes Publishing Group), 1988.
Sanderson, HF. *Railway Commercial Practice Supplement to Volumes One and Two.* Chapman & Hall, 1955.
Tufnell, RM. *The British Railcar : AEC to HST.* David and Charles (Publishers) Limited, 1984.
Whittle, G. *The Railways of Consett and North-West Durham.*
Yeadon, WB. *LNER Locomotive Allocations. The Last Day 1947.* Irwell Press Limited, 1989.
Young, A. *Suburban Railways of Tyneside.* Martin Bairstow, 1999.

Privately-published Journals
British Railways North Eastern Region Magazine.
Engineering, including :
   Discharging Iron Ore from Ship to Wagon.
                                   13 August 1954.
   Mills, HR. *Railway Wagons for Iron Ore*
      and other Bulk Materials. 18 March 1955.
Modern Railways.
North Eastern Express, including :
   Addyman, JF. *Tyne Dock – The NER Cinderella.*
                                     May 1995.
   Crawley, MC. *Tyne Dock – Consett Iron Ore*
      Operations with 56 ton Hopper Wagons.
                                  December 2003.

Railway Gazette, The.
Railway Magazine, The, including :
   Special Wagons for Iron-Ore Traffic between
      Tyne Dock and Consett. April 1952.
   Service to the Steel Industry. July 1974.
   Denholm, MJ. *Shadows of Consett.* October 1982.
Railway World, including :
   Denholm, MJ. *The Last Railway to Consett.*
                                     June 1984.
Supplement to the London Gazette, August 25 1916.
The Railway Observer.
Trains Illustrated, including :
   Ransome-Wallis, P. *The Tyne Dock -*
      Consett Ore Traffic. October 1955.

Index

Area Board, North Eastern .... 10 *et seq.,*
   18, 21, 31, 32, 34, 41, 48, 58, 61, 87, 97, 111, 114,
   133, 140, 152, 154, 167 *et seq.,* 179, 183, 187
Beeching Report (*The Re-shaping of BR*) 21, 24,
   48, 53, 82, 85, 96, 99, 104, 108, 112, 114, 152, 158
Brakes, wagon / train 13, 15, 16, 40, 44, 45
   et seq., 50, 58, 59 *et seq.,* 65, 67, 122
British Rail Engineering Limited 144
British Railways Board, formation .... 18 *et seq.*
British Transport Commission
   Formation 6
   Abolition 18
Civil Engineering
   Bonus Incentives .... 156 *et seq.*
   Bridge Renewals and Repairs 155
   Colliery Subsidence 155
   Continuous Welded Rails .... 16, 147 *et seq.*
   Depots and Workshops .... 151 *et seq.*
   Drainage 151
   Gauging and Standard Cross Sections . 155 *et seq.*
   Leeds City Modernisation 154
   Mechanised Maintenance ... 16, 148 *et seq.,* 151
   Modernisation Plan ...... 12 *et seq.,* 152 *et seq.*
   Rails and Fastenings
   (see also Continuous Welded Rails) . . 146 *et seq.*
   Switch and Crossing Manufacture 148
   Switch Heaters 152
   Track Abandonments 158
   Track Quality, Monitoring ....156 *et seq.*
Central Electricity Generating Board . 22, 54 *et seq.,* 59
Containers / Containerisation .. 16, 22, 45, 48 *et seq.,*
   50 *et seq.,* 144
Docks and Inland Waterways Executive 6, 18, 29
DMU Depots
   Blaydon 140
   Bradford (Hammerton Street) . . 76 *et seq.,* 135, 140
   Darlington 79, 135, 140
   Hull (Botanic Gardens) 78, 135, 140
   Leeds (Neville Hill) ..... 87, 136 *et seq.,* 140, 163
   Manningham 140
   Middlesbrough....................... 140
   South Gosforth .... 77 *et seq.,* 85, 114, 140
   Sunderland 140

Electrification .... 9, 13, 16, 33, 48, 87 *et seq.,* 90,
   132 (caption), 155, 165, 166, 189 (caption)
Freight Traffic
   Brakes, wagon / train 13, 15, 16, 40, 44,
      45 *et seq.,* 50, 58, 59 *et seq.,* 65, 67, 122
   Coal ...... 13, 22, 23, 35, 36, 39, 41, 44 *et seq.,*
      46 *et seq.,* 52, *et seq.,* 59, 61 *et seq.,* 63
   Computerisation .... 61 *et seq.*
   Containers / Containerisation 16, 22, 45,
      48 *et seq.,* 50 *et seq.,* 144
   Iron Ore (Tyne Dock - Consett) ...... 64 *et seq.*
   Liner Trains ....22, 48, 50 *et seq.*
   Merchandise / Sundries 12, 13, 16, 18, 21,
      22, 36, 39, 40, 41, 45, 47, 48, 49 *et seq.,* 61,
      62 *et seq.,* 163, 184, 186
   Merry-Go-Round (MGR) .... 57 *et seq.*
   Oil .... 59 *et seq.*
   Roadrailer .... 49 *et seq.,* 55
   Tyneside Central Freight Depot 45
Hotels Executive 6, 24
Liner Trains .... 22, 48, 50 *et seq.*
Marshalling Yards
   Healey Mills 16, 41,
      44, 48, 63, 137, 152 *et seq.,* 170
   Stourton 16, 41, 48, 152
   Tees Yard (Newport) 13, 16, 34,
      41, 63, 152 *et seq.,* 178
   Tyne Yard (Lamesley) 16, 41,
      43 *et seq.,* 63, 152
Merry-Go-Round (MGR) .... 57 *et seq.*
Modernisation Plan ...... 11 *et seq.,* 17, 24, 40 *et seq.,*
   46, 47, 53, 72, 77 *et seq.,* 83 *et seq.,* 85,
   87 *et seq.,* 95, 111, 124, 144, 146, 152, 154, 163,
   165, 167, 168, 178 *et seq.,* 187
Motive Power Depots
   Gateshead.....................132, 136 *et seq.*
   Healey Mills .... 137 *et seq.*
   Knottingley .... 58 *et seq.,* 139
   Leeds (Holbeck) 136
   Leeds (Neville Hill) ..... 87, 136 *et seq.,* 140, 163
   Thornaby .... 132 *et seq.,* 163
National Coal Board 7, 22, 36, 44,
   46, 53 *et seq.,* 58, 62, 155

Nationalisation, railway . . . . 5 *et seq.*
North Eastern Area Board. . . . . . 10 *et seq.*, 18, 21, 31,
    32, 34, 41, 48, 58, 61, 87, 97, 111, 114, 133, 140,
    152, 154, 167 *et seq.*, 179, 183, 187
North Eastern Region
    Description 7
    Map 20
    Merger with Eastern Region 9, 23
    Regional colour 9, 19, 30
North Eastern Regional Railway Board 18, 21,
    23, 24, 27, 34, 58, 183
Passenger Traffic
    Closures and Economies 12, 21, 107
    Cross-Country 94
    Diesel Multiple-Units . . . . 12 *et seq.*, 16 *et seq.*,
        21, 24, 32 *et seq.*, 72, 75
    East Coast Main Line 87
    Fares, Marketing and Tickets 11, 115
    Holidays, Excursions, *etc.* 103
    Sleeper Services,
        including Car-Sleepers and Car-Carriers 101
    Trans-Pennine 97
    Tyneside Electrics 84, 113
Personalities
    Beeching, Sir Richard . . . . . . 17 *et seq.*, 21 *et seq.*,
        24, 28, 45, 59, 82, 84, 85, 89, 90, 96, 99,
        103 *et seq.*, 108, 111, 114, 115, 145, 151,154
    Bond, Roland C 15, 143, 144
    Burrows, MG 31, 144
    Butland, AN 146
    Carslake, Charles 164
    Castle, Barbara 23, 111
    Cook, KJ 31, 144
    Curtis, Dr Frederick Francis Charles 169
    Dean, Arthur . . . . 21, 23, 27 *et seq.*,
        34, 145, 146, 154, 156, 160, 163
    Elliot, John 26, 32
    Ellison, Charles C 179
    Fiennes, Gerard F . . . . 23, 27 *et seq.*
    Fraser, John Holden 164, 181
    Gladstone, William Ewart, MP 5
    Hardy, Sydney 161, 163, 170
    Harrison, JF 31, 143
    Hick, Frank 33, 75, 77, 78, 79,
        84, 85, 97, 108
    Hochen, HO 144
    Hopkins, Charles P 7, 9, 27, 32
    Horler, Frank 172
    Hurcomb, Sir Cyril 6, 8, 26
    Margetts, Frederick C . . . . 18 *et seq.*, 21,
        27 *et seq.*, 33, 34, 95, 104, 108, 168
    Marples, Ernest, MP . . . . 17 *et seq.*, 154
    McMurdo, Archibald William 145
    Missenden, Sir Eustace 6, 9, 26, 28, 30, 32
    Mitchell, Sir Steuart 18, 144
    Ormiston, Harold 145
    Peppercorn, Arthur H 8, 31, 122
    Pope, Frank A 12, 75
    Purves, Robert James 181
    Raymond, Stanley E 23
    Reeves, L 144
    Riddles, Robert A . . . . . 8 *et seq.*, 12, 15, 142 *et seq.*

Robertson, Sir Brian 10, 12, 18, 33
Robson, AE 31, 144
Short, Herbert A . . . . 9, 27 *et seq.*,
    32, 33 *et seq.*, 72, 78, 176, 183
Sinclair, J 144
Summerson, Thomas H 11, 18, 21, 22, 32,
    33 *et seq.*, 61, 133, 136
Tattersall, Arthur Ewart . . . . 164, 166 *et seq.*
Thew, George Charlton 167, 181
Thompson, Edward 122
Thompson, John Taylor 145, 160
Thorpe, Albert Newton . . . . . .160 *et seq.*, 169, 170
Triffitt, Edwin 145
Watkinson, Harold, MP 132, 167, 173
Wigram, Arthur Frederic 164, 167, 181
Railway Executive . . . . 6 *et seq.*, 10,
    12, 23, 26, 32, 34, 36, 46, 52, 65, 75, 87, 142, 146,
    148, 164, 167, 169
Railway Nationalization Society 5
Region, North Eastern
    Description 7
    Map 20
    Merger with Eastern Region 9, 23
    Regional colour 9, 19, 30
Regional Railway Board, North Eastern 18, 21,
    23, 24, 27, 34, 58, 183
Regions, formation of . . . . 6 *et seq.*
Roadrailer . . . . .49 *et seq.*, 55
Shipping 182
Signal & Telecommunications
    Automatic Train Control /
        Automatic Warning System . . . 16, 167 *et seq.*
    Centralised Traffic Control . . . . . . 12, 168 *et seq.*
    Level Crossings . . . . 16, 172 *et seq.*
    Modernisation Plan . . . . 12 *et seq.*, 165
    Signal Box Design . . . . 169 *et seq.*
    Signalling Technology
        Individual Function Switch 164, 181
        Entrance – Exit . . . . . 166, 172 (caption), 181
        One Control Switch . . 164, 165 (caption), 181
    Signalling Schemes . . . . 13, 16, 164 *et seq.*
    Telecommunications 12, 178
Stations, major re-building of
    Harrogate 161
    Leeds Central replaced by modernised Leeds City .
        . . . . . . 16, 33, 71, 96, 108, 111, 154, 160 *et seq.*
    Middlesbrough 71, 72, 160
    Sunderland . . . . 16, 71, 160 *et seq.*,
        rear cover (caption)
    Wakefield Westgate 16, 161
Tyneside Central Freight Depot 45
Works
    Darlington North Road 123, 124,
        126, 132, 140 *et seq.*
    Faverdale . . . . .49, 125, 132, 142 *et seq.*
    Gateshead 141
    Shildon . . . . 49, 50, 53, 142 *et seq.*
    York . . . . 103, 142 *et seq.*
    Walker Gate . . . . 142 *et seq.*